About Island Press

Island Press is the only nonprofit organization in the United States whose principal purpose is the publication of books on environmental issues and natural resource management. We provide solutions-oriented information to professionals, public officials, business and community leaders, and concerned citizens who are shaping responses to environmental problems.

In 2003, Island Press celebrates its nineteenth anniversary as the leading provider of timely and practical books that take a multidisciplinary approach to critical environmental concerns. Our growing list of titles reflects our commitment to bringing the best of an expanding body of literature to the environmental community throughout North America and the world.

Support for Island Press is provided by The Nathan Cummings Foundation, Geraldine R. Dodge Foundation, Doris Duke Charitable Foundation, Educational Foundation of America, The Charles Engelhard Foundation, The Ford Foundation, The George Gund Foundation, The Vira I. Heinz Endowment, The William and Flora Hewlett Foundation, Henry Luce Foundation, The John D. and Catherine T. MacArthur Foundation, The Andrew W. Mellon Foundation, The Moriah Fund, The Curtis and Edith Munson Foundation, National Fish and Wildlife Foundation, The New-Land Foundation, Oak Foundation, The Overbrook Foundation, The David and Lucile Packard Foundation, The Pew Charitable Trusts, The Rockefeller Foundation, The Winslow Foundation, and other generous donors.

Alternative Futures for Changing Landscapes

THE UPPER SAN PEDRO RIVER BASIN IN ARIZONA AND SONORA

Alternative Futures for Changing Landscapes

THE UPPER SAN PEDRO RIVER BASIN IN ARIZONA AND SONORA

Carl Steinitz
Hector Manuel Arias Rojo
Scott Bassett
Michael Flaxman
Tomas Goode
Thomas Maddock III
David Mouat
Richard Peiser
Allan Shearer

Foreword by Robert L. Anderson III

ISLAND PRESS • WASHINGTON • COVELO • LONDON

Library of Congress Cataloging-in-Publication Data
Alternative futures for changing landscapes : the Upper San Pedro River Basin in Arizona and Sonora / Carl Steinitz ... [et al.] ; foreword by Robert L. Anderson III.
p. cm.
ISBN 1-55963-335-2 (hardcover : alk. paper) —
ISBN 1-55963-222-4 (pbk. : alk. paper)
1. Regional planning—San Pedro River Watershed (Mexico and Ariz.)—Case studies. 2. Urbanization—San Pedro River Watershed (Mexico and Ariz.)—Case studies. 3. Land use—San Pedro River Watershed (Mexico and Ariz.)—Case studies. 4. Regional planning—Environmental aspects—San Pedro River Watershed (Mexico and Ariz.)—Case studies. 5. San Pedro River Watershed (Mexico and Ariz.)
I. Steinitz, Carl.
HT395.S175 A47 2002
307.1'2'0972—dc21
2002014978

British Cataloguing-in-Publication Data available

Book design by Joyce C. Weston

Printed on recycled, acid-free paper ♻

Manufactured in the United States of America

09 08 07 06 05 04 03 8 7 6 5 4 3 2 1

Contents

List of Tables

List of Figures

Foreword

> In the process of finding solutions to our transportation, settlement, agriculture, energy and other material needs, remaining natural environments have been placed under enormous stress, and continue to be fragmented, polluted or damaged in other ways. . . . This decline in habitat has led to a widespread crisis not confined to any one country or region.
>
> — Commission on Environmental Cooperation, *The North American Mosaic: A State of the Environment Report*

North America is facing a widespread crisis due to its shrinking biodiversity. Half of North America's most biodiverse ecoregions are now severely degraded, and the region now has at least 235 threatened species of mammals, birds, reptiles, and amphibians.

The pervasive and worldwide conflict between conservation and development is not new, and it is not newly recognized. The three NAFTA partners—Canada, Mexico, and the United States—formed the Commission on Environmental Cooperation (CEC) to respond to the threat posed by rapid decline in biodiversity.

The three countries have enacted a number of conservation strategies in the past few decades. Overall, the total protected area in North America has increased from less than 100 million hectares in 1980 to 300 million hectares now, or about 15 percent of the continent's land surface. Yet, despite these accomplishments, looming threats overshadow these positive achievements. Natural areas in all three countries are in danger of being overwhelmed by multiple factors. The North American situation can be seen all around the world, frequently in even more critical conditions.

The future of the Upper San Pedro River Basin in Arizona and Sonora is just one example of the tensions between conservation and development, and it is further complicated by the presence of a major military installation. In 1994, the Department of Defense directed military installations to begin managing their environmental programs from an ecosystem perspective.

In 1996, the Department of Defense sent representatives to the Biodiversity Research Consortium, a partnership of government agencies and universities. BRC's goal is to develop databases and analytical methods for assessing and managing risks to biodiversity. Winifred Rose and Robert Lozar of the U.S. Army Engineer Research and Development Center represented the Army. Consequently, the groundwork was in place when I expressed interest in applying the Alternative Futures process to the Upper San Pedro River region. In 1997, my proposal to the Department of Defense's Legacy Resources Management Program was approved. Legacy is a Congressional program to foster proactive natural and cultural resources projects outside routine environmental funding channels.

While the scientific community still debates the meaning of ecosystem management, the concern for the military is managing installations in the context of how they interact with and impact the environmental processes—biological and physical—of their surrounding landscapes. The Army Training and Doctrine Command's Fort Huachuca, enmeshed in the volatile and highly publicized environmental issues in the Upper San Pedro River Valley of Arizona, seemed to be the Army's best candidate installation for such a study.

Environmental issues from an army perspective within the Upper San Pedro River valley include:

- Fort Huachuca's location adjacent to the San Pedro Riparian National Conservation Area; the SPRNCA's originating legislation requires a base flow to be maintained in the river.

- The presence of a number of water-dependent endangered species on and near the installation.
- The widespread concern for balancing water use between conservation concerns and growth in this growing and attractive high-desert environment.
- Litigation involving the alleged impacts on the watershed.

In further support of a study of alternative futures for this changing landscape, the Environmental Protection Agency initiated the Federal Clean Water Action Plan in October 2000. The plan directs federal agencies to assume a watershed perspective for environmental management and improve natural resources stewardship through an increase in public involvement in watershed management on federal lands. It also calls on federal agencies to work together with states, tribes, local governments, private landowners, and other interested parties to take a watershed approach to federal land and resource management. Watershed planning includes assessment and monitoring of watershed conditions and identification of priority watersheds on which to focus budget and other resources. Carl Steinitz's alternative futures framework is a major component of this approach.

Although the alternative futures approach increases somewhat the complexity of the installation planning and management process, it compensates by making the planning evaluation process for the region more seamless, especially for those many aspects of the environment that do not respect property boundaries. It does require greater agency and community interaction: in this example requiring international cooperation because the watershed originates in Mexico. The rewards of such an analysis lie in the remarkable perspectives it provides. The case study in this book illustrates a potentially efficacious way of considering and assessing policy scenarios aimed at planning for future change while diminishing its harmful impacts.

This study is not an attempt to steer the community in a particular direction. It is, rather, a means to help local planners predict the consequences of the region's potential alternative futures, and therefore improve their foresight in choosing among them. It is our hope that it will be viewed as a framework to better enable the region's leaders to work together in planning the environmental future of this richly diverse and scenic high-desert environment. The study's extensive analysis is a tool that should aid this dynamic community in realizing "smart growth" in the future. The study has already influenced Fort Huachuca to be the first army installation to devote significant funding to purchase conservation easements.

I am very grateful to all of the planners, researchers, agency personnel and interested local citizens in the United States and Mexico who have worked together with us to make this project both possible and, I hope, successful. But I wish to especially thank the members of the research team for their efforts, talent, and camaraderie.

Robert L. Anderson III
U.S. Army Training and Doctrine Command
Conservation and Natural Resources Program
Fort Monroe, Virginia

Preface

The research described in this book was conducted by a team of investigators from the Harvard University Graduate School of Design, the Desert Research Institute, the University of Arizona, Instituto del Medio Ambiente y el Desarrollo Sustentable del Estado de Sonora (IMADES), the United States Army Training and Doctrine Command, and the United States Army Engineer Research and Development Center.

This study makes use of the work of others, especially in its descriptions of the region and the issues that it faces. We are grateful for the cooperation and permissions that have been granted to us by the region's planning agencies, the Semi-Arid Land-Surface-Atmosphere Program, the Commission for Environmental Cooperation, the United States Bureau of Land Management, and Fort Huachuca. We also appreciate the many persons from the study area who participated in the scenario guide survey and those who provided comments at our public presentations.

The research was funded by a grant obtained by the U.S. Army Training and Doctrine Command's Environmental Division, Fort Monroe, Virginia, from the Department of Defense Legacy Resources Management Program, Project Number 981702. However, there is no contractual obligation or consultative relationship between the investigators and any sponsoring groups or governing jurisdictions. The information herein is believed to be reliable, but the investigators and their institutions do not warrant its completeness or accuracy. Opinions and estimates are the judgments of the research team. The sole purpose of this research publication is educational: to provide information to the many stakeholders and jurisdictions of the region regarding issues, strategic planning choices, and their possible consequences related to the built and natural environment.

Alternative Futures for Changing Landscapes

THE UPPER SAN PEDRO RIVER BASIN IN ARIZONA AND SONORA

CHAPTER 1

Alternative Futures for a Changing Region

When regions face changing conditions and environmental crises, new policies and plans are required. Usually, there are several simultaneous causes of these crises, and each requires consideration in terms of policy and planning options. Decision makers, and stakeholders in general, have a difficult problem. They must try to foresee the potential consequences of their choices, and policies and plans must be seen together, as a set. Studies of alternative futures based on different assumptions provide a way to investigate the possible outcomes of current policy options and decisions.

If the future were easily knowable, planning for it would be a simple task. However, no one can know what the actual future of a region will be, and therefore planning for the future is a complicated and uncertain process. Since no single vision of the future is likely to be accurate, it is helpful to consider a set of alternative futures that encompasses a spectrum of possibilities. Therefore, this study, and others like it, examines several alternative possible futures for the region.

There are two main ways of thinking about alternative futures (figure 1.1). The most common approach postulates or designs a small number of alternative plans for future land use and/or land cover and comparatively assesses their potential consequences. These alternative futures are often based on geometrically defined development patterns (compact, diffuse, linear, etc.), on political interest group priorities (the conservationists' plan, the developers' plan, etc.), or on single dominant policies (sewer alternatives, transport alternatives, etc.). The advantage of this approach is its simplicity, although a danger is that a misleading simplification often results. Its principal disadvantage is that while a sense of what the future might be is created, it may be impossible to identify the full set of policies needed to achieve that future.

Many planning studies have used this approach. These include most of the spatially oriented land use modeling studies carried out beginning in the 1960s. See, for example, Steinitz and Rogers 1970.

The other approach, which forms the basis of this study of the Upper San Pedro River Basin, more closely resembles the typical decision-making processes of the many governmental, organizational, and individual choices that shape the future for a region. This approach aims to identify the several most important issues responsive to policy and planning decisions, along with the widest range of options pertaining to each issue. As is the case in any policy debate, these are not taken one at a time, but rather as a simultaneous set, with each seen in the context of others. A scenario is then created to reflect choices among the possible options for each policy in the set. The word *scenario* is usually understood to mean an outline of events, typically the plot of a story, play, or film. Similarly, for the purposes of this study, a scenario is an outline or plot that can generate a hypothetical future of the Upper San Pedro River Basin.

In a scenario-based study of alternative futures, each single policy option either alters a spatially varied characteristic that can attract or repel future development or alters a parameter in one of the several process models that assess the impacts of future change. Choices are made, and the resulting scenarios are used to direct the allocation of future land uses using a model of the process of development. The alternatives are then assessed for their consequences. This approach provides for the creation of a variety of alternative futures for a region and gives guidance on how to achieve them

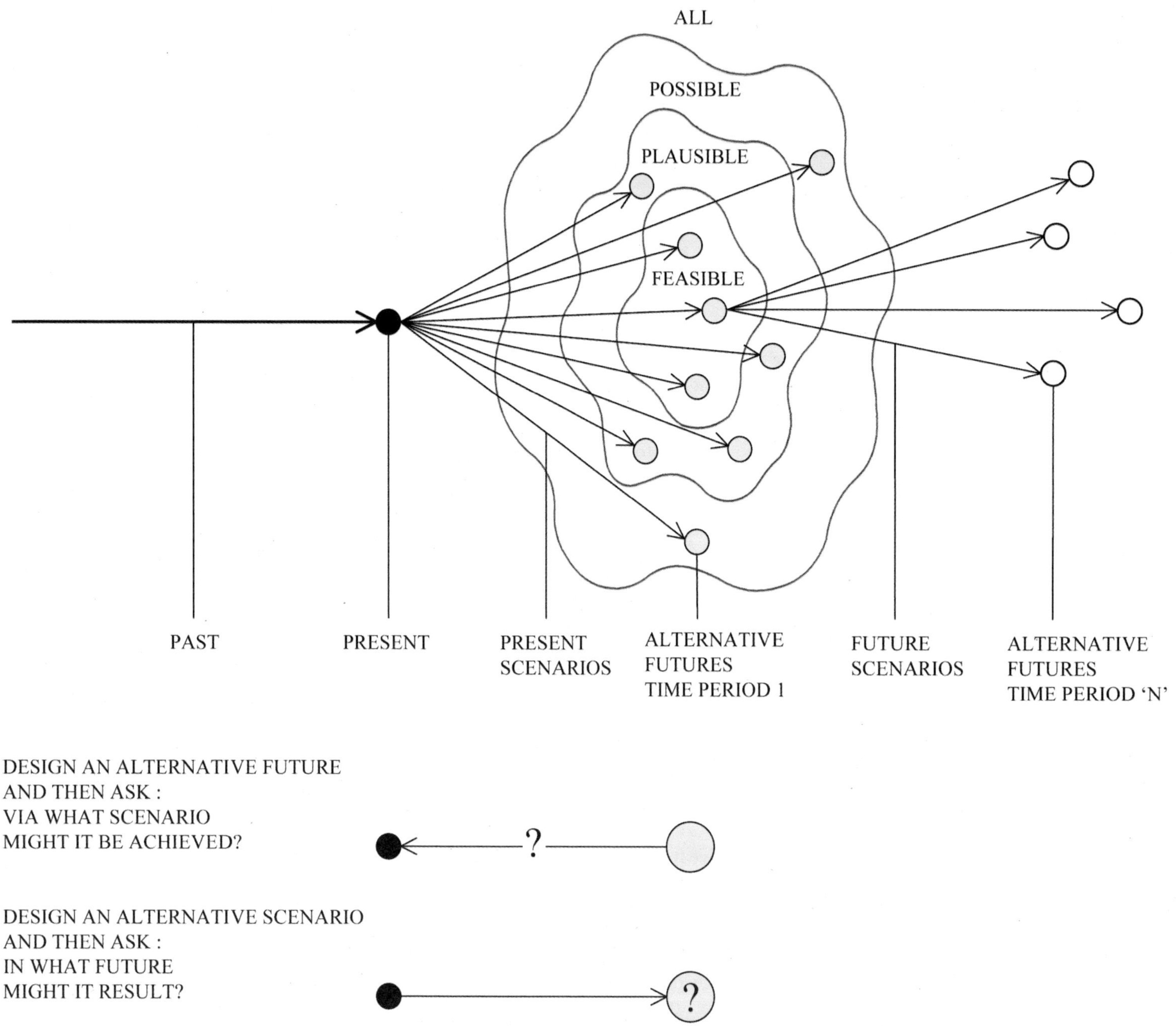
ALL
POSSIBLE
PLAUSIBLE
FEASIBLE
PAST
PRESENT
PRESENT SCENARIOS
ALTERNATIVE FUTURES TIME PERIOD 1
FUTURE SCENARIOS
ALTERNATIVE FUTURES TIME PERIOD 'N'
DESIGN AN ALTERNATIVE FUTURE AND THEN ASK : VIA WHAT SCENARIO MIGHT IT BE ACHIEVED?
?
DESIGN AN ALTERNATIVE SCENARIO AND THEN ASK : IN WHAT FUTURE MIGHT IT RESULT?
?

Figure 1.1 ■ Two strategies for considering the future

because the alternatives themselves are based on a set of assumed policy decisions. An additional benefit is the ability to test the effects of individual policy choices by using sensitivity analysis.

Both approaches to the study of alternative futures for changing regions allow consideration of the past and the present. Both recognize that there are an infinite number of future options. Both must reduce the number of alternatives for study from the infinite to a manageable number that includes the most important issues and an appropriate range of policy choices. Both approaches can be used in studies of alternative futures, and both approaches can provide important insights.

Several important and changing landscape regions have recently been studied using scenario-based alternative futures. These include Monroe County, Pennsylvania; the region of Camp Pendleton, California; the Willamette River Basin in western Oregon; the Southern Rocky Mountains in Alberta; the California Mojave Desert; and the Iowa Corn Belt.

Monroe County, Pennsylvania

Alternative Futures for Monroe County, Pennsylvania was a study conducted in 1993 by researchers from the Harvard University Graduate School of Design in collaboration with representatives of the U.S. Environmental Protection Agency (EPA) and the county government (Steinitz et al. 1994; Steinitz and McDowell 2001).

Monroe County in northeastern Pennsylvania lies in the heart of the Poconos. Its beautiful scenery and year-round recreational opportunities have made it an ideal destination for tourists for the past hundred years. Recently, these valuable landscape resources and improved transportation have attracted new residential development, making Monroe County the second-fastest-growing county in Pennsylvania. An estimated 90,000 additional people were expected to locate there by 2020, doubling the current population. As a result, Monroe County faced a crisis, the classic dilemma of conservation versus urban development. In addition, New York City and Philadelphia are only 90 mi (149 km) away, putting 60 million people within a four-hour drive of the recreational attractions of the area.

The study analyzed the trends of growth in Monroe County, determined the possible effects of that growth, and provided some insight into how that growth might best be managed. It identified six key processes (geologic, biologic, visual, demographic, economic, and political) as necessary points of evaluation, discussion, decision, and action. The research prepared six alternative futures for 2020. These were determined by modeling the results of (1) following the county's comprehensive plan, (2) allowing development to be market-driven, (3) pursuing the strategic development interests of each township, (4) adopting a policy of land conservation with an emphasis on outdoor recreational opportunities, (5) concentrating new development in a corridor served by public transportation, and (6) conserving all existing undeveloped land. Models of the six key processes produced maps of expected development impact outcomes, allowing people to visualize the consequences of the alternative futures. This process allowed decision makers to consider how change might affect the future of their county. Tangible results included the later preparation of a plan by Monroe County for its development and conservation, and the passing of a twenty-five million dollar bond issue for conservation.

The Region of Camp Pendleton, California

Biodiversity and Landscape Planning: Alternative Futures for the Region of Camp Pendleton, California explored how urban growth and change in the rapidly developing area located between San Diego and Los Angeles might influence the biodiversity of the area (Steinitz et al.1996; Adams and Steinitz 2000). The study was conducted in 1994–96 by a team of investigators from the Harvard University Graduate School of Design, Utah State

University, the National Biological Service, the U.S. Forest Service, the U.S. Environmental Protection Agency (EPA), the Nature Conservancy, and the Biodiversity Research Consortium, with the cooperation of the two relevant regional agencies, the San Diego Association of Governments (SANDAG) and the Southern California Association of Governments (SCAG), and Marine Corps Base (MCB) Camp Pendleton. The research was supported by the Strategic Environmental Research and Development Program (SERDP), a joint program of the U.S. Department of Defense, the U.S. Department of Energy, and the U.S. EPA, through a grant to the Western Ecology Division of the EPA's National Health and Environmental Effects Research Laboratory.

The study region was an 80 by 134 km (50 by 83 mi) rectangle that encompasses the five major river drainage basins directly influencing Camp Pendleton: San Juan, San Mateo, San Onofre, Santa Margarita, and San Luis Rey. The research strategy was based on the hypothesis that the major stressors causing biodiversity change are related to urbanization. The study area is one of the most biologically diverse environments in the continental United States. Within the region are more than 200 plants and animals listed by federal or state agencies as endangered, threatened, or rare. These include the least Bell's vireo, the coastal cactus wren, and the California gnatcatcher. In addition, a number of plants and animals are of local concern because of declining populations, such as the California cougar. The region is also one of the country's most desirable places to live and work, and it continues to grow and develop. Its population in 1990 was about 1.1 million. The regional planning agencies forecast that by 2010 the population will grow to 1.6 million, and it is expected to continue to grow beyond that date. The effects on biodiversity will depend on several factors, including where and how people build homes, where new industry will be located, where new infrastructure will be built to support urbanization, and whether and where land will be conserved.

Future change was studied at four scales: several restoration projects, a subdivision, a third-order watershed, and the region as a whole. Regional change was simulated via six alternative projections of development to 2010 and to subsequent "build-out." The first scenario was based upon the current local and regional plans as summarized by SCAG and SANDAG and those of Camp Pendleton. Five additional scenarios provided a method to explore and compare the impacts of different land use and development policies relating to biodiversity. Alternative 2 illustrated what may be considered the dominant spread pattern of low-density growth. Alternative 3 also followed the spread pattern, but introduced a conservation strategy in 2010. Alternative 4 proposed private conservation of biodiversity by encouraging large-lot ownership adjacent to and encompassing important habitat areas. Alternative 5 focused on concentrating centers of development and new communities. Alternative 6 concentrated growth in a single new city. All alternatives accommodated the population forecast for the region.

A set of process models was used to assess each alternative. The soils model evaluated the agricultural productivity of the area's soils. The hydrology models predicted the 25-year storm hydrographs for each of the rivers and their watersheds, flooding heights and water discharge, and resultant soil moisture. The fire models assessed both the need for fire in maintaining vegetation habitat and the risks of fire and fire suppression. The visual model assessed scenic preferences for the region's landscape. Biodiversity was assessed in three ways: a landscape ecological pattern model, ten selected single species potential habitat models, and a species richness model.

The evaluations of the alternative futures were used by stakeholders, including MCB Camp Pendleton, to assess the desirability of the policies that generated them and to devise and compare additional development scenarios and conservation strategies.

The Willamette River Basin, Oregon

The Pacific Northwest Ecosystem Research Consortium (PNW-ERC) is a regional research consortium involving researchers at the University of Oregon, Oregon State University, the University of Washington, and the U.S. EPA, and is supported under a 1996 cooperative agreement between the EPA and the universities. The research of the consortium is designed to create a regional landscape context for interpreting trajectories of regional ecosystem change in western Oregon's Willamette River Basin, to identify and understand critical ecological processes, and to develop approaches for evaluating outcomes of alternative future land use, management, and policy (Hulse et al. 2002).

The Willamette River Basin encompasses 12 percent of the state of Oregon, but it is the home of 68 percent of Oregon's population and accounts for 31 percent of the timber harvested and 45 percent of the market value of agricultural production in the state. By 2050, an additional 1.7 million people are expected to live in the Willamette River Basin, bringing the total to around 4 million. That is equivalent to adding three more cities the size of Portland. The high quality of life and quality of the environment are major factors in attracting people to the region. The key challenge will be to accommodate the expected population growth while sustaining and improving the highly valued features of the basin. Already at least 1400 mi (2253 km) of streams in the basin do not meet water quality standards, largely because of runoff associated with human use of the land. Seventeen plant and animal species in the basin are listed under the Federal Endangered Species Act.

Three alternative visions for the future of the region were prepared in 10-year increments through 2050. These were based on basin stakeholder input regarding policies for urban and rural residential, agricultural, forestry, and natural lands and their associated water uses. The Plan Trend scenario represents the expected future landscape if current policies are implemented as written, and, where no policies exist, recent trends continue. The Development alternative reflects a loosening of current policies, across all aspects of the landscape, to allow freer rein to market forces. The Conservation alternative places greater emphasis on ecosystem protection and restoration, although still reflecting a plausible balance between ecological, social, and economic considerations as defined by the stakeholders.

These alternative futures were compared for their impacts on ecological conditions of the Willamette River (including projected changes in river channel structure, streamside vegetation, and fish communities), water availability and use (including whether future demands can be satisfied by the finite water supply in the basin), ecological conditions of streams (including projected changes in stream habitat and the composition and diversity of native fish and benthic invertebrate communities), and terrestrial wildlife (including changes in habitat and abundance and distribution of selected wildlife species).

A central aim of the research has been to communicate to decision makers the system-level implications of positions and policies being modeled. A group appointed by the governor of Oregon and charged with creating a restoration plan for endangered salmon used the Conservation 2050 scenario as the centerpiece of its recommendations to the Oregon legislature (Jerrick et al. 2001).

The Southern Rocky Mountains, Alberta

The Southern Rockies Landscape Planning Project was initiated in 1996 by the Ecological Landscape Division of Alberta Environment, Its purpose is to develop and test computerized planning support tools that may be used to evaluate the ecological and socioeconomic impacts of alternative future regional landscapes by 2018 and 2048 (Alberta Environment and Olson and

Olson 2000). The 5000 sq km (1930 sq mi) pilot study area is in the Southern Rocky Mountains of Alberta.

In order to test both the planning framework and the suite of impact models, several landscape futures have been developed, visualized, and assessed. The Trend scenario assumes that existing protection and management policies would be continued and that forest harvesting location, intensity, and extent will be based on current policies. The Disturbance scenario assumes that catastrophic fires similar in extent to historic events (burning 65 percent of the forested land in 30 years) will reoccur in the area. The Fiber scenario explores future conditions if current planning is overwhelmed by economic pressures and the area is managed for the maximization of forest fiber production with little or no regard for other forest values. The Preservation scenario assumes that the area is managed for preservation as a quasi-wilderness area, with prescribed burning as the primary management tool. This alternative was used to identify the economic costs of a moratorium on forest industrial activity. The Full Recreation scenario emphasizes recreation as the primary land use and projects a wide range of backcountry and frontcountry recreational uses while severely limiting fiber extraction.

All alternatives were comparatively evaluated by a series of impact models, including single species potential habitat abundance; landscape ecological pattern; protection of rare, unique, and valued elements; watershed risk; surface water quantity and timing; flammability and head fire intensity; visual quality; cultural resource protection; and several economic impacts.

The prototype project already is influencing integrated resource planning in Alberta because of its emphasis on spatially explicit integration of multisectoral interests and its recognition of landscapes as important regional planning units.

The Mojave Desert, California

Funded largely by a grant from the Strategic Environmental Research and Development Program (SERDP) of the Department of Defense, a team of researchers from the Desert Research Institute, Utah State University, Oregon State University, and the U.S. Forest Service developed and assessed alternative future scenarios within the California Mojave Desert (Mouat et al. 2002, Toth et al. 2002).

The California Mojave Desert is becoming increasingly important for several reasons. Its diverse physiographic features make it ecologically significant. There are high levels of endemic species, and a growing number of high-visibility species that are considered threatened or endangered or are likely to attain such status under current trends. The Mojave Desert's traditional importance for military training is perhaps unrivaled by any other region of the country. These ecological and military uses are increasingly threatened by the rapid pace of current and projected urbanization.

The research is based on the hypothesis that three main drivers are responsible for growth and change within any given region. In a broad sense, the drivers are classified as sociodemographic, economic, and biophysical factors. As an example of the interactions among the drivers, regional economic shifts can bring population redistribution, which, in turn, impacts biodiversity through attendant land-use change. This study makes use of the triad of interactions and cause-and-effect relationships to model a range of alternative futures for the California Mojave region.

To reflect the region's sociodemographic future, population projections from the California Department of Finance were adjusted to apply to the 75,000 sq km (29,000 sq mi) study region. To reflect economic change, a development prediction model generated spatially explicit probabilities for future development using a logistic regression model incorporating several characteristics, such as new development over a 10-year interval, distance to existing development, and distance to primary roads. The biophysical models assessed the potential distribution, richness, diversity, endemism, and rarity of terrestrial vertebrates within the Californian Mojave. These models incorporate data based on California Wildlife Habitat Relationship species distributions that were refined using detailed landform data, elevation ranges, riparian systems, and spring locations.

The alternative futures fall into two broad categories: (1) the likely trend of future development to 2020, with an additional population of 877,000 persons, under current development policies and patterns, and (2) several alternatives to the trend that meet specific stakeholder interests, concerns, and proposals, such as different population growth assumptions, new urban encroachment buffers, infrastructure upgrades, ecologically based restrictions on development, and public/private land exchanges. These demonstrate the ability of the approach to both adapt to a wide range of issues and to provide policy-relevant information to various publics and the military.

The Iowa Corn Belt

Agricultural policy implies new future scenarios for agricultural landscapes each time a new federal farm bill or emergency aid to farmers is debated. Alternative futures studies are one tool to make the implications of proposed policy apparent, as well as to suggest new policy combinations that could achieve specific policy goals. Agricultural policies and practices in the Iowa Corn Belt have been the focus of *Modeling Effects of Alternative Landscape Design and Management on Water Quality and Biodiversity in Midwest Agricultural Watersheds* (Santelmann et al. 2001), a research program begun in 1997 and supported by the U.S. EPA's Science to Achieve Results Program.

Two study areas that exemplify different soil and relief conditions in second-order watersheds in Iowa were chosen as research foci: the 87.9 sq km (33.9 sq mi) Buck Creek Watershed in Poweshieck County (8790 ha [21,700 ac]) and the 56 sq km (21.6 sq mi) Walnut Creek Watershed in Story and Boone Counties. Future population growth in both Walnut and Buck Creek watersheds were assumed to be typical of rural Iowa, which will suffer population loss under current trends.

The base condition is the 1994 Corn Belt landscape. Agricultural policy goals that affected that landscape included income support to farmers based on past crop production areas, incentives for soil and water conservation, best management practices, and incentives for voluntary 10-year set-aside of highly erodible fields into conservation reserves that also created habitat. Agricultural production required high use of fossil fuels and high use of chemical and technological inputs. Public concerns for food safety and demand for choice in food quality paralleled increasing skepticism about the health of agricultural landscapes and recognition of the value of rural places.

Three alternative futures for 2025 were prepared with stakeholder participation, each assuming different primary policy goals for federal agricultural policy (Nassauer et al. 2002). All assume that policy supports profitable agricultural production by private landowners in 2025. Scenario 1 illustrates landscape changes that could result if increased production from agricultural enterprises is the dominant policy concern. Scenario 2 focuses on landscape change that could result if water quality dominates public concern, and Scenario 3 focuses on landscape change that could result if loss of biodiversity dominates public concern.

Each of the alternative futures was assessed for its spatial impacts on the landscape ecological pattern, biodiversity, hydrology, soil erosion, the economics of agricultural production, and public acceptance. Public acceptance was evaluated by a survey of Iowa farmers who viewed digital image simulations of the alternative futures. The research results show that these policy choices would have dramatic effects, just as the early nineteenth-century

General Land Office survey, the early twentieth-century establishment of the Soil Conservation Service, and the mid-twentieth-century price support programs dramatically affected the agricultural landscape.

Scenario-based studies of alternative futures such as these, and the current study of the Upper San Pedro River Basin, have several advantages. The use of multiple scenarios allows the investigation of differing points of view. Scenarios allow choices to vary within the selected areas of policy concern, and different points of view are represented by specific choices. The process intentionally investigates several futures and accommodates a diversity of opinion within the same study. Additionally, because each scenario describes the future in similar terms of policy choices, there is an opportunity to investigate the outcome of a single, specific policy decision.

The most important reason to use a scenario-based approach is the benefit to decision-making processes. For elected officials and public administrators, scenarios can be used to test current planning ideas and to explore the implications of public concerns. For landowners, alternative futures derived from scenarios can help anticipate the range of potential impacts to their lands that may result from regional changes. They also can help to assess how the multiple actions of property owners or the policies of local, regional, and national governments might affect the regional environment.

For all the members of a community, scenarios can help to better understand how today's decisions—or the failure to make important decisions—act together to change the future. The use of scenarios allows communities to assess the relative impacts of several alternative sets of choices. What are the relative merits and faults of a group of policies that promote some land uses over others, that concentrate some land uses in a single area rather than distribute them over the region, or that favor some policies over others? Given limited resources and complex issues, residents and elected officials must be able to address these types of questions. Scenario-based studies of alternative futures offer a tool to help make better-informed decisions today, for an improved future.

CHAPTER 2

The Upper San Pedro River Basin

The San Pedro River begins in Sonora, Mexico, and flows northward through Arizona, United States, before joining the Gila River, which flows into the Colorado, and finally empties into the Gulf of California (figure 2.1). The Upper San Pedro River Basin in Sonora and Arizona is the focus of a number of urgent, complex, interrelated, and controversial issues, including its international importance as bird habitat, its attractiveness to development, and the vulnerability of its landscape to changes caused directly by development and indirectly via continued lowering of the groundwater table.

The Upper San Pedro River Basin is located within an extremely diverse semiarid environment. It is diverse not only in terms of its abiotic geologic, geomorphic, and climatic environment, but also in terms of the associated edaphic and vegetation characteristics. This unique biogeographic setting defines habitat for a unique faunal assemblage. The basin provides breeding or migration habitat for 389 bird species (almost half of those seen in North America), 84 species of mammals (second in diversity only to those found in the rainforests of Costa Rica), and 47 species of reptiles and amphibians (Kunzmann n.d.). Several are listed as threatened or endangered species. Most of these species are completely dependent on the continued functioning of this rare ecosystem. In 1988, the San Pedro Riparian National Conservation Area (SPRNCA) was established by the United States Congress. So important is the region—the last free-flowing

Nevada
Utah
Colorado
Colorado River
Arizona
New Mexico
California
Gila River
Texas
San Pedro River
Study Area
Sonora
Chihuahua
Pacific
Ocean
Gulf
of
California
Baja
California
Sinaloa
Durango
0 50 100 Kilometers
0 50 100 Miles

Figure 2.1 ■ Location of the region

river in the Southwest—that the Nature Conservancy has placed the San Pedro River Basin on its list of "Last Great Places in the Western Hemisphere." *Wild Bird Digest* lists the area as the number one birding site in the United States (U.S. Dept. of Interior 1998). The potential disruption of this system by future patterns of land use and their anticipated effects forms the basis for intense debate among the various stakeholders in the region.

The San Pedro River can be characterized in part by the presence of shallow groundwater and intermittent stream flows. Small changes in either the groundwater level or river flow can greatly impact riparian vegetation and the animal species of the region. Water extraction and the concomitant lowering of the water table are threatening critical habitat and other environmental concerns.

In addition to the San Pedro riparian corridor, the uplands of the Upper San Pedro River Basin are also of value. The native perennial grasslands, along with the unique woodlands and forests of the higher elevations, are of significant importance in supporting the region's high biodiversity.

There are major policy and legal conflicts in the region over water use and water rights in the Upper San Pedro River Basin. In Sonora, the mining at Cananea pumps groundwater, uses it in its several mining processes, and discharges wastewater outside the San Pedro River Basin and into the south-flowing Rio de Sonora River Basin. In Arizona, and under Arizona law, surface water must be appropriated and uses must not interfere with those of senior or prior appropriations. However, in most of the rural areas of the state, including the basin, groundwater does not require appropriation. Irrigated agriculture and some domestic water users are of long standing, as is Fort Huachuca. An explicit federal reserved right to enough water for the Bureau of Land Management to fulfill the purposes of the San Pedro Riparian National Conservation Area was granted by Congress in 1988 (USDI BLM 1998).

The Gila River Indian Community is also a claimant to the San Pedro Sub-basin water. Although they draw water from far downstream on the Gila River, they consider that all water in the Upper San Pedro River Basin contributes to the supply of water to their reservation, and they include it in their very senior claims.

In Arizona, the pace of development is increasing. Fort Huachuca is unavoidably enmeshed in the controversy surrounding the fate of the San Pedro River. Local perception places much of the responsibility for growth and water impacts on the fort due to its link to 38 percent of Cochise County's employment (Crandall et al. 1992). The fort has been the subject of lawsuits alleging that it stimulates regional growth that in turn threatens endangered species by lowering the level of the aquifer supplying the San Pedro River.

Understanding the hydrologic processes that define the relationships between land use changes, ground water recharge, stream flow, vegetation, and habitat is of critical importance to the decision makers responsible for land management throughout the region.

These and other land use–related issues require integrated planning for long-term management. To deal with the decisions at hand, the United States and Mexico, Arizona and Sonora, their counties and towns, and Fort Huachuca need a long-term regional planning approach based on knowledge of local ecosystems.

This study is designed to develop an array of possible alternative future patterns of land uses for the region of the Upper San Pedro River Basin, Arizona, and Sonora, and to assess the resultant impacts that these alternative futures might have on patterns of biodiversity and related environmental factors, including vegetation, hydrology, and visual preference. A basic premise of the research is that issues related to land use and ecosystem planning can best be understood on a regional basis.

The research area (figure 2.2) includes the Upper San Pedro River Basin from its headwaters near Cananea, Sonora, to

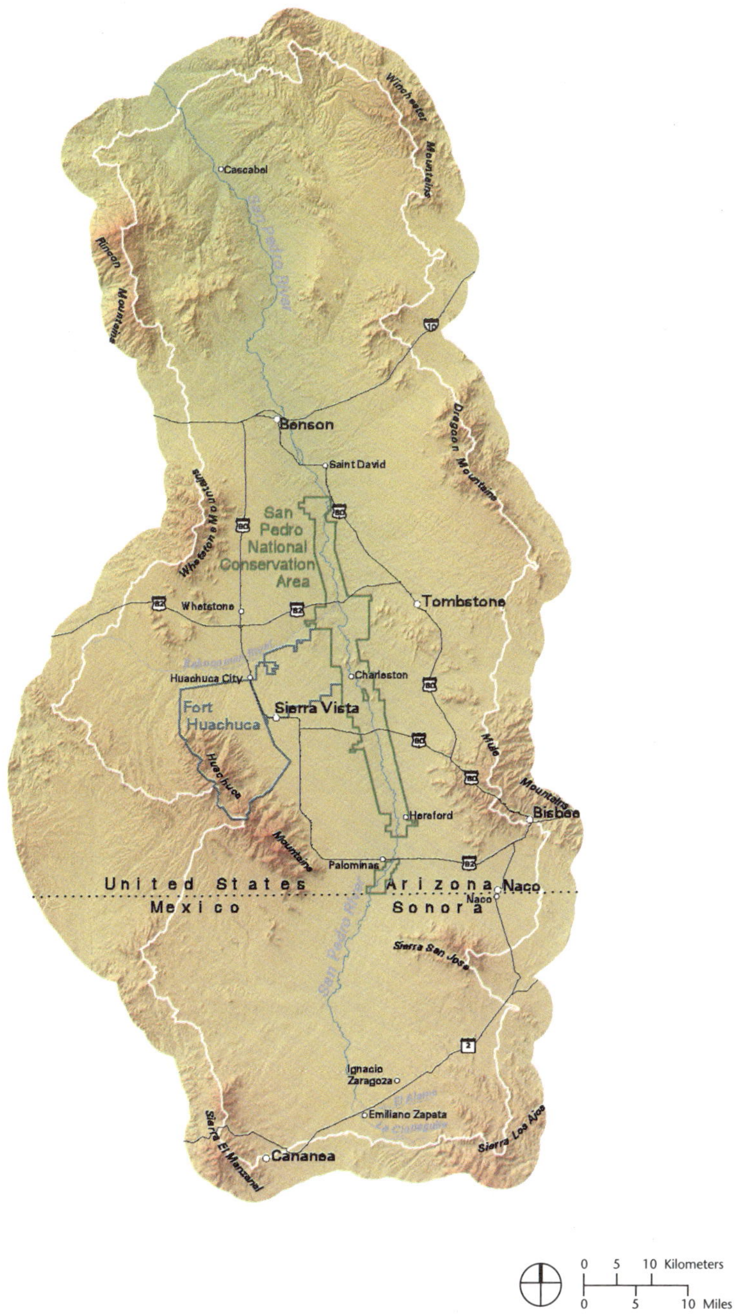
Cascabel
San Pedro River
Winchester Mountains
Rincon Mountains
Benson
Saint David
Dragoon Mountains
Whetstone Mountains
San Pedro National Conservation Area
Tombstone
Whetstone
Huachuca City
Charleston
Fort Huachuca
Sierra Vista
Huachuca Mountains
Mule Mountains
Bisbee
Hereford
Palominas
United States
Mexico
Arizona
Sonora
Naco
Naco
Sierra San Jose
Ignacio Zaragoza
Emiliano Zapata
Sierra Los Ajos
Sierra El Manzanal
Cananea
0 5 10 Kilometers
0 5 10 Miles

Figure 2.2 ■ The Upper San Pedro River Basin study area

Redington, Arizona. Areas adjacent to the basin that are integral for the maintenance of regional biodiversity are also included in the investigation. In total, the study includes 10,660 sq km (nearly 4100 sq mi). Arizona encompasses 74 percent of the study area, and the remaining 26 percent is in Sonora.

This research on the Upper San Pedro River Basin builds on earlier work on biodiversity and related issues in southeast Arizona, carried out by Mexican and American government agencies, universities, research institutions, and other groups such as the Nature Conservancy. Paramount among the research efforts is the coordinated investigations of the Semi-Arid Land-Surface-Atmosphere (SALSA) program. SALSA is an international effort that includes government agencies, universities, and research centers working to evaluate the consequences of natural and human-induced changes in semiarid environments focused on the Upper San Pedro River Basin. The San Pedro River Basin has been the focus of several prior regional planning studies, most recently by the Commission on Environmental Cooperation (CEC 1999) created by the North American Free Trade Agreement. The CEC report *Ribbon of Life* (1999) makes several conservation, planning, and related recommendations that are based principally on current conditions and the foresight of the several expert authors.

It is the aim of this study of alternative futures for the Upper San Pedro River Basin to investigate issues relating to possible future development in Arizona and Sonora and its potential impacts on regional hydrology and biodiversity. The study is solely a research project and should not be considered to be a part of a consulting or planning service. The study can aid decision making by identifying and evaluating regional ecosystem and water management options, by assessing the impacts of future land use patterns on the environment, and by demonstrating a flexible and practical planning approach to aid cooperative decision making in the region. The objective of this research is increased understanding of the risks and benefits implicit in a range of policy decisions for the Upper San Pedro River Basin.

The products of this research, including the scenarios and alternative futures, are not intended to be comprehensive analyses of the region. The planning assumptions used in this study rely mainly on publicly available documents and on local peoples' responses to policy choices as contained in the Scenario Guide (appendix A). There were six public presentations and many meetings, but the study did not include widespread community consultation in Arizona and in Sonora. Individual private property boundaries and local government jurisdictions are not considered except as related to hypothetical future development patterns. There are several important projects that have been proposed in the study area that have not been considered, including several very large private development proposals in Arizona; water recharge proposals related to Fort Huachuca and Sierra Vista; changes in water use related to mining in Sonora; and the importation of water into the San Pedro River Basin from outside sources.

In summary, there are many reasons to study the Upper San Pedro region. First, it has some of the highest levels of biodiversity in North America. Second, it is experiencing dramatic change and will have to manage increasing development pressures. Third, much information about the area had been compiled, but had not yet been assessed across international boundaries or applied to regional management of hydrology and biodiversity. Fourth, there is still time to make a difference.

CHAPTER 3

The Framework for Alternative Futures Studies

This study of the Upper San Pedro River Basin is organized according to the framework for alternative futures studies developed by Carl Steinitz (1990, 1993) and shown in figure 3.1. The framework consists of six questions that are asked several times during the course of a study. In designing a study of alternative futures for an area, the answers—the models and their applications—are particular to the case study. Some modeling approaches can be general, but model parameters and data are local to the place and time of the study, as are the issues and options whose consequences are being studied.

The six questions are:

1. How should the state of the landscape be described in content, space, and time? This question is answered by representation models, the data upon which the study relies.
2. How does the landscape operate? What are the functional and structural relationships among its elements? This question is answered by process models that provide information for the several analyses that are the content of the study.
3. Is the current landscape working well? This question is answered by evaluation models, which are dependent on cultural knowledge of the decision-making stakeholders.
4. How might the landscape be altered, by what policies and actions, where and when? This question is answered by the change models that will be tested in the research. They are also data, as assumed for the future.
5. What difference might the changes cause? This question is answered by impact models, which are information produced by the process models under changed conditions.
6. How should the landscape be changed? This question is answered by decision models, which, like the evaluation models, are dependent on the cultural knowledge of the responsible decision-makers.

During the course of the study, each of the six questions and its subsidiary questions are asked at least three times: first to define the context and scope of the work; second to identify the methods of study; and third, to implement the study method.

First Iteration: Describe Scope

The study process begins with a broad survey of major issues and the physical setting of the study. The six questions framework is used from top to bottom. Existing descriptions and representations of the region are examined and a general knowledge of how the landscape works is developed. Areas of concern, existing plans and policy interventions and their potential impacts, and decision-making processes and criteria are investigated.

Some typical initial questions include:

Representation:
Where is the study area?
What is its history?
What is its physical, economic, and social geography?

Process:
What are the area's major natural processes?
How are they linked to each other?

Evaluation:
Is the area seen as attractive? Why? Why not?
Are there current environmental "problems" in the area?

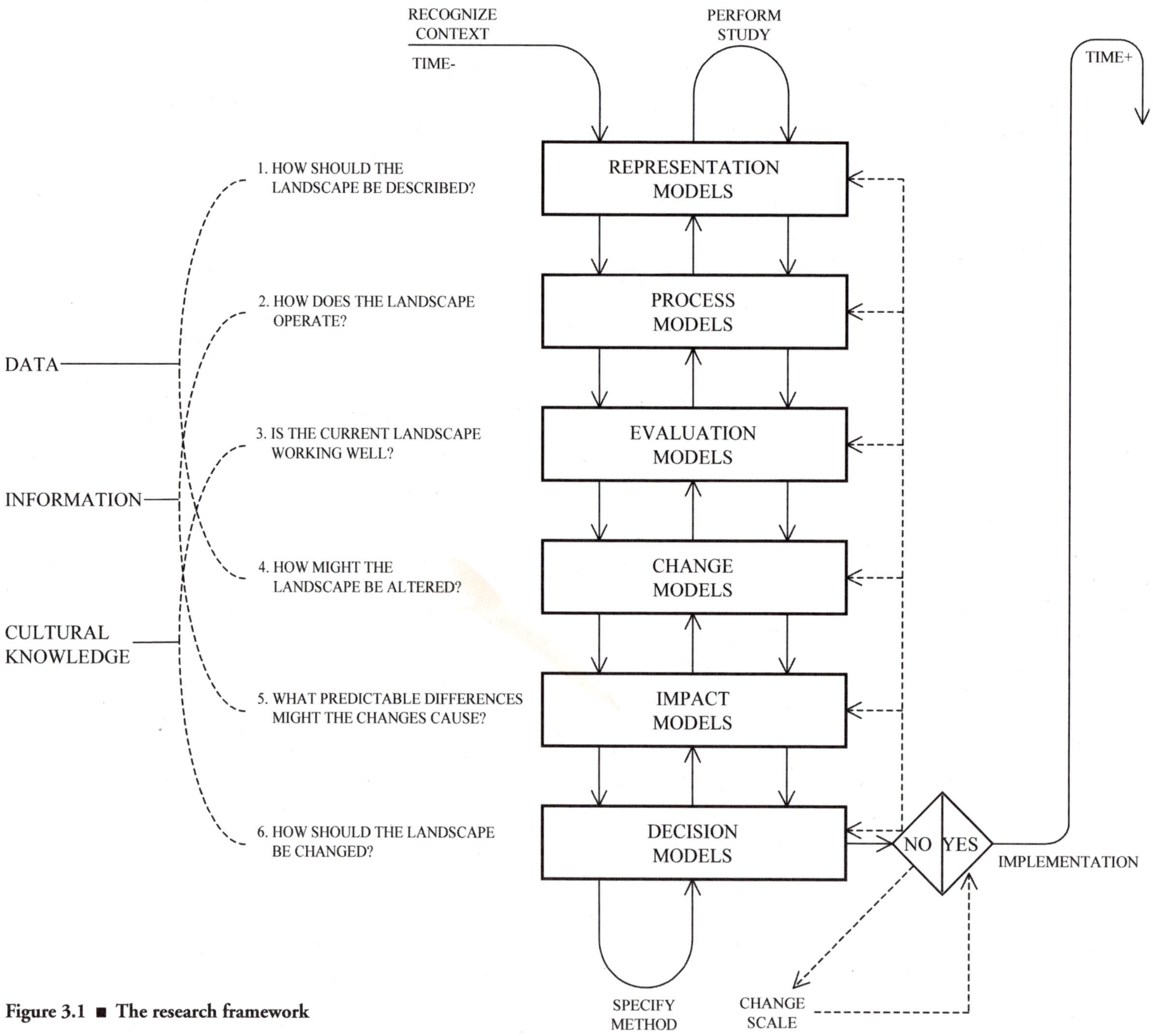
RECOGNIZE CONTEXT
TIME-
PERFORM STUDY
TIME+
DATA
INFORMATION
CULTURAL KNOWLEDGE
1. HOW SHOULD THE LANDSCAPE BE DESCRIBED?
2. HOW DOES THE LANDSCAPE OPERATE?
3. IS THE CURRENT LANDSCAPE WORKING WELL?
4. HOW MIGHT THE LANDSCAPE BE ALTERED?
5. WHAT PREDICTABLE DIFFERENCES MIGHT THE CHANGES CAUSE?
6. HOW SHOULD THE LANDSCAPE BE CHANGED?
REPRESENTATION MODELS
PROCESS MODELS
EVALUATION MODELS
CHANGE MODELS
IMPACT MODELS
DECISION MODELS
NO
YES
IMPLEMENTATION
SPECIFY METHOD
CHANGE SCALE

Figure 3.1 ■ The research framework

Change:
What major changes are foreseen for the region?
Are they related to growth or decline?
Are the pressures for change from inside or outside?

Impact:
Are foreseen changes seen as beneficial or harmful?
Are they seen as serious? Irreversible?

Decision:
Who are the major stakeholders? Are they public or private?
Are "positions" known? Are they in conflict?

Second Iteration: Define Method

In the second stage, the framework is used from bottom to top.

Designing the methodology for a study of alternative futures involves decisions that are especially complex and that are most often based on experience and judgment. Some overarching questions, which apply to any planning-related study, include:

- Who should participate and how? Local residents and/or outside experts?
- What is the purpose? Scientific advancement and/or public action?
- What is the trade-off between faster study results and action, versus possibly better research and later decisions?
- Will the study "product" be a single effort or a continuing decision support process?
- What is the appropriate cost? How much time, money, and basic research are needed?

Basic to developing the methodology is an understanding of how public and private decisions to change the landscape are made. The issues and the criteria defining acceptable impacts that decision makers and their constituents apply are investigated. Ways of identifying planning and policy choices that may influence future change are identified. Existing landscape conditions must be understood and considered. Structural and functional landscape processes are studied and models are specified. Once the processes are understood and their data needs identified, requirements for data and appropriate means of representation can be identified.

Decision:
What do the decision makers need to know?
What are their bases of evaluation? Are they scientific evaluations? Cultural norms? Legal standards?
Are there issues of public communication? Of visualization?

Impact:
Which impacts, how much, where, when, and to whom are seen as "good" versus "bad"?

Change:
Who defines the scenarios for change? How?
Which scenarios are selected? Toward which time horizon?
At what scale(s)?
Which issues are beyond the capabilities of the research models?
Are the alternative future outcomes simulated, or are they normative allocations?

Evaluation:
What are the measures of evaluation? In ecology?
In development economics? In politics?

Process:
Which models should be included?
How complex should the models be?

Representation:
Which data are needed? For which geography? At what spatial

scale? At which classification? For which times?
From which sources? At which cost? In which mode of representation?

Third Iteration: Implement Method

In the third stage, the framework is again used from top to bottom in carrying out the study.

Representation
Process
Evaluation
Change
Impact
Decision

Data are gathered and represented in a format useful for study purposes. Process models are implemented, and they evaluate the existing landscape as a baseline from which to assess impacts of change; a number of alternative futures are simulated, and their impacts are assessed. Decision makers can then better understand the likely future impacts of their choices.

At the extreme, two decision choices present themselves: no and yes. A no implies a backward feedback loop in the framework and the need to alter a prior level. All six levels can be the focus of feedback; "better data," "a better model," and "redesign of the proposed changes" are frequently applied feedback strategies.

A contingent yes decision (still a no) may also trigger a shift in the scale or size or timing of the study. In a scale shift, the study will again proceed through the six levels of the framework, but the several types of model will be different. The study will then continue until it achieves a potential positive (yes) decision. A yes decision implies implementation, and (one assumes) a forward-in-time change to new representation models.

When repeated and linked over scale and time, the framework may be the organizing basis of a very complex study. Regardless of complexity, the same questions are posed again and again. However, the models, their methods, and their answers vary according to the context in which they are used.

Although the framework and its set of questions and models looks orderly and sequential, it is frequently not so in application. The path through any study is not always smooth. There are false starts, dead ends, and serendipitous discoveries, but the path does pass through the questions and models of the framework as described herein before decisions can be made.

Figure 3.2 shows the relationship between the research team and the stakeholders. Decision making is the responsibility of the region's stakeholders, from the individual citizen to the federal level (and in this case study, the international level). In order to make decisions, questions must be asked and answered, and options for choice must be framed and deliberated. This study is shaped to respond to the issues and choices posed by the stakeholders. The alternative futures and the results of the assessments of their impacts are presented for stakeholder review and for the many decision processes that must precede any major action.

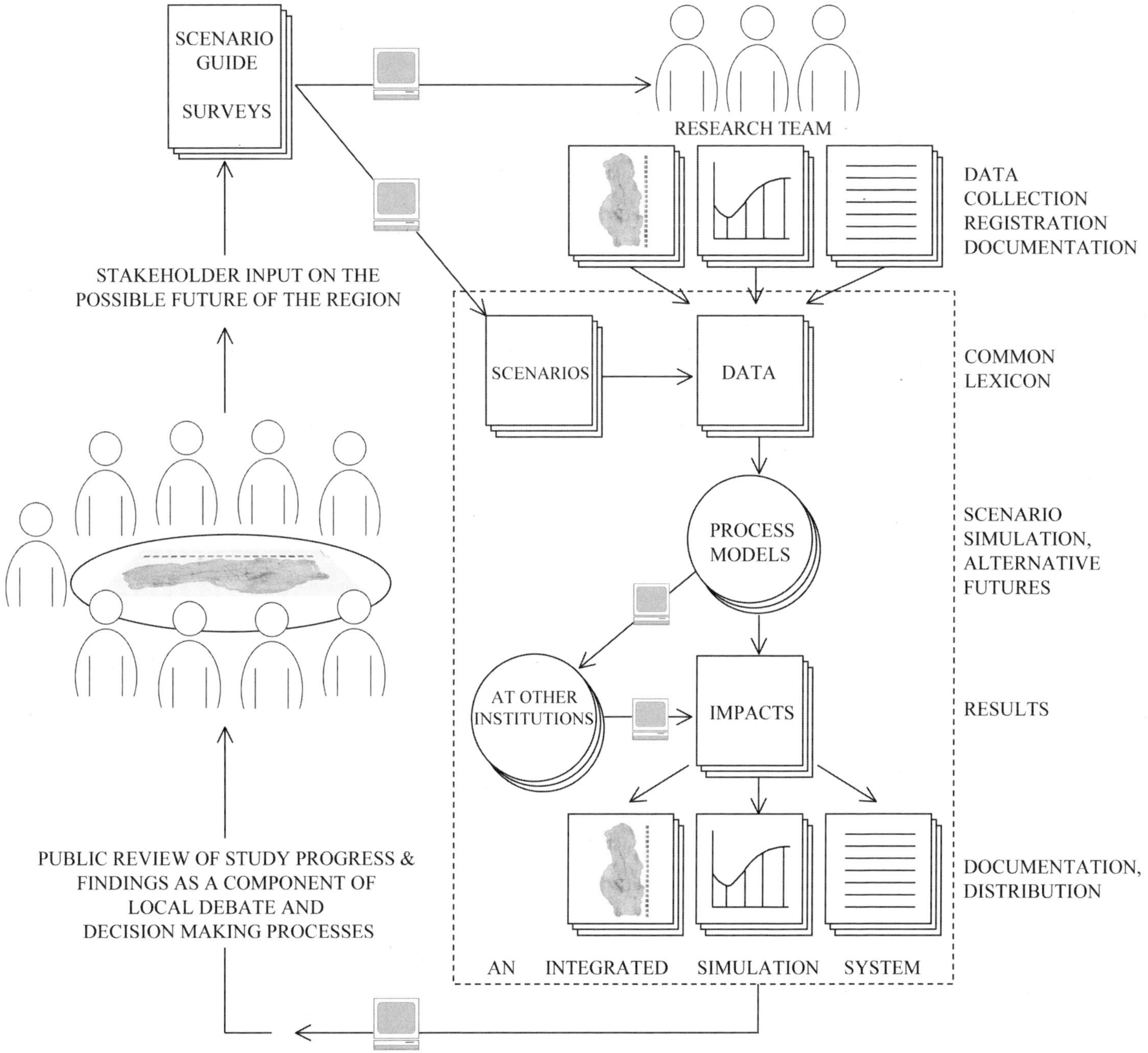
SCENARIO GUIDE
SURVEYS
RESEARCH TEAM
DATA COLLECTION REGISTRATION DOCUMENTATION
STAKEHOLDER INPUT ON THE POSSIBLE FUTURE OF THE REGION
SCENARIOS
DATA
COMMON LEXICON
PROCESS MODELS
SCENARIO SIMULATION, ALTERNATIVE FUTURES
AT OTHER INSTITUTIONS
IMPACTS
RESULTS
PUBLIC REVIEW OF STUDY PROGRESS & FINDINGS AS A COMPONENT OF LOCAL DEBATE AND DECISION MAKING PROCESSES
DOCUMENTATION, DISTRIBUTION
AN INTEGRATED SIMULATION SYSTEM

Figure 3.2 ■ The stakeholders and the research

CHAPTER 4

The Organization of the Research

This study of alternative futures for the Upper San Pedro River Basin applies the six-question framework in the organization of the research and in carrying it forward.

How should the state of the landscape be described in content, space, and time?

The question of describing the landscape is answered by representation models, the data upon which the study relies.

The research area includes the Upper San Pedro River Basin from the headwaters near Cananea, Sonora, to Redington, Arizona. Areas adjacent to the basin that are integral for the maintenance of regional biodiversity are also included in the investigation. In total, the analysis covers 10,660 sq km (or nearly 4100 sq mi). To describe the geography and the dynamic processes at work in this large study area, a computer-based geographic information system was organized to contain spatially explicit and publicly available data on the region. Digital data have been collected from a variety of public sources, including the United States Geological Survey, the Environmental Protection Agency, the United States Army, the Arizona Land Resource Information System, the Arizona GAP program, and the Semi-Arid Land-Surface-Atmosphere program. The 2000 land use/land cover classification was produced by the Desert Research Institute based on an interpretation of LANDSAT satellite imagery and color infrared aerial photography. Additional information, such as Natural Resources Conservation Service Soil Reports for the area, have been transferred into digital form at the Harvard Graduate School of Design. The information is coordinated on a 30-m (98.5 ft) grid using the Universal Transverse Mercator georeferencing system.

How does the landscape operate? What are the functional and structural relationships among its elements?

Questions about how the landscape operates are answered by process models that provide information for the several analyses that are the content of the study (figure 4.1).

A suite of computer-based process models is used to describe and evaluate the current landscape and also to assess the potential impacts of each of the alternative futures relative to the conditions in 2000.

The development model evaluates the attractiveness of the available land for five kinds of development: commerce-industry and four residential types: urban, suburban, rural, and exurban. It then simulates the development pattern of the region in accordance with several different scenarios for change. Each scenario includes assumptions about future population, the demand for different housing types, and policies and plans that might constrain or attract new private urban development.

The hydrological model simulates flow processes in the groundwater system of the Upper San Pedro River Basin. These include the interactions of groundwater with surface water and evapotranspiration. Unlike previous studies in Arizona, and in order to provide a more complete basis for evaluation, the hydrological model integrates data on the Sonoran part of the study area. After modeling current conditions, the hydrological model evaluates possible future impacts to the hydrologic system resulting from stresses inherent in each of the alternative futures. Five summary impact evaluations are made for each alternative: change in agricultural pumping; change in municipal and industrial pumping; average daily groundwater storage change based on

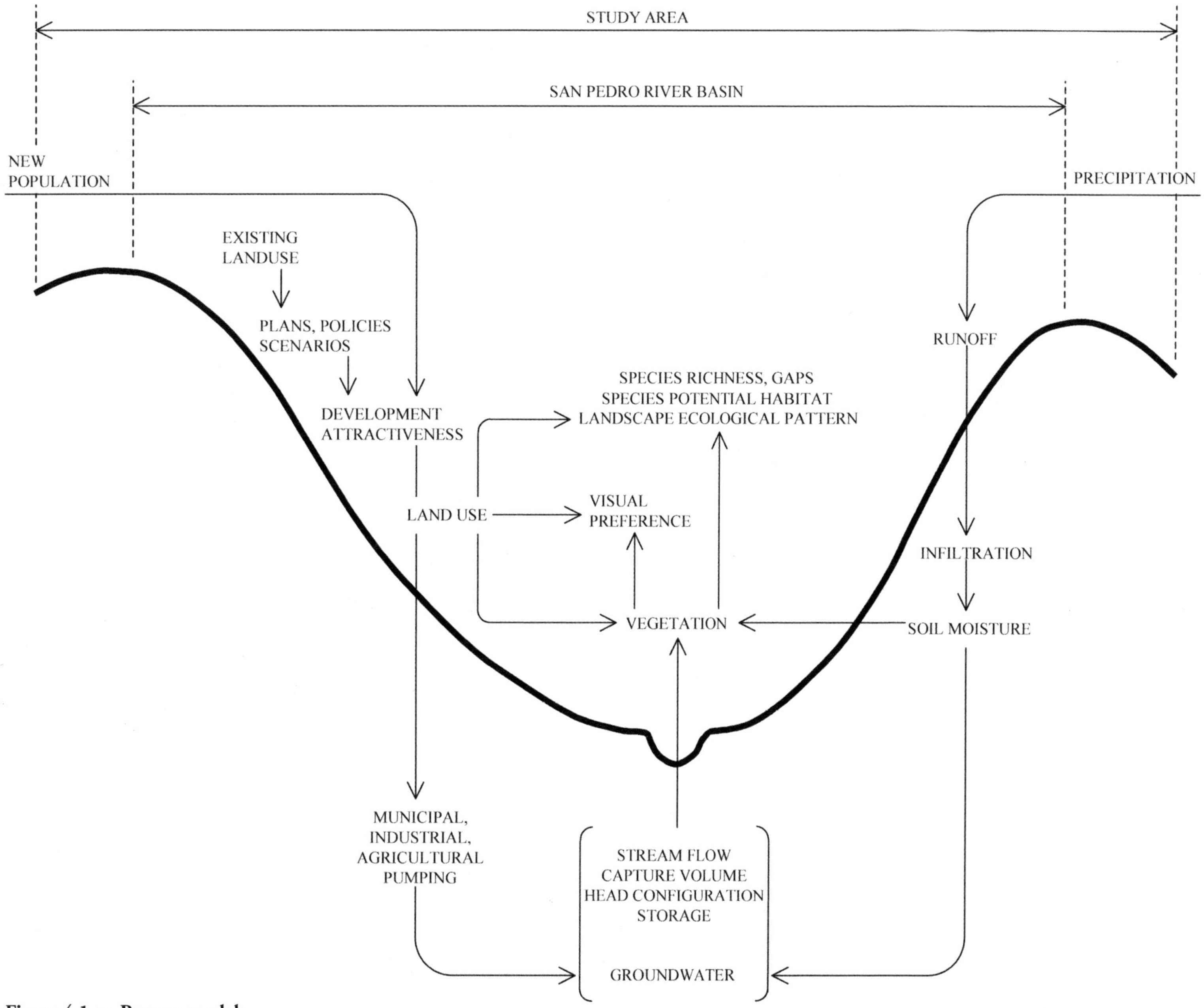
STUDY AREA
SAN PEDRO RIVER BASIN
NEW POPULATION
PRECIPITATION
EXISTING LANDUSE
PLANS, POLICIES SCENARIOS
DEVELOPMENT ATTRACTIVENESS
RUNOFF
SPECIES RICHNESS, GAPS
SPECIES POTENTIAL HABITAT
LANDSCAPE ECOLOGICAL PATTERN
LAND USE
VISUAL PREFERENCE
INFILTRATION
VEGETATION
SOIL MOISTURE
MUNICIPAL, INDUSTRIAL, AGRICULTURAL PUMPING
STREAM FLOW
CAPTURE VOLUME
HEAD CONFIGURATION
STORAGE
GROUNDWATER

Figure 4.1 ■ Process models

changes in the water table; change in flow in the San Pedro River; and change in the length of perennially flowing segments of the river.

The vegetation model then assesses several of the major stresses on vegetation and forecasts changes in the type and spatial distribution of vegetation within the study area. Factors accounted for in the model include urban development; addition, alteration, or removal of irrigated agriculture or grazing; managed fire or the absence of fire; lowering of the water table; changes in soil moisture; and changes in riparian corridors resulting from flooding and/or reduced stream flows.

The predicted new vegetation patterns form the basis for a three-part assessment of regional biodiversity: the landscape ecological pattern, a group of single species potential habitat models, and vertebrate species richness.

The focus of the landscape ecological pattern model is the spatial relationships between structural and functional elements of the landscape. Any type of landscape at any scale can be described as a mosaic--a background matrix and patches connected by corridors. Evaluation of the landscape ecological pattern presents the hypothesis that there are spatial landscape patterns that will conserve the majority of natural processes in any landscape.

Single-species models of six terrestrial vertebrates evaluate the impacts of future changes on their potential habitat. The species were chosen so that each of the vegetation communities within the study area was represented by at least one animal inhabitant. Additional criteria for selection included threatened or endangered species status (southwestern willow flycatcher, Sonoran pronghorn), existing or proposed reintroduction programs (beaver, jaguar), and species requiring large areas or unique features (northern goshawk, Gila monster).

The species richness approach to assessing biodiversity examines the distribution of potential habitat of all resident terrestrial vertebrates: amphibians, reptiles, birds, and mammals. The analysis of species richness involves identifying the vegetation and land cover types in which a given species can be expected to occur, a Wildlife Habitat Relations model. Species richness represents the total number of individual terrestrial vertebrate animals that might inhabit a given area. The method is based on the premise that it is possible to use the large sample size of all vertebrate species to provide general patterns of species richness and response to change, even though there is not a great deal of information on each particular species. Some natural habitat in the Upper San Pedro River Basin is already managed for wildlife conservation. However, not all species have protected habitats. GAP analysis uses habitat information from species richness analysis and land management information to identify areas of potential habitat for species that currently have no habitat in the region's protected areas.

The effect of change in the Upper San Pedro River Basin on visual preference is assessed by the visual preference model. The visual model identifies areas of scenic attractiveness in terms of the preferences expressed by residents of the San Pedro region, and evaluates how visual preference might change in the future by combining attractiveness with patterns of visibility to determine the overall visual preference of the area.

Is the current landscape working well?

Whether the current landscape is working well or not is answered by evaluation models, which are dependent on cultural knowledge of the stakeholders to decision making.

Each of the process models is applied to data on conditions in the study area during the period 1997–2000, referred to here as 2000. This establishes the reference period against which the impacts of future change are measured.

How might the landscape be altered—by what policies and actions, where and when?

How the landscape will be altered is answered by the change models that will be tested in this research. They are also data, as assumed for the future.

Because no single vision of the future can be certain, it is preferable to consider a set of alternative futures that encompass a spectrum of possibilities. Therefore, this study generates several alternative policy scenarios and examines the resulting range of alternative futures that the region might experience.

To help generate the scenarios in Arizona, the Scenario Guide questionnaire was developed. It was based on three groups of issues central to debate in the region that are currently being considered by area residents and elected officials. The questions addressed the development of the area, water use, and land management. The answers, interpreted into a set of assumptions and choices about policy, became a range of scenarios. A separate but similar question set that concerns the Sonoran part of the basin was applied to the Mexican portion.

Three groups of scenarios are projected from 2000 to 2020 in 5-year increments by the allocation portion of the development model. The first, called PLANS, is based on interpretation of the existing planning documents and land use practices of the region. The second, CONSTRAINED, investigates lower-than-forecast population growth and tightly controlled development zones. The third, OPEN, anticipates greater-than-forecast population growth and low-density development across the region. Each of these is expanded by variations that alter key policy positions, resulting in a total of ten different scenarios, each of which results in an alternative future. By comparing the effects caused by changing these key policies, the variations provide a basis for better understanding which actions will produce the greatest effects.

What difference might the changes cause?

What the possible differences might be is answered by impact models, information produced by the process models under changed conditions.

Applying the process models to the alternative futures for 2020 and comparing the results with the reference year 2000 yields impact assessments. Urbanization and agriculture are the major environmental stresses affecting the San Pedro River Basin. Direct impacts on hydrology and habitat are caused by activities such as grading, paving, plowing, grazing, irrigation, and water use. Indirect effects include modified hydrology, fire suppression, and vegetation change. Indirect effects may remain unnoticed by the casual observer, but their cumulative effects can be as detrimental to biodiversity as the direct impacts. Both direct and indirect impacts are assessed, with each of the impact assessments revealing one aspect of how an alternative future is predicted to change the landscape.

How should the landscape be changed?

How the landscape should be changed is answered by decision models, which, like the evaluation models, are dependent on the cultural knowledge of the decision makers.

Every decision-making process implies the existence of a decision model, based on the cultural knowledge of those bearing the responsibility for making choices. This research is intended to inform these decision-making processes, rather than to recommend specific solutions or policies. The projected impacts of the alternative futures can be used by stakeholders in Sonora and Arizona, including Fort Huachuca, to assess the desirability of the various policies that generated them. The criteria by which choices are made will vary among individuals and among different interest groups, but the decision-making responsibility is theirs.

Figure 4.2 shows the overall organization of the research.

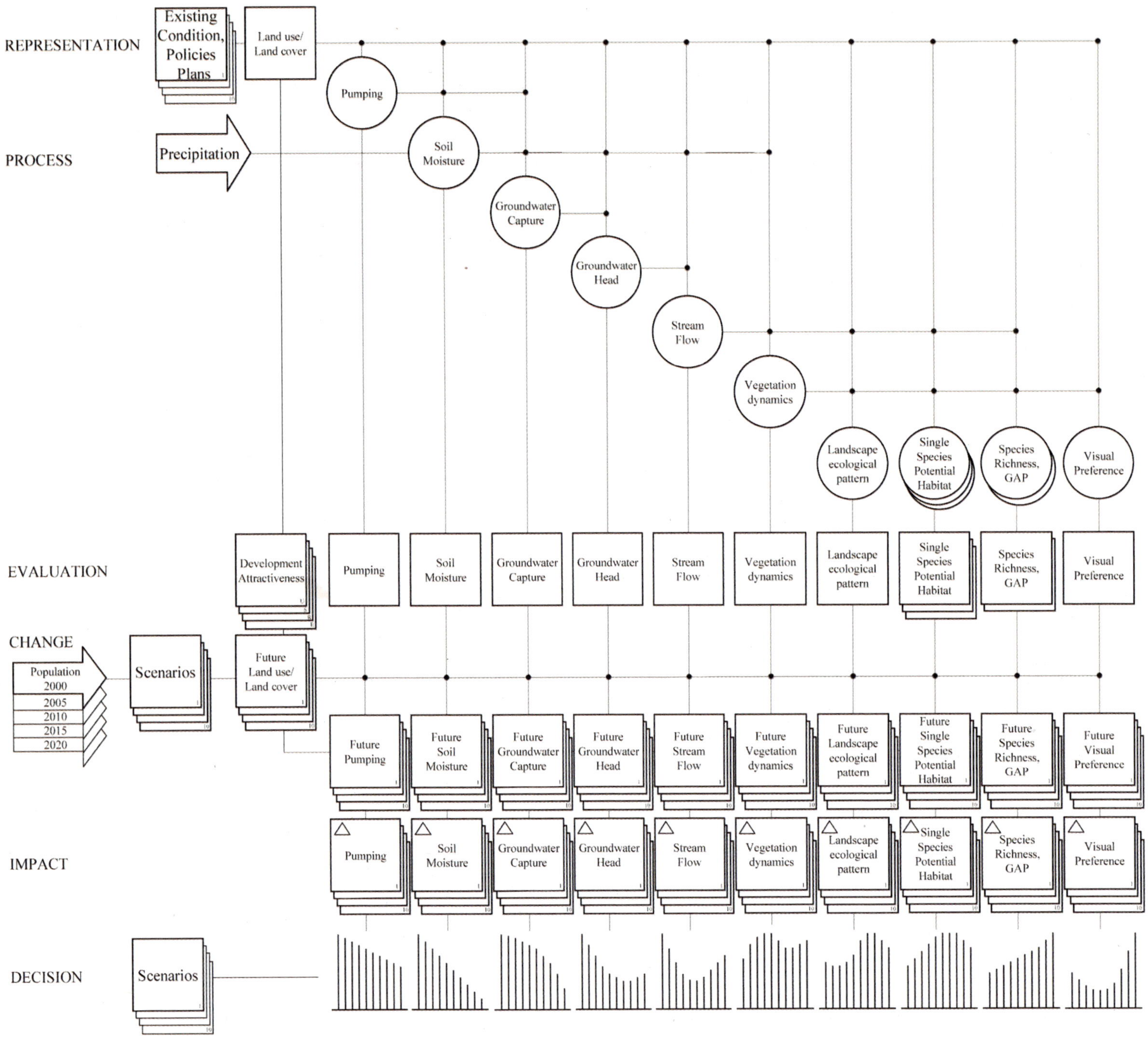
REPRESENTATION
Existing Condition, Policies Plans
Land use/ Land cover
PROCESS
Precipitation
Pumping
Soil Moisture
Groundwater Capture
Groundwater Head
Stream Flow
Vegetation dynamics
Landscape ecological pattern
Single Species Potential Habitat
Species Richness, GAP
Visual Preference
EVALUATION
Development Attractiveness
CHANGE
Population
2000
2005
2010
2015
2020
Scenarios
Future Land use/ Land cover
Future Pumping
Future Soil Moisture
Future Groundwater Capture
Future Groundwater Head
Future Stream Flow
Future Vegetation dynamics
Future Landscape ecological pattern
Future Single Species Potential Habitat
Future Species Richness, GAP
Future Visual Preference
IMPACT
DECISION
Scenarios

Figure 4.2 ■ The organization of the research

CHAPTER 5

Natural and Cultural History

The Upper San Pedro River Basin is located within the basin and range physiographic province. This topography is characterized by short narrow isolated mountain ranges (island mountains or sky islands) separated by extensive basins (bolsons) consisting of bajadas (or alluvial fans), valley fill, and occasional lacustrine (lake bed) deposits. The alluvial fans may be of very recent origin and unconsolidated, or of older age (Pleistocene: 10,000 to 1.7 million years ago, and Pre-Pleistocene: 1.7 to 5 million years ago) and more indurated. Many of these older fans have hardened layers of calcium carbonate or caliche that restricts both root development of vegetation and infiltration of water. In addition, the older fans are often deeply incised by the ephemeral channels that cross them, providing both habitat and movement corridors. Hillside slopes are typically rocky with shallow soils. The soils developed on these substrates are highly variable. Along with microclimatic factors, they lead to highly diverse vegetation types and an equally diverse assemblage of habitats.

The Upper San Pedro River Basin is situated in a trough formed by a down-dropped block fault between two groups of mountains. To the west, the prominent Huachuca, Whetstone, Mariquita, and Elenita Mountains rise as much as 1520 m (5000 ft) above the surrounding plains. The Dragoon, Mule, and Los Ajos Mountains border the basin to the east. Although the mountain ranges are typically deeply incised by streams, and the bajadas are crossed by arroyos, none are perennial. The only perennial watercourse is the San Pedro River, but only for a part of its

Photo 5.1 ■ San Pedro River Corridor

Photo 5.2 ■ Upper San Pedro River cottonwood-willow habitat

Photo 5.3 ■ Mouth of Garden Canyon

course. Even its largest tributary, the Babocomari River, is dry much of the year. The other two principal tributaries, Walnut Gulch and Greenbush Draw, are also ephemeral. Rock types include Pre-Cambrian metamorphosed schists and gneisses; a wide variety of granites, extrusive rhyolites, and andesites; and sedimentary shale, sandstone, and limestone units from Paleozoic to Tertiary. All of these rock types are distributed throughout the region. These rock units have a wide range of both geochemical and hydrologic characteristics that contribute to the diversity of associated vegetation and habitat types.

The region occupies a unique climatic situation. It is affected by two quite different and distinct air masses and wind circulation systems. In winter, the area is affected by the southward migration of the westerlies, bringing frontal precipitation. The northward advance of the sun brings with it a northward migration of high pressure systems that result in extreme drought in late spring and early summer. By mid-summer, a global readjustment of the subtropical highs occurs and results in moisture-laden winds moving into the region. The associated convectional storms of the summer monsoons can bring very intense storms over short periods of time to the study area. As a result, the region experiences a bimodal precipitation pattern: winter and summer rains separated by extensive periods of drought.

The animals and plants in the region are adapted to this highly heterogeneous landscape, diverse in terrain, rock type, soils, and climate (both in ranges and in variability of precipitation and temperature). Life must adapt to very hot temperatures in summer and annual precipitation as low as 250 mm (10 in.), enduring long periods of drought that is exacerbated by high annual precipitation variability. Sierra Vista, with an annual precipitation of 430 mm (17 in.), may experience years of less than 200 mm (8 in.) and years of over 750 mm (30 in.). Although the basin's vegetation reflects the general aridity of the region, it also exhibits great diversity based on the region's variations in climate and

Photo 5.4 ■ Grassland oak woodland transition

Photo 5.5 ■ Chihuahua desert scrub

Photo 5.6 ■ Retired agriculture on SPRNCA

elevation. Other factors influence microclimate and need to be considered in order to understand the type and distribution of vegetation. The steepness of a slope, the orientation of the plane on which it lies with respect to the sun (aspect), and the reflectivity (albedo) of the surface can modify considerably the small-scale climate over an area that might otherwise be considered homogeneous. Microclimates, soils, and landforms interact to form a multitude of plant communities providing habitat for the unique fauna of the region. The present vegetation of the region also shows the influence of human activity.

The first European to enter the Upper San Pedro River Basin was probably Fray Marcos de Niza in 1539. He was followed in 1540 by Francisco Vásquez de Coronado, who traveled north from Mexico searching for the Seven Cities of Cäbola, where the streets were thought to be paved with gold. Coronado entered a lush river valley that had been occupied by human settlements from as early as 12,000 B.C., or shortly after the end of the last Ice Age. Mammoth bones with embedded spear points indicate early Clovis culture settlements. Later, Cochise culture existed along the river from about 9000 B.C. to 1000 B.C. Ancient irrigation diversion systems and pottery shards indicate occupation by the Hohokam culture from about 450 B.C. to about A.D. 1450. Archaeological evidence suggests that prehistoric peoples used fire to a large degree, perhaps maintaining the grassland ecosystem. They also gathered fuelwood in large quantities, practiced agriculture, and hunted. The Sobaipuri Indians, ancestors of the Pima and Tohono O'Odham, followed the Hohokam. At the time of Coronado's visit, approximately 2000 indigenous people lived in the San Pedro Valley (McGuire 1997). Sauer (in Bahre 1991) estimated the prehistoric population of southeast Arizona at 10,000. That population decreased substantially after A.D.1500 as a result of the introduction of European diseases and tribal wars.

In 1686, Cananea was a settlement inhabited by Pima Indians loyal to the Spanish. Mining for gold and silver had begun at "La Cananea," but failed to prosper (Rodriguez in SALSA 1999). During the late 1690s, the Jesuit missionary Eusebio Kino established missions and introduced European tools, crops, and livestock along with the Catholic faith (Hadley in SALSA 1999). Small Mexican ranches, missions, and Indian farm plots dotted the valley in the 1700s, but were gradually abandoned after constant raids. The San Pedro valley had fallen under the influence of the Apache, who moved in from the north and east. They dominated the area from the mid-1700s, attacking farms, missions, settlements, miners, and soldiers and repressing or eliminating development in the region. The Sobaipuri remained in the valley until 1762 when the Spanish moved them to safer areas in the Santa Cruz valley near Tucson (Bahre 1991). Native Americans never again formed a major portion of the resident population of the basin (Bahre 1991).

Anglos entered the region in 1826 as beaver trappers, but did not settle. Anglo fur trappers called the San Pedro "Beaver River," and in a week in March 1833, they collected 1200 beaver skins there (Hadley in SALSA 1999). It was not until after the Mexican War of 1846–1848 that Anglos began to settle in the valley and confront the Apache. Most of the study area fell into American hands following the War of 1846, but the area remained largely unsettled until about 1870. In 1854, the Gadsden Purchase transferred an area that includes most of the Upper San Pedro River Basin to the United States. To protect the new settlers, military posts were built in southern Arizona from 1856 to 1876. In 1877, the U.S. Cavalry established a camp overlooking the San Pedro River valley at the mouth of Huachuca Canyon, which subsequently became Fort Huachuca.

The first important Anglo settlement was established at St. David by Mormon farmers as authorized by the Church of Jesus Christ of Latter-day Saints. In the same year, silver was discovered in the Tombstone Hills, and copper and other minerals at Bisbee, inaugurating the region's important mining industry. By 1879, a

Photo 5.7 ■ Upper San Pedro River

Photo 5.8 ■ Parade grounds on Fort Huachuca

mill at Charlestown was processing ore from Tombstone. Organized mining on an industrial scale dates to 1899 in the Cananea region of Sonora. The city of Cananea, located near the headwaters of the San Pedro, took its water from the spring at the river's source, later supplemented by wells driven near the river (Lopez in SALSA 1999).

In 1880, the city of Benson was founded and became an important station on the Southern Pacific Railroad, which was completed in 1881. The railway aided the expansion of mining and provided for efficient importation of livestock. By 1885, the watershed's grazing ranges were stocked to capacity. Serious overstocking of cattle soon followed (Hastings and Turner 1965). In May 1887, a major earthquake caused large cracks in the valley floor and disrupted the flow of springs. During the open range cattle boom, periodic droughts decimated the huge herds, with as many as 50 to 75 percent dying of starvation in 1893. Drought was interspersed with wet years, resulting in erosion and serious flooding by the late 1880s (Hadley in SALSA 1999).

In 1886, the famous warrior Geronimo surrendered to Don Mariano Avila, administrator of the Cuchuta hacienda, ending the Apache wars (Rodriguez in SALSA 1999). By this time, Tombstone had grown into a town of 8000. Many of the miners who lived there went to work at the successful new mine, at Cananea in Mexico. William Cornell Greene arrived in the region at about this time. Initially involved in mining, he moved into cattle ranching after suffering repeated Apache attacks. In 1899, he bought his first cattle. His holdings expanded to include 137,593 ha (340,000 ac) in the San Pedro River Basin and in Cananea Valley, and thousands of head of cattle and horses.
He returned to mining and in 1899 formed the Cananea Consolidated Copper Company based on his discovery of a large copper ore deposit. In 1907, Greene passed control of his mining interests to the Anaconda Copper Company and returned to ranching. His Cananea Cattle Company occupied an area extending 68 km (42 mi) from north to south and 110 km (68 mi) from east to west. This huge ranch was well managed, but pressure existed on the Mexican government to expropriate the land. After the Mexican Revolution of 1910, the 1917 constitution enabled the government to expropriate lands from large landowners and give them to agrarian communities. In the desert north of the country, the ejido is the predominant form of land tenure. Ejidos are communally held and include land used by individuals as well as by the community as a whole (Corcuera et al. 2000). In 1959, the

Photo 5.9 ■ Lavender Pit Copper Mine, Bisbee

Photo 5.10 ■ Saint David

Photo 5.11 ■ Agricultural fields south of Benson

Photo 5.12 ■ Mesquite Chihuahua desert scrub in grassland

Photo 5.13 ■ Copper mine at Cananea

Photo 5.14 ■ Ejido in Sonora

Table 5.1 Land use/land cover types

Land use/land cover type	Notes
Water	Free standing water
Coniferous Forest	Includes aspens although mainly comprised of various evergreen conifers (e.g. ponderosa pine and pinyon pine)
Oak Woodland	Contains various encinal oaks
Upland Mesquite	Comprised of scrub mesquite and grasses
Southern Desert Scrub	Mainly composed of creosote and white thorn acacia with small amounts of grasses
Northern Desert Scrub	Contains many desert shrubs and grasses, but must have saguaro cacti
Grassland	Includes both annual and perennial grasses
Barren	Areas largely absent of above-ground vegetation
Riparian	Composed of cottonwood-willow and mesquite bosque vegetative communities. Mesquite bosque represents mesquite trees over 2 m in height; not to be confused with scrub mesquite < 2 m in height.
Agriculture	Includes both active and inactive fields
Golf Course	
Exurban Residential	*Housing at a density of 1 house per > 4 acres
Rural Residential	*Housing at a density of 1 house per 1–4 acres
Urban Residential	*Housing at a density of 1 house per < 1 acre
Commercial	Generally takes the form of strip development along major roads
Industrial	Includes airports
Open Pit Mine	Includes tailing piles

*Zones of ownership and influence are considerably larger

Photo 5.15 ■ Sierra Vista

Photo 5.16 ■ Grassland south of Naco, Sonora

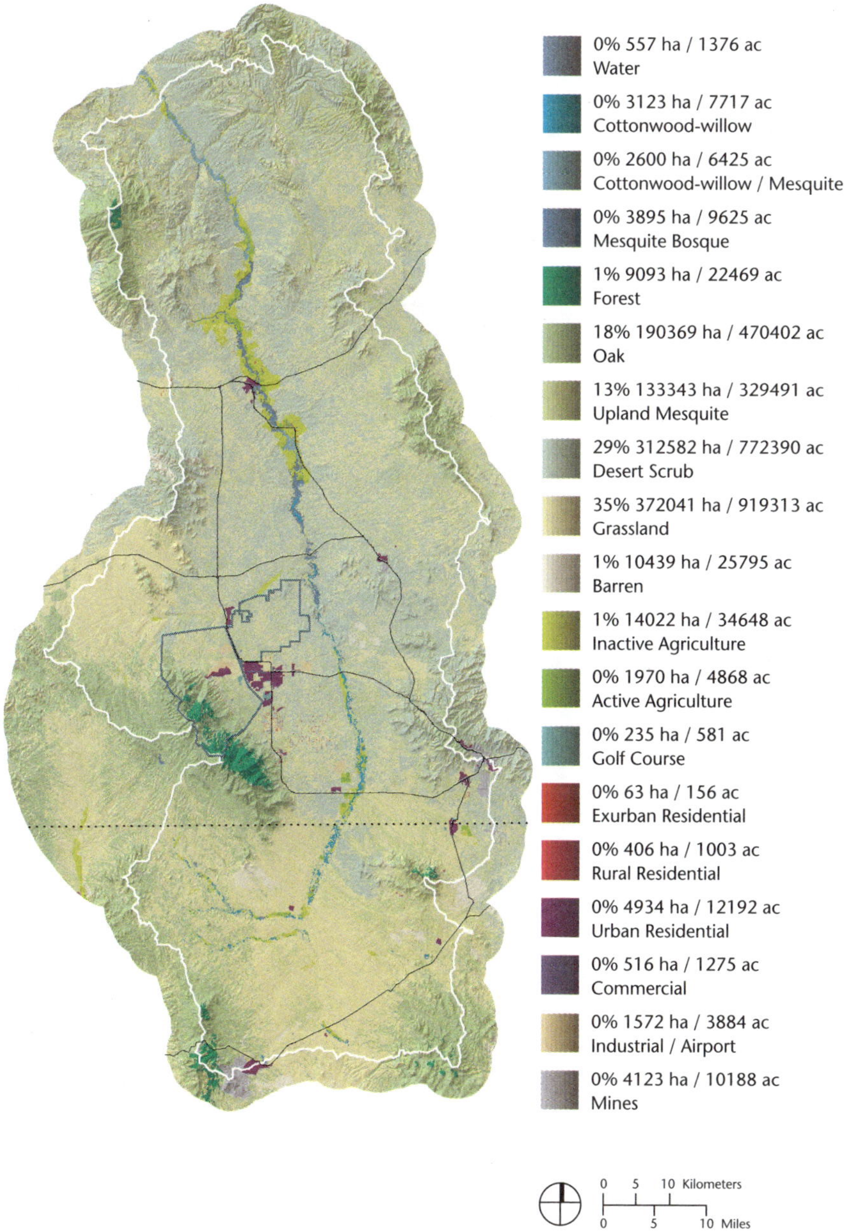
0% 557 ha / 1376 ac
Water
0% 3123 ha / 7717 ac
Cottonwood-willow
0% 2600 ha / 6425 ac
Cottonwood-willow / Mesquite
0% 3895 ha / 9625 ac
Mesquite Bosque
1% 9093 ha / 22469 ac
Forest
18% 190369 ha / 470402 ac
Oak
13% 133343 ha / 329491 ac
Upland Mesquite
29% 312582 ha / 772390 ac
Desert Scrub
35% 372041 ha / 919313 ac
Grassland
1% 10439 ha / 25795 ac
Barren
1% 14022 ha / 34648 ac
Inactive Agriculture
0% 1970 ha / 4868 ac
Active Agriculture
0% 235 ha / 581 ac
Golf Course
0% 63 ha / 156 ac
Exurban Residential
0% 406 ha / 1003 ac
Rural Residential
0% 4934 ha / 12192 ac
Urban Residential
0% 516 ha / 1275 ac
Commercial
0% 1572 ha / 3884 ac
Industrial / Airport
0% 4123 ha / 10188 ac
Mines
0 5 10 Kilometers
0 5 10 Miles

Figure 5.1 ■ Land use/land cover, 2000

Main St.
ANTIQUES
&
Collectables
BISBEE GRAND

Photo 5.17 ■ Bisbee

Photo 5.18 ■ Irrigated agriculture, Sonora

Photo 5.19 ■ Cananea

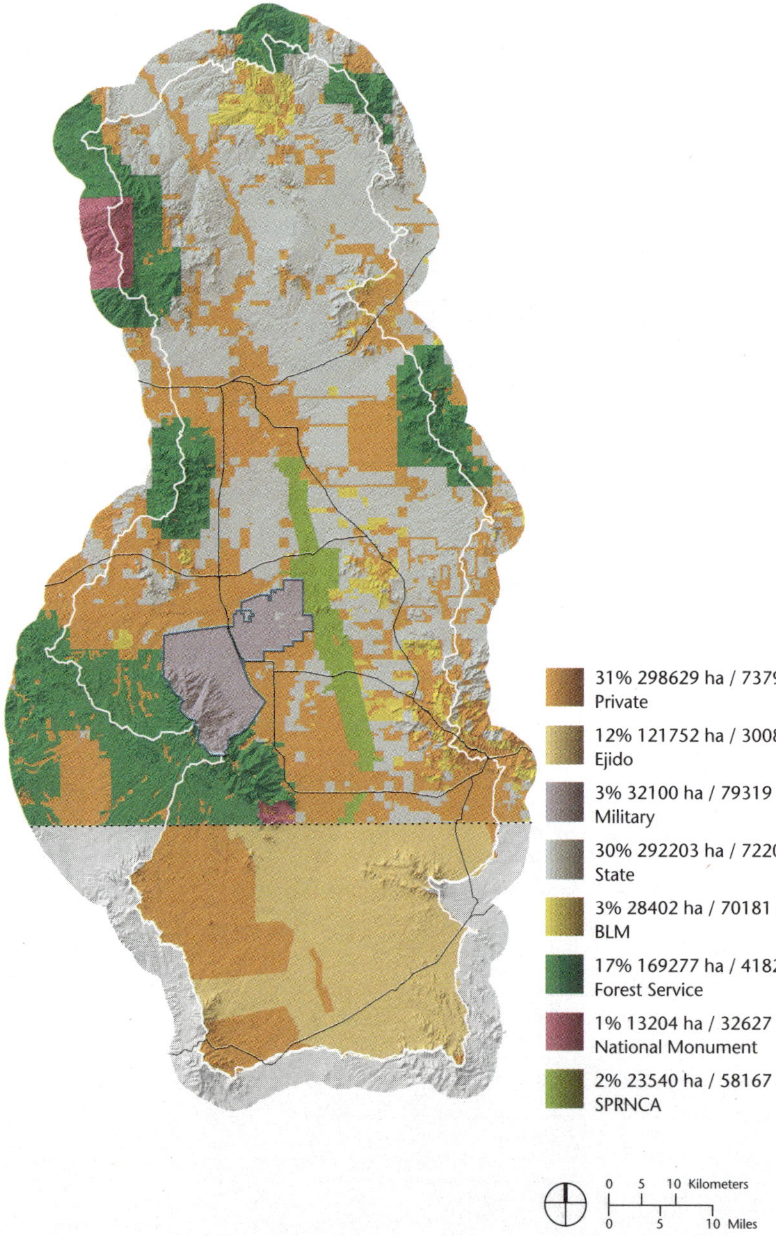
31% 298629 ha / 737912 ac
Private
12% 121752 ha / 300849 ac
Ejido
3% 32100 ha / 79319 ac
Military
30% 292203 ha / 722034 ac
State
3% 28402 ha / 70181 ac
BLM
17% 169277 ha / 418283 ac
Forest Service
1% 13204 ha / 32627 ac
National Monument
2% 23540 ha / 58167 ac
SPRNCA
0 5 10 Kilometers
0 5 10 Miles

Figure 5.2 ■ Land management, 2000

253,000 ha of the Ranchos de Cananea were expropriated to form 853 ejidos (Rodriguez in SALSA 1999).

Fort Huachuca continued as a military installation. From 1913, the fort was home to the Buffalo Soldiers, the Native Americans' name for the segregated black military units that had defended the region against the Apache. In 1955, Fry, a small town established in 1912 to serve the fort, was renamed Sierra Vista.

The 2000 U.S. Arizona census statistics reported that 177,755 people resided in Cochise County, with about 38,000 of them in Sierra Vista. Other settlements in the Arizona portion of the study area include Benson, Tombstone, Bisbee, and Huachuca City. In the Sonora portion of the study area, the principal settlements include Cananea (somewhat smaller than Sierra Vista) and Naco.

A map of the present land use/land cover of the study area is shown in figure 5.1. The information used to create this map is derived from several sources and translated into a 30 m (98.5 ft) grid. This map shows the reference condition to which the various scenarios are applied to generate the alternative futures. It also is the benchmark against which impacts are measured. Table 5.1 describes the land use/land cover map categories.

About 40 percent of the Arizona study area is private land, 35 percent is administered by the state of Arizona, and the remaining 25 percent is in U.S. Forest Service, Bureau of Land Management, U.S. Department of Defense, or other public ownership (figure 5.2). Fort Huachuca occupies 29,450 ha (73,000 ac) (Kent in SALSA 1999). In Sonora, and in the rest of Mexico, a large proportion of the land is under communal land tenure. The ejido can be very large, and it is made up of lands surrounding a small rural settlement. Land includes urban plots for residential uses, parcels for individual work sites, and communal lands, including agricultural, cattle range, and forestry areas for collective use (Corcuera et al. 2000).

The land is used for a variety of purposes, with grazing predominating in both Arizona and Sonora. Agriculture, primarily along the San Pedro River flood plain and lower bajadas, is still significant but declining. Other uses include military purposes, conservation, and settlement.

Much of the Arizona portion of the study area is used for recreation and tourism. The fine scenery, exceptional birding (especially in Ramsey, Carr, and Miller canyons), the newly opened Kartchner Caverns State Park (already attracting 200,000 visitors a year), the historic towns of Tombstone and Bisbee, and the transportation hub at Benson attract considerable numbers of tourists, recreationalists, and other visitors. The expansion of nearby Tucson and the high level of amenity are increasingly attracting development pressure.

While agriculture, grazing, and mining are declining in importance and extent within the Arizona portion of the Upper San Pedro River Basin, they are fairly stable and may even be increasing in the Sonoran portion of the basin. Several hundred hectares of fertile and potentially productive land near Naco, Sonora, may soon be brought into agricultural production, further reducing surface flow and exacerbating wastewater management problems. The copper mine at Cananea is one of Mexico's two largest, and it is growing at a rapid rate. However, fluctuations in the market price of copper may result in an increase or decrease in production and its related workforce. With biosphere reserves demarcated in the mountains near Cananea, and growing awareness of the need to protect both the extensive upland grasslands and the San Pedro River riparian zone, the potential for conflicts over appropriate land use increases. The demands of rapidly increasing population in Sonora must be balanced against needs to maintain the grasslands and the riparian zone for recreation, conservation, agriculture, or grazing. Decisions on the future land uses of the region are now at a critical juncture.

CHAPTER

6

The Issues for Research

A review of public planning reports, the media, and several interviews conducted in 1997–1998 resulted in the identification of three major groups of issues facing the region: population growth and planning, water management, and land management and conservation. The list of issues includes:

Increasing population
Increasing development
Growth of Cananea and its mining industry
Growth of Naco and its agriculture
Types of future residential development
Rural residential development in Arizona
Status of Fort Huachuca
Kartchner Caverns State Park
Domestic water use
Lowered groundwater levels
Reduced flow in the San Pedro River
Irrigated agriculture
Vegetation management for stream flow
Ranching
Conservation leasing of Arizona state land
Expansion of riparian conservation land
Fire management
Landscape ecological pattern
Protection of habitats
Threatened and endangered species
Visual quality

These issues require decisions that will shape the future of the region. The research is based on local input in shaping the scenarios that incorporate the widest range of options within these issues. Choices among these options have been developed into the several alternative futures and in framing the questions listed below, which are among those tested in the research.

- What is the widest range of environmental impacts that might be expected by 2020?
- What is the variance between the scenario that is most development/least conservation oriented and the one that is least development/most conservation?
- What will be the impacts upon future conditions in Arizona and Sonora if the current population forecast for the Arizona portion of the study area is doubled?
- What will be the impacts on future conditions in Arizona and in Sonora if there is unexpectedly rapid growth in Sonora?
- What will be the impacts of strict enforcement of policies that guide future development in Arizona into development zones around existing urban areas?
- In a policy climate that favors development and is less focused on conservation, what will be the impacts of accelerated growth in population and development in Arizona and in Sonora?
- In a scenario that constrains development for assumed environmental benefits, what are the impacts of doubling Fort Huachuca's on-base population?
- In the most development-constraining and conservation-favoring scenario, what will be the impacts of closing Fort Huachuca?
- What will be the impacts of closing Fort Huachuca in an environment of accelerated and less-constrained growth in Arizona and one that favors rural and exurban development?
- What will be the variance in impacts caused by closing Fort Huachuca or doubling its on-base population?
- What differences will there be for Sierra Vista if existing development regulation is changed to allow more development?
- What differences will there be for Benson if existing development regulation is changed to allow more development?

CHAPTER 7

The Scenarios for Change

After investigation of the environmental issues facing the San Pedro region, a questionnaire called the Scenario Guide was developed for use in the Arizona part of the study area (appendix A). It was given out at public meetings and was available via the project Web site. The Scenario Guide gave respondents the opportunity to select from a set of options (or to suggest their own strategies) related to planning issues and priorities for the future of the region. It was based on issues under discussion throughout the community, municipal meetings, and reports in local media. It contained questions relating to land development, water use, and land management. The answers were used to guide the creation of several sets of interrelated policy choices, each of which in turn became a scenario. A similar set of issues was investigated within the Sonoran part of the study area, generating two sets of policies and assumptions used as input to the scenarios. Each assumption or policy choice implies either attractions or constraints to future land use changes that can be simulated in the geographical information system.

A 20-year period, 2000 to 2020, was chosen for the study and for the Scenario Guide. A 20-year period is frequently used in planning studies, and demographic forecasts are generally limited to a 20-year period. Improvement and financing plans for infrastructure, such as roads, bridges, sewage treatment facilities, etc., are often developed in 20-year phases. Study periods of longer than 20 years become subject progressively to higher levels of uncertainty.

Analysis of the Scenario Guides revealed several recognizable patterns of response that generally represented the observed interests of the respondents. Each of these patterns was developed into a base scenario, and some variations. One scenario, referred to as PLANS, is based on current plans in Arizona and accepts current population forecasts. Another, called CONSTRAINED, directs development in Arizona into currently developed areas and reduces the forecast population. The third, OPEN, removes most constraints on land development and assumes higher population than forecast. Each scenario is further modified by selected policy changes resulting in additional but closely related scenarios. Examination of these related scenarios highlights the effect of individual and important policy changes.

In Mexico, consultation in Sonora resulted in two scenarios for the Mexican part of the study area. One assumes the town of Naco doubles in population, based on expanded irrigated agriculture, and establishes a conservation corridor along the San Pedro River. This was used in all but two of the scenarios, PLANS 2 and OPEN 2. The second, high-growth scenario for Sonora assumes Naco doubling with expanded agriculture and Cananea doubling because of increased mining, but no new conservation areas.

Table 7.1 summarizes the issues raised in the Scenario Guide and indicates the choices used to create each of the scenarios. (Note that the material in table 7.1 appears in appendix A as well.) In the table, P stands for PLANS, C for CONSTRAINED, and O for OPEN. An appended number indicates a related scenario. Each group of scenarios represents a pattern of responses to the issues and policy choices in the Scenario Guide. The scenarios are used to create the alternative futures. Some of the choices offered in the Scenario Guide were not selected by any respondents.

Ten scenarios guide the model of how development could take place, creating the ten alternative futures. The ten scenarios result from changes to important components of the three main scenarios, PLANS, CONSTRAINED, and OPEN, made in order to examine the changes in the alternative futures when various policy choices are changed.

- PLANS is based on interpretation of the current Arizona and Sonora plans, and a forecast population of 95,000 in 2020 in the Arizona portion of the study area.
- PLANS 1 increases the Arizona population at a rate double the present forecast, but is otherwise the same as PLANS.
- PLANS 2 maintains the predicted Arizona population growth, and doubles the population in Sonora, with corresponding increases in mining activity, but no change to Sonoran conservation areas.
- PLANS 3 maintains the predicted Arizona and Sonora population growth, but constrains growth in Arizona to urbanized areas.
- CONSTRAINED assumes lower than forecast population growth in Arizona. Development is concentrated in existing developed areas. It includes very large lot residential development.
- CONSTRAINED 1 varies in that the on-base population of Fort Huachuca is doubled.
- CONSTRAINED 2 varies in that Fort Huachuca is closed.
- OPEN assumes higher than forecast population growth in Arizona, with major reductions of development control. Sonora remains as forecast.
- OPEN 1 is the same as OPEN, except that Fort Huachuca closes, and there are increased controls on rural residential development.
- OPEN 2 doubles the on-base population of Fort Huachuca and doubles the population of Sonora, with corresponding increases in mining activity, but no change to Sonora's conservation areas.

Table 7.1 Responses to the Scenario Guide

POPULATION FORECAST

P	P1	P2	P3	C	C1	C2	O	O1	O2	
				■	■	■				Population increase should be one-half less than as forecast (2020 population of 78,500)
										Population increase should be one-third less than as forecast (2020 population of 84,000)
■		■	■							Population increase should be as forecast (2020 population of 95,000)
										Population increase should be one-third greater than as forecast (2020 population of 106,000)
							■	■	■	Population increase should be one-half greater than as forecast (2020 population of 111,500)

DISTRIBUTION OF NEW RESIDENTS

P	P1	P2	P3	C	C1	C2	O	O1	O2	
80	80	80	70	90	90	90	15	15	15	urban
15	15	15	10	00	00	00	15	15	15	suburban
03	03	03	10	00	00	00	60	60	60	rural
02	02	02	10	10	10	10	10	10	10	exurban

RURAL RESIDENTIAL ZONING

P	P1	P2	P3	C	C1	C2	O	O1	O2	
										The minimum size of a rural residential lot should be 40 ac in the Upper San Pedro River Basin
										The minimum size of a rural residential lot should be 20 ac in the Upper San Pedro River Basin
										The minimum size of a rural residential lot should be 10 ac in the Upper San Pedro River Basin
■	■	■	■	■	■	■				The minimum size of a rural residential lot should be 4 ac in the Upper San Pedro River Basin
							■	■	■	The minimum size of a rural residential lot should be 1 ac in the Upper San Pedro River Basin
										There is no minimum lot size for a rural residential lot in the Upper San Pedro River Basin

P	P1	P2	P3	C	C1	C2	O	O1	O2	
				■	■	■				The minimum size of a rural residential lot should be 40 ac if within 1 mi of the San Pedro Riparian National Conservation Area (SPRNCA)
										The minimum size of a rural residential lot should be 20 ac if within 1 mi of the SPRNCA
										The minimum size of a rural residential lot should be 10 ac if within 1 mi of the SPRNCA
■	■	■	■							The minimum size of a rural residential lot should be 4 ac if within 1 mi of the SPRNCA
							■	■	■	The minimum size of a rural residential lot should be 1 ac if within 1 mi of the SPRNCA
										There is no minimum lot size for a rural residential lot if within 1 mi of the SPRNCA

STATUS OF FORT HUACHUCA

P	P1	P2	P3	C	C1	C2	O	O1	O2	
				■						The fort remains open but is reduced to only those units and activities associated with the Electronics Proving Ground; all other units and activities are transferred to other facilities (approximately 1500 active duty troops, civilian contractors, and support personnel would remain at Fort Huachuca)
■	■	■	■							The fort remains open and should stay at its current size
					■				■	The fort remains open and should double its current resident population
										The fort closes and its built facilities should be reused by the Arizona National Guard; and all training areas should continue to be dual-managed for conservation and training
										The fort closes and its built facilities should be used for economic growth in the civilian sector with all the training area managed for conservation
						■				The fort closes and its built facilities should be used for economic growth in the civilian sector with half of the training area managed for conservation and half used for economic growth
							■	■		The fort closes and all its built facilities and land should be used for economic growth in the civilian sector

KARTCHNER CAVERNS

P	P1	P2	P3	C	C1	C2	O	O1	O2	
										Kartchner Caverns should attract 100,000 people per year in 2020
■	■	■	■				■	■	■	Kartchner Caverns should attract 200,000 people per year in 2020
										Kartchner Caverns should attract 400,000 people per year in 2020
				■	■	■				Kartchner Caverns should attract 1,000,000 people per year in 2020

DOMESTIC WATER USE

P	P1	P2	P3	C	C1	C2	O	O1	O2	
										Domestic per capita consumption from public/company sources should decrease from 995 levels by 40 percent (36 gallons per person per day)
■	■	■	■	■	■	■				Domestic per capita consumption from public/company sources should decrease from 1995 levels by 20 percent (48 gallons per person per day)
							■	■	■	Domestic per capita consumption from public/company sources should remain at 1995 levels (60 gallons per person per day)
										Domestic per capita consumption from public/company sources should increase from 1995 levels by 20 percent (72 gallons per person per day)
										Domestic per capita consumption from public/company sources should increase from levels by 40 percent (84 gallons per person per day)

Table 7.1 Responses to the Scenario Guide, continued

P	P1	P2	P3	C	C1	C2	O	O1	O2	Response
■	■	■	□	□	□	□	□	□	□	Domestic per capita consumption from individually owned sources should decrease from 1995 levels by 40 percent (75 gallons per person per day)
□	□	□	□	■	■	■	□	□	□	Domestic per capita consumption from individually owned sources should decrease from 1995 levels by 20 percent (100 gallons per person per day)
□	□	□	■	□	□	□	■	■	■	Domestic per capita consumption from individually owned sources should remain at 1995 levels (125 gallons per person per day)
□	□	□	□	□	□	□	□	□	□	Domestic per capita consumption from individually owned sources should increase from 1995 levels by 20 percent (150 gallons per person per day)
□	□	□	□	□	□	□	□	□	□	Domestic per capita consumption from individually owned sources should increase from 1995 levels by 40 percent (175 gallons per person per day)

IRRIGATED AGRICULTURE

P	P1	P2	P3	C	C1	C2	O	O1	O2	Response
□	□	□	□	□	□	□	□	□	□	Irrigated agriculture in the Upper San Pedro River Basin should be continued at its present level of intensity and locations
□	□	□	□	■	■	■	□	□	□	All irrigated agriculture in the Upper San Pedro River Basin should be removed
□	□	□	□	□	□	□	■	■	■	An irrigation nonexpansion area (INA) should be created within the Upper San Pedro River Basin; all existing irrigated agriculture remains, but proposed irrigated agriculture within 1 mile of the Upper San Pedro River is prohibited
■	■	■	■	□	□	□	□	□	□	An irrigation exclusion area should be created within the Upper San Pedro River Basin; all proposed irrigated agriculture within 1 mi of the Upper San Pedro River is prohibited; existing water rights for irrigated agriculture within 1 mi of the San Pedro River are purchased and retired
□	□	□	□	□	□	□	□	□	□	Irrigated agriculture in the Upper San Pedro River Basin should be increased by 50 percent (in area)

VEGETATION MANAGEMENT FOR STREAM FLOW

P	P1	P2	P3	C	C1	C2	O	O1	O2	Response
□	□	□	□	□	□	□	□	□	□	Cottonwood and willow trees in the riparian zone along the San Pedro should be removed and the land managed to maintain a grassland ecosystem
□	□	□	□	■	■	■	□	□	□	Approximately half of the cottonwood and willow trees in the riparian zone along the San Pedro should be removed by the clearing of selected areas and that land managed to maintain a grassland ecosystem
■	■	■	■	□	□	□	■	■	■	Cottonwood and willow trees in the riparian zone along the San Pedro should not be removed
□	□	□	□	□	□	□	□	□	□	Upland mesquite should be removed and the land should be managed to maintain a grassland ecosystem
□	□	□	□	■	■	■	□	□	□	Approximately half the upland mesquite should be removed by clearing selected areas and that land managed to maintain a grassland ecosystem
■	■	■	■	□	□	□	■	■	■	Upland mesquite should not be removed

RANCHING

P	P1	P2	P3	C	C1	C2	O	O1	O2	Response
■	■	■	□	□	□	□	□	□	□	Ranching in the San Pedro River Basin on state- and federal-owned lands should be increased to the full extent (in area) that is possible
□	□	□	□	□	□	□	■	■	■	Ranching in the San Pedro River Basin should be continued at its current intensity and locations
□	□	□	□	□	□	□	□	□	□	All ranching in the San Pedro River Basin should be removed
□	□	□	□	■	■	■	□	□	□	Ranching in the San Pedro River Basin on state-owned lands should be removed
■	■	■	□	□	□	□	□	□	□	Ranching in the San Pedro River Basin on federal-owned lands should be removed
□	□	□	■	□	□	□	□	□	□	Ranching in the San Pedro River Basin on state- and federal-owned lands should be removed

LEASING OF STATE LAND FOR CONSERVATION

P	P1	P2	P3	C	C1	C2	O	O1	O2	Response
■	■	■	■	■	■	■	□	□	□	The leasing of state-owned land in the San Pedro River Basin for conservation purposes should be allowed by competitive bidding
□	□	□	□	□	□	□	■	■	■	The leasing of state-owned land in the San Pedro River Basin for conservation purposes should not be allowed

SAN PEDRO RIPARIAN NATIONAL CONSERVATION AREA

P	P1	P2	P3	C	C1	C2	O	O1	O2	Response
□	□	□	□	□	□	□	□	□	□	The SPRNCA should be dissolved and the land sold to private interests
□	□	□	□	□	□	□	□	□	□	The SPRNCA should be maintained as is
■	■	■	□	□	□	□	■	■	■	Areas along the San Pedro River to the south that are not protected as part of the SPRNCA should be purchased for conservation purposes (that is, the SPRNCA will span from its current northern edge to the Mexican border)
□	□	□	□	□	□	□	□	□	□	Areas along the San Pedro River that are not protected as part of the SPRNCA between Cascabel and the Mexican border should be purchased for conservation purposes (that is, the SPRNCA will span from Cascabel to the Mexican border)
□	□	□	■	■	■	■	□	□	□	Areas along the San Pedro River that are not protected as part of the SPRNCA between Cascabel and the Mexican border should be purchased for conservation purposes (that is, the SPRNCA will span from Cascabel to the Mexican border); additionally, Mexico should establish and manage an extension of the SPRNCA in Sonora; conserved habitat should extend to the town of José Maria Morelos, Mexico (that is, near the headwaters of the San Pedro River)

FIRE MANAGEMENT

P	P1	P2	P3	C	C1	C2	O	O1	O2	Response
■	■	■	■	■	■	■	□	□	□	Fires should be prescribed as a part of a vegetation management plan for the Upper San Pedro River Basin
□	□	□	□	□	□	□	□	□	□	Fires should not be prescribed as a part of vegetation management plan, but when they occur, they are allowed to burn
□	□	□	□	□	□	□	■	■	■	Fires should not be prescribed, and all fires are suppressed

Table 7.1 Responses to the Scenario Guide, continued

LANDSCAPE ECOLOGICAL PATTERN

P	P1	P2	P3	C	C1	C2	O	O1	O2	Response
□	□	□	■	□	□	□	□	□	□	Large natural patches (natural areas that are greater than 10,000 ac) and their connecting corridors should be protected
■	■	■	□	■	■	■	□	□	□	Large natural patches (natural areas that are greater than 5,000 ac) and their connecting natural corridors should be protected
□	□	□	□	□	□	□	■	■	■	Large natural patches and their connecting corridors should not be protected

PROTECTION OF SPECIES HABITAT

P	P1	P2	P3	C	C1	C2	O	O1	O2	Response
■	■	■	■	■	■	■	□	□	□	Southwestern willow flycatcher habitat should be protected
□	□	□	□	□	□	□	■	■	■	Southwestern willow flycatcher habitat should not be protected
■	■	■	□	■	■	■	□	□	□	Northern goshawk habitat should be protected
□	□	□	■	□	□	□	■	■	■	Northern goshawk habitat should not be protected
■	■	■	□	■	■	■	□	□	□	Gila monster habitat should be protected
□	□	□	■	□	□	□	■	■	■	Gila monster habitat should not be protected
■	■	■	□	■	■	■	□	□	□	Beaver habitat should be protected
□	□	□	■	□	□	□	■	■	■	Beaver habitat should not be protected
■	■	■	■	■	■	■	□	□	□	Sonoran pronghorn habitat should be protected
□	□	□	□	□	□	□	■	■	■	Sonoran pronghorn habitat should not be protected
■	■	■	□	■	■	■	□	□	□	Jaguar habitat should be protected
□	□	□	■	□	□	□	■	■	■	Jaguar habitat should not be protected

PROTECTION OF HABITAT FOR LISTED SPECIES

P	P1	P2	P3	C	C1	C2	O	O1	O2	Response
■	■	■	■	■	■	■	■	■	■	Potential habitat (as defined by AZ Species Richness Analysis) for endangered species should be protected
□	□	□	□	□	□	□	□	□	□	Potential habitat (as defined by AZ Species Richness Analysis) for endangered species should not be protected (the Endangered Species Act is amended)
■	■	■	■	■	■	■	□	□	□	Potential habitat (as defined by AZ Species Richness Analysis) for threatened species should be protected
□	□	□	□	□	□	□	■	■	■	Potential habitat (as defined by AZ Species Richness Analysis) for threatened species should not be protected (the Endangered Species Act is amended)

SPECIES DIVERSITY

P	P1	P2	P3	C	C1	C2	O	O1	O2	Response
□	□	□	■	■	■	■	□	□	□	Contiguous habitat areas that contain at least 250 vertebrate species should be protected
■	■	■	□	□	□	□	■	■	■	No areas should be protected based on species diversity

PROTECTION OF GAPs

P	P1	P2	P3	C	C1	C2	O	O1	O2	Response
■	■	■	■	■	■	■	□	□	□	Basin scale GAPs (from Arizona GAP Analysis) should be protected
□	□	□	□	□	□	□	■	■	■	Basin scale GAPs (from Arizona GAP Analysis) should not be protected

VISUAL QUALITY

P	P1	P2	P3	C	C1	C2	O	O1	O2	Response
■	■	■	■	■	■	■	□	□	□	Views of mountain ridge lines as seen from major state roads should be protected
□	□	□	□	□	□	□	■	■	■	Views of mountain ridge lines as seen from major state roads should not be protected
■	■	■	■	■	■	■	□	□	□	Views of the San Pedro River riparian vegetation corridor as seen from major state roads should be protected
□	□	□	□	□	□	□	■	■	■	Views of the San Pedro River riparian vegetation corridor as seen from major state roads should not be protected

In Sonora

URBAN GROWTH IN SONORA

P	P1	P2	P3	C	C1	C2	O	O1	O2	Response
■	■	□	■	■	■	■	■	■	□	Cananea remains at its current size
□	□	■	□	□	□	□	□	□	■	Cananea doubles in size based on mining economy
■	■	□	■	■	■	■	■	■	□	Naco remains at its current size
□	□	■	□	□	□	□	□	□	■	Naco doubles in size based on a services and agricultural economy

SAN PEDRO RIPARIAN ZONE CONSERVATION IN SONORA

P	P1	P2	P3	C	C1	C2	O	O1	O2	Response
□	□	□	□	■	■	■	□	□	□	The riparian zone of the Upper San Pedro River in Sonora is conserved
■	■	■	■	□	□	□	■	■	■	The riparian zone of the Upper San Pedro River in Sonora is not conserved

Table 7.2 The PLANS Scenario

POPULATION

- Population increase is as forecast (2020 population of 95,000).
- 80 percent of the new population live in urban homes.
- 15 percent of the new population live in suburban homes.
- 3 percent of the new population live in rural homes.
- 2 percent of the new population live in exurban homes.
- The minimum size of a rural residential lot is 1.62 ha (4 ac) in the Upper San Pedro River Basin.
- The minimum size of a rural residential lot is 1.62 ha (4 ac) if within 1.61 km (1 mi) of the SPRNCA
- The fort remains open and stays at its current size.
- Kartchner Caverns attracts 200,000 people per year in 2020.
- Growth in Sonora is moderate.

WATER MANAGEMENT

- Domestic per capita consumption from public and water company sources decreases from 1995 levels by 20 percent (182 L or 48 gallons per person per day).
- Domestic per capita consumption from individually owned sources decreases from 1995 levels by 40 percent (284 L or 75 gallons per person per day).
- An irrigation exclusion area is created within the Upper San Pedro River Basin; all proposed irrigated agriculture within 1.61 km (1 mi) of the Upper San Pedro River is prohibited; existing water rights for irrigated agriculture within 1.61 km (1 mi) of the San Pedro River are purchased and retired.
- Cottonwood and willow trees in the riparian zone along the San Pedro are not removed.
- Upland mesquite is not removed.

LAND MANAGEMENT

- Ranching in the San Pedro River Basin on federal-owned lands is removed.
- The leasing of state-owned land in the San Pedro River Basin for conservation purposes is allowed by competitive bidding.
- Fires are prescribed as a part of a vegetation management plan for the Upper San Pedro River Basin.
- Areas along the San Pedro River to the Mexican border that are not protected as part of the SPRNCA are purchased for conservation purposes.
- Large natural patches (greater than 2023 ha or 5,000 ac) and their connecting natural corridors are protected.
- Potential habitat for endangered species is protected.
- Potential habitat for threatened species is protected.
- Gila monster, southwestern willow flycatcher, northern goshawk, beaver, Sonoran pronghorn, and jaguar potential habitat is protected.
- No areas are protected based on species diversity.
- Basin scale GAPs (from Arizona GAP analysis) are not protected.
- Views of mountain ridge lines as seen from major state roads are protected.
- Views of the riparian vegetation corridor as seen from major state roads are protected.

Table 7.3 The CONSTRAINED Scenario

POPULATION

- Population increase will be 50 percent less than the current forecast (2020 population of 78,500).
- 90 percent of the new population will live in urban homes.
- 10 percent of the new population will live in exurban homes.
- The minimum size of a rural residential lot is 1.62 ha (4 ac) in the Upper San Pedro River Basin.
- The minimum size of a rural residential lot is 16.2 ha (40 ac) if within 1.61 km (1 mi) of the SPRNCA.
- The fort remains open but is reduced to only those units and activities associated with the Electronic Proving Ground; all other units and activities are transferred to other facilities. (Approximately 1500 active duty troops, civilian contractors, and support personnel remain at Fort Huachuca.)
- Kartchner Caverns attracts 1,000,000 people per year in 2020.
- Growth in Sonora is moderate.

WATER MANAGEMENT

- Domestic per capita consumption from public/company sources decreases from 1995 levels by 20 percent (182 L or 48 gallons per person per day).
- Domestic per capita consumption from individually owned sources decreases from 1995 levels by 20 percent (379 L or 100 gallons per person per day).
- All irrigated agriculture in the Upper San Pedro River Basin is removed.
- Approximately half of the cottonwood and willow trees in the riparian zone along the San Pedro River are removed by the clearing of selected areas that are then managed to maintain a grassland ecosystem.
- Approximately half the upland mesquite is removed by clearing selected areas that are managed to maintain a grassland ecosystem.

LAND MANAGEMENT

- Ranching in the San Pedro River Basin on state-owned lands is removed.
- The leasing of state-owned land in the San Pedro River Basin for conservation purposes is allowed by competitive bidding.
- Fires are prescribed as a part of a vegetation management plan for the Upper San Pedro River Basin.
- Areas along the San Pedro River that are not protected as part of the SPRNCA between Cascabel and the Mexican border are purchased for inclusion in the SPRNCA.
- Mexico will establish and manage an extension of the SPRNCA in Sonora; conserved habitat will extend to the town of José Maria Morelos, Mexico.
- Large natural patches (greater than 2023 ha or 5000 ac) and their connecting natural corridors are protected.
- Potential habitat for endangered species is protected.
- Potential habitat for threatened species is protected.
- Gila monster, southwestern willow flycatcher, northern goshawk, beaver, Sonoran pronghorn, and jaguar potential habitat is protected.
- Contiguous habitat areas that contain at least 195 vertebrate species are protected.
- Basin scale GAPs are protected.
- Views of mountain ridge lines as seen from major state roads are protected.
- Views of the riparian vegetation corridor as seen from major state roads are protected.

Table 7.4. The OPEN Scenario

POPULATION

- Population increase is 50 percent greater than the current forecast (2020 population of 111,500).
- 15 percent of the new population live in urban homes.
- 15 percent of the new population live in suburban homes.
- 60 percent of the new population live in rural homes.
- 10 percent of the new population live in exurban homes.
- The minimum size of a rural residential lot is .41 ha (1 ac) in the Upper San Pedro River Basin.
- The minimum size of a rural residential lot is .41 ha (1 ac) if within 1.61 km (1 mi) of the SPRNCA.
- The fort closes, and all its facilities and land are used for economic growth in the civilian sector.
- Kartchner Caverns attracts 200,000 people per year in 2020.
- Growth in Sonora is moderate.

WATER MANAGEMENT

- Domestic per capita consumption from public or water company sources remains at 1995 levels (227 L or 60 gallons per person per day).
- Domestic per capita consumption from individually owned sources remains at 1995 levels (473 L or 125 gallons per person per day).
- An INA is created within the Upper San Pedro River Basin; all existing irrigated agriculture remains, but proposed irrigated agriculture within 1.61 km (1 mi) of the Upper San Pedro River is prohibited.
- Cottonwood and willow trees in the riparian zone along the San Pedro River are not removed.
- Upland mesquite is not removed.

LAND MANAGEMENT

- Ranching in the San Pedro River Basin continues at its current intensity and locations.
- The leasing of state-owned land in the San Pedro River Basin for conservation purposes is not allowed.
- Fires are not prescribed, and to the greatest extent possible, all fires are suppressed.
- Areas along the San Pedro River to the Mexican border south of the current SPRNCA are purchased for conservation purposes.
- Large natural patches and their connecting natural corridors are not protected.
- Potential habitat for endangered species is protected.
- Potential habitat for threatened species is not protected.
- There is no conservation or management of individual species.
- No areas are protected based on species diversity.
- Basin scale GAPs (from Arizona GAP Analysis) are not protected.
- Views of mountain ridge lines as seen from major state roads are not protected.
- Views of the riparian vegetation corridor as seen from major state roads are not protected.

CHAPTER

8

The Development Model

The development model selects the locations for residential and commercial/industrial projects that developers would likely make under the several scenarios. The model takes into account various population projections, policies, and plans in accordance with the ten scenarios.

Developers select locations for subdivisions and other types of development based on their experience with a variety of factors. For residential development, home buyers' preferences for proximity to various amenities are important. Developers also carefully consider the locations of roads and utilities because they will have to build connections to off-site sewer and water lines and roads. If the distances are too great, the costs can become prohibitive. The limits to the amount that developers can afford to spend on infrastructure are usually related to size of development. In general, the larger the subdivision, the greater the off-site costs that can be supported.

Because demand for new homes in the San Pedro River Basin is low compared to major metropolitan areas, most subdivisions are small—fewer than 100 homes. Of subdivisions recently approved in Sierra Vista, only three of eighteen are larger than 100 homes. Most are between 25 and 50 homes. It is important to note that the development model is based on development practice typical within the region. Very large projects that are proposed in the Arizona part of the San Pedro River Basin, such as the Bachman Springs project (1125 homes, etc.) and the Castle and Cooke

GOODYEAR

Photo 8.1 ■ Commercial development

Photo 8.2 ■ Tract homes

Photo 8.3 ■ Custom homes

project (6140 homes, etc.) are not taken into consideration in this study. However, the sites that these projects are proposed to occupy are treated by the model as land available for development.

Home builders fall into two main categories—tract or production builders and custom builders. Most homes are built by production builders, in groups of 25 to 50 homes at a time. Cost efficiencies and financing are determinants of the number of homes built at one time. Tract homes may range greatly in price, from low-cost starter homes to luxury retirement housing. Custom builders build individually designed homes tailored to specific lots. They are generally much more expensive than production homes. Normally, the more expensive the home, the more developers can afford to pay for land. Since land cost is related to proximity to desirable features, more expensive homes tend to be located in areas with more amenities.

The development model contains one commercial/industrial land use category and four housing categories:

urban on .41 ha (1 ac) lots;
suburban on .41 ha (1 ac) lots within 3.2 km (2 mi) of an incorporated town;
rural on 1.62 ha (4 ac) lots; and
exurban areas with 5 homes on 16.2 ha (40 ac).

Urban and suburban plots of land that are 10 ha (25 ac) or larger are likely to be developed into subdivisions by production builders. This type of development dominates most urban and suburban growth. Individual infill urban lots are likely to be developed as custom built homes, especially those lots situated in higher priced parts of Sierra Vista. Rural and exurban homes are likely also to be built individually rather than in subdivisions. Many rural and exurban homes will be manufactured housing or trailer homes placed on the owner's lot. Manufactured housing tends to be low in cost. It is attractive in rural and exurban situations because it can be delivered in a finished state to the owner's lot, placed on a prepared foundation, and finished in a matter of days by professional crews.

A survey of home builders and real estate professionals in Arizona was conducted in order to obtain estimates for weighting the various characteristics that affect attractiveness for development. These estimates were used in the housing allocation model through equations that generate an attractiveness score for each grid cell within the study area.

Respondents were asked about their preferences for being near desirable amenities or away from unattractive features. Developers place differing degrees of importance on various site location factors depending on whether they are building tract homes or custom homes. Survey respondents were asked to distinguish between tract and custom housing in their evaluations of the various factors (table 8.1).

Forty percent of developers considered 4/10 km (1/4 mi) the maximum feasible distance from utilities. Another 40 percent were willing to use sites up to 1.2 km (3/4 mi) away from utilities, and 20 percent would use sites up to 3.2 km (2 mi) away. Proximity to some types of existing land use would make otherwise usable sites undesirable. Both tract home builders and custom home builders prefer locations distant from industrial parks, trailer parks, and mines. When asked for the minimum distance from these land uses that they would build, answers ranged from .8 km (1/2 mi) away from a busy highway or shopping center to 1.6 km (1 mi) from an industrial park, trailer park, or mine.

Developers consider close distance from a major highway to be critical both for access and for visibility. Home buyers, on the other hand, do not like to be too close to a highway because of traffic, noise, and pollution. Distance from the edge of town was expected to be important because most home buyers like to be near the amenities and activities found in town, and developers want to be near existing utility lines. Interestingly, the preference gradient falls off slowly. Distances of up to 16.1 km (10 mi) from the edge of town are apparently acceptable in the San Pedro region.

Table 8.1 Responses to the developer survey

1.What is the maximum acceptable distance from utilities?

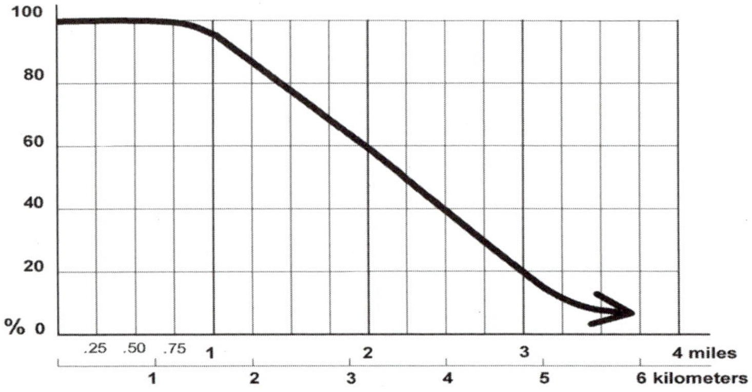
100
80
60
40
20
% 0
.25 .50 .75 1 2 3 4 miles
1 2 3 4 5 6 kilometers

2. How close to a major highway do you want to be located?

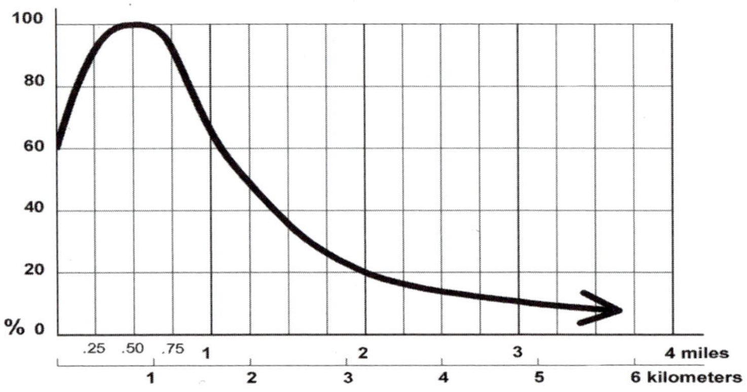
100
80
60
40
20
% 0
.25 .50 .75 1 2 3 4 miles
1 2 3 4 5 6 kilometers

3. What is the farthest location from the edge of town?

100
80
60
40
20
% 0
.50 1 2 3 4 5 6 7 8 9 10 miles
1 2 3 4 5 6 7 8 9 10 11 12 13 14 15 16 kilometers

4. Importance of being near amenities

Amenity	Tract Homes	Custom Homes
High Priced Houses	6.8	8.1
Mountains	6.7	7.8
Lake	6.9	7.2
Preserve	6.7	7.1
Golf Course	5.5	8.1
Park	6.7	6.1
Forest	5.1	5.5
Higher Elevation	4.3	5.7
Long Distance View	4.1	5.9
River	3.2	5.1

5. Importance of being away from disamenities

Negative Factor	Tract Homes	Custom Homes
Industrial Park	8	9+
Mine	8	9
Trailer Park	8	9
Busy Highway	5	8
Adjacent to Shopping Center	5	6

6. Distance below which you would not build (deal killer)

Industrial Park	1.0 miles	1.0 miles
Mine	1.0 miles	1.0 miles
Trailer Park	1.0 miles	1.0 miles
Busy Highway	0.5 miles	0.5 miles
Shopping Center	0.5 miles	0.5 miles

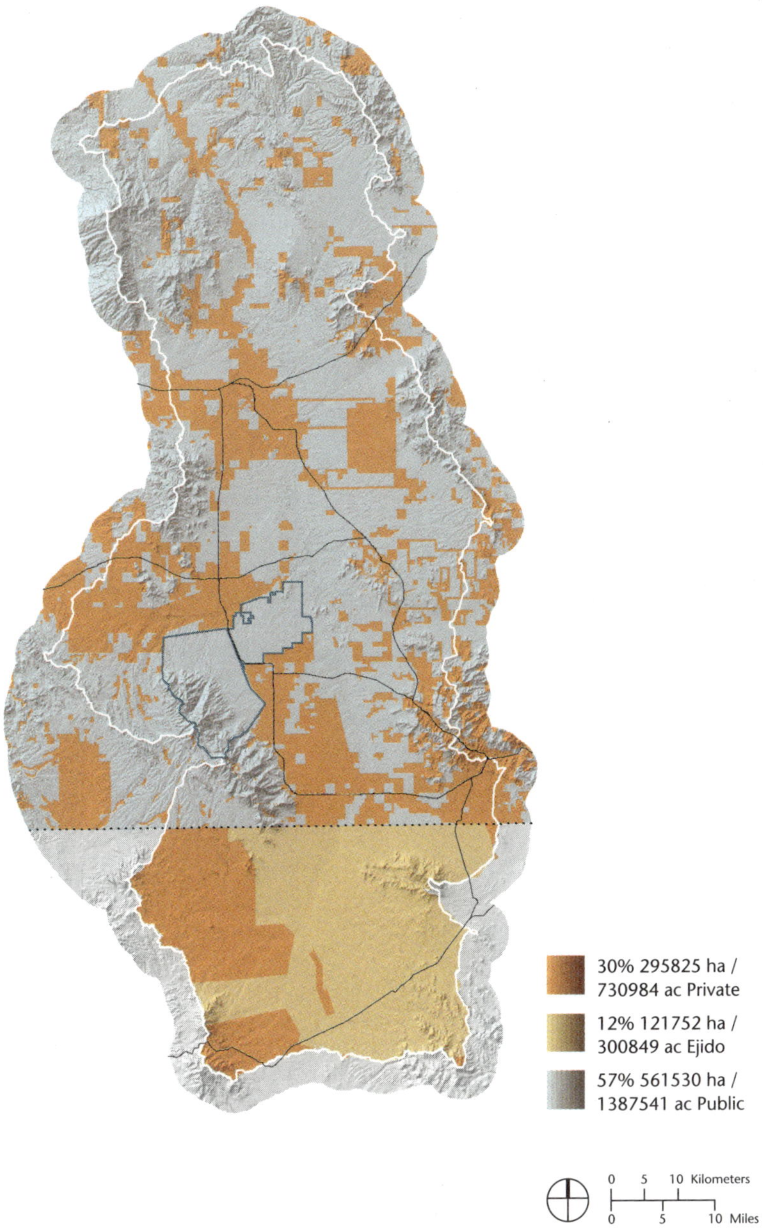
30% 295825 ha /
730984 ac Private
12% 121752 ha /
300849 ac Ejido
57% 561530 ha /
1387541 ac Public
0 5 10 Kilometers
0 5 10 Miles

Figure 8.1 ■ Public and private ownership, 2000

Respondents were asked to indicate the importance of locating near or having views of various land uses. Not surprisingly, custom home builders gave the highest preferences to having views of golf courses and mountains and to being near existing expensive homes. Tract home builders gave the highest preferences to sites that have water, mountain, or protected open space views and to being near expensive homes. The range of scores was lower than for the custom home builders. Greater price sensitivity in most production residential development makes it difficult for developers to find land that offers the desired amenities at a price home buyers can afford.

The survey results are used in the development model to evaluate attractiveness for residential development. Land is classed as either developable or not developable based on policies in the various scenarios, such as prohibition of development on steep slopes or in conservation areas. In Arizona, only privately owned land is considered to be developable (figure 8.1). The land that is developable is evaluated based on proximity to features as evaluated in the survey.

Figure 8.2a–d shows the development attractiveness for each of the four types of housing. The maps are based on evaluation of all land in the Arizona portion of the study area, regardless of thc assumptions of land availability in the individual scenarios.

The Allocation of Development

The development model is used to allocate the five kinds of development—one commercial/industrial and four residential types: urban, suburban, rural, and exurban.

The development model allocates future development using the process described below for the part of the study area in Arizona. The model assumes that preference for a housing type is based on density of development (urban, suburban, etc.) and that this dominates preference for specific features of a location such as

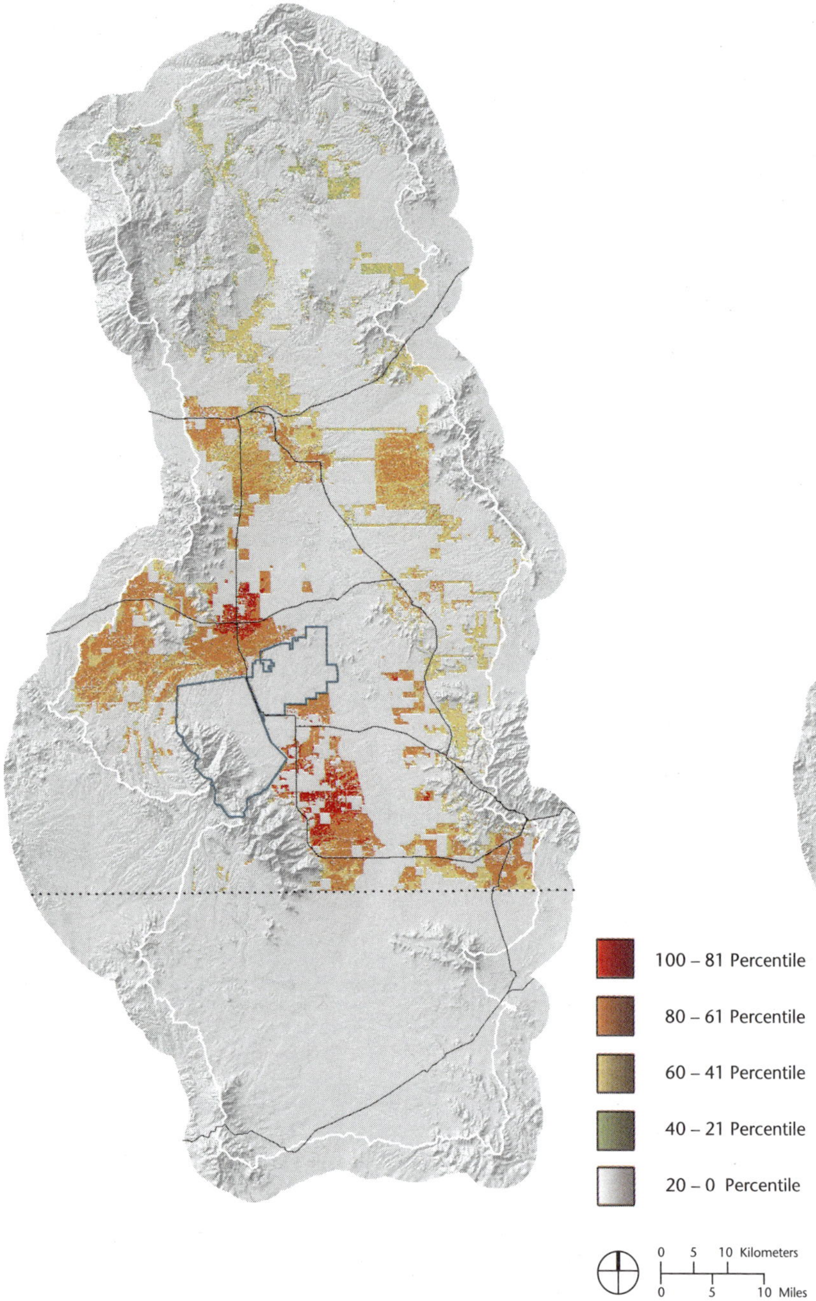
100 – 81 Percentile
80 – 61 Percentile
60 – 41 Percentile
40 – 21 Percentile
20 – 0 Percentile
0 5 10 Kilometers
0 5 10 Miles

Figure 8.2a ■ Urban residential attractiveness, 2000

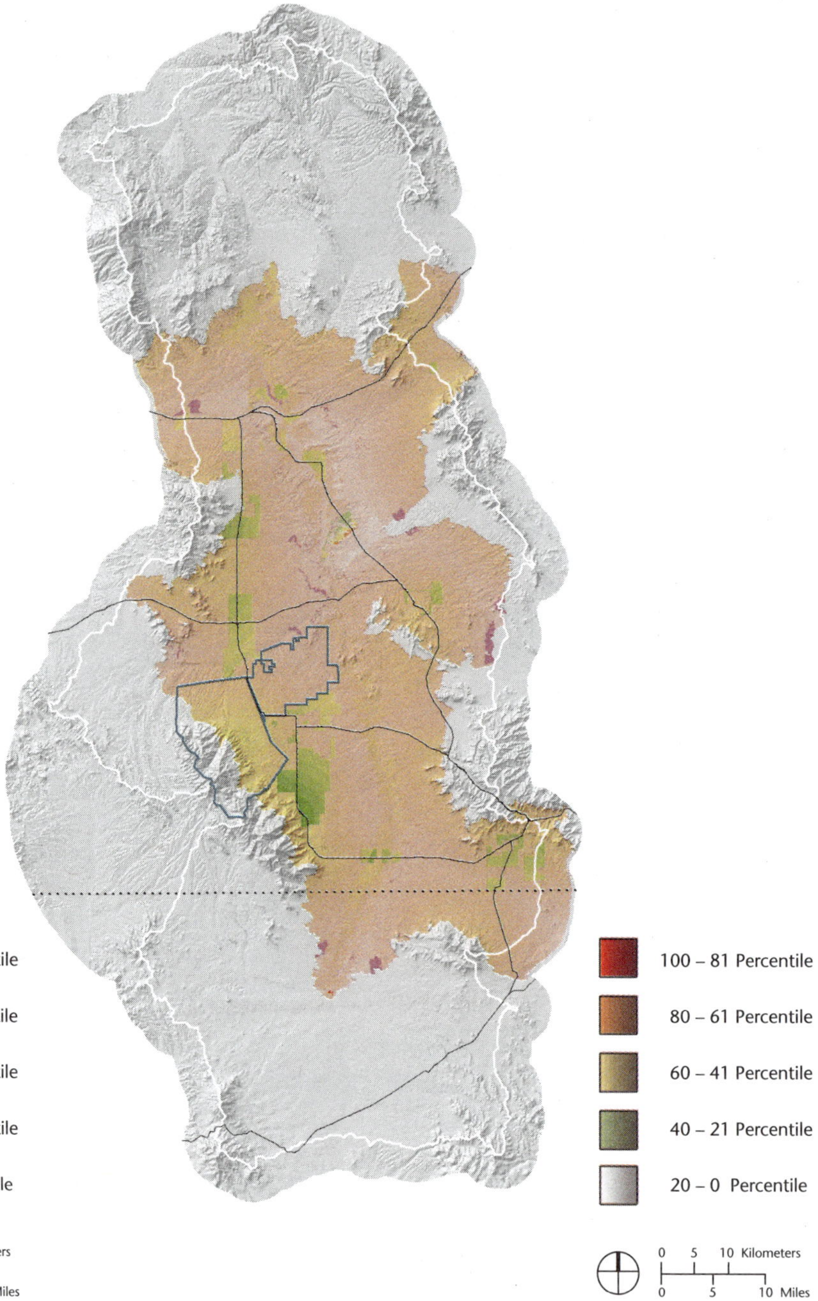
100 – 81 Percentile
80 – 61 Percentile
60 – 41 Percentile
40 – 21 Percentile
20 – 0 Percentile
0 5 10 Kilometers
0 5 10 Miles

Figure 8.2b ■ Suburban residential attractiveness, 2000

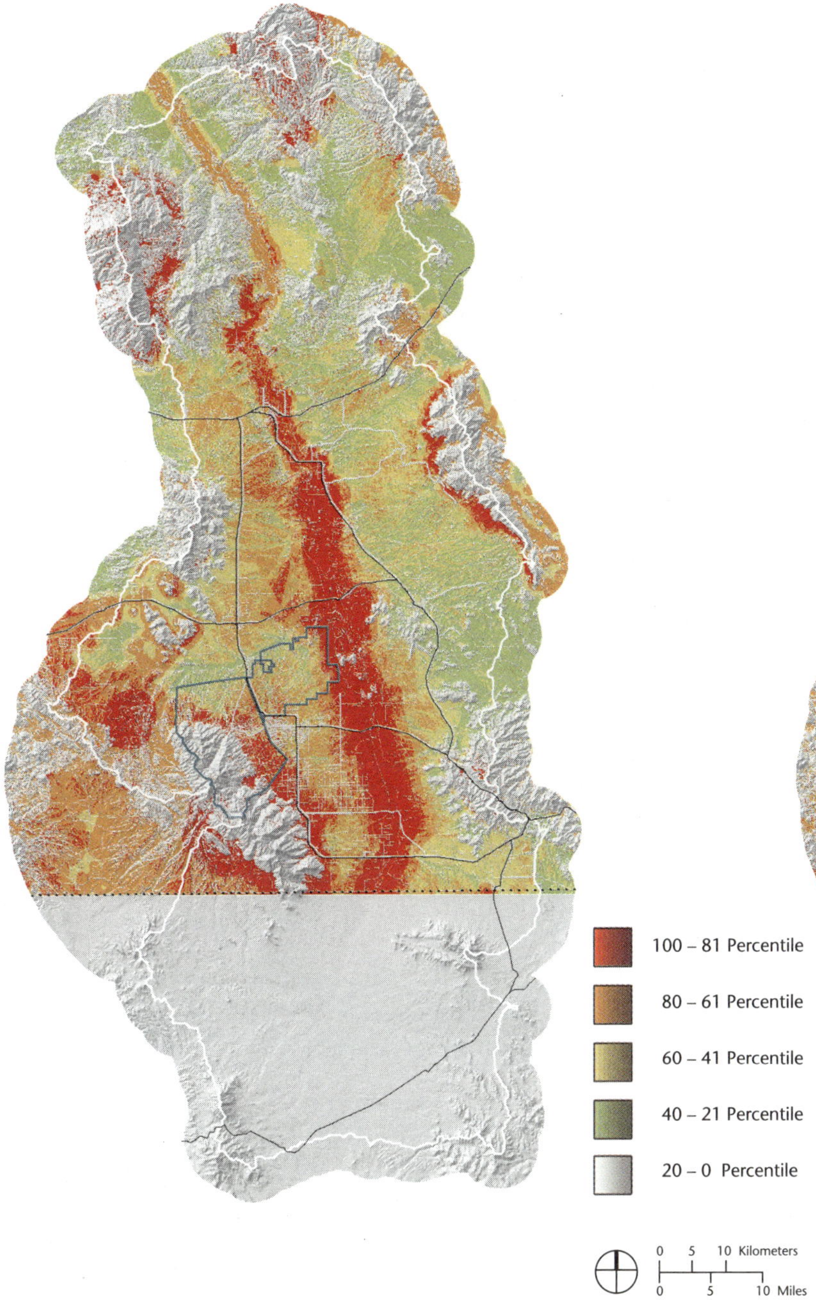
100 – 81 Percentile
80 – 61 Percentile
60 – 41 Percentile
40 – 21 Percentile
20 – 0 Percentile
0 5 10 Kilometers
0 5 10 Miles

Figure 8.2c ■ Rural residential attractiveness, 2000

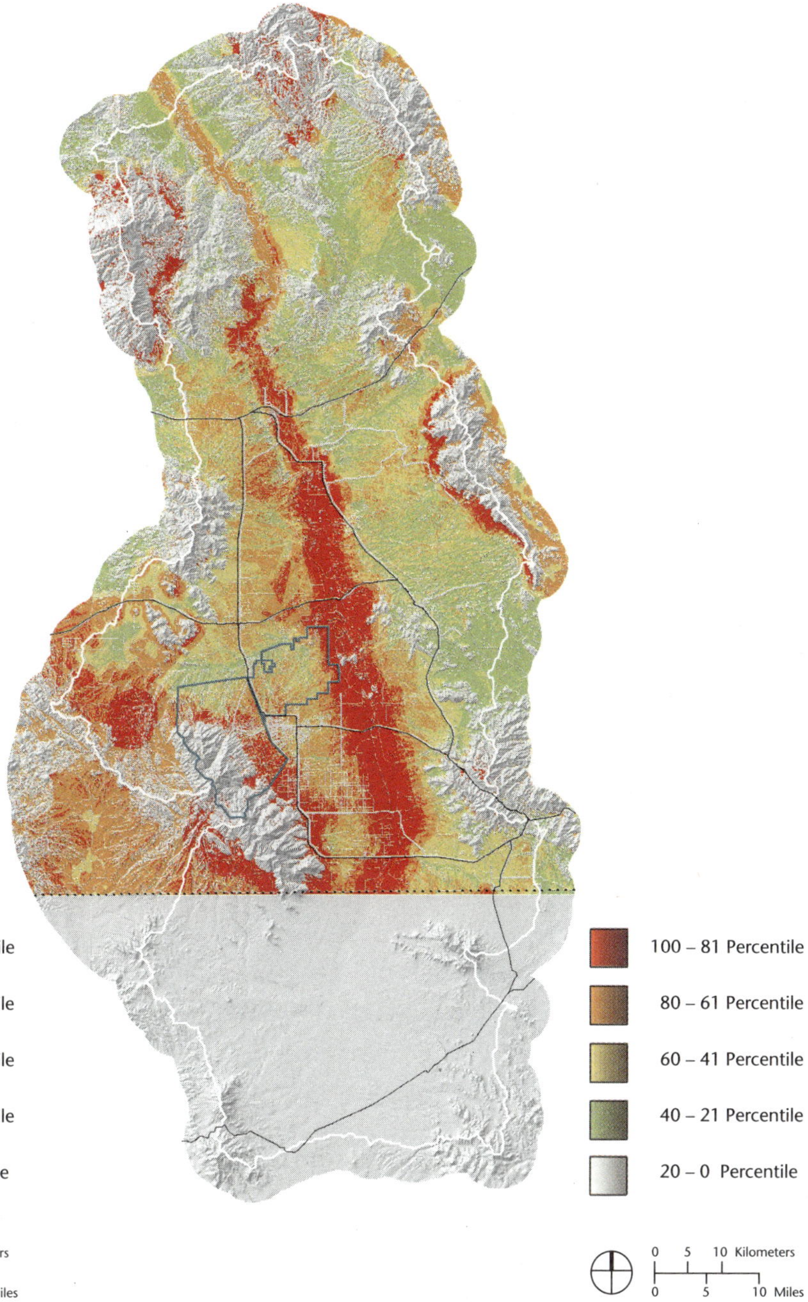
100 – 81 Percentile
80 – 61 Percentile
60 – 41 Percentile
40 – 21 Percentile
20 – 0 Percentile
0 5 10 Kilometers
0 5 10 Miles

Figure 8.2d ■ Exurban residential attractiveness, 2000

Photo 8.4 ■ Commercial development

GAS CITY

Photo 8.5 ■ I-10 commercial development near Karchner Caverns

a view. For each type of residential development, allocation is made to the most attractive locations for that type, within the areas where that type is allowed by the zoning pattern and other constraints selected in each scenario. In Sonora, developable land contiguous to existing urban areas is expanded in a manner consistent with Mexican urban development policy.

The development model is a simple Lowry-type model. It is iterative, "designed to generate estimates of retail employment, residential population, and land use for sub-areas of a bounded region" (Lowry 1964). Such a model is appropriate here because

Photo 8.6 ■ Urban housing

Photo 8.7 ■ Suburban housing

the new population to be allocated is small in relation to the size of the study area. This study is primarily concerned with the location of land that is most likely to be developed, rather than with the income, workforce, or demographic characteristics of future residents. In spite of the simplicity of the development types, the development model is powerful because allocations are based on a much more comprehensive set of physical characteristics than one typically finds in Lowry-type models of urban location. The allocation process of the development model is conducted from the reference year 2000 in 5-year iterations to 2020.

Photo 8.8 ■ Rural housing

Photo 8.9 ■ Exurban housing

The development model is subject to several limitations. Consistent pricing and amenity data for residential housing, commercial property, and land values are unavailable. Consequently, a hedonic pricing approach for estimating property values is inappropriate. Instead, 1980 and 1990 U.S. Census data are used as indicators of neighborhood characteristics and trends. However, these data are collected in unequal spatial sampling units. Because the sampling units vary widely in size and are based on historic population patterns, small but rapidly growing towns are poorly characterized. Finally, the model does not take into account the social or demographic characteristics of communities, potential future road and other infrastructure development, or the impact of growth in adjacent areas outside of the study area.

The model proceeds by first allocating commercial/industrial land uses. These are represented by a single land use category that combines office, retail, and industrial activities. Demand for commercial/industrial land is derived by extrapolating the current ratio of commercial/industrial developed land to all developed land to 2020. The ratio of the amount of commercial/industrial land to population is assumed to remain constant throughout the study period. Land located within 120 m (393 ft) of primary and secondary roads is considered prime for commercial/industrial development. New commercial/industrial land use is allocated to areas near existing population centers.

Kartchner Caverns State Park is expected to attract many visitors in the next 20 years and to create a demand for new hotel and motel rooms. These new accommodations and other supporting commercial activities are allocated to land along Arizona Highway 90 near Interstate 10 and the caverns.

Next, the development model allocates residential land uses. The allocation process combines the two most common modeling approaches: probabilistic and deterministic. In the former, locations are evaluated for their likelihood of development, and a random process is used to make the allocation. In a deterministic approach, a set of criteria is combined, usually in a GIS mapping system, to produce a mapped index of priority, and allocation is made in priority order.

Development is allocated by weighted randomness. All of the developable 30 m (98.5 ft) square grid cells (approximately .1 ha or .25 ac) are divided into five equal subgroups based on their attractiveness for development. Although there is a range of scores within each of the five subgroups, all cells within a subgroup are considered equally likely to attract development. Housing demand is then randomly allocated with 80 percent to the highest

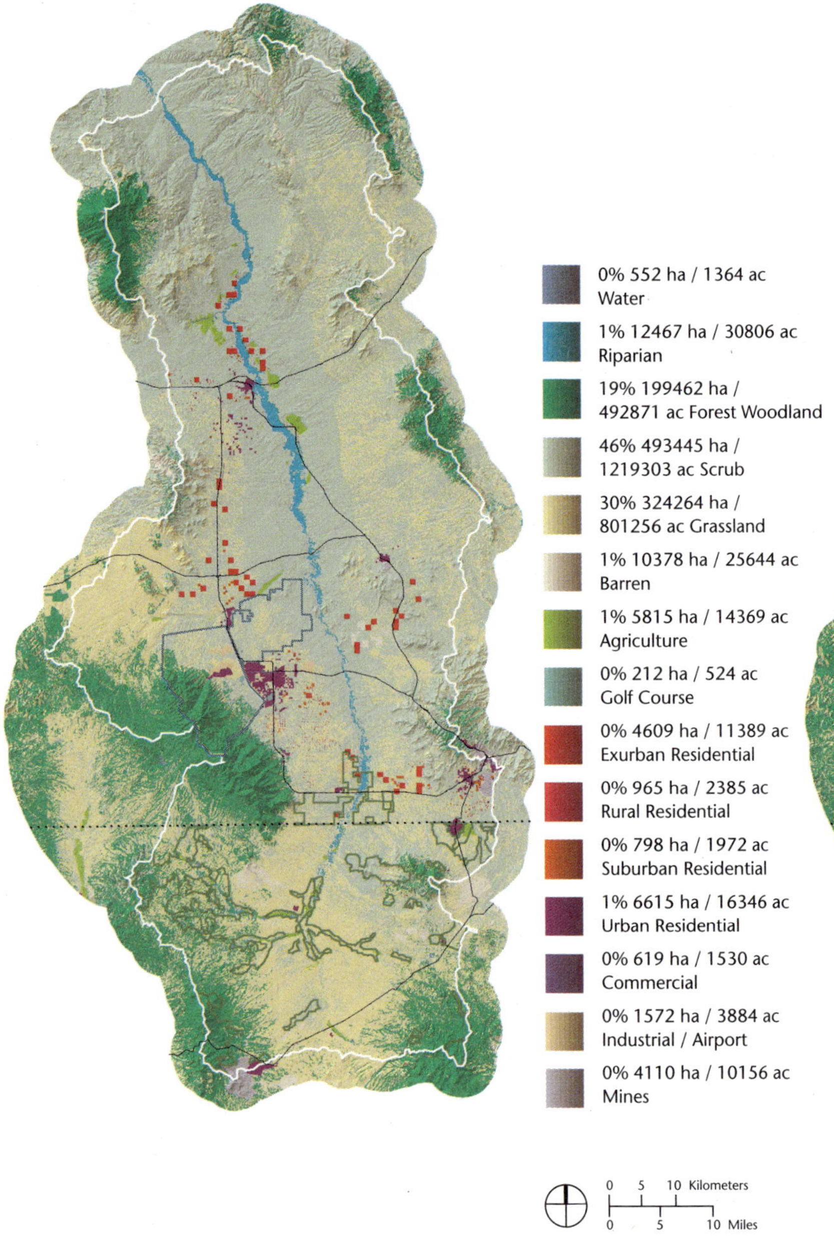
0% 552 ha / 1364 ac
Water
1% 12467 ha / 30806 ac
Riparian
19% 199462 ha /
492871 ac Forest Woodland
46% 493445 ha /
1219303 ac Scrub
30% 324264 ha /
801256 ac Grassland
1% 10378 ha / 25644 ac
Barren
1% 5815 ha / 14369 ac
Agriculture
0% 212 ha / 524 ac
Golf Course
0% 4609 ha / 11389 ac
Exurban Residential
0% 965 ha / 2385 ac
Rural Residential
0% 798 ha / 1972 ac
Suburban Residential
1% 6615 ha / 16346 ac
Urban Residential
0% 619 ha / 1530 ac
Commercial
0% 1572 ha / 3884 ac
Industrial / Airport
0% 4110 ha / 10156 ac
Mines
0 5 10 Kilometers
0 5 10 Miles

Figure 8.3a ■ PLANS, New development, 2000–2020

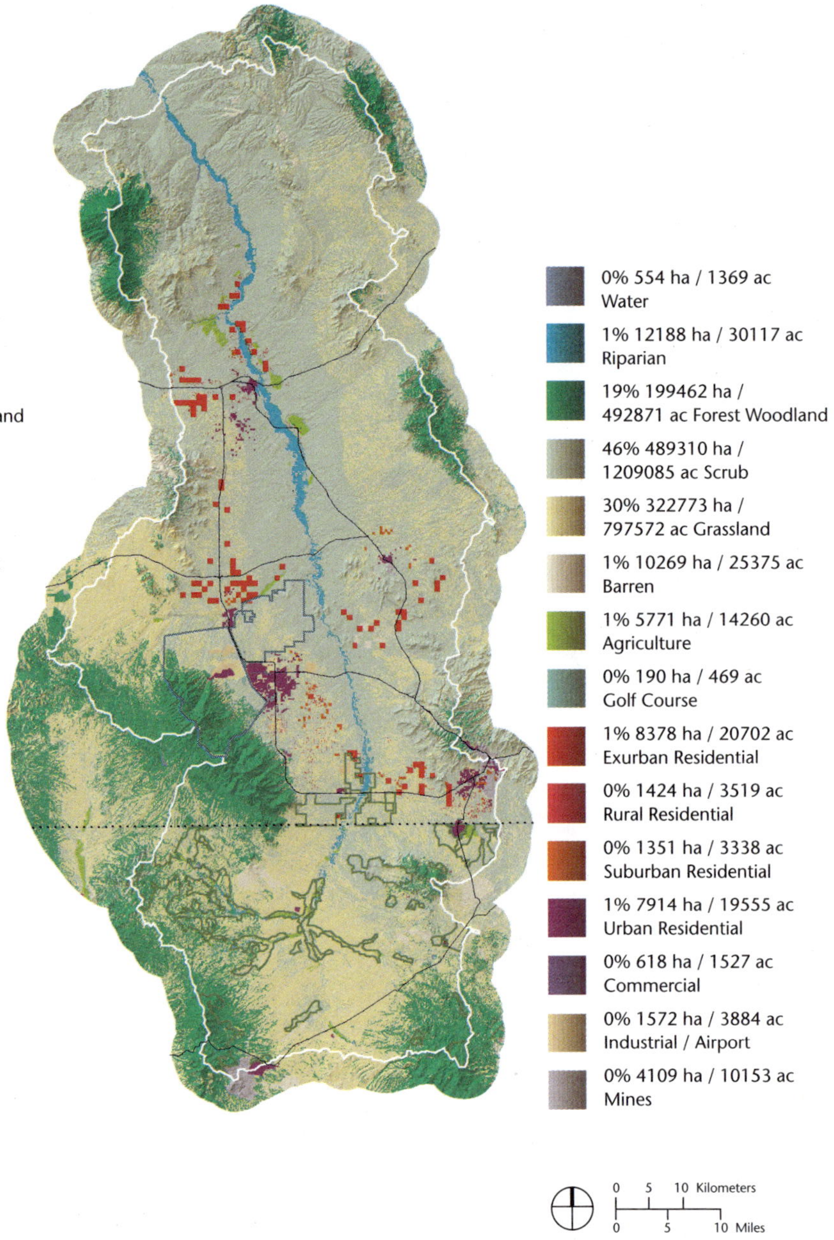
0% 554 ha / 1369 ac
Water
1% 12188 ha / 30117 ac
Riparian
19% 199462 ha /
492871 ac Forest Woodland
46% 489310 ha /
1209085 ac Scrub
30% 322773 ha /
797572 ac Grassland
1% 10269 ha / 25375 ac
Barren
1% 5771 ha / 14260 ac
Agriculture
0% 190 ha / 469 ac
Golf Course
1% 8378 ha / 20702 ac
Exurban Residential
0% 1424 ha / 3519 ac
Rural Residential
0% 1351 ha / 3338 ac
Suburban Residential
1% 7914 ha / 19555 ac
Urban Residential
0% 618 ha / 1527 ac
Commercial
0% 1572 ha / 3884 ac
Industrial / Airport
0% 4109 ha / 10153 ac
Mines
0 5 10 Kilometers
0 5 10 Miles

Figure 8.3b ■ PLANS 1, New development, 2000–2020

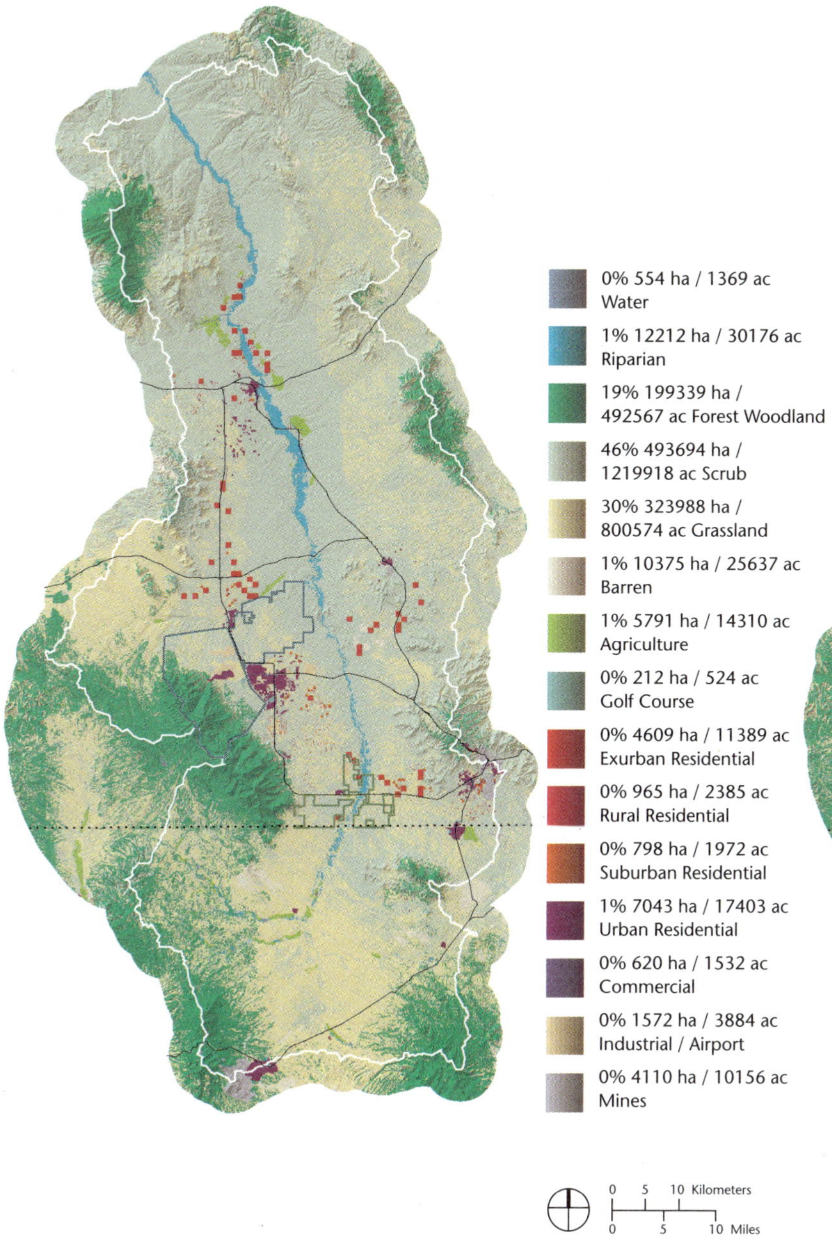
0% 554 ha / 1369 ac
Water
1% 12212 ha / 30176 ac
Riparian
19% 199339 ha /
492567 ac Forest Woodland
46% 493694 ha /
1219918 ac Scrub
30% 323988 ha /
800574 ac Grassland
1% 10375 ha / 25637 ac
Barren
1% 5791 ha / 14310 ac
Agriculture
0% 212 ha / 524 ac
Golf Course
0% 4609 ha / 11389 ac
Exurban Residential
0% 965 ha / 2385 ac
Rural Residential
0% 798 ha / 1972 ac
Suburban Residential
1% 7043 ha / 17403 ac
Urban Residential
0% 620 ha / 1532 ac
Commercial
0% 1572 ha / 3884 ac
Industrial / Airport
0% 4110 ha / 10156 ac
Mines
0 5 10 Kilometers
0 5 10 Miles

Figure 8.3c ■ PLANS 2, New development, 2000–2020

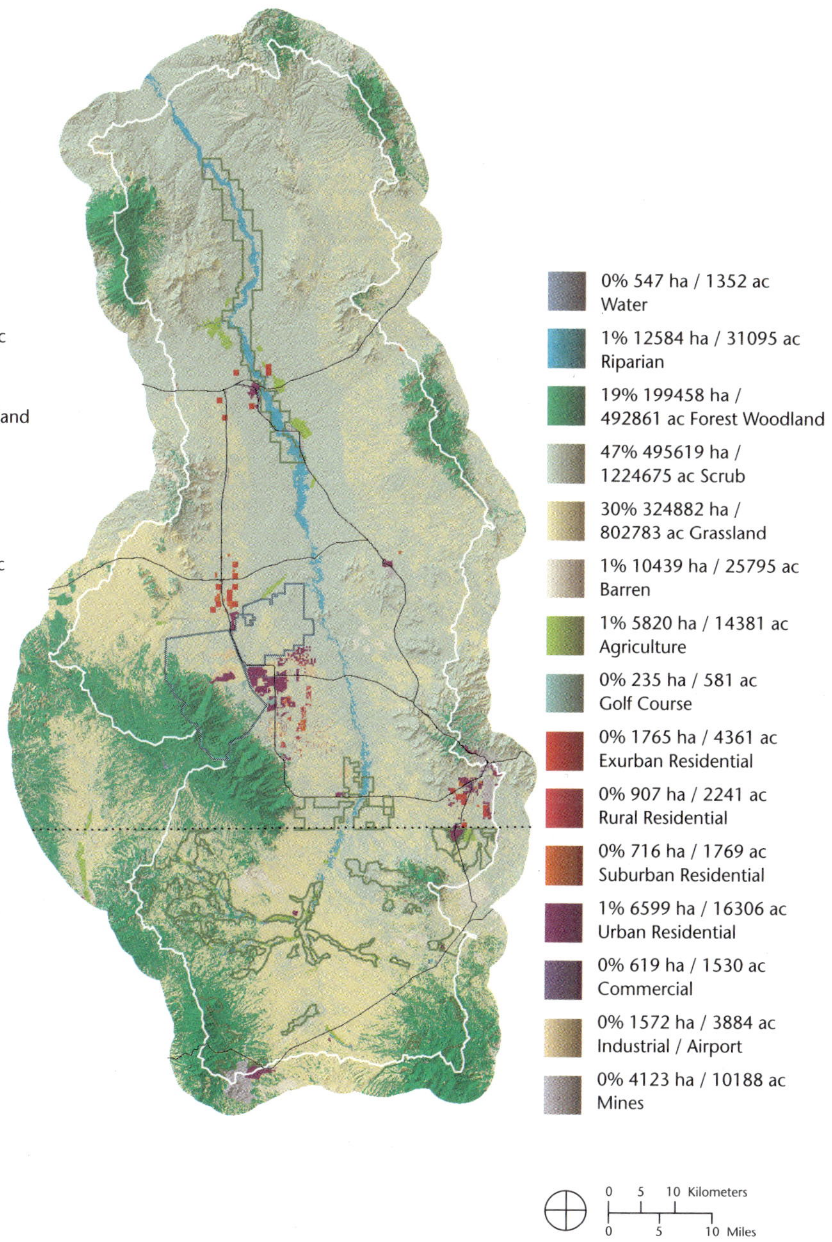
0% 547 ha / 1352 ac
Water
1% 12584 ha / 31095 ac
Riparian
19% 199458 ha /
492861 ac Forest Woodland
47% 495619 ha /
1224675 ac Scrub
30% 324882 ha /
802783 ac Grassland
1% 10439 ha / 25795 ac
Barren
1% 5820 ha / 14381 ac
Agriculture
0% 235 ha / 581 ac
Golf Course
0% 1765 ha / 4361 ac
Exurban Residential
0% 907 ha / 2241 ac
Rural Residential
0% 716 ha / 1769 ac
Suburban Residential
1% 6599 ha / 16306 ac
Urban Residential
0% 619 ha / 1530 ac
Commercial
0% 1572 ha / 3884 ac
Industrial / Airport
0% 4123 ha / 10188 ac
Mines
0 5 10 Kilometers
0 5 10 Miles

Figure 8.3d ■ PLANS 3, New development, 2000–2020

subgroup, and 20 percent to the next highest subgroup, until all of the demand for the 5-year period is completely allocated and all of the land within the highest available subgroup is used. Only 80 percent of the demand is allocated to the highest available subgroup. Withholding 20 percent of the best land from the initial allocation recognizes that some portion of the most attractive land is normally not available for development. Sellers may prefer to wait for future price increases, or they may not want to sell their property at the first opportunity for personal reasons. Sales of farmland often occur because the farmer wishes to retire or dies, and no heir wants to continue farming.

In each five-year time period, the evaluation and allocation process is repeated for the four types of housing: urban, suburban, rural, and exurban. Urban homes, including multifamily dwellings, are located within an incorporated municipal boundary and on lots smaller than .41 ha (1 ac). Urban homes are connected to the municipal sewer and use the municipal water supply. Suburban homes are built on lots of .41 to 1.62 ha (1 to 4 ac), and are within 3 km (1.9 mi) of an incorporated municipal area. Suburban homes use septic tanks and are connected to the municipal water supply. Rural homes are built on lots of 1.62 ha (4 ac) or larger. They are built in generally open areas, such as ranching or agricultural areas. They have private, on-site wells and use septic tanks. Exurban homes, frequently built in so-called wildcat subdivisions, are also built in generally open areas. Built on lots of .41 to .9 ha (1 to 2 ac), they are typically found clustered together in groups of five within a 16 ha (40 ac) parcel. Exurban homes use septic tanks and a shared water supply, usually provided by a private water company. Exurban homes are generally reached by dirt roads or low-volume paved roads.

Housing types are considered to be specific submarkets. Urban, suburban, rural, and exurban housing types each define density, location, and whether tract or custom built. A limitation of the model is that the allocation of demand among housing types is

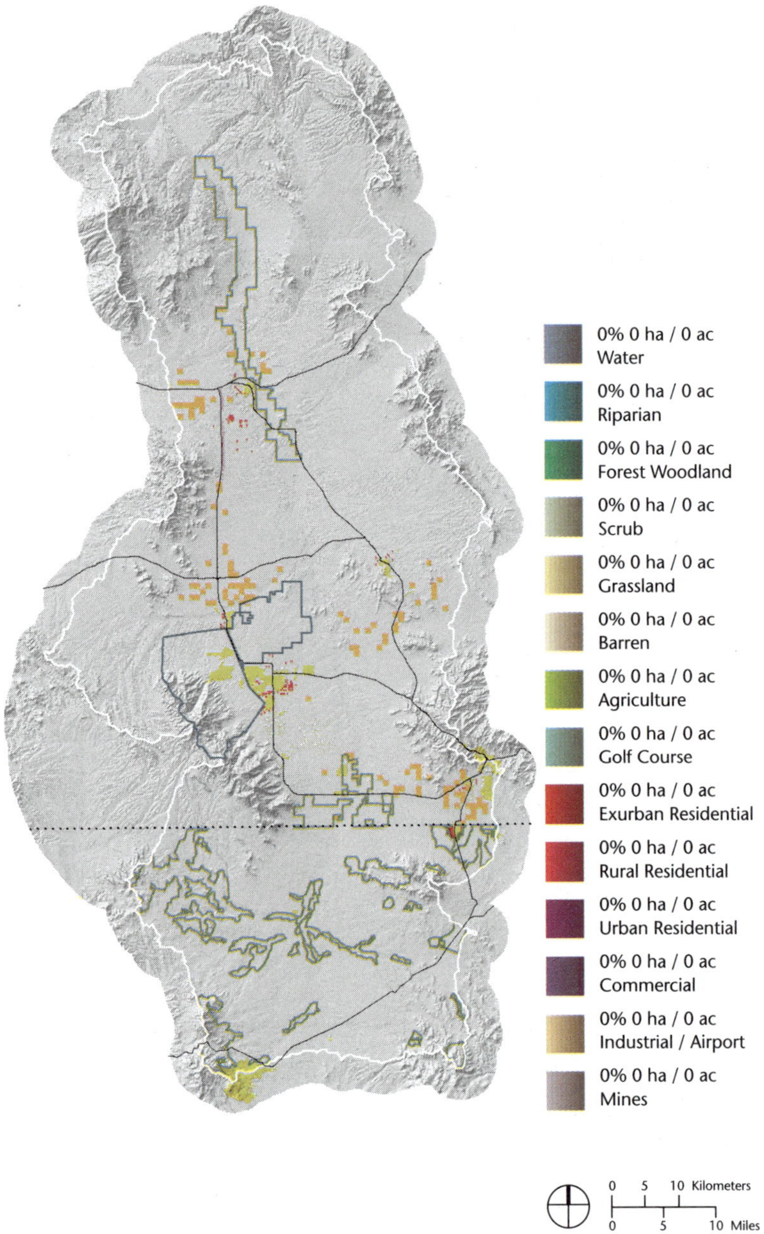
0% 0 ha / 0 ac
Water
0% 0 ha / 0 ac
Riparian
0% 0 ha / 0 ac
Forest Woodland
0% 0 ha / 0 ac
Scrub
0% 0 ha / 0 ac
Grassland
0% 0 ha / 0 ac
Barren
0% 0 ha / 0 ac
Agriculture
0% 0 ha / 0 ac
Golf Course
0% 0 ha / 0 ac
Exurban Residential
0% 0 ha / 0 ac
Rural Residential
0% 0 ha / 0 ac
Urban Residential
0% 0 ha / 0 ac
Commercial
0% 0 ha / 0 ac
Industrial / Airport
0% 0 ha / 0 ac
Mines
0 5 10 Kilometers
0 5 10 Miles

Figure 8.3e ■ CONSTRAINED, New development, 2000–2020

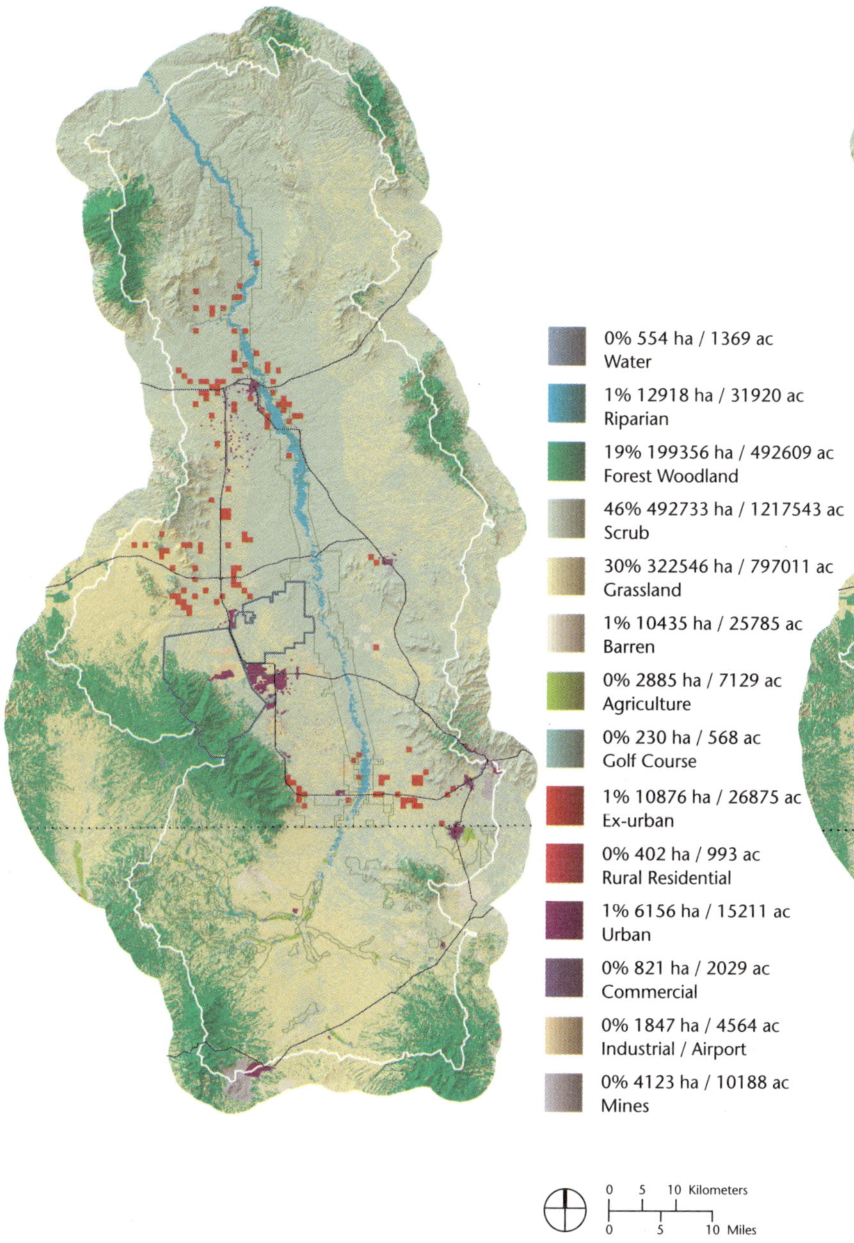
0% 554 ha / 1369 ac
Water
1% 12918 ha / 31920 ac
Riparian
19% 199356 ha / 492609 ac
Forest Woodland
46% 492733 ha / 1217543 ac
Scrub
30% 322546 ha / 797011 ac
Grassland
1% 10435 ha / 25785 ac
Barren
0% 2885 ha / 7129 ac
Agriculture
0% 230 ha / 568 ac
Golf Course
1% 10876 ha / 26875 ac
Ex-urban
0% 402 ha / 993 ac
Rural Residential
1% 6156 ha / 15211 ac
Urban
0% 821 ha / 2029 ac
Commercial
0% 1847 ha / 4564 ac
Industrial / Airport
0% 4123 ha / 10188 ac
Mines
0 5 10 Kilometers
0 5 10 Miles

Figure 8.3f ■ CONSTRAINED 1, New development, 2000–2020

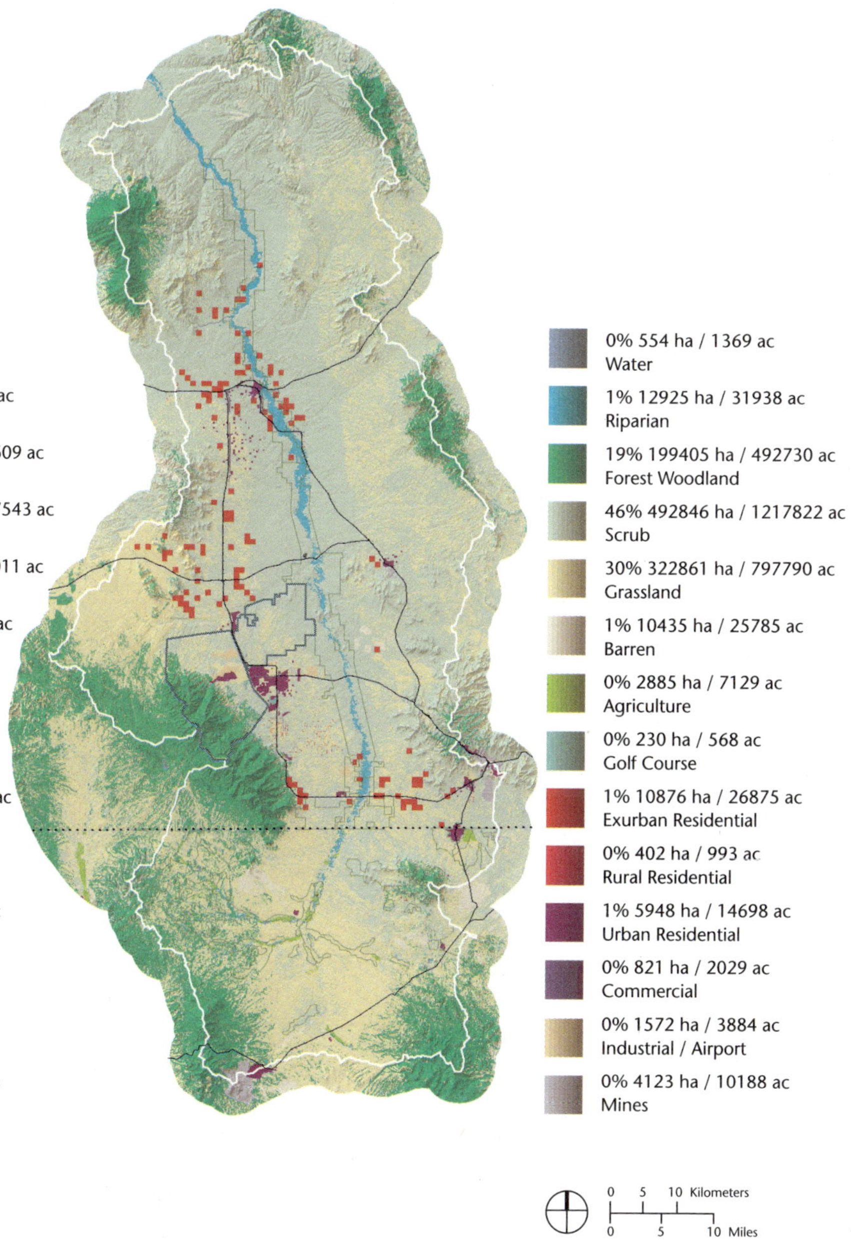
0% 554 ha / 1369 ac
Water
1% 12925 ha / 31938 ac
Riparian
19% 199405 ha / 492730 ac
Forest Woodland
46% 492846 ha / 1217822 ac
Scrub
30% 322861 ha / 797790 ac
Grassland
1% 10435 ha / 25785 ac
Barren
0% 2885 ha / 7129 ac
Agriculture
0% 230 ha / 568 ac
Golf Course
1% 10876 ha / 26875 ac
Exurban Residential
0% 402 ha / 993 ac
Rural Residential
1% 5948 ha / 14698 ac
Urban Residential
0% 821 ha / 2029 ac
Commercial
0% 1572 ha / 3884 ac
Industrial / Airport
0% 4123 ha / 10188 ac
Mines
0 5 10 Kilometers
0 5 10 Miles

Figure 8.3g ■ CONSTRAINED 2, New development, 2000–2020

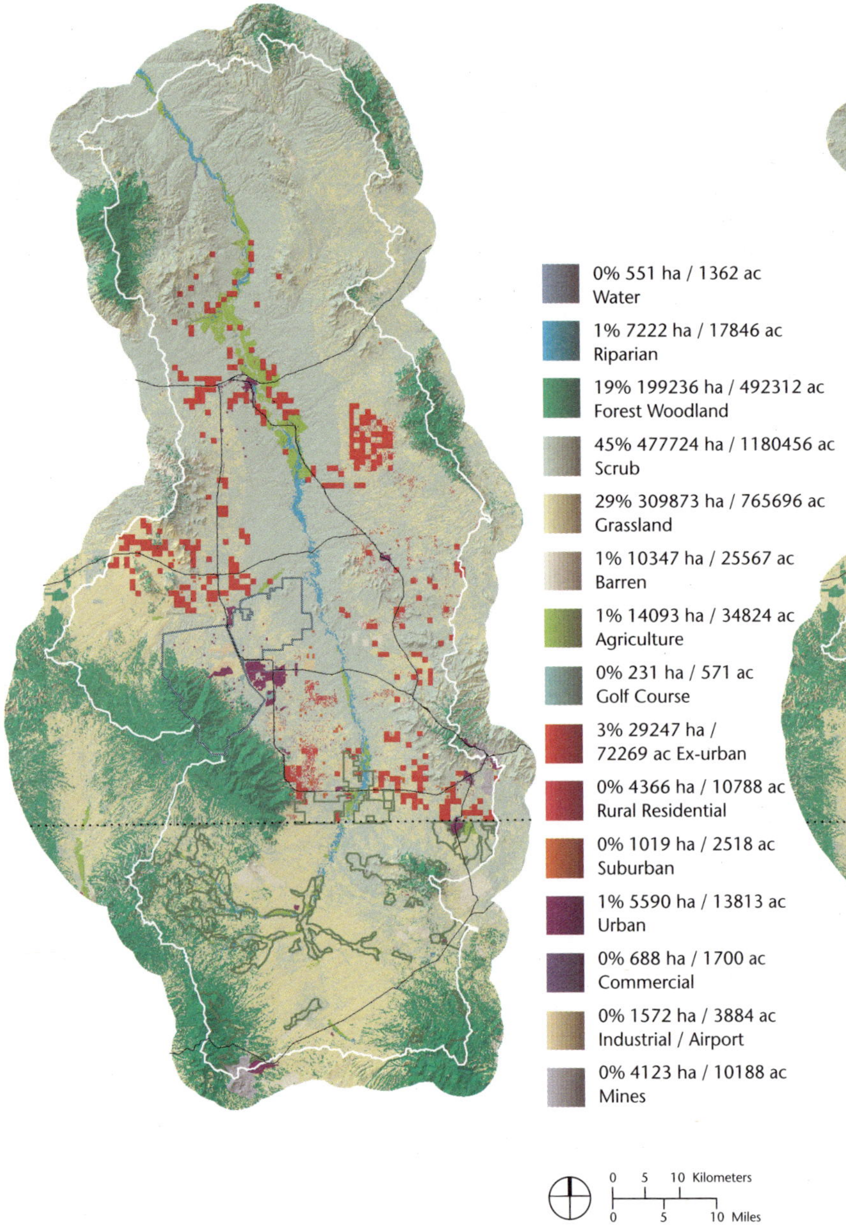
0% 551 ha / 1362 ac
Water
1% 7222 ha / 17846 ac
Riparian
19% 199236 ha / 492312 ac
Forest Woodland
45% 477724 ha / 1180456 ac
Scrub
29% 309873 ha / 765696 ac
Grassland
1% 10347 ha / 25567 ac
Barren
1% 14093 ha / 34824 ac
Agriculture
0% 231 ha / 571 ac
Golf Course
3% 29247 ha /
72269 ac Ex-urban
0% 4366 ha / 10788 ac
Rural Residential
0% 1019 ha / 2518 ac
Suburban
1% 5590 ha / 13813 ac
Urban
0% 688 ha / 1700 ac
Commercial
0% 1572 ha / 3884 ac
Industrial / Airport
0% 4123 ha / 10188 ac
Mines
0 5 10 Kilometers
0 5 10 Miles

Figure 8.3h ■ OPEN, New development, 2000–2020

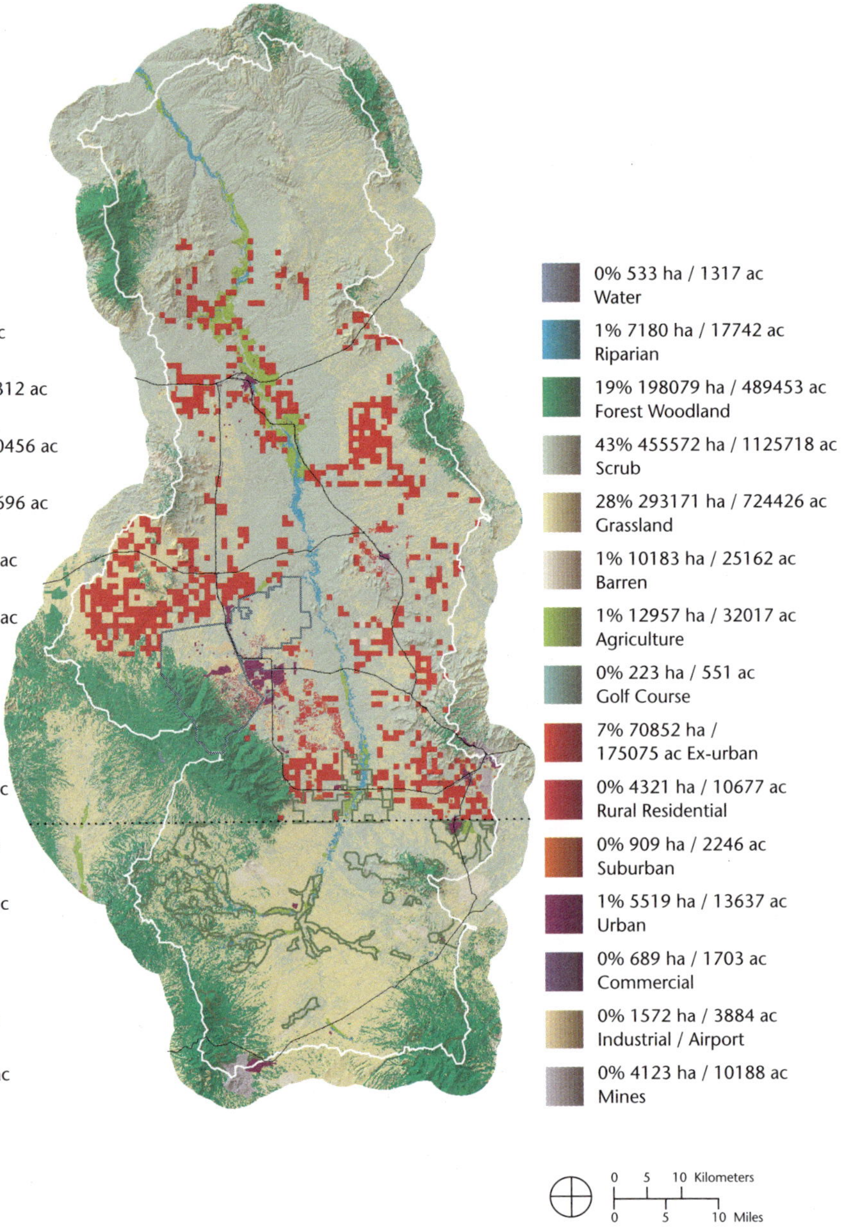
0% 533 ha / 1317 ac
Water
1% 7180 ha / 17742 ac
Riparian
19% 198079 ha / 489453 ac
Forest Woodland
43% 455572 ha / 1125718 ac
Scrub
28% 293171 ha / 724426 ac
Grassland
1% 10183 ha / 25162 ac
Barren
1% 12957 ha / 32017 ac
Agriculture
0% 223 ha / 551 ac
Golf Course
7% 70852 ha /
175075 ac Ex-urban
0% 4321 ha / 10677 ac
Rural Residential
0% 909 ha / 2246 ac
Suburban
1% 5519 ha / 13637 ac
Urban
0% 689 ha / 1703 ac
Commercial
0% 1572 ha / 3884 ac
Industrial / Airport
0% 4123 ha / 10188 ac
Mines
0 5 10 Kilometers
0 5 10 Miles

Figure 8.3i ■ OPEN 1, New development, 2000–2020

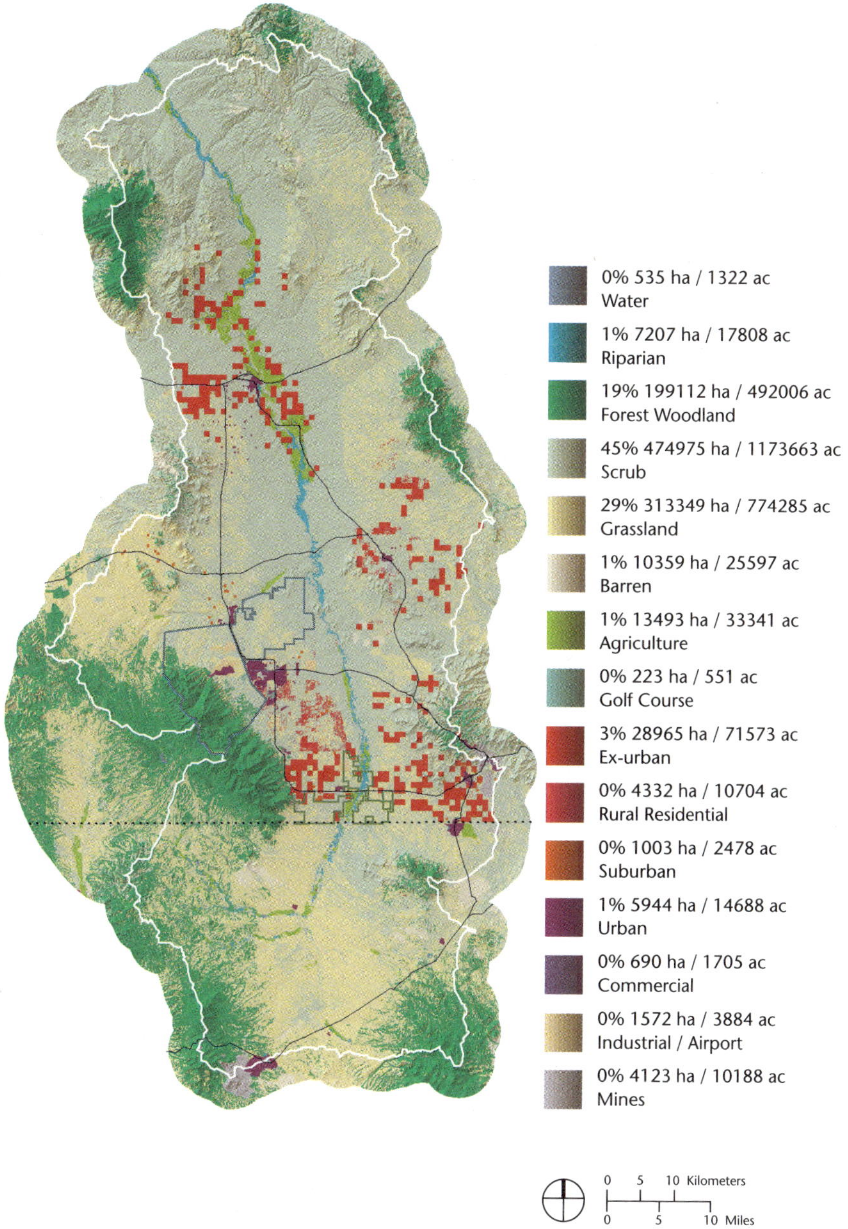
0% 535 ha / 1322 ac
Water
1% 7207 ha / 17808 ac
Riparian
19% 199112 ha / 492006 ac
Forest Woodland
45% 474975 ha / 1173663 ac
Scrub
29% 313349 ha / 774285 ac
Grassland
1% 10359 ha / 25597 ac
Barren
1% 13493 ha / 33341 ac
Agriculture
0% 223 ha / 551 ac
Golf Course
3% 28965 ha / 71573 ac
Ex-urban
0% 4332 ha / 10704 ac
Rural Residential
0% 1003 ha / 2478 ac
Suburban
1% 5944 ha / 14688 ac
Urban
0% 690 ha / 1705 ac
Commercial
0% 1572 ha / 3884 ac
Industrial / Airport
0% 4123 ha / 10188 ac
Mines
0 5 10 Kilometers
0 5 10 Miles

Figure 8.3j ■ OPEN 2, New development, 2000–2020

determined outside the model. The model does not allow demand to be reallocated to other types. If the supply of land for a given housing type is insufficient, the excess demand is unmet.

In Sonora, the development allocation process was less complex. Two alternative projections of population, one the current forecast and the second assuming a higher than forecast population increase based on increased mining in Cananea and agriculture near Naco, were used to estimate the amount of development. Development was then allocated adjacent to existing urban areas, in accordance with current patterns.

The three groups of scenarios—PLANS, CONSTRAINED, and OPEN—create very different patterns of new development, as shown in figure 8.3a–j. Differences in the patterns of development are largely attributable to the combination of constraints on developable land, the attractiveness of the available land for each of the four housing types, and the differing housing demands under each scenario.

The PLANS scenario is based on interpretation of the current Arizona and Sonora plans and a forecast population of 95,000 in 2020 in the Arizona portion of the study area (figure 8.3a). The PLANS 1 scenario increases the Arizona population at a rate double the present forecast, but is otherwise the same as PLANS (figure 8.3b). The PLANS 2 scenario maintains the predicted Arizona population growth and doubles the population in Sonora, with corresponding increases in mining activity but no change to Sonoran conservation areas (figure 8.3c). The PLANS 3 scenario maintains the predicted Arizona and Sonora population growth, but constrains growth in Arizona to urbanized areas (figure 8.3d).

The CONSTRAINED scenario assumes lower than fore-

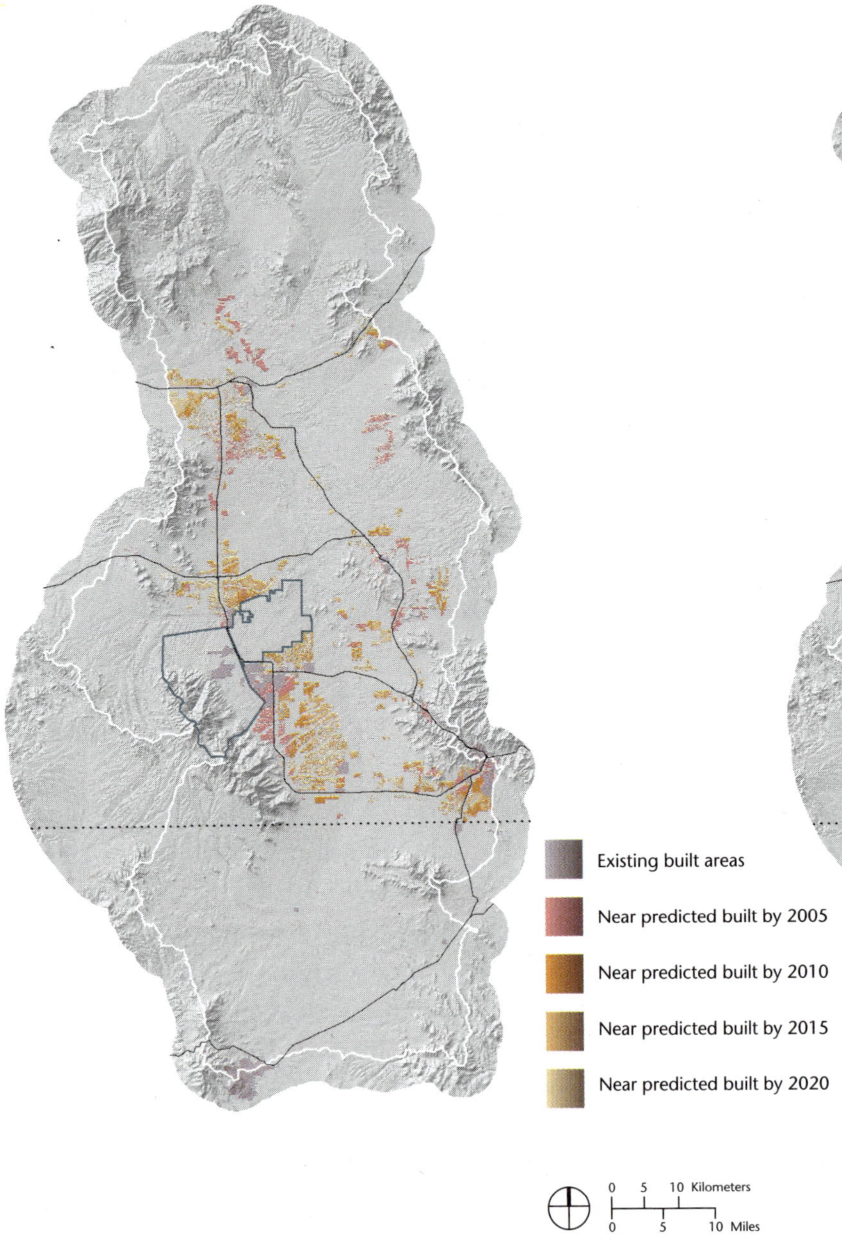
Existing built areas
Near predicted built by 2005
Near predicted built by 2010
Near predicted built by 2015
Near predicted built by 2020
0 5 10 Kilometers
0 5 10 Miles

Figure 8.4a ■ PLANS, Time stages of development

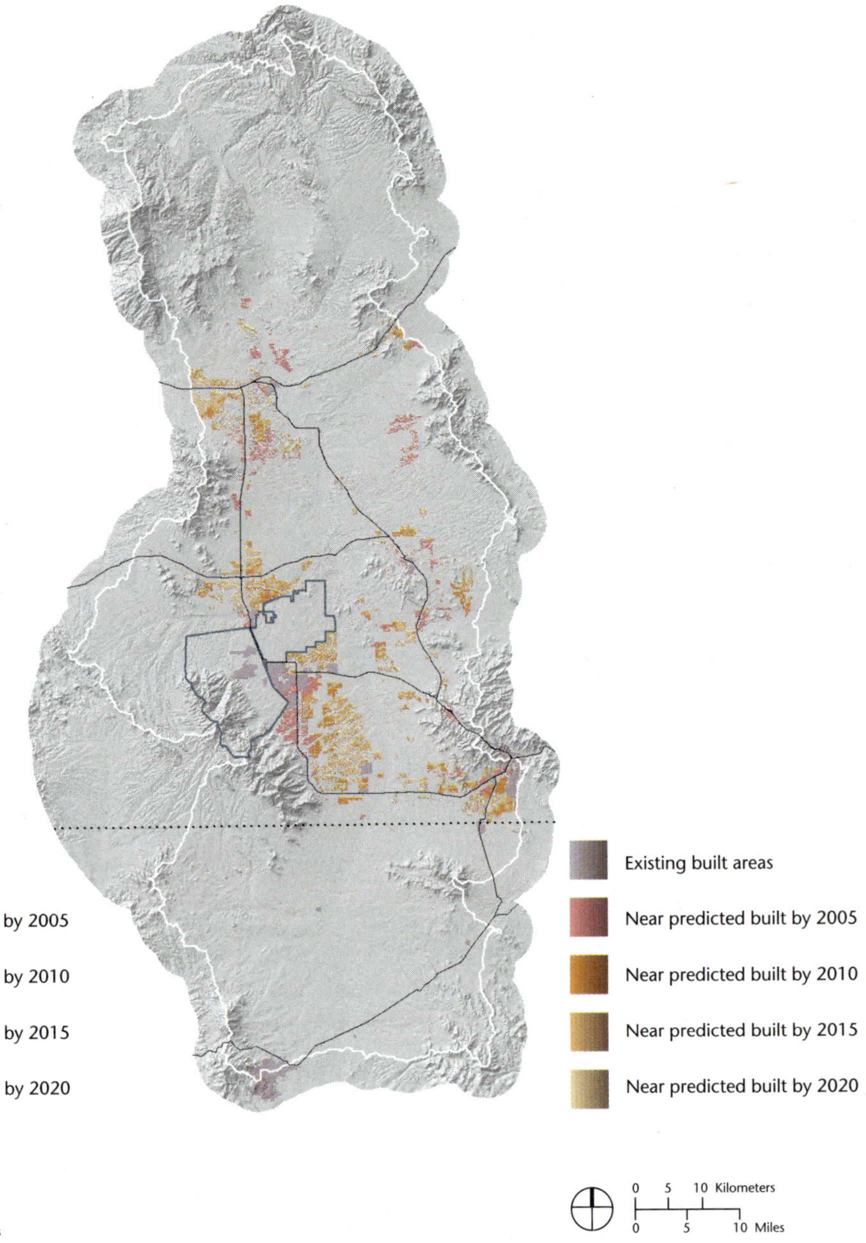
Existing built areas
Near predicted built by 2005
Near predicted built by 2010
Near predicted built by 2015
Near predicted built by 2020
0 5 10 Kilometers
0 5 10 Miles

Figure 8.4b ■ CONSTRAINED, Time stages of development

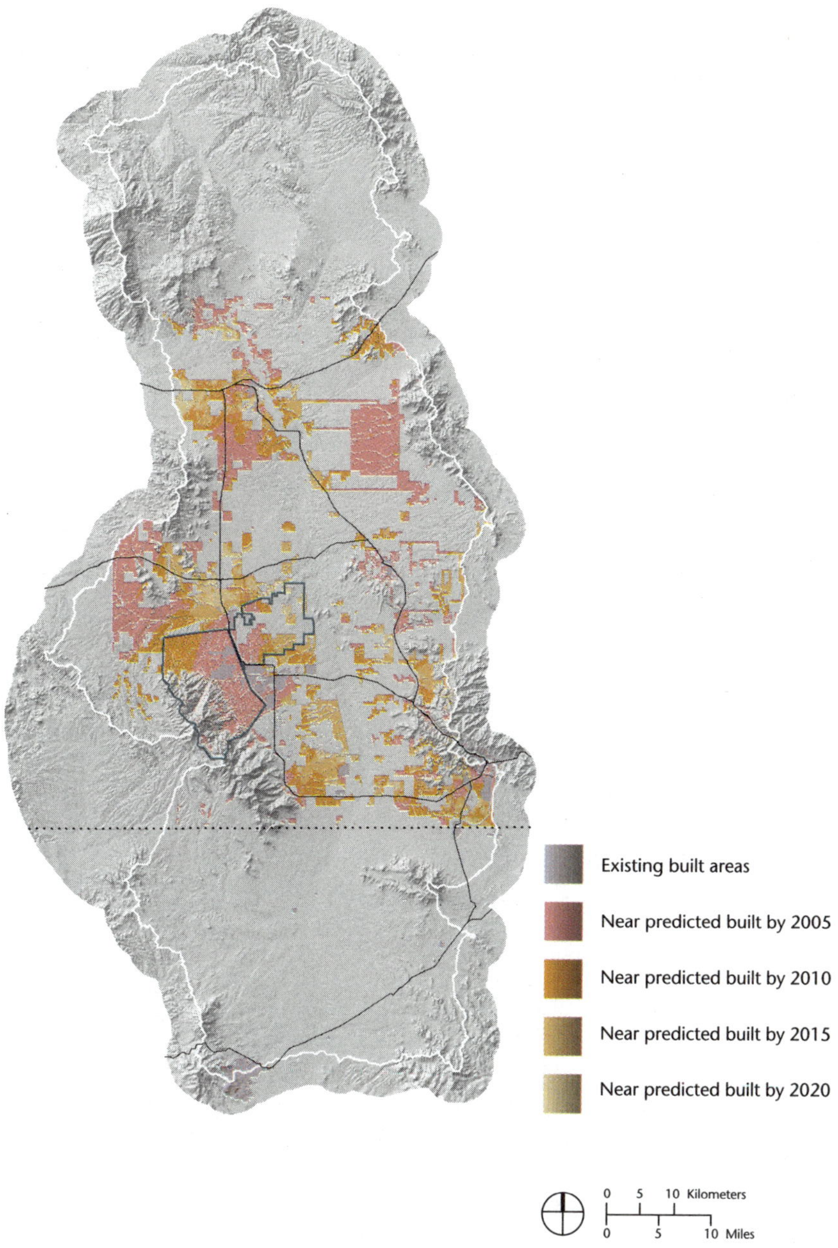
Existing built areas
Near predicted built by 2005
Near predicted built by 2010
Near predicted built by 2015
Near predicted built by 2020
0 5 10 Kilometers
0 5 10 Miles

Figure 8.4c ■ OPEN, Time stages of development

cast population growth in Arizona. Development is concentrated in existing developed areas. It includes very large lot residential development (figure 8.3e). The CONSTRAINED 1 scenario varies in that the on-base population of Fort Huachuca is doubled (figure 8.3f). The CONSTRAINED 2 scenario varies in that Fort Huachuca is closed (figure 8.3g).

The OPEN scenario assumes higher than forecast population growth in Arizona, with major reductions of development control. Sonora remains as forecast (figure 8.3h). The OPEN 1 scenario is the same as OPEN, except that Fort Huachuca closes, and there are increased controls on rural residential development (figure 8.3i). The OPEN 2 scenario doubles the on-base population of Fort Huachuca and doubles the population of Sonora, with corresponding increases in mining activity but no change to Sonora's conservation areas (figure 8.3j).

Figure 8.4a–c shows the 5-year time stages in which the PLANS, CONSTRAINED, and OPEN alternative futures are developed.

Figure 8.5a–c shows the land use/land cover patterns resulting from the alternative futures PLANS 2020, CONSTRAINED 2020, and OPEN 2020.

Impacts of the ten alternative futures are summarized in each of chapters 8 through 16 in three ways. The first is by summary statistics of conditions in 2020 relative to baseline conditions in 2000.

Among the impacts caused by the alternative futures is change in overall attractiveness for residential development. One measure of consumer satisfaction is the average attractiveness for all new residential development of each type.

Table 8.2 shows the attractiveness scores for each housing type weighted by the population living in each

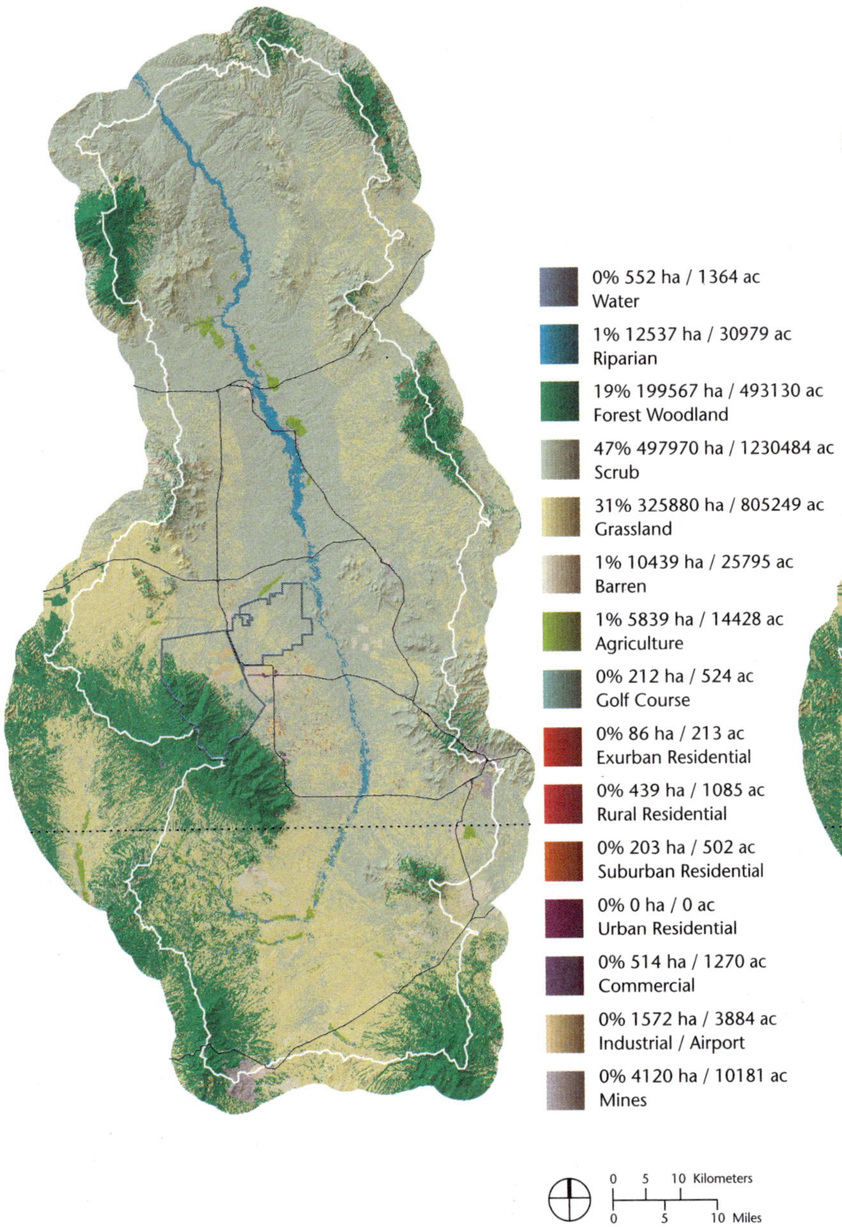
0% 552 ha / 1364 ac
Water
1% 12537 ha / 30979 ac
Riparian
19% 199567 ha / 493130 ac
Forest Woodland
47% 497970 ha / 1230484 ac
Scrub
31% 325880 ha / 805249 ac
Grassland
1% 10439 ha / 25795 ac
Barren
1% 5839 ha / 14428 ac
Agriculture
0% 212 ha / 524 ac
Golf Course
0% 86 ha / 213 ac
Exurban Residential
0% 439 ha / 1085 ac
Rural Residential
0% 203 ha / 502 ac
Suburban Residential
0% 0 ha / 0 ac
Urban Residential
0% 514 ha / 1270 ac
Commercial
0% 1572 ha / 3884 ac
Industrial / Airport
0% 4120 ha / 10181 ac
Mines
0 5 10 Kilometers
0 5 10 Miles

Figure 8.5a ■ PLANS, Land use/land cover, 2002

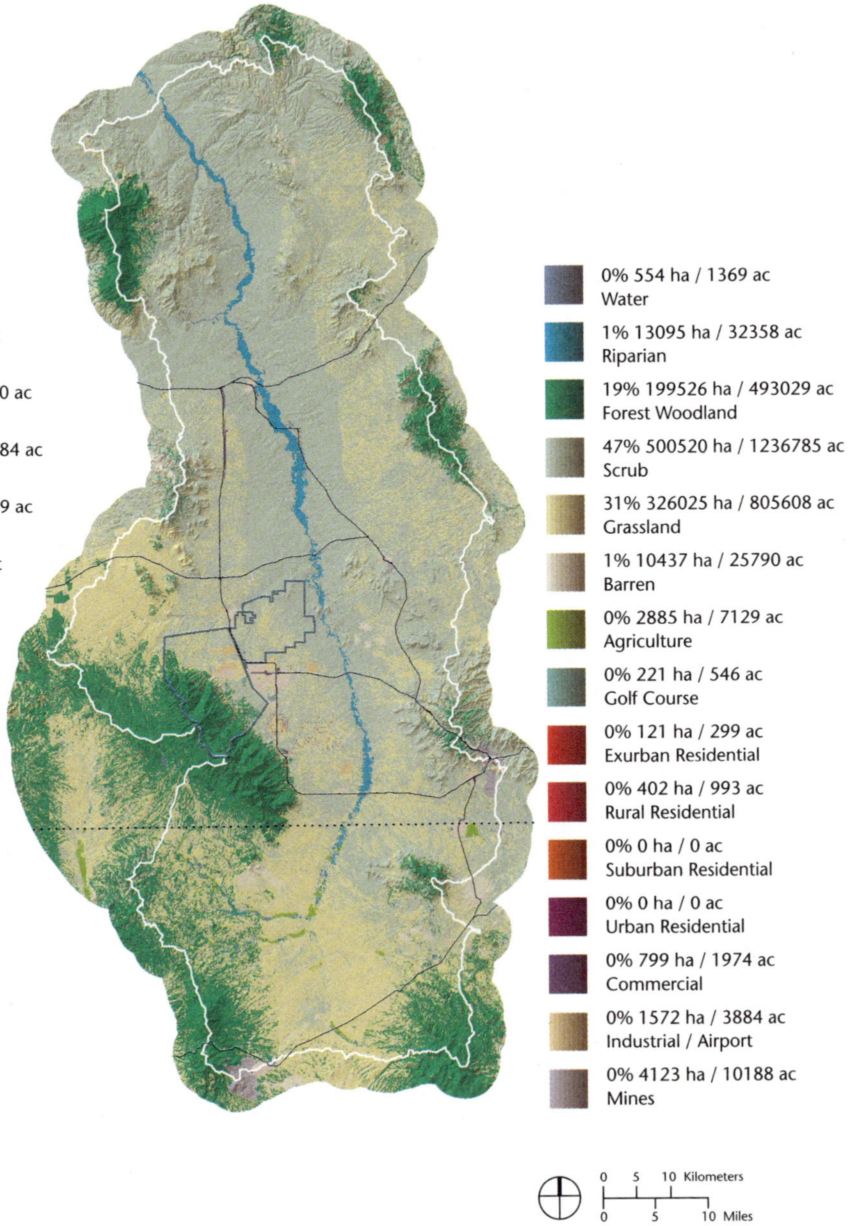
0% 554 ha / 1369 ac
Water
1% 13095 ha / 32358 ac
Riparian
19% 199526 ha / 493029 ac
Forest Woodland
47% 500520 ha / 1236785 ac
Scrub
31% 326025 ha / 805608 ac
Grassland
1% 10437 ha / 25790 ac
Barren
0% 2885 ha / 7129 ac
Agriculture
0% 221 ha / 546 ac
Golf Course
0% 121 ha / 299 ac
Exurban Residential
0% 402 ha / 993 ac
Rural Residential
0% 0 ha / 0 ac
Suburban Residential
0% 0 ha / 0 ac
Urban Residential
0% 799 ha / 1974 ac
Commercial
0% 1572 ha / 3884 ac
Industrial / Airport
0% 4123 ha / 10188 ac
Mines
0 5 10 Kilometers
0 5 10 Miles

Figure 8.5b ■ CONSTRAINED, Land use/land cover, 2002

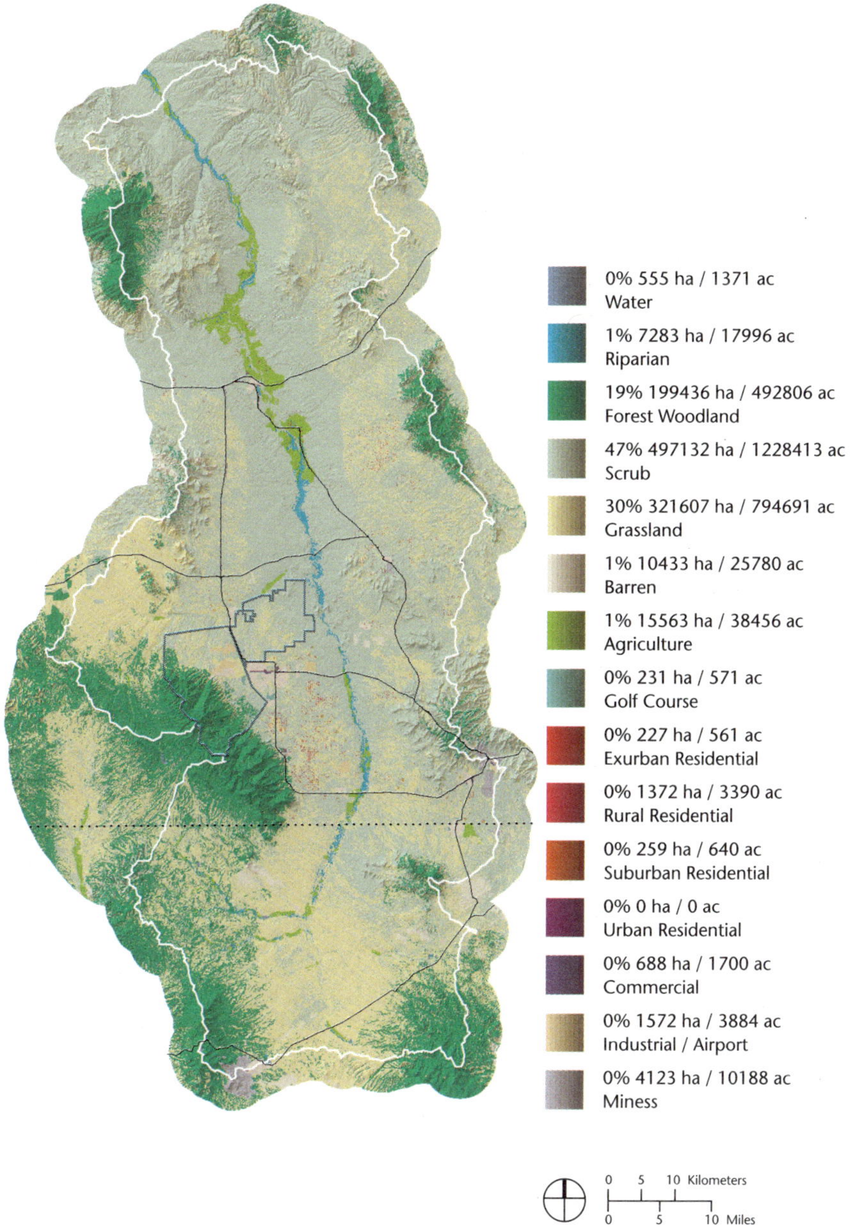
0% 555 ha / 1371 ac
Water
1% 7283 ha / 17996 ac
Riparian
19% 199436 ha / 492806 ac
Forest Woodland
47% 497132 ha / 1228413 ac
Scrub
30% 321607 ha / 794691 ac
Grassland
1% 10433 ha / 25780 ac
Barren
1% 15563 ha / 38456 ac
Agriculture
0% 231 ha / 571 ac
Golf Course
0% 227 ha / 561 ac
Exurban Residential
0% 1372 ha / 3390 ac
Rural Residential
0% 259 ha / 640 ac
Suburban Residential
0% 0 ha / 0 ac
Urban Residential
0% 688 ha / 1700 ac
Commercial
0% 1572 ha / 3884 ac
Industrial / Airport
0% 4123 ha / 10188 ac
Miness
0 5 10 Kilometers
0 5 10 Miles

Figure 8.5c ■ OPEN, Land use/land cover, 2002

type. For example, the weighted attractiveness score for all housing types in the PLANS alternative future is 8.4. The column titled "attractiveness" gives the average attractiveness of all new residential allocations for that type of residential development in Arizona. For example, in PLANS, 14,250 new occupants of suburban housing occupy sites with an average attractiveness of 9.1, a high level. The column titled "attractiveness weighted by population" shows the overall level of attractiveness for all development occupied by new residents. Population is defined by each scenario. The weighted attractiveness scores are comparable. The higher the score, the more attractive the development sites are for home builders.

Comparison of the attractiveness for development of the three PLANS alternative futures shows that attractiveness for tract housing is highest under PLANS 3 because of the proximity and availability of infrastructure (roads and utilities). Attractiveness for rural residential and exurban residential, however, is significantly lower because PLANS 3 restricts the development of land by constraining growth to existing urbanized areas.

There is no significant difference in attractiveness between PLANS and PLANS 1, which double the forecasted population growth. Except for exurban land, there seems to be sufficient desirable land to accommodate the doubled growth.

In the CONSTRAINED alternative futures, a smaller increase in population occurs in only two residential types, urban and exurban. Ninety percent of new homes are urban, and 10 percent are exurban. The attractiveness of the three CONSTRAINED alternative futures is virtually identical. Average attractiveness is lower than the PLANS alternative futures because no new suburban or rural development is allowed. Nevertheless, the scores for

Table 8.2 Attractiveness of residential development in Arizona

Scenario	Baseline 2000	PLANS	PLANS 1	PLANS 2	PLANS 3	CONSTR	CONSTR 1	CONSTR 2	OPEN	OPEN 1	OPEN 2
Urban Attractiveness Index	8.3	8.3	8.4	8.9	8.9	8.3	8.1	8.2	8.2	8.4	8.2
Suburban Attractiveness Index	9.1	9.1	9.2	9.8	9.8	N/A	N/A	N/A	8.8	7.4	9.1
Rural Attractiveness Index	9.0	9.0	9.1	6.6	6.6	N/A	N/A	N/A	8.8	9.2	7.0
Exurban Attractiveness Index	7.8	7.8	7.0	6.4	6.4	6.5	7.6	8.5	7.4	5.8	6.0
Overall Residential Attractiveness	8.4	8.4	8.5	8.9	8.9	8.1	8.1	8.2	8.3	8.1	8.0

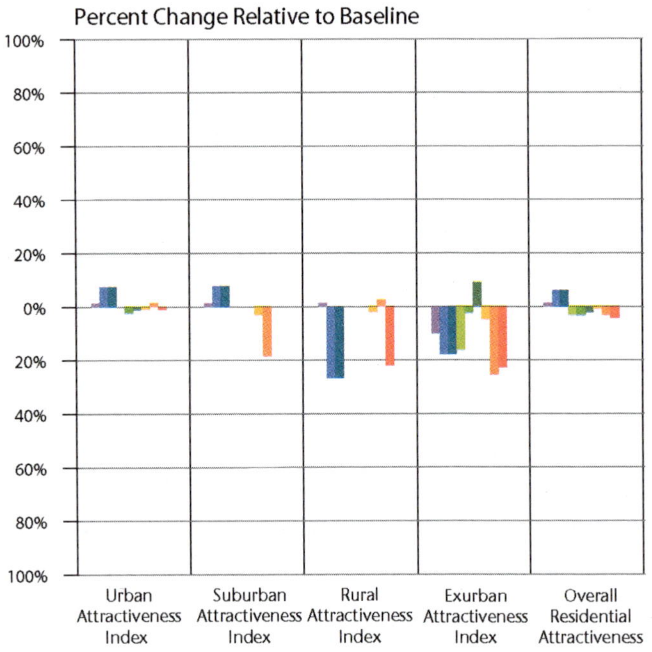

Percent Change Relative to Baseline
100%
80%
60%
40%
20%
0%
20%
40%
60%
80%
100%
Urban Attractiveness Index
Suburban Attractiveness Index
Rural Attractiveness Index
Exurban Attractiveness Index
Overall Residential Attractiveness

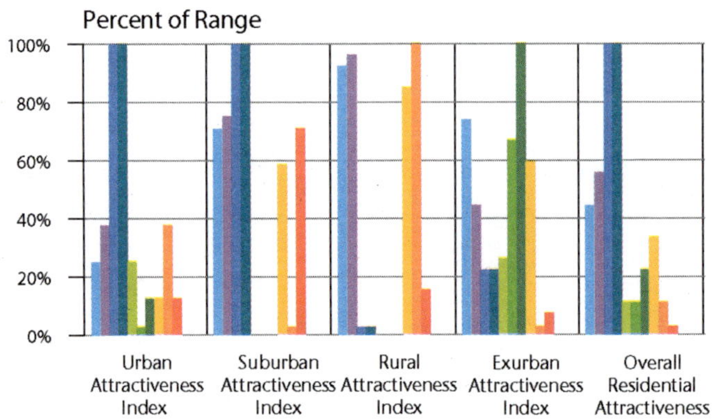

Percent of Range
100%
80%
60%
40%
20%
0%
Urban Attractiveness Index
Suburban Attractiveness Index
Rural Attractiveness Index
Exurban Attractiveness Index
Overall Residential Attractiveness

development in the urban zone are only slightly lower in the CONSTRAINED alternative futures than in the PLANS alternative futures. This reveals that there is sufficient desirable land available for development in the urban zone.

In the CONSTRAINED 2 alternative future, the closure of Fort Huachuca marginally increases the attractiveness for both urban and exurban development because highly desirable land inside Fort Huachuca becomes available for development.

The OPEN alternative futures show the impact of reduced development constraints. Except for PLANS l, growth is higher than in the other scenarios. Average attractiveness is lower than for the PLANS scenarios primarily because in the OPEN scenarios, more housing is allocated to rural and exurban locations. Rural and exurban development is less costly since there is less regulation of subdivisions. The increased demand more rapidly consumes the most attractive locations.

A potentially harmful pattern of development in exurban areas is the wildcat subdivision. Current zoning allows owners of 16.2 ha (40 ac) to subdivide their property into five residential lots without subdivision approval, in effect allowing unregulated subdivision at an average density of one home on 3.2 ha (8 ac). This practice allows rural landowners to legally subdivide their property with no obligation to provide paved roads or other utilities. Buyers of such property often expect the county to pave the roads and provide utility services. The county, however, has no obligation to do so. The resulting exurban development is frequently substandard in terms of infrastructure and can be especially damaging to the environment.

The OPEN 1 scenario attempts to control wildcat development by allowing rural development only on 16.2 ha (40 ac) parcels, rather than at the present effective density of 3.2 ha (8 ac) per home. The OPEN 1 scenario assumes the same number of new rural homes as the OPEN scenario, but because of the increase in parcel size, the resulting exurban land demand requires five times more area than in the OPEN scenario. Because much less desirable exurban land must be used to provide the larger area, the average attractiveness score for exurban land drops from 7.4 to 5.8 in the OPEN 1 alternative future. Attractiveness for suburban development is higher in OPEN 1 because Fort Huachuca closes, opening more highly desirable land for suburban development. The OPEN 1 scenario shows the greatest effect of accelerated sprawl.

Comparison of the alternative futures in 2020 for PLANS, CONSTRAINED, and OPEN shows that the greatest expansion of exurban development comes under the OPEN scenario. It creates much more development in and near Sierra Vista, the Palominas/Bisbee area, and in the lower slopes of all the mountain areas in Cochise County. The CONSTRAINED scenario produces more exurban development than the PLANS scenario, because the CONSTRAINED scenario does not allow rural residential development.

Under all the scenarios, new development is located mainly on the west side of the San Pedro river. This tendency is most pronounced under the PLANS scenario.

CHAPTER 9

The Hydrological Model

The hydrological model simulates the flow processes in the groundwater system and the baseflow processes of the surface water system in the Upper San Pedro River Basin. Until about 1940, water users in the San Pedro Basin relied upon spring discharge, streamflow, artesian wells, and shallow wells to supply their water needs. By about 1940, the completion of rural electrification had provided power to operate modern electric high-powered hydraulic lift pumps. With the large volumes of water taken from underground by these pumps, equilibrium in the hydrologic cycle in the basin was disrupted. Before 1988, most pumping was for agricultural purposes. Pumping from the floodplain and close to regional aquifers has had an adverse effect on the San Pedro River over the entire basin. Pumping from wells near the river has caused naturally losing portions of the river to lose more water and naturally gaining portions to gain less water. With the creation of the San Pedro Riparian National Conservation Area (SPRNCA) in 1988, the U.S. Bureau of Land Management acquired significant amounts of agricultural land within the floodplain and retired the related pumping. The effect on the San Pedro River has been dramatic, and parts of the stream show improved conditions.

Widespread pumping is still a major problem in the basin. It is exacerbated by the location of major centers of pumping, such as Sierra Vista and Benson, which lie between the source of recharge (the rainfall in the surrounding mountains), and the discharge from the basin (the San Pedro River). Because of surface water diversions and depletions of surface water caused by groundwater pumping, the previously perennial streamflow of the San Pedro River has become intermittent in some areas. Groundwater withdrawals threaten to lower the water table in riparian areas along the river, potentially eliminating the currently available areas of shallow water and the plant life there. This could substantially reduce the quality of wildlife habitat in the SPRNCA. The lowering of the water table caused by groundwater pumping can result in aquifer compaction and produce subsidence problems similar to those seen in the urban area of nearby Tucson. Agriculture along the floodplain of the river that formerly relied on the readily available streamflow now relies more heavily on groundwater withdrawals, compounding water problems near the river. Increased population in the basin is also creating a demand for more water, which at present can only be satisfied by increased pumping from groundwater in the regional aquifer. Since the regional aquifer is hydraulically connected to the floodplain aquifer, effects in the regional aquifer are transferred to the river.

The hydrological model simulates flow processes, including the interactions of groundwater with surface water and evapotranspiration. Unlike in earlier studies, the hydrological model integrates data on the Sonoran part of the study area to provide a more complete basis for the evaluation of alternative futures in the Upper San Pedro River Basin.

Improvements to methodology were of primary concern in creating a new model of this already highly investigated area. An extensive expansion of the geographical information system (GIS) was developed for land surface, geology, hydraulic properties, mountain front recharge, riparian evapotranspiration, irrigated agriculture, well locations, and stream network. The GIS enabled several important changes in methods and information management to be used in this study. Estimated pumping rates are distributed to known well locations, corresponding to records held

Photo 9.1 ■ Irrigated agriculture on San Pedro floodplain

Photo 9.2 ■ Residential development

by the state of Arizona. Mountain front recharge is given a weighted distribution based on elevation and the average precipitation of contributing subbasins. Results from recent studies of evapotranspiration were applied in riparian areas. Model boundaries are extended toward mountain front areas and include the entire Mexican portion of the Upper San Pedro River Basin as well as the headwaters of the Babocomari River watershed (figure 9.1). These changes allow for a more comprehensive hydrologic evaluation of alternative futures for the Upper San Pedro River Basin than was previously possible. The model integrates new

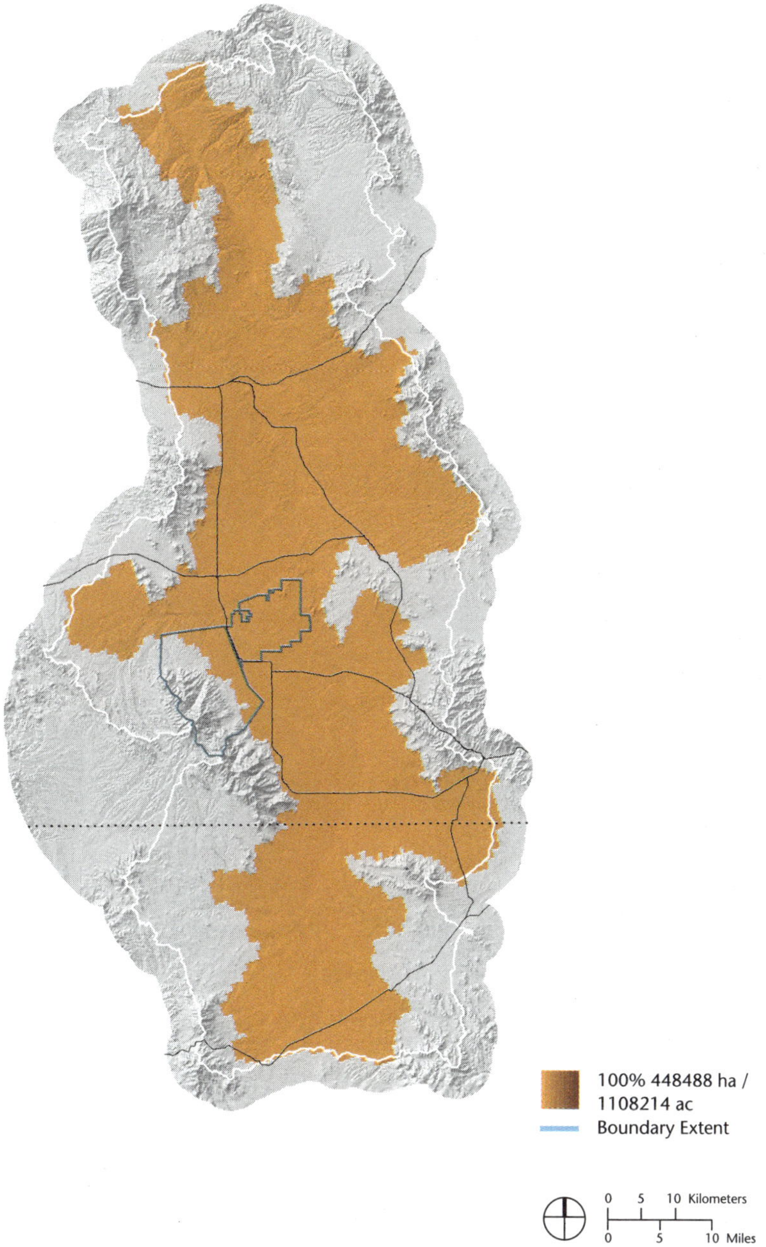
100% 448488 ha /
1108214 ac
Boundary Extent
0 5 10 Kilometers
0 5 10 Miles

Figure 9.1 ■ Hydrological model boundaries

hydrologic information developed for the basin by the U.S. Geological Survey (USGS) and other entities such as the Semi-Arid Land-Surface-Atmosphere Program.

Precipitation falls in the upper regions of the mountains of the San Pedro Basin, flows in streams winding down through the mountain valleys, and infiltrates into the groundwater system below the alluvial fans at the base of the mountains (figure 9.2). The infiltrated water percolates downward through the regional aquifer and flows slowly across and down the valley through the porous material. Most of the water continues to flow underground northward toward the Gila River, but a portion of it flows upward to recharge the river as baseflow (that portion of streamflow that is supplied by ground water). The baseflow between Palominas and Charleston gauges increases by nearly an order of magnitude by this process.

The regional aquifer is typically divided into two parts. The lower basin fill is an important water-bearing unit throughout the basin. It overlies impermeable bedrock (the Pantano Formation) and consists of interbedded sands and gravels. Its thickness ranges from a few meters along the valley edge to possibly more than 300 m (1000 ft) in the center of the basin. The upper basin fill overlies the lower basin fill, up to a depth of over 200 m (660 ft). The

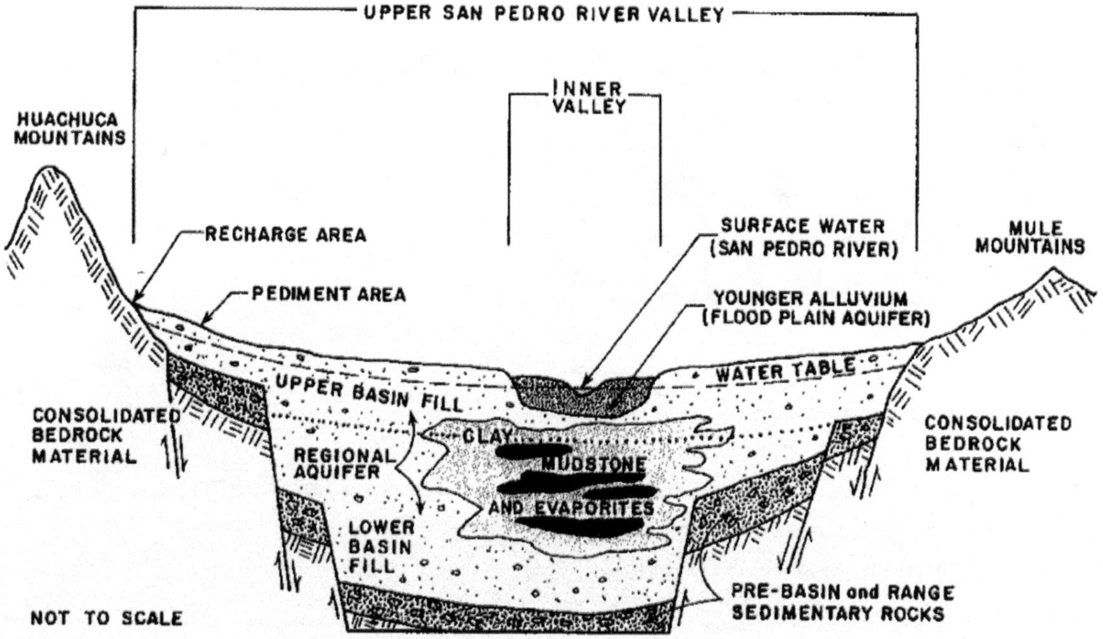
UPPER SAN PEDRO RIVER VALLEY
INNER VALLEY
HUACHUCA MOUNTAINS
RECHARGE AREA
PEDIMENT AREA
SURFACE WATER (SAN PEDRO RIVER)
MULE MOUNTAINS
YOUNGER ALLUVIUM (FLOOD PLAIN AQUIFER)
WATER TABLE
UPPER BASIN FILL
CONSOLIDATED BEDROCK MATERIAL
CLAY, MUDSTONE AND EVAPORITES
REGIONAL AQUIFER
LOWER BASIN FILL
CONSOLIDATED BEDROCK MATERIAL
PRE-BASIN and RANGE SEDIMENTARY ROCKS
NOT TO SCALE

Figure 9.2 ■ Conceptual cross section of the Upper San Pedro River Basin

upper basin fill contains a multitude of clay and silt layers interbedded among sands and gravels.

Where saturated, the lower and upper alluvial units of the basin fill are in direct hydraulic connection with each other. Because of vertical and horizontal changes in composition, the upper and lower basin fill units behave as one hydrologic unit (Freethy 1982). Silt and clay layers within the basin fill split the groundwater into deep and shallow flow systems (Pool and Coes 1999). A large clay unit (the St. David Formation) exists near the St. David and Benson area (Gray 1965). It consists of nearly 300 m (1000 ft) of clays, silts, and some freshwater limestones. The clay layers up to 100 m (330 ft) thick form an aquitard between the coarse grained sediments of the overlying flood plain aquifer and the regional aquifer below (Jahnke 1994). The earthquake of 1887 is believed to have caused cienegas (swamps) in the St. David area to disappear and to have changed the pattern of springs. It caused artesian pools to appear and wells to begin to flow under artesian conditions (Hadley in Salsa 1999; ADWR 1991).

The floodplain alluvium, consisting of unconsolidated gravel, sand, and silt, forms a lon,g narrow, and relatively shallow aquifer beneath and on both sides of the San Pedro River. The floodplain generally overlies the regional aquifer and confining clays, ranging from over 50 m (165 ft) thick to nonexistent where the river flows directly over exposed bedrock. The river itself has a variable entrenched channel that meanders through its floodplain and riparian forest area. Streamflow is variable. The reaches from Hereford to Charleston are generally gaining and perennial. From Fairbank to the "Narrows," a geologic formation north of Benson, flow is intermittent. At the Benson Narrows, a geologic constriction forces regional groundwater upward into the floodplain. Further downstream, streamflow is generally intermittent except in short perennial segments where bedrock is at or near the surface (Huckleberry 1996).

The hydrological model consists of a set of mathematical equations, based on hydrologic principles for groundwater flow and stream baseflow processes. These equations predict changes in groundwater levels, storage, stream-aquifer interactions, and baseflow caused by the stresses of groundwater pumping and surface water diversions.

The building of the hydrological model proceeds in two stages. First, a conceptual model of the groundwater system is created. For groundwater systems, the conceptual model specifies geologic boundaries and layers, stream and diversion locations, riparian and agricultural areas, mountain front recharge distribution zones, and well site locations.

The conceptual model uses GIS software, in this case ArcView (ESRI, Redlands, Calif.), to view and create point, line, and polygon shapes. These shapes are spatial representations of physical entities such as well points, linear stream segments, and riparian and agricultural cover areas. These shapes are linked to attribute information (i.e., well pumping rates, streamflow and shape characteristics, and evapotranspiration rates associated with differing types of vegetative cover) contained in a geographical database.

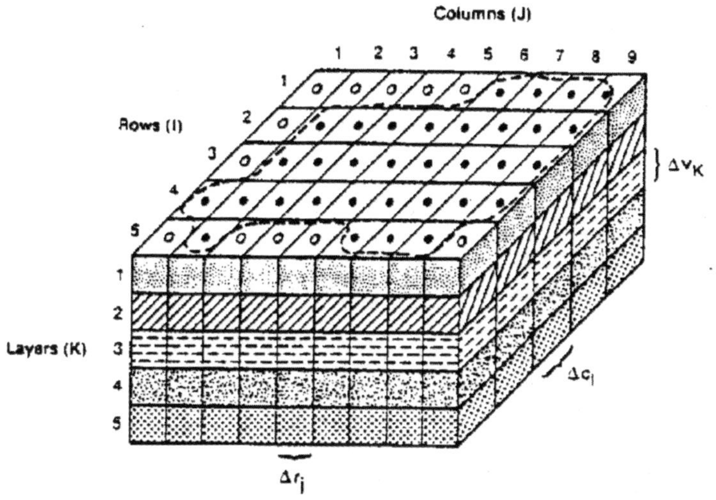
Columns (J)
1 2 3 4 5 6 7 8 9
Rows (I)
1 2 3 4 5
Layers (K)
1 2 3 4 5
Δv_K
Δc_I
Δr_j

Figure 9.3 ■ A discretized hypothetical aquifer system

The second stage of building the hydrological model is the application of a numerical approximation to the conceptual model. This approximation leads to the creation of a numerical computer model. This is accomplished by merging the conceptual model, with all its attributes, onto a three-dimensional finite difference grid representing the surface and subsurface geology of the study region (figure 9.3). The infusion of the two models (conceptual and numerical) is aided through the use of U.S. Department of Defense Groundwater Modeling System (GMS) software. GMS is an interface between GIS applications and numerical computer models. The numerical computer model used in this study is MODFLOW groundwater software originating from the USGS (McDonald and Harbaugh 1988). MODFLOW computes the hydraulic head (water level) for each cell within a finite difference grid. The program has a modular structure allowing the user to incorporate a series of packages or modules to simulate different processes associated with groundwater. Packages used in this study include evapotranspiration, recharge, well pumping, and stream-aquifer interaction.

GMS also assists in editing the conceptual model by generating

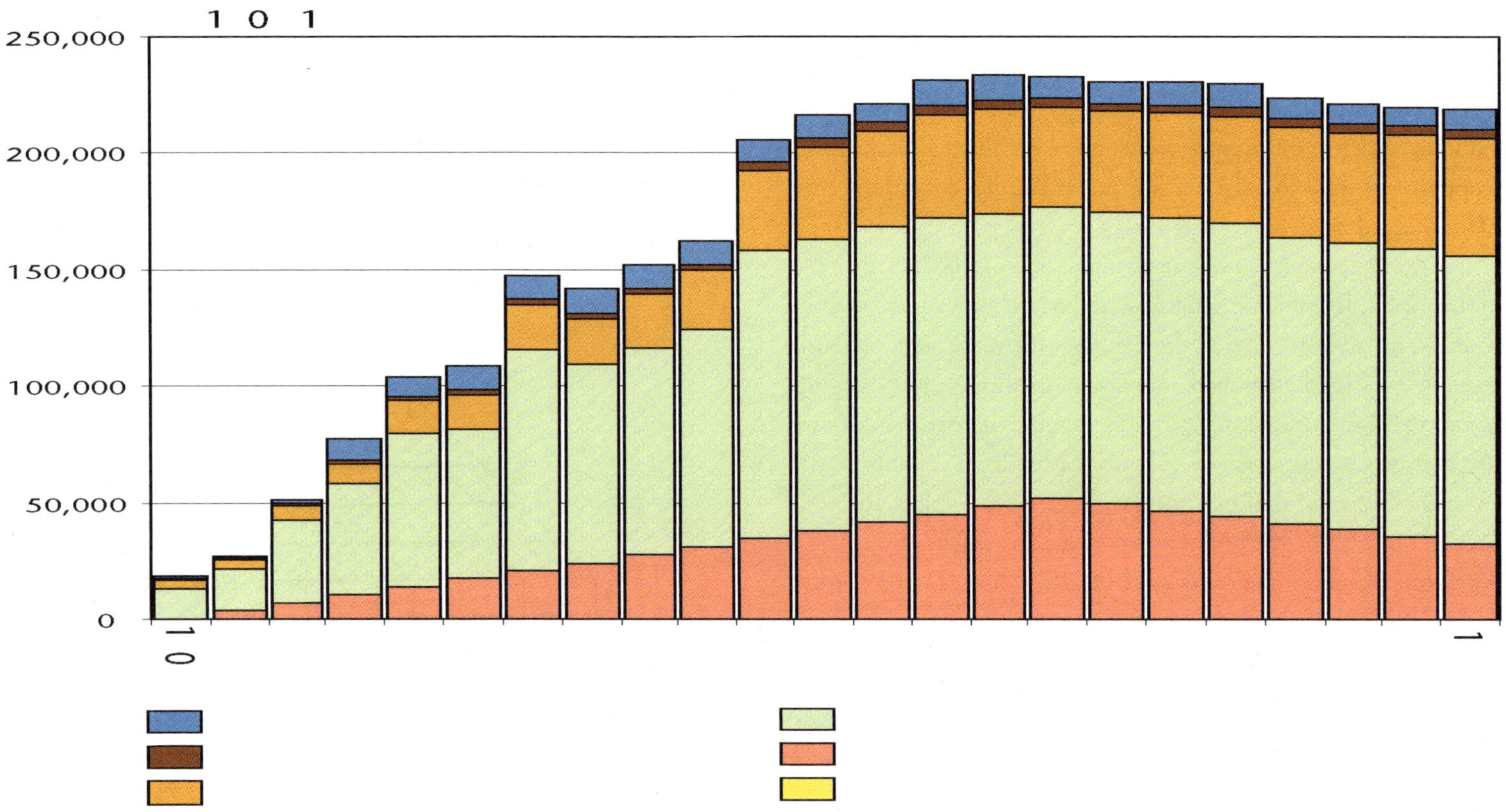
1 0 1
250,000
200,000
150,000
100,000
50,000
0

Figure 9.4 ■ Total pumping distribution, 1940–1997

a three-dimensional grid, geostatistics, and postprocessing. The map module within GMS is used extensively in conforming the conceptual model to the three-dimensional finite difference grid used by MODFLOW packages. GMS was selected for this study because it automates grid construction, facilitates generation of head contours, and allows model representation in real-world coordinates consistent with the GIS applications mentioned above.

To establish a baseline against which the alternative futures are evaluated, groundwater is modeled to represent predevelopment conditions. This is intended to represent the "steady state" of the region's hydrology before the introduction of significant human-caused stresses. Steady-state conditions are assumed to have existed in 1940, an assumption shared with other prior hydrological studies of the area. The steady state is used to define the baseline condition for subsequent transient analysis. The transient simulation models the effect of change on ground and surface water by applying historical and current information on anthropogenic stresses to the system from 1940 to the present. The transient simulation is divided into a series of twenty-three stress periods. Within each stress period all parameters remain constant (i.e., pumping rates do not change). Each stress period is divided into a series of 1-year time steps.

Modeled groundwater and stream conditions in both the steady state and in the transient simulations are calibrated against measurements of observed water levels and stream baseflow conditions. Hydrologic and geologic parameters are adjusted within the model in order for the computer simulation to better represent historic and current groundwater conditions. Figure 9.4 shows the total pumpage distribution by type of use for each of the stress periods during the period 1940 through 1997 (Goode and Maddock 2000). Dominant uses in the Arizona portion of the study area include agricultural irrigation and increasing amounts of pumping to provide supply for the increased population. In

Photo 9.3 ■ High water

Photo 9.4 ■ Low water

Sonora, pumping is chiefly related to changes in water use associated with mining activity.

The model replicates the groundwater flow behavior for trends from 1940 to 1997. It indicates that there is a reduction of streamflow in the San Pedro River, a reduction of evapotranspiration by riparian vegetation along the floodplain of the San Pedro River, and the formation of significant cones of depression of groundwater levels near many communities. The model indicates large losses from groundwater storage associated with these trends.

The depletion of streamflows in the San Pedro River by ground-

Photo 9.5 ■ Copper mine, Cananea

water pumping is seen in some of the reaches near the Benson area. By 1997, these reaches have no baseflow—there is no perennial surface streamflow present in the river bed. This is a result of the large increases in pumping. By 1997, nearly 20 percent of the water pumped in the Upper San Pedro Basin is taken from the San Pedro River. Although baseflow still exists in the Charleston area in 1997, the model indicates that the flow has been reduced by more than 30 percent since 1940. Since the creation of the SPRNCA, water levels along the protected portion of the floodplain have seen some recovery. However, water is still being taken from the riparian area outside the SPRNCA.

Cones of depression in the level of groundwater can be observed in excess of 25 m (80 ft) in depth beneath Sierra Vista, Arizona, and greater than 40 m (130 ft) in depth near Cananea, Sonora, in 1997. Smaller declines in the water table level can be seen along the floodplain near the communities of St. David and Benson and near the town of Naco. The water level declines are indicative of losses from groundwater storage. By 1997, over 65 percent of the water pumped is taken from storage.

After modeling current conditions, anticipated future conditions are projected by modifying current stresses or by adding new ones. By using the alternative futures developed under each

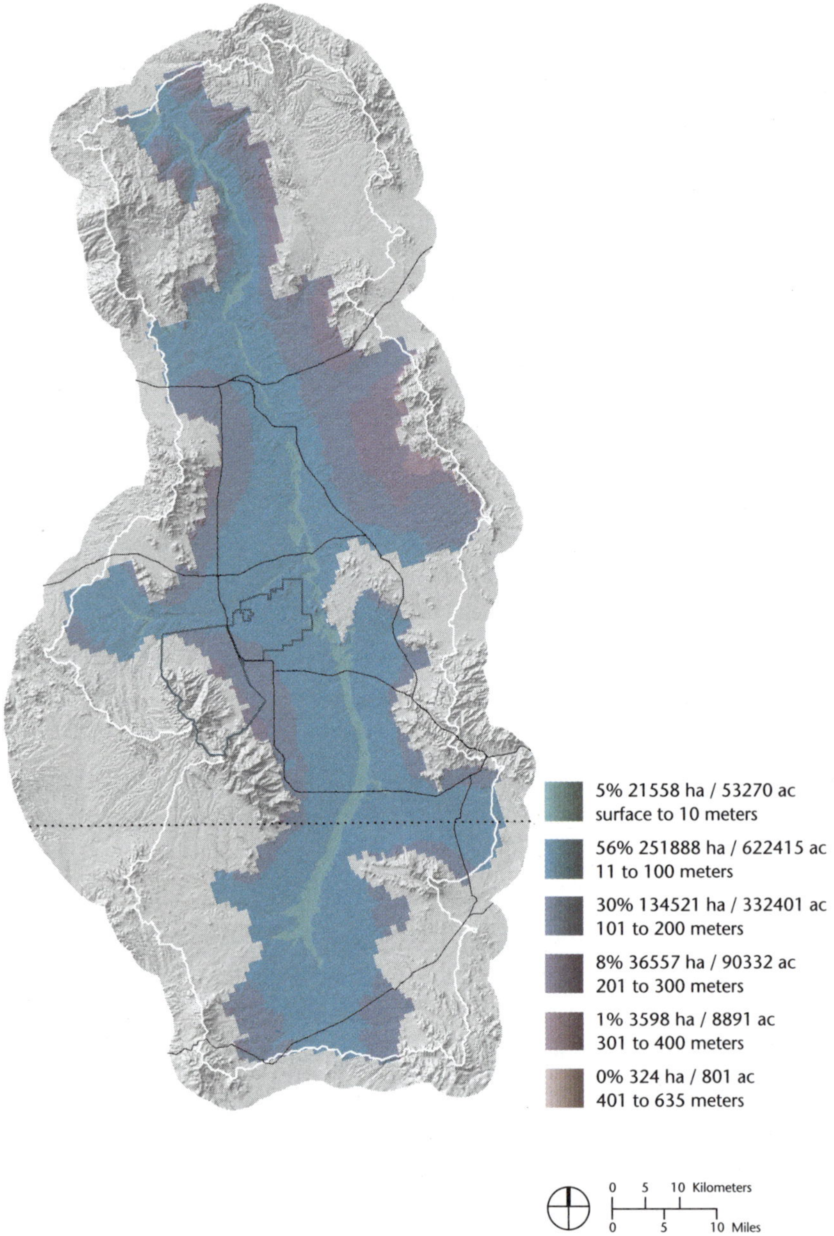
5% 21558 ha / 53270 ac
surface to 10 meters
56% 251888 ha / 622415 ac
11 to 100 meters
30% 134521 ha / 332401 ac
101 to 200 meters
8% 36557 ha / 90332 ac
201 to 300 meters
1% 3598 ha / 8891 ac
301 to 400 meters
0% 324 ha / 801 ac
401 to 635 meters
0 5 10 Kilometers
0 5 10 Miles

Figure 9.5 ■ Groundwater, 2000

Table 9.1 Groundwater: Impacts, 2000–2020

	change in agricultural pumping over 20 years m^3/day	change in municipal and industrial pumping over 20 years m^3/day	loss from groundwater storage over 20 years m^3/day	capture from the San Pedro River System over 20 years m^3/day
Baseline 2000	113,153	94,614	-131,494	38,279
Plans	-92,190	-2,759	-76,133	27,634
Plans 1	-92,190	17,941	-92,058	30,087
Plans 2	-89,496	30,737	-106,991	30,218
Plans 3	-92,533	-816	-78,735	27,259
Constrained	-110,859	-1,370	-55,726	20,901
Constrained 1	-110,859	5,140	-61,493	21,185
Constrained 2	-110,859	-9,000	-47,515	21,050
Open	-6,382	15,083	-142,102	38,096
Open 1	-6,382	19,213	-147,114	37,523
Open 2	-3,294	49,975	-179,707	38,267

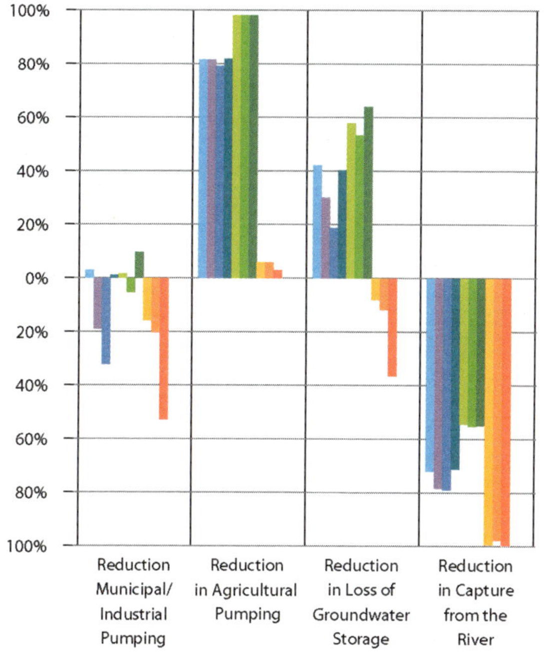
100%
80%
60%
40%
20%
0%
20%
40%
60%
80%
100%
Reduction Municipal/ Industrial Pumping
Reduction in Agricultural Pumping
Reduction in Loss of Groundwater Storage
Reduction in Capture from the River

Percent impacts

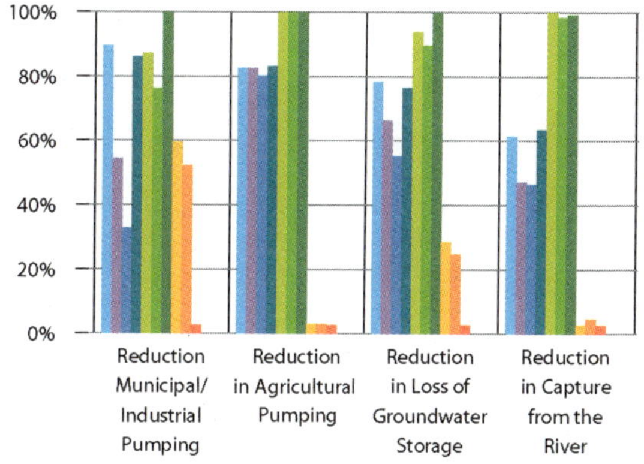
100%
80%
60%
40%
20%
0%
Reduction Municipal/ Industrial Pumping
Reduction in Agricultural Pumping
Reduction in Loss of Groundwater Storage
Reduction in Capture from the River

Relative impacts

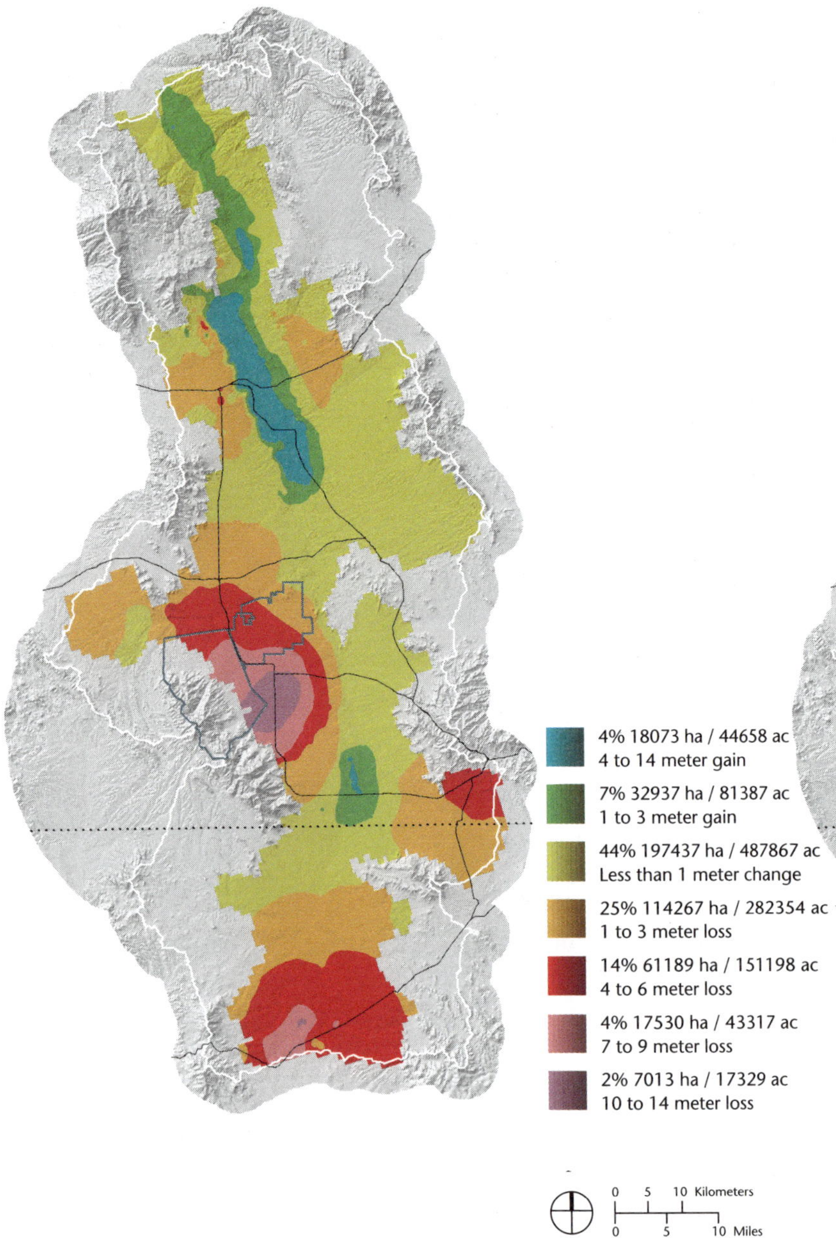
4% 18073 ha / 44658 ac
4 to 14 meter gain
7% 32937 ha / 81387 ac
1 to 3 meter gain
44% 197437 ha / 487867 ac
Less than 1 meter change
25% 114267 ha / 282354 ac
1 to 3 meter loss
14% 61189 ha / 151198 ac
4 to 6 meter loss
4% 17530 ha / 43317 ac
7 to 9 meter loss
2% 7013 ha / 17329 ac
10 to 14 meter loss
0 5 10 Kilometers
0 5 10 Miles

Figure 9.6a ■ PLANS, Groundwater impacts, 2000–2020

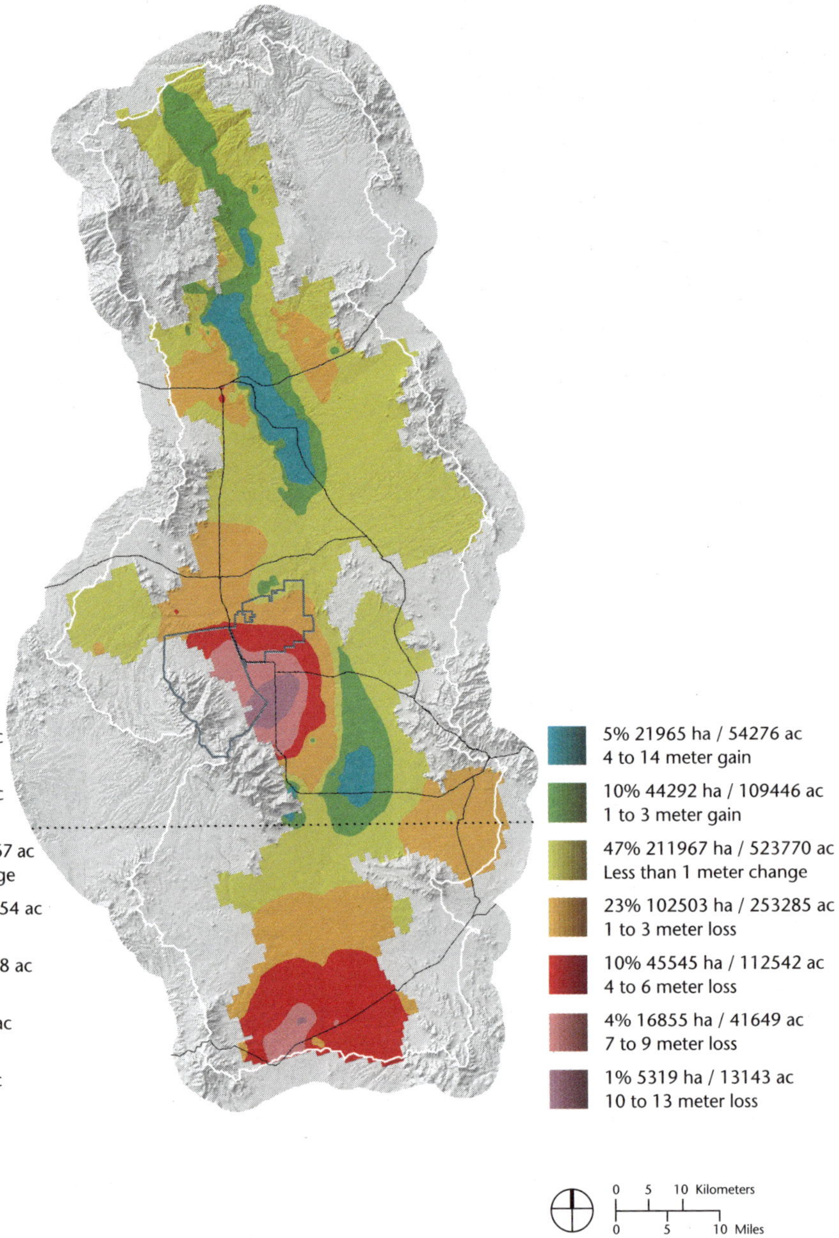
5% 21965 ha / 54276 ac
4 to 14 meter gain
10% 44292 ha / 109446 ac
1 to 3 meter gain
47% 211967 ha / 523770 ac
Less than 1 meter change
23% 102503 ha / 253285 ac
1 to 3 meter loss
10% 45545 ha / 112542 ac
4 to 6 meter loss
4% 16855 ha / 41649 ac
7 to 9 meter loss
1% 5319 ha / 13143 ac
10 to 13 meter loss
0 5 10 Kilometers
0 5 10 Miles

Figure 9.6b ■ CONSTRAINED, Groundwater impacts, 2000–2020

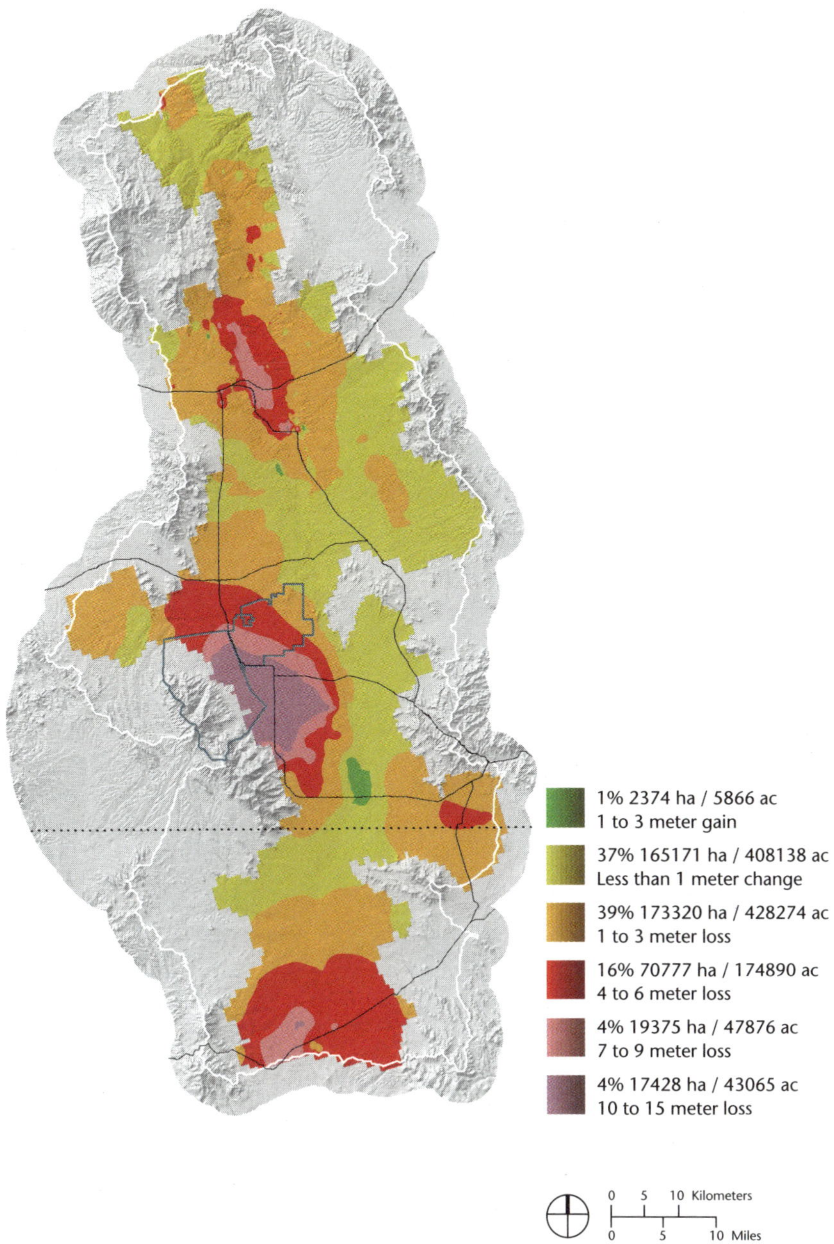
1% 2374 ha / 5866 ac
1 to 3 meter gain
37% 165171 ha / 408138 ac
Less than 1 meter change
39% 173320 ha / 428274 ac
1 to 3 meter loss
16% 70777 ha / 174890 ac
4 to 6 meter loss
4% 19375 ha / 47876 ac
7 to 9 meter loss
4% 17428 ha / 43065 ac
10 to 15 meter loss
0 5 10 Kilometers
0 5 10 Miles

Figure 9.6c ■ OPEN, Groundwater impacts, 2000–2020

scenario, the model is able to predict hydrologic changes caused by differing policies and patterns of development, agriculture, mining, vegetation change, and so forth. The hydrological model evaluates possible future impacts to the hydrologic system resulting from the applied stresses inherent in each of the alternative futures. Five summary impact evaluations are made for each alternative: change in agricultural pumping; change in municipal and industrial pumping; average daily groundwater storage; change in flow in the San Pedro River; and change in the length of flowing river. Figure 9.6a–c shows the changes in the groundwater table for the PLANS, CONSTRAINED, AND OPEN alternative futures (table 9.1).

The results of this study are similar to the results of previous studies of the hydrology of the San Pedro Basin. Previous studies have all indicated deepening cones of depression of the groundwater, reduction of streamflows, and loss from groundwater storage and evapotranspiration (Vionnet 1992; Jahnke 1994; Correll et al. 1996). This study serves to further substantiate the evidence of previous hydrological studies as well as to provide the means to evaluate the hydrological impacts of the alternative futures.

All the alternative futures have adverse impacts on the river (figure 9.7). All cause groundwater losses. The size of the impact depends on whether or not there is an increase in groundwater pumping or in the diversion of surface water. The CONSTRAINED scenarios produce the least reduction of groundwater storage and cause the least amount of water to be captured from the river, resulting in the greatest length of flowing stream in comparison to the other scenarios. The OPEN scenarios produce the greatest loss of groundwater storage and cause the largest amounts of water to be captured from streamflow, resulting in the greatest increase in length of dried-up streambed. The impacts of the PLANS scenarios, although all show storage loss and stream capture increases, are generally similar to the hydrological impacts of the CONSTRAINED scenarios.

The greatest changes in stress are caused by the reduction of irrigated agriculture. Even the OPEN scenario anticipates a reduction in irrigated agriculture, although a small one in relation to the CONSTRAINED scenario. For example, in 2000, agricultural pumping in the subbasin is 113,153 cu m (91.74 ac ft) per day. By 2020, in the PLANS scenario, pumping is reduced by 92,190 cu m (74.75 ac ft) per day, anticipating an agricultural pumping rate of 20,863 cu m (16.91 ac ft) per day. In comparison, the OPEN scenario anticipates a reduction in agricultural pumping of 6382 cu m (5.71 ac ft) per day, leaving active pumping at the rate of 106,771 cu m (86.57 ac ft) per day by 2020.

Because the PLANS and CONSTRAINED scenarios have similar amounts of reduction in agricultural pumping (92,190 cu m and 110,859 cu m, respectively, or 74.75 ac ft and 89.88 ac ft), the capture of surface water caused by pumping is similar (27,634 cu m and 20,901 cu m, respectively, or 22.4 ac ft and 16.94 ac ft), and the length of dry river bed expected to result is also nearly equal (table 9.2 and figure 9.8a–c).

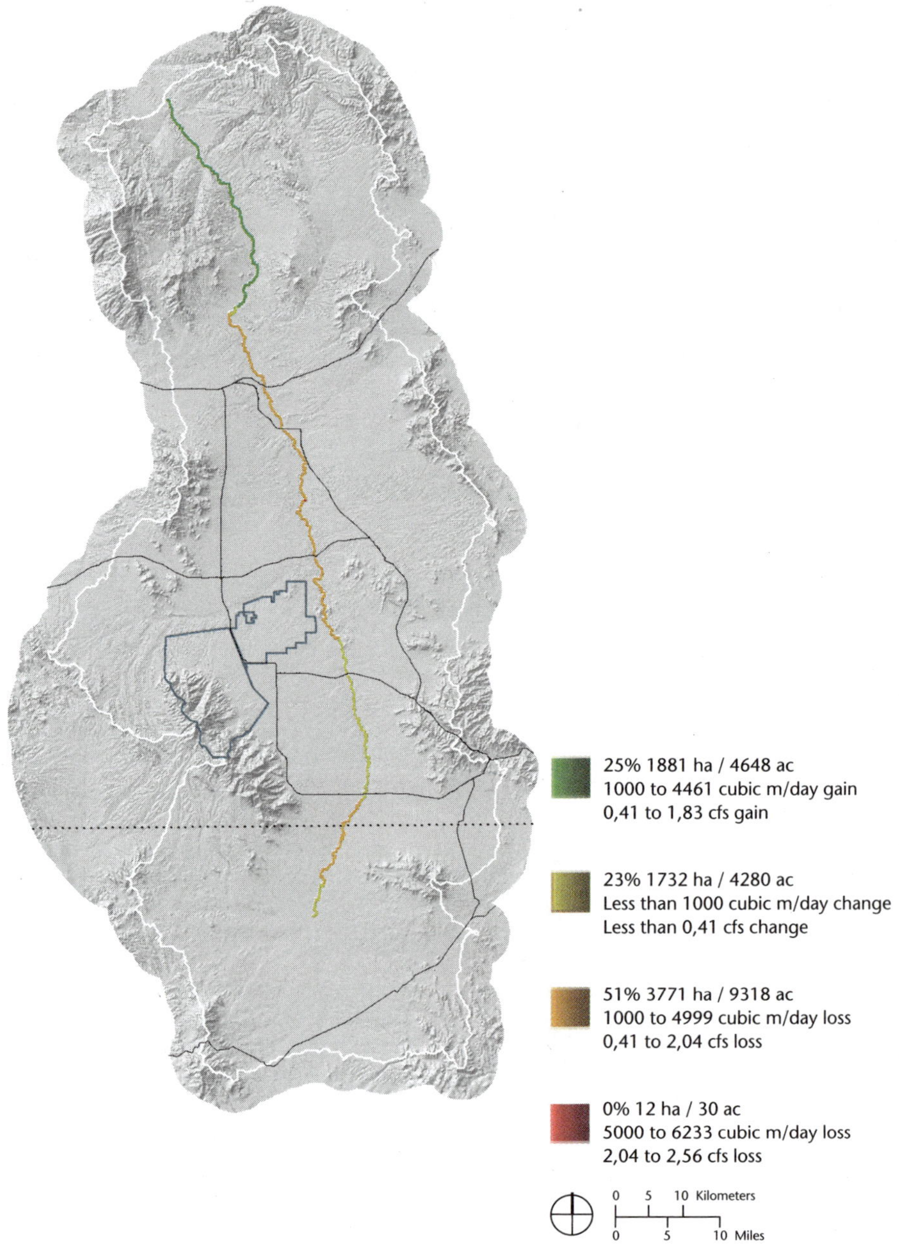
25% 1881 ha / 4648 ac
1000 to 4461 cubic m/day gain
0,41 to 1,83 cfs gain
23% 1732 ha / 4280 ac
Less than 1000 cubic m/day change
Less than 0,41 cfs change
51% 3771 ha / 9318 ac
1000 to 4999 cubic m/day loss
0,41 to 2,04 cfs loss
0% 12 ha / 30 ac
5000 to 6233 cubic m/day loss
2,04 to 2,56 cfs loss
0 5 10 Kilometers
0 5 10 Miles

Figure 9.8a ■ PLANS, Stream flow impacts, 2000–2020

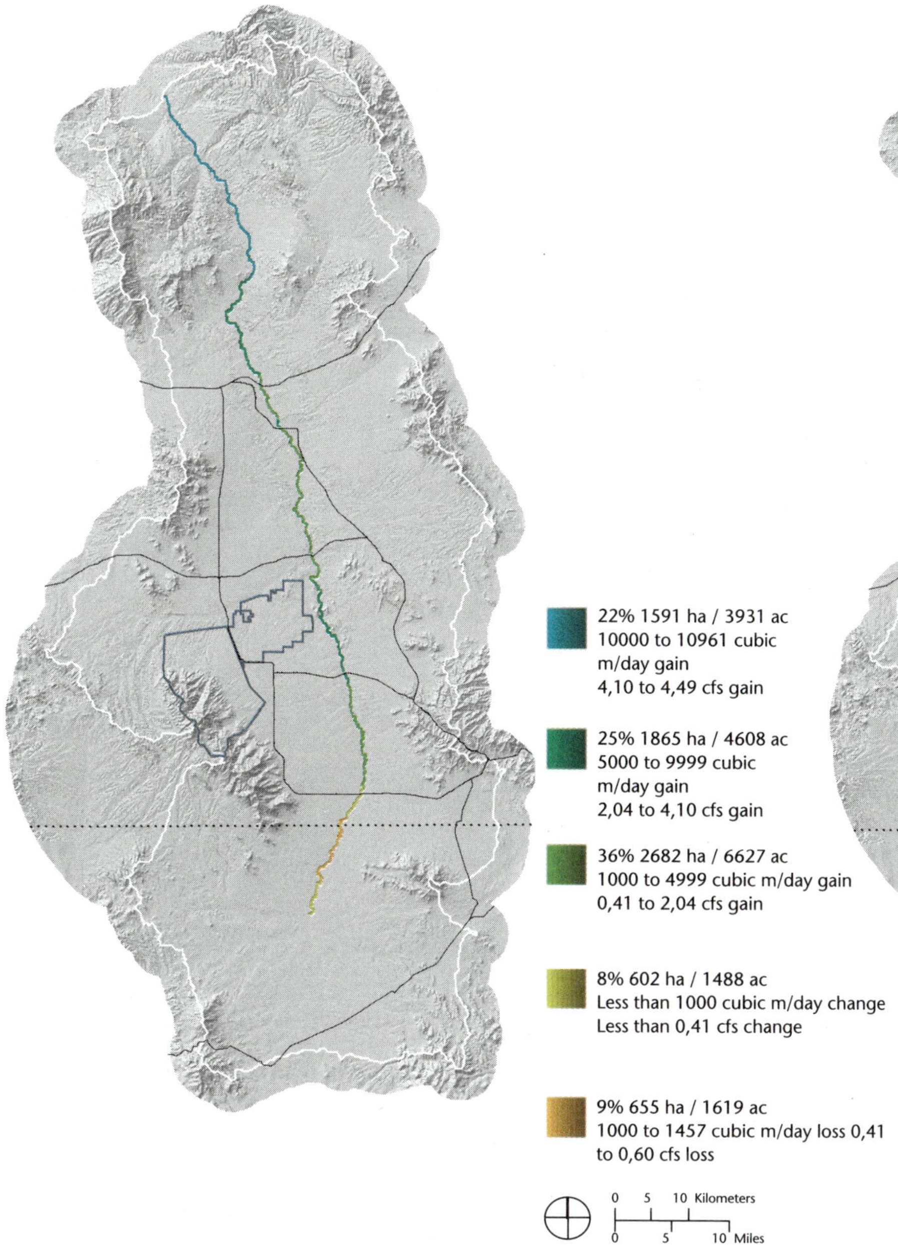
22% 1591 ha / 3931 ac
10000 to 10961 cubic m/day gain
4,10 to 4,49 cfs gain
25% 1865 ha / 4608 ac
5000 to 9999 cubic m/day gain
2,04 to 4,10 cfs gain
36% 2682 ha / 6627 ac
1000 to 4999 cubic m/day gain
0,41 to 2,04 cfs gain
8% 602 ha / 1488 ac
Less than 1000 cubic m/day change
Less than 0,41 cfs change
9% 655 ha / 1619 ac
1000 to 1457 cubic m/day loss 0,41 to 0,60 cfs loss
0 5 10 Kilometers
0 5 10 Miles

Figure 9.8b ■ CONSTRAINED, Stream flow impacts, 2000–2020

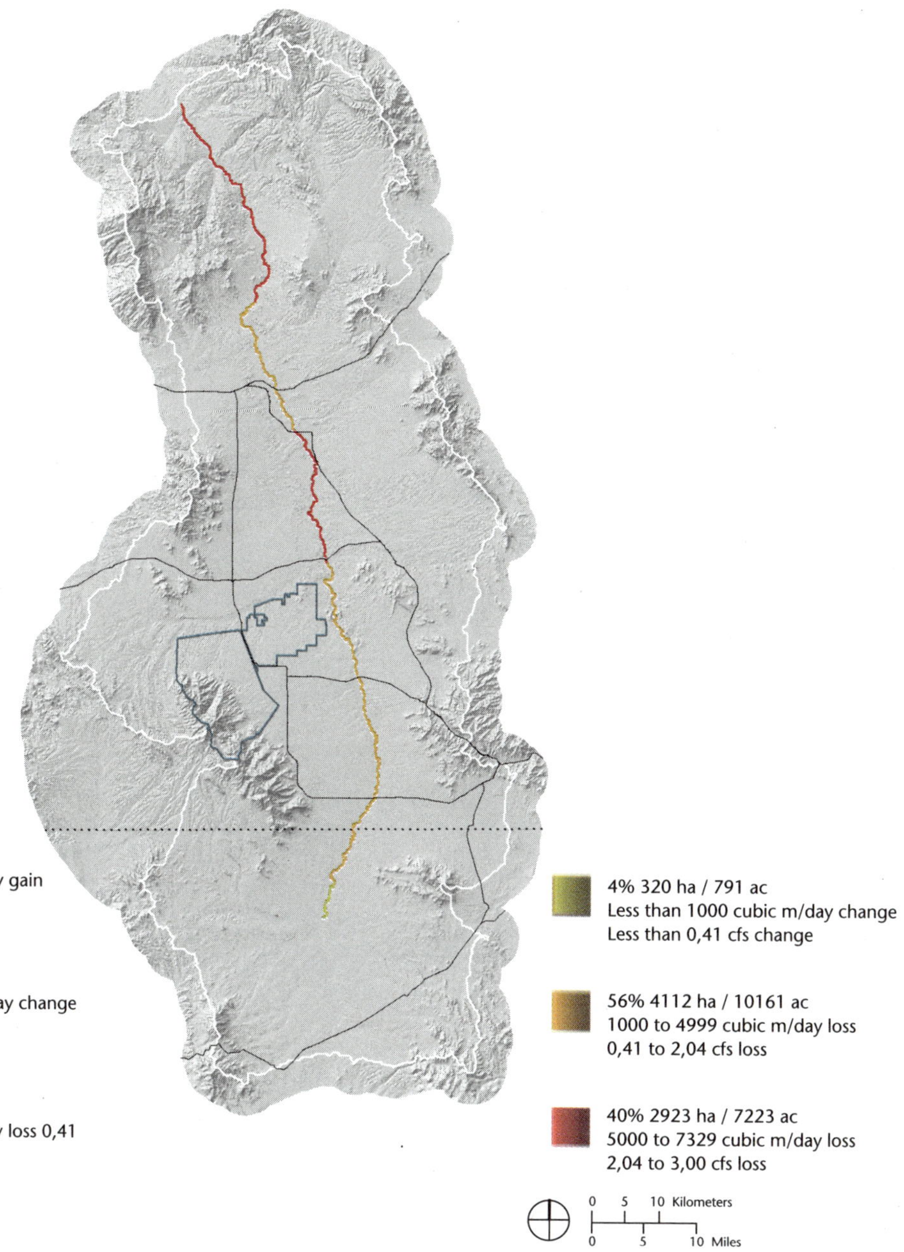
4% 320 ha / 791 ac
Less than 1000 cubic m/day change
Less than 0,41 cfs change
56% 4112 ha / 10161 ac
1000 to 4999 cubic m/day loss
0,41 to 2,04 cfs loss
40% 2923 ha / 7223 ac
5000 to 7329 cubic m/day loss
2,04 to 3,00 cfs loss
0 5 10 Kilometers
0 5 10 Miles

Figure 9.8c ■ OPEN, Stream flow impacts, 2000–2020

Table 9.2 Streamflow: Impacts, 2000–2020

	San Pedro River length of dry river: km
Baseline 2000	7.7
Plans	2.6
Plans 1	2.6
Plans 2	3.4
Plans 3	2.6
Constrained	2.6
Constrained 1	2.6
Constrained 2	2.6
Open	39.5
Open 1	38.0
Open 2	40.8

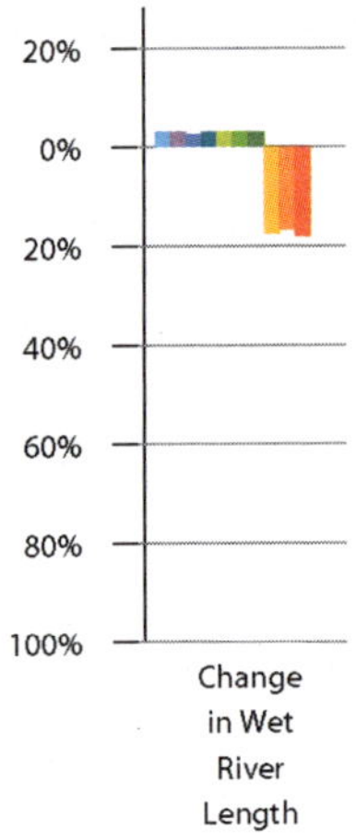
20%
0%
20%
40%
60%
80%
100%
Change in Wet River Length

Relative impacts

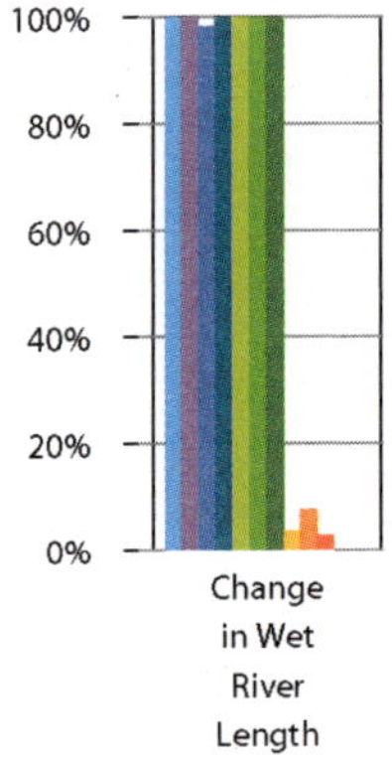
100%
80%
60%
40%
20%
0%
Change in Wet River Length

Percent impacts

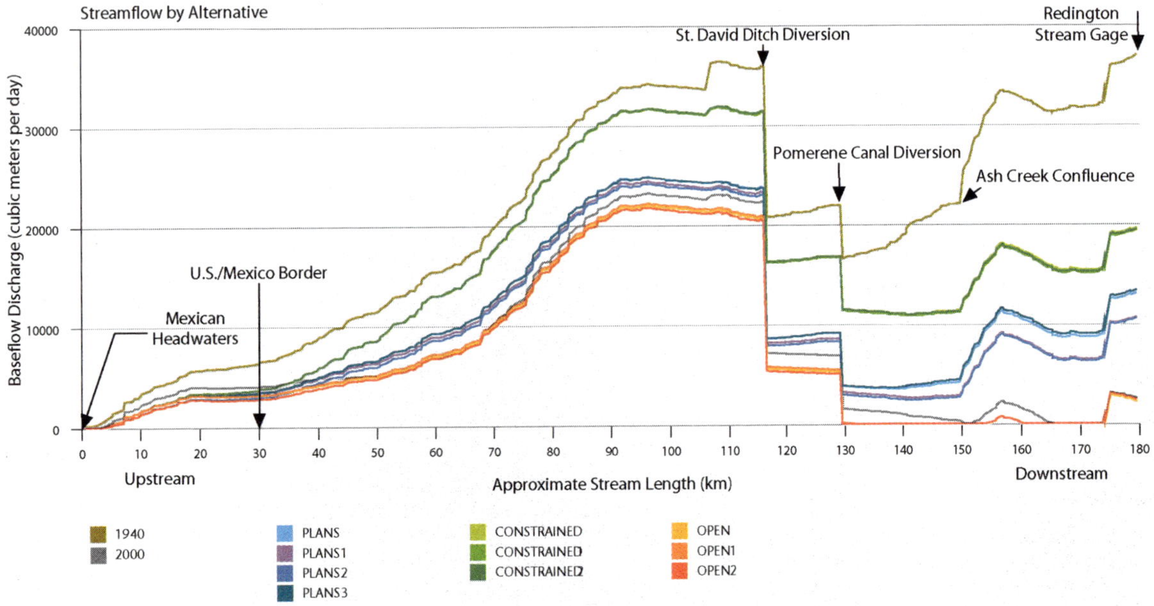
Streamflow by Alternative
Baseflow Discharge (cubic meters per day)
40000
30000
20000
10000
0
St. David Ditch Diversion
Redington Stream Gage
Pomerene Canal Diversion
Ash Creek Confluence
U.S./Mexico Border
Mexican Headwaters
0 10 20 30 40 50 60 70 80 90 100 110 120 130 140 150 160 170 180
Upstream
Approximate Stream Length (km)
Downstream
1940
2000
PLANS
PLANS1
PLANS2
PLANS3
CONSTRAINED
CONSTRAINED1
CONSTRAINED2
OPEN
OPEN1
OPEN2

Figure 9.7 ■ Simulated stream flow of the Upper San Pedro River, 1940–2020

CHAPTER 10

The Vegetation Model

Vegetation in the study area (Figure 10.1) can be classified or examined in a number of ways, from general (forest, grassland, desert) to specific (a vegetation assemblage defined by its three or four most dominant or reliable species). To define regional habitat types, a classification based on overall appearance with one or two common species as indicators is useful.

The study area is divided into six separate habitat types. Conifer forests dominated by Douglas fir, ponderosa pine, and white fir, with an admixture of grasses and broadleaf trees, occur at the highest elevations (above 2130 m or 7000 ft). Oak- and juniper-dominated woodlands are more prominent at the lower elevations of the island mountains (1520 to 2280 m or 5000 to 7500 ft). The oak-juniper woodland intergrades to an oak-juniper savannah with large patches of grassland occurring between the trees. Occasionally, pinyon pine becomes co-dominant with either oak or juniper. At somewhat lower elevations, the oak-juniper woodland/savanna is replaced by a mesquite dominated woodland or savanna (1460 to 1830 m or 4800 to 6000 ft). The savannas give way to desert grassland. This grassland is dominated by species such as grama that typically turn green following summer rains. The watershed at its lowest elevations (below 1460 m or 4800 ft) is dominated by two types of desert scrub: one predominantly whitethorn acacia, mesquite, and saguaro cactus; and another predominantly whitethorn acacia, mesquite, tarbush, and

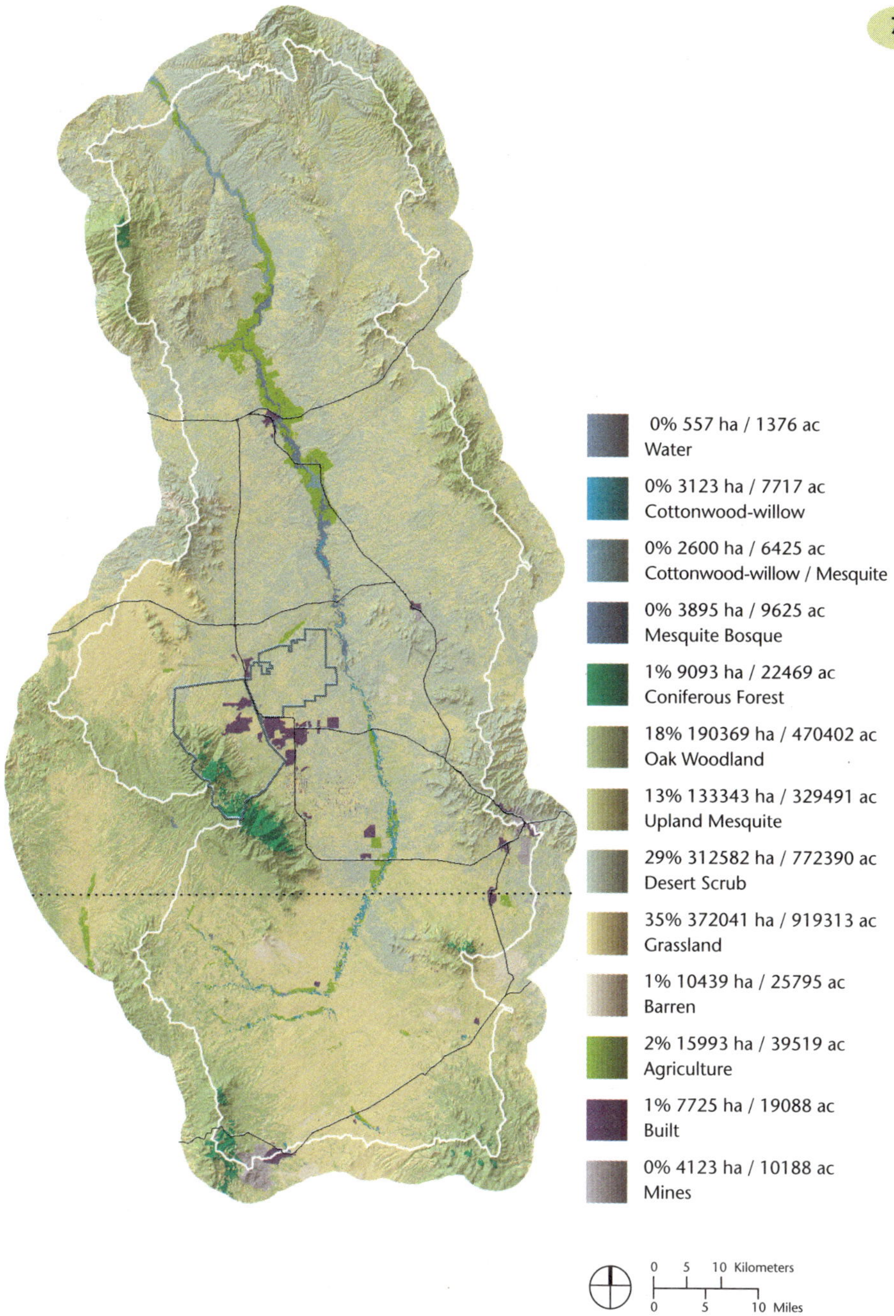
0% 557 ha / 1376 ac
Water
0% 3123 ha / 7717 ac
Cottonwood-willow
0% 2600 ha / 6425 ac
Cottonwood-willow / Mesquite
0% 3895 ha / 9625 ac
Mesquite Bosque
1% 9093 ha / 22469 ac
Coniferous Forest
18% 190369 ha / 470402 ac
Oak Woodland
13% 133343 ha / 329491 ac
Upland Mesquite
29% 312582 ha / 772390 ac
Desert Scrub
35% 372041 ha / 919313 ac
Grassland
1% 10439 ha / 25795 ac
Barren
2% 15993 ha / 39519 ac
Agriculture
1% 7725 ha / 19088 ac
Built
0% 4123 ha / 10188 ac
Mines
0 5 10 Kilometers
0 5 10 Miles

Figure 10.1 ■ Vegetation, 2000

creosote bush. The differences are subtle, with more cactus in the first type. These two types represent an intergradation between the Sonoran Desert influence to the west and the Chihuahuan Desert influence to the east. Riparian woodland dominates the watercourses of the San Pedro River floodplain, and to a lesser degree the Babocomari River. The riparian woodland, also known as gallery forest (galleria in Spanish), consists of cottonwood, willow, and mesquite. Riparian woodland is subdivided into cottonwood-willow, mesquite bosque, cottonwood-willow-mesquite, and an invasive type, salt cedar. Riparian grassland, although important for habitat, occurs in areas too small to be delineated.

A full understanding of the vegetation of the watershed requires not only an understanding of its spatial distribution but also an understanding of its dynamics. A number of researchers (Hastings and Turner 1965; Bahre 1991; McClaren and Van Devender 1995; Mouat and Lancaster 1996; and Kepner et al. 2000, among others) have described vegetation changes in the region. In the nineteenth and early twentieth centuries, cattle grazing, woodcutting, mining, and agriculture caused extensive change, including removal of large woody species in riparian zones and in conifer forests and woodlands. Some grasslands were heavily impacted and suffered severe surface and gully erosion. The grasslands above 1460 m (4800 ft) were generally resilient and were able to reestablish themselves. Below 1460 m (4800 ft), however, grasslands were less resilient and were frequently replaced by desert scrub. The riparian zones were almost completely degraded, with the cienegas, or riparian grasslands, being almost completely extirpated. By the mid-twentieth century, riparian zones began to recover with cottonwoods, willows, and mesquite once again becoming predominant.

Three important changes over the past 50 years have resulted in considerable alterations to vegetation and associated habitat: the suppression of fire, the reduction of grazing, and lowering of the water table caused by ground water pumping. These changes have

Photo 10.1 ■ Oak woodland, Sierra El Manzanal

Photo 10.2 ■ Desert grassland

Photo 10.3 ■ Sonoran desert scrub

Photo 10.4 ■ Desert grassland

Photo 10.5 ■ Desert grassland with yucca

Photo 10.6 ■ Tamarisk in a San Pedro River cienega

altered vegetation community composition. The natural succession of vegetation communities is disrupted, potentially causing localized extinction of native species.

Historically, the grassland vegetation type was largely maintained by fire. Periodic fires resulted in the effective removal of shrubby vegetation and were a critical force in nutrient cycling. Suppression of fire has led to what some researchers (see, especially, McClaren and Van Devender 1995) consider to be an irreversible shift of vegetation from grassland to desert shrub. Shrub and cactus species (such as mesquite, acacia, cholla, and prickly pear) outcompete the perennial native grasses for water and soil nutrients and eventually replace them. A concomitant change in the spatial distribution of soil nutrients from homogeneous to heterogeneous, along with increased sheet and rill erosion, effectively results in the change becoming irreversible. It is highly unlikely that under these conditions the desert shrub vegetation could revert to grassland. At the higher elevations and in Sonora, where fire has not been suppressed as much as in Arizona, the grassland vegetation has maintained itself. For a considerable time, the effect of fire was accomplished by grazing. Ranchers, in trying to maintain grassland, worked to remove invading shrubs, primarily mesquite and acacia. By the 1970s, however, increased urbanization near Sierra Vista led to a gradual disappearance of grazing and maintenance of the grassland. This situation continues. Groundwater withdrawal has resulted in riparian changes. Cottonwood and willow are being lost and replaced by riparian desert scrub.

In the lower San Pedro River floodplain, salt cedar (tamarisk) is moving up the river, successfully displacing cottonwood and willow. Both riparian mesquite bosque and cottonwood-willow vegetation associations tend to be replaced by salt cedar. Riparian vegetation increases with rises in the water table. Cottonwood, willow, and mesquite bosques all become more prominent. With water table reductions of only a few meters, those species are replaced by riparian scrub in the Upper San Pedro and by salt cedar in the lower San Pedro, below Saint David.

The decision to alter or to restore a landscape in which vegetation changes have occurred is predicated on a number of factors. Chief among these is the notion that "natural" is better than "changed," and that the attendant fauna are dependent on the vegetation and changes along with it. A "natural" habitat with native vegetation and wildlife is often valued more highly than an altered one because of its biodiversity and for aesthetic reasons. In this study, grassland is more highly valued than the altered desert scrub that is replacing it; mesquite riparian forest is more important than the salt cedar that is replacing it; grama grasses are more valuable than the Lehmann's lovegrass that is replacing them; and the Sonoran pronghorn are more valuable than the introduced European cattle.

The vegetation model assesses several of the major stresses on vegetation and forecasts changes in the type and spatial distribution of vegetation within the study area. Factors accounted for in the model include urban development; addition, alteration, or removal of irrigated agriculture or grazing; managed fire or the absence of fire; lowering of the water table; changes in soil moisture; and changes in riparian corridors resulting from flooding and/or reduced streamflows. Removing the influence of fire eliminates the single most important factor in maintaining grasslands. Fire eliminates invasive woody shrubs (upland mesquite, whitethorn acacia, and cactus). Grazing cattle also help to maintain grassland. Removal of both fire and grazing results in expansion of desert scrub.

Two groups of scenarios, PLANS and CONSTRAINED, include a policy assumption that prescribed burning will be used as a vegetation management tool. The other group of scenarios, OPEN, maintains the status quo, assuming that prescribed burning will not be a management tool. The grassland vegetation areas will be rapidly converted into developed areas or will change into desert

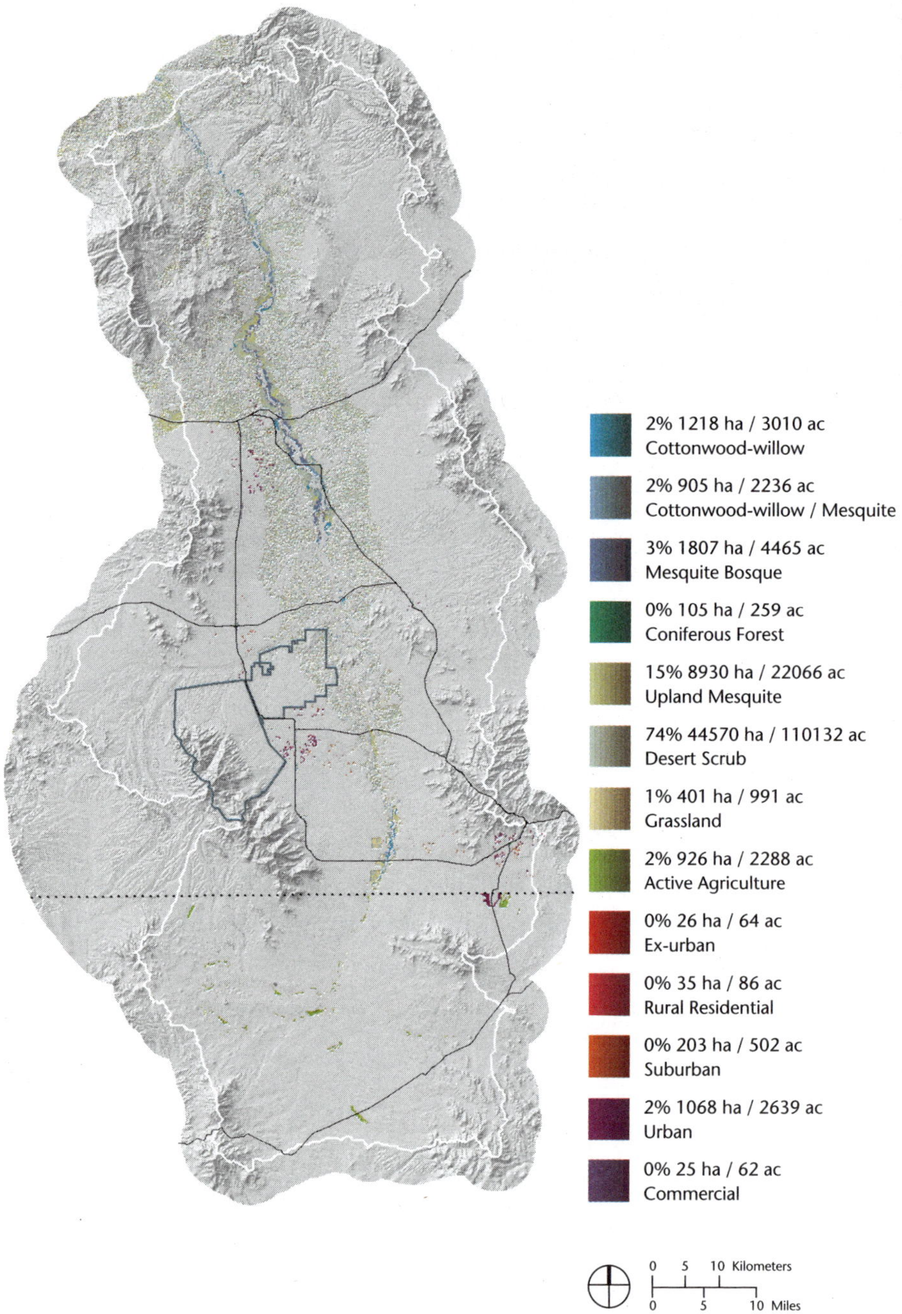
2% 1218 ha / 3010 ac
Cottonwood-willow
2% 905 ha / 2236 ac
Cottonwood-willow / Mesquite
3% 1807 ha / 4465 ac
Mesquite Bosque
0% 105 ha / 259 ac
Coniferous Forest
15% 8930 ha / 22066 ac
Upland Mesquite
74% 44570 ha / 110132 ac
Desert Scrub
1% 401 ha / 991 ac
Grassland
2% 926 ha / 2288 ac
Active Agriculture
0% 26 ha / 64 ac
Ex-urban
0% 35 ha / 86 ac
Rural Residential
0% 203 ha / 502 ac
Suburban
2% 1068 ha / 2639 ac
Urban
0% 25 ha / 62 ac
Commercial
0 5 10 Kilometers
0 5 10 Miles

Figure 10.2a ■ PLANS, Vegetation impacts, 2000–2020

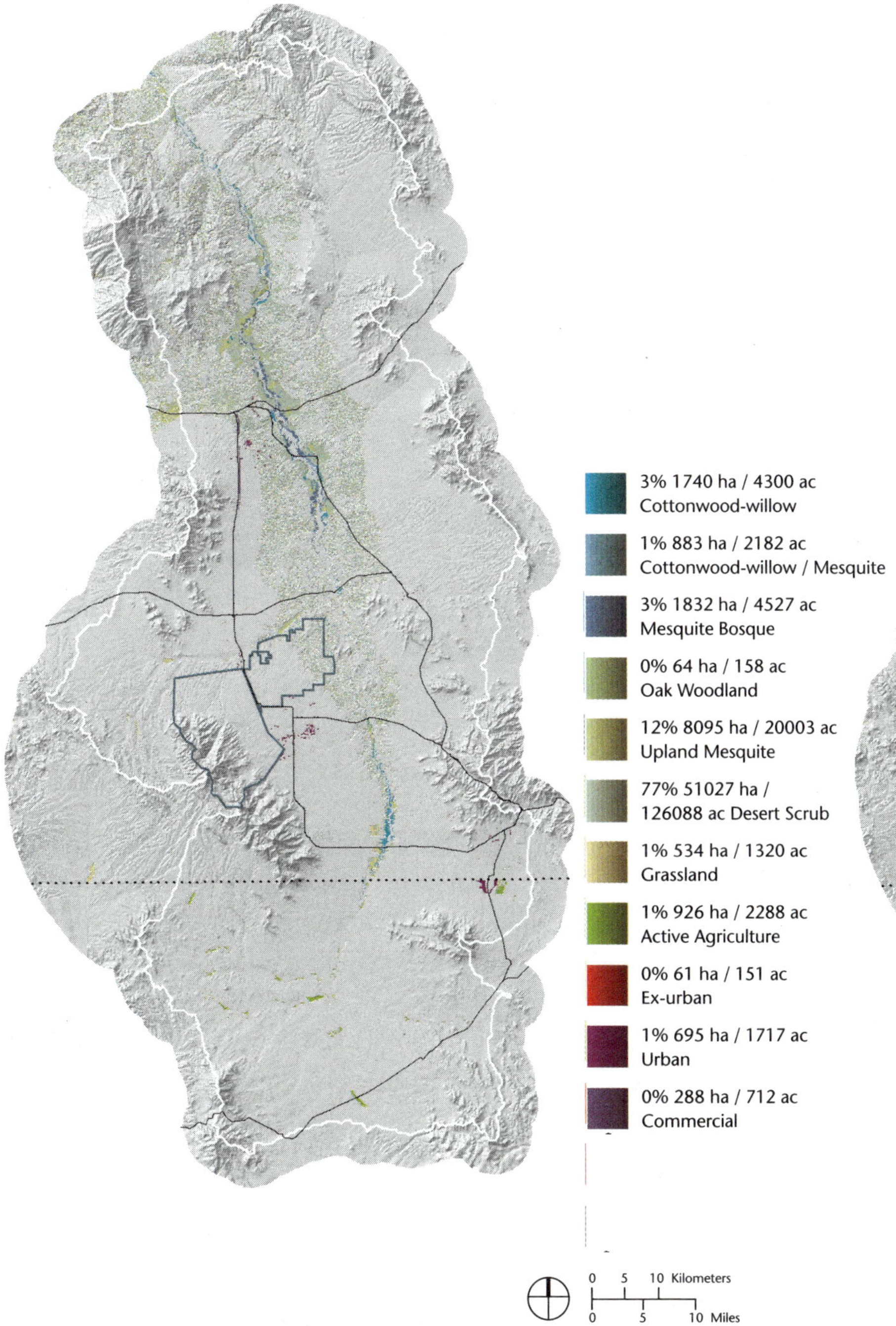
3% 1740 ha / 4300 ac
Cottonwood-willow
1% 883 ha / 2182 ac
Cottonwood-willow / Mesquite
3% 1832 ha / 4527 ac
Mesquite Bosque
0% 64 ha / 158 ac
Oak Woodland
12% 8095 ha / 20003 ac
Upland Mesquite
77% 51027 ha /
126088 ac Desert Scrub
1% 534 ha / 1320 ac
Grassland
1% 926 ha / 2288 ac
Active Agriculture
0% 61 ha / 151 ac
Ex-urban
1% 695 ha / 1717 ac
Urban
0% 288 ha / 712 ac
Commercial
0 5 10 Kilometers
0 5 10 Miles

Figure 10.2b ■ CONSTRAINED, Vegetation impacts, 2000–2020

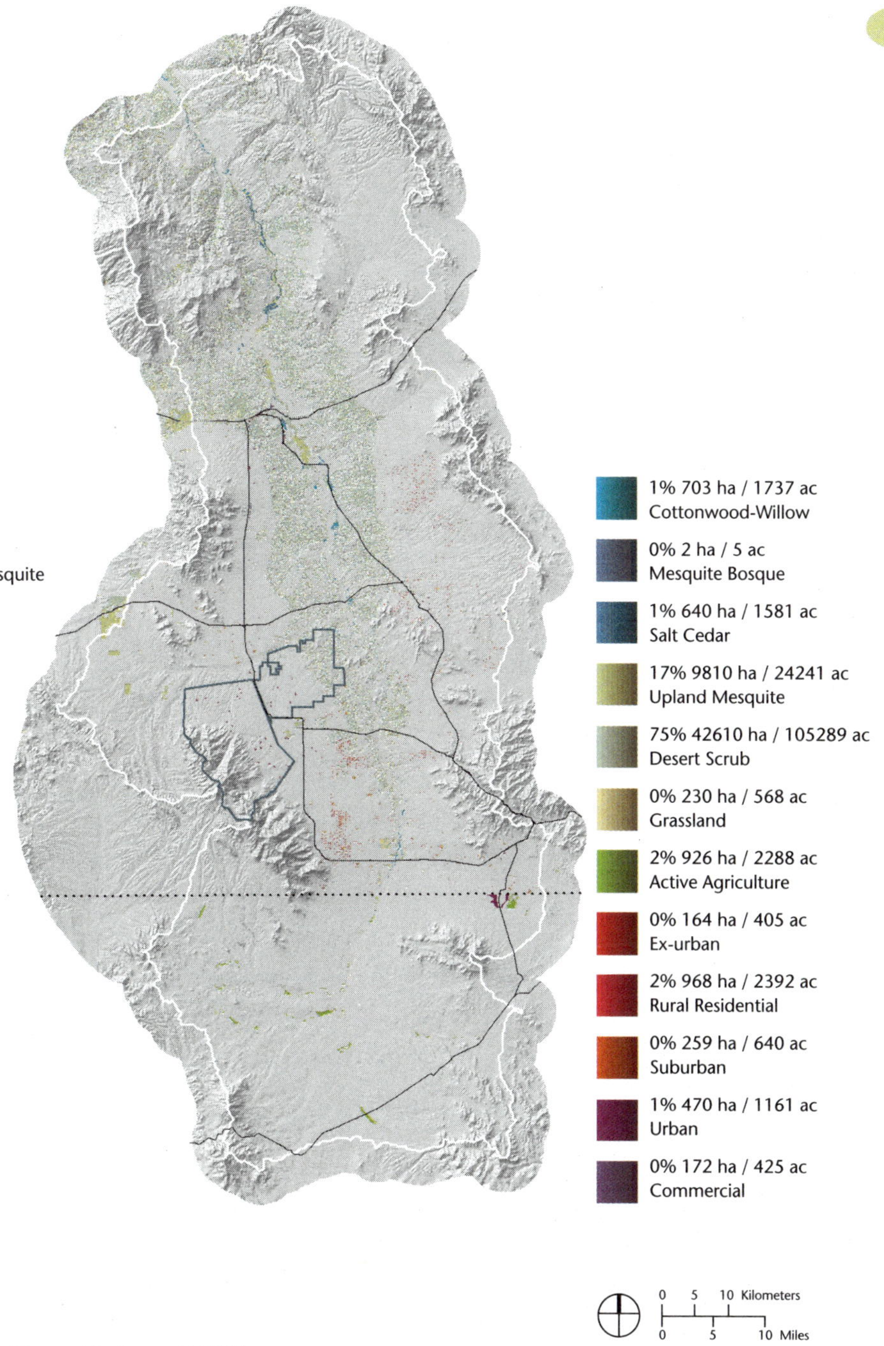
1% 703 ha / 1737 ac
Cottonwood-Willow
0% 2 ha / 5 ac
Mesquite Bosque
1% 640 ha / 1581 ac
Salt Cedar
17% 9810 ha / 24241 ac
Upland Mesquite
75% 42610 ha / 105289 ac
Desert Scrub
0% 230 ha / 568 ac
Grassland
2% 926 ha / 2288 ac
Active Agriculture
0% 164 ha / 405 ac
Ex-urban
2% 968 ha / 2392 ac
Rural Residential
0% 259 ha / 640 ac
Suburban
1% 470 ha / 1161 ac
Urban
0% 172 ha / 425 ac
Commercial
0 5 10 Kilometers
0 5 10 Miles

Figure 10.2c ■ OPEN, Vegetation impacts, 2000–2020

Table 10.1 Vegetation: Impacts, 2000–2020

	change in riparian vegatation ha	change in grassland vegatation ha
Baseline 2000	9618	372,041
Plans	2,920	-46,161
Plans 1	2,669	-46,421
Plans 2	2,659	-46,437
Plans 3	2,967	-46,103
Constrained	3,477	-46,016
Constrained 1	3,438	-46,056
Constrained 2	3,444	-46,056
Open	-2,334	-50,434
Open 1	-2,369	-50,408
Open 2	-2,348	-50,731

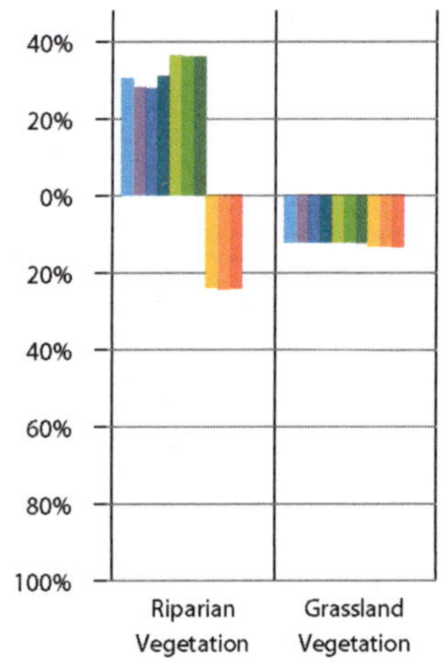
40%
20%
0%
20%
40%
60%
80%
100%
Riparian Vegetation
Grassland Vegetation

Percent impacts

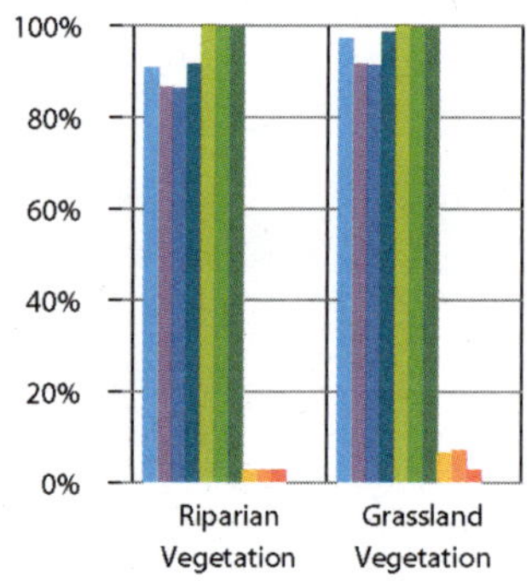
100%
80%
60%
40%
20%
0%
Riparian Vegetation
Grassland Vegetation

Relative impacts

scrub in the absence of management by fire and grazing. Because of the fire management policies, grassland vegetation suffers somewhat less under PLANS and CONSTRAINED scenarios than under the OPEN scenarios. The loss, however, is only reduced by about 10 percent. It is likely that the woodland and forested vegetation types will be affected more by the lack of fire management under the OPEN scenario. Catastrophic fires, such as occurred in the Huachuca Mountains in 1976, are likely to recur under a policy that ignores fuel buildup in wooded areas. At the highest elevations, vegetation types are not likely to change regardless of the policy on fire.

The scenarios produce widely differing effects on riparian vegetation. Increased development means increased demand for groundwater and lowering of the water table, reducing the perennial flow of the San Pedro River. Under all scenarios, riparian vegetation between St. David and the Mexican border will degrade and be converted to some degree to riparian scrub and salt cedar. However, a policy included in PLANS and CONSTRAINED scenarios to retire agriculture between St. David and Pomerene (a small town north of Benson) will have the effect of remediating riparian vegetation in that area. Under the OPEN scenarios, no such policy is included. The modeled results of the OPEN scenarios are disastrous to riparian vegetation. Under the OPEN scenarios, riparian vegetation declines significantly, while under both the PLANS and CONSTRAINED scenarios, riparian vegetation increases. As might be expected, riparian vegetation under the CONSTRAINED scenario increases about 15 percent more than under the PLANS scenario. Within all three groups of alternative futures, the variation within each group is minor, with small differences resulting from their changes in development policies.

CHAPTER 11

The Landscape Ecological Pattern Model

Landscape ecology is based on the concept that spatial landscape patterns of land use and land cover define the relationship among structural and functional elements in any landscape. These patterns can be described as a mosaic made up of a background matrix, and natural and disturbed patches, either isolated or linked by corridors. The composition of the mosaic supports the diversity of plants and animals found in an area. The usefulness of landscape ecology is not for the preservation of any one species, but rather for the maintenance of the current mosaic to preserve the ecological diversity present in a given locale (Dramstad et al. 1996; Forman 1995).

Viewed from the air, the San Pedro basin is a patchwork of desert vegetation communities in the lowlands, forested areas in the mountains, and small towns and cities interconnected by a network of roads. This picture would, in landscape ecological terms, be referred to as the mosaic. To maintain the ecological functioning of the mosaic one needs to define the relevant factors.

Elements that form the landscape ecological pattern in the San Pedro study area include:

- Contiguous natural vegetation occurring in areas larger than 5000 ha (12,360 ac), creating large natural patches
- Isolated natural vegetation occurring in areas less than 5000 ha (12,360 ac), creating small patches
- Stream corridors and arroyos up to 180 m (200 yd) in width
- Disturbed landscapes resulting from arable agriculture or grazing
- Built landscapes made up of developed land and roads
- Water

Photo 11.1 ■ Large natural patches and corridors, toward Mexico

The patch-corridor model must contain two essential pattern elements to provide for critical landscape functions: large patches of natural vegetation that protect the species diversity of a landscape by providing large habitat areas, and wide corridors or clusters of small patches to provide for species movement between large patches.

In the San Pedro Basin, large natural patches and their associated connecting corridors are important (figure 11.1). Preserving large natural patches is the best way to maintain the overall mosaic of an area. The connections between large patches ensure that some of the ecological functions, such as migration, will continue.

The landscape ecological pattern model identifies large natural patches by excluding development, agriculture, and roads, and their effects. In the model, heavily traveled roads and developed areas create adjacent impact zones. Within the San Pedro study area, Interstate Highway 10 and developed areas are assigned an

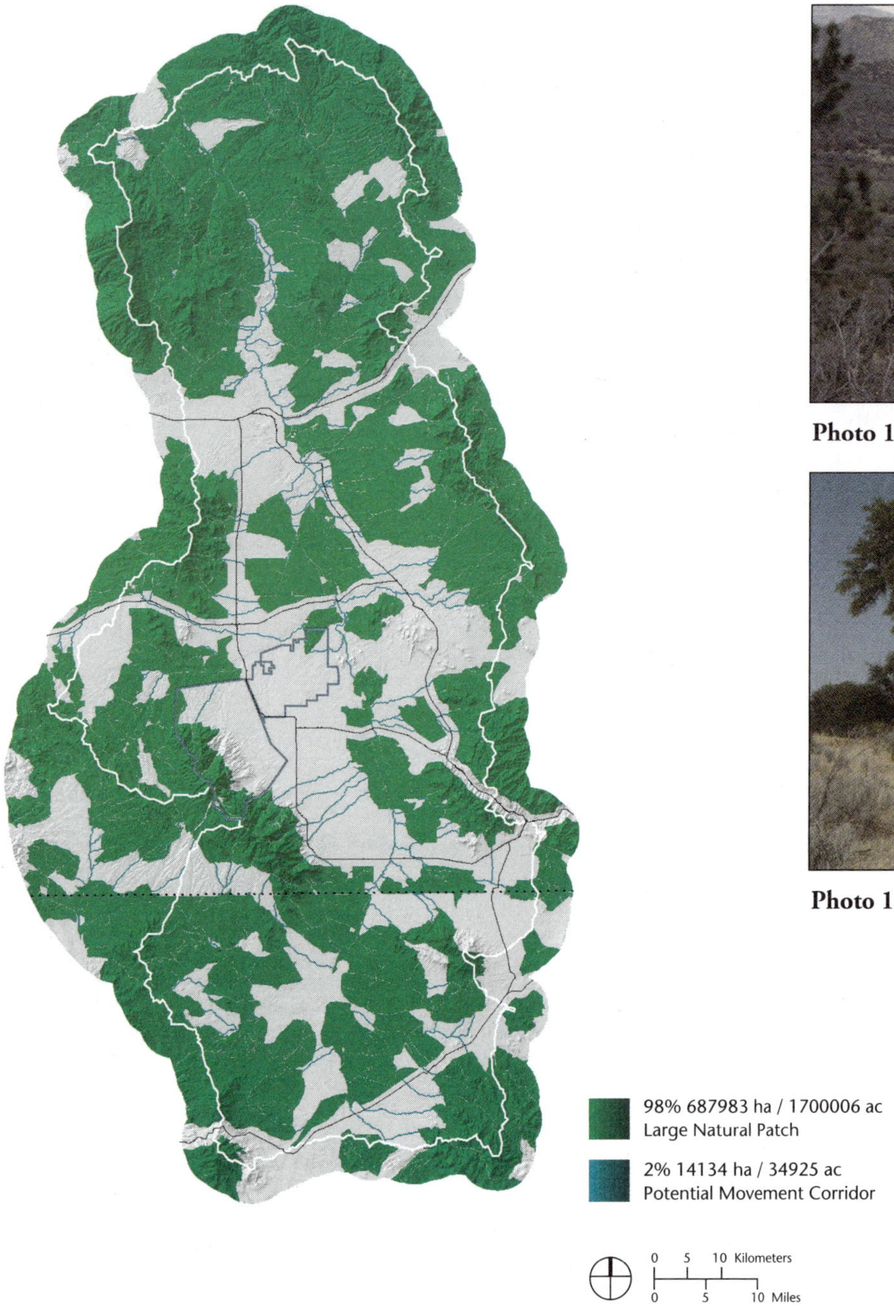
98% 687983 ha / 1700006 ac
Large Natural Patch
2% 14134 ha / 34925 ac
Potential Movement Corridor
0 5 10 Kilometers
0 5 10 Miles

Figure 11.1 ■ Landscape ecological pattern, 2000

Photo 11.2 ■ Large natural patch (oak woodland)

Photo 11.3 ■ Arroyo on Bobocomari Ranch

Table 11.1 Landscape ecological pattern: Impacts, 2000–2020

	change in area of large patches / ha
Baseline 2000	687,983
Plans	-5,466
Plans 1	-9,632
Plans 2	-9,302
Plans 3	-1,601
Constrained	-4,232
Constrained 1	-15,503
Constrained 2	-15,503
Open	-67,486
Open 1	-101,455
Open 2	-49,991

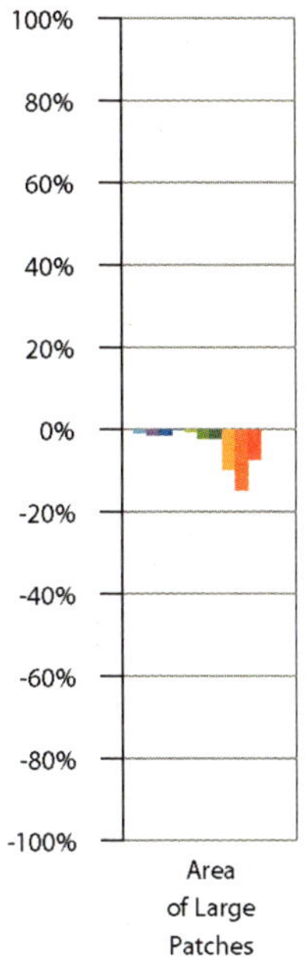
100%
80%
60%
40%
20%
0%
-20%
-40%
-60%
-80%
-100%
Area of Large Patches

Relative impacts

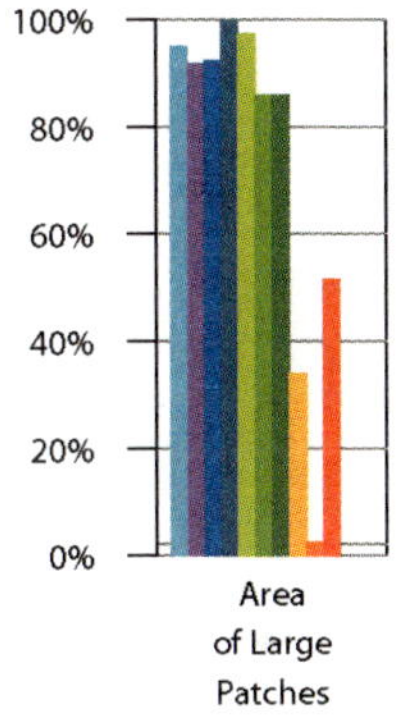
100%
80%
60%
40%
20%
0%
Area of Large Patches

Percent impacts

impact zone extending 930 m (1017 yd) into surrounding areas. Less busy secondary roads and Arizona highways are assigned an impact zone of 810 m (885 yd). These impact zones are excluded from the area of large patches (Reijnen et al. 1996; Reijnen et al. 1995).

Corridors connect the large patches through a series of streams and major arroyos. Unlike large patches, corridors are not eliminated by roads or impact zones. If, however, development extends more than 50 percent of the width of the corridor, the connectivity is compromised and the corridor is eliminated. Even small amounts of development, if located in a narrow section of corridor, can compromise connectivity among large patches. Loss of connecting corridors resulting in increases in distance of travel between or among large natural patches is considered detrimental to the landscape ecological pattern.

All of the scenarios create alternative futures that have negative impacts on the landscape ecological pattern (figures 11.2a–c and table 11.1). The impacts are caused by the future development pattern resulting from each scenario. All the alternative futures eliminate the species movement potential of some existing corridors, and reduce the extent of large patches. In all the alternative futures, the ability of species to move among the existing large patches is reduced.

The most dramatic impacts result from the OPEN scenarios. Corridor length is increased and some existing movement corridors are lost. The area of large patches decreases by between 7 and 15 percent. Loss occurs in foothill and valley locations. The OPEN 1 scenario causes the most loss, resulting from changes to exurban development patterns. Under OPEN 1, exurban homes do not occur in clusters of five homes; rather, regulation allows only a single home on each 16 ha (40 ac) lot. This results in exurban homes being more spread out, increasing the amount of impact. The OPEN and OPEN 2 scenarios are roughly similar in impact and

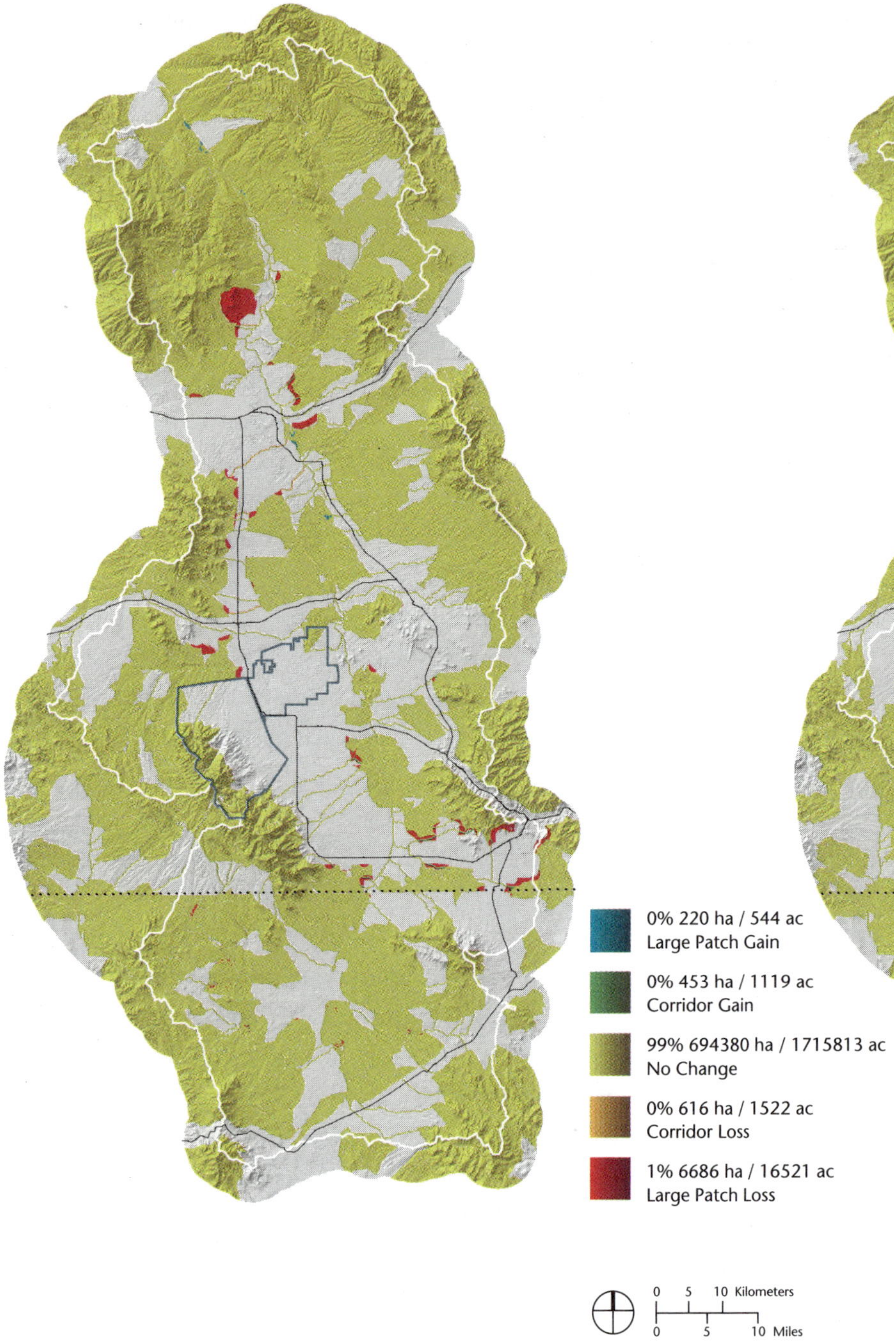
0% 220 ha / 544 ac
Large Patch Gain
0% 453 ha / 1119 ac
Corridor Gain
99% 694380 ha / 1715813 ac
No Change
0% 616 ha / 1522 ac
Corridor Loss
1% 6686 ha / 16521 ac
Large Patch Loss
0 5 10 Kilometers
0 5 10 Miles

Figure 11.2a ■ PLANS,
Landscape ecological pattern impacts, 2000-2020

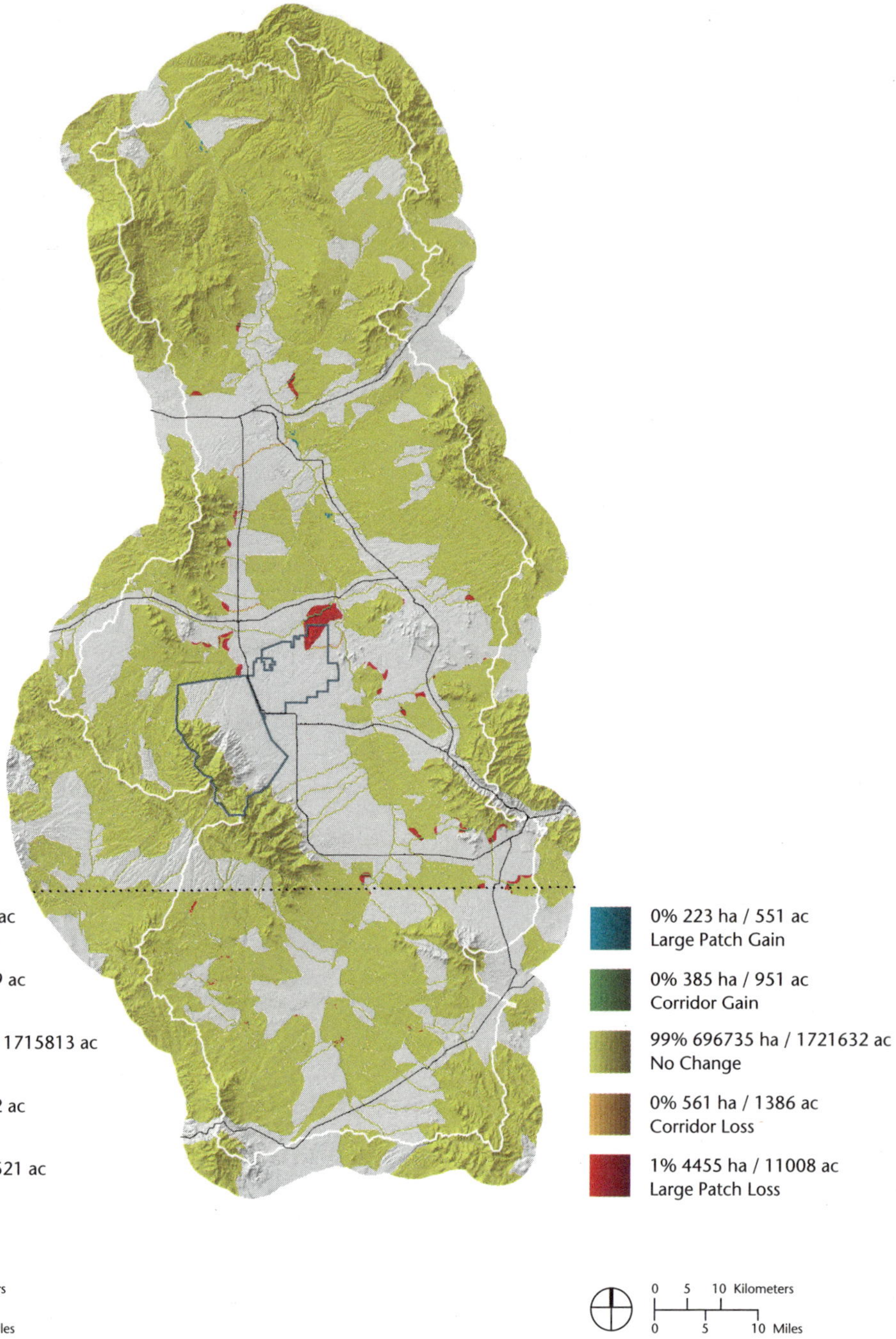
0% 223 ha / 551 ac
Large Patch Gain
0% 385 ha / 951 ac
Corridor Gain
99% 696735 ha / 1721632 ac
No Change
0% 561 ha / 1386 ac
Corridor Loss
1% 4455 ha / 11008 ac
Large Patch Loss
0 5 10 Kilometers
0 5 10 Miles

Figure 11.2b ■ CONSTRAINED,
Landscape ecological pattern impacts, 2000-2020

are less damaging than OPEN 1, but more damaging than either the PLANS or CONSTRAINED alternative futures.

The PLANS and CONSTRAINED scenarios result in generally similar and smaller reductions in large patch size. Loss occurs mainly in foothill and valley locations. Most of the differences can be explained by the availability of a vast amount of land to accommodate more compact development types, allowing for many possible distributions of new development.

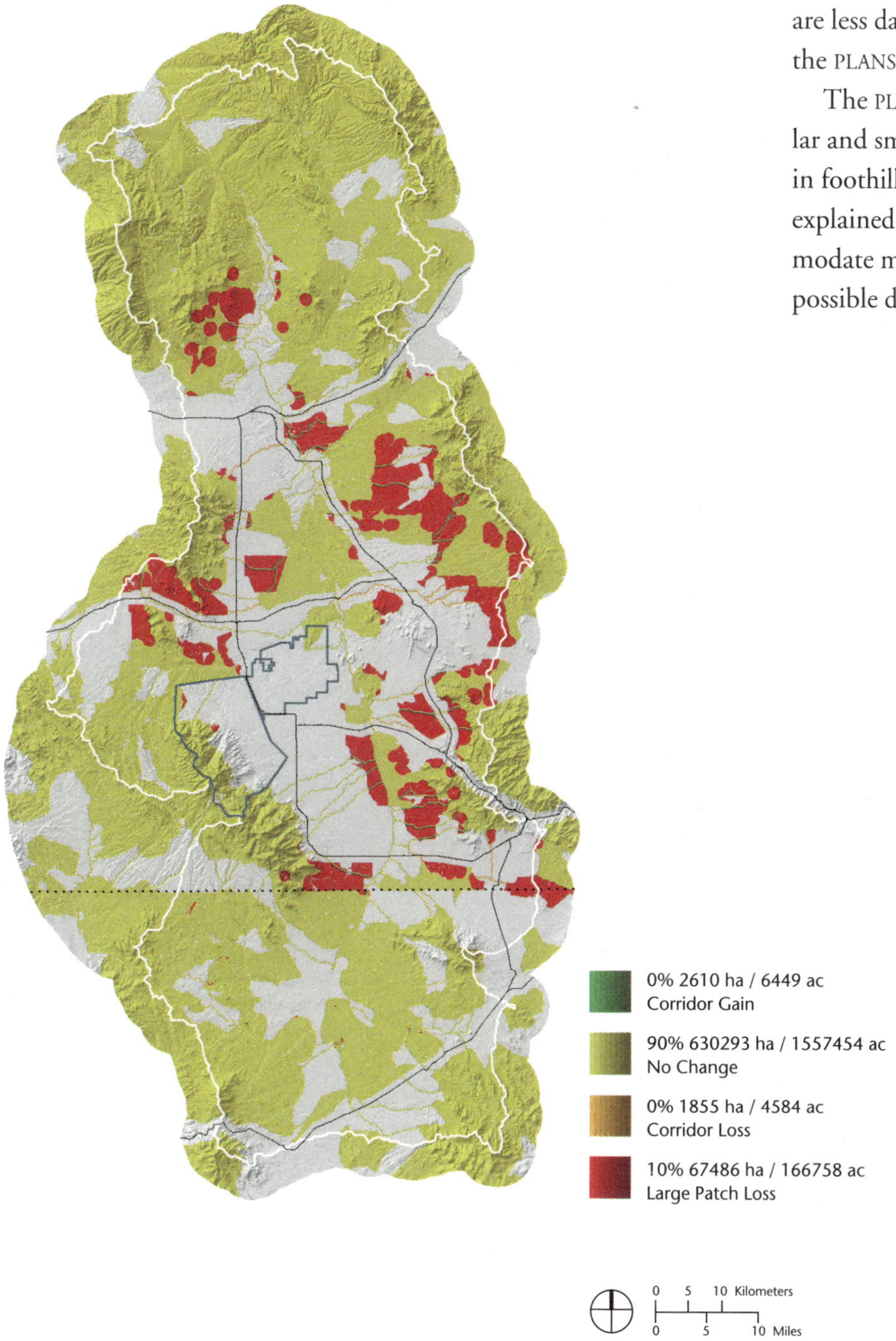
0% 2610 ha / 6449 ac
Corridor Gain
90% 630293 ha / 1557454 ac
No Change
0% 1855 ha / 4584 ac
Corridor Loss
10% 67486 ha / 166758 ac
Large Patch Loss
0 5 10 Kilometers
0 5 10 Miles

Figure 11.2c ■ OPEN,
Landscape ecological pattern impacts, 2000-2020

CHAPTER 12

Single Species Potential Habitat Models

Six species of terrestrial vertebrates were selected for detailed study. The species were chosen so that each of the vegetation communities in the study area was represented by at least one animal inhabitant. Additional criteria for selection included threatened or endangered status (southwestern willow flycatcher, Sonoran pronghorn), existing or proposed reintroduction programs (beaver, jaguar), and species requiring large areas or unique features (northern goshawk, Gila monster). The potential habitat model for each wildlife species is specified according to standards for the development of Habitat Suitability Index (HSI) models of the U. S. Fish and Wildlife Service (USFWS) and its Habitat Evaluation Procedures (USFWS 1980). The HSI format emphasizes the quantitative relationships between environmental variables and habitat suitability. HSI models focus on spatially explicit habitat data, including vegetation type, stand age, percent cover, vertical and horizontal structure, patch size, patch configuration, edge, juxtaposition of plant community types, disturbance, elevation, aspect, soil, special features, and other spatially explicit factors. Behavioral data with spatial implications are also incorporated into each model.

Each potential habitat model was based on research literature and on personal communications from wildlife scientists. The models were reviewed by biologists familiar with the subject species and with the ecology of the study area. The models vary in level of precision in part because of varying availability of life history and habitat-related information. Each species' potential habitat map, based on HSI standards, delineates the total estimated potential habitat for that species in 2000. The subsequent impact maps show the estimated changes to the extent of the potential habitat in 2020, based on the changed vegetation pattern and other characteristics, in each of the alternative futures.

Photo 12.1 ■ Desert grassland near Sonoita

Southwestern Willow Flycatcher Potential Habitat

The southwestern willow flycatcher, *Empidonax traillii extimus*, is a small passerine bird that frequents riparian areas. Measuring 15 cm (5.75 in.) in height and weighing 11 g (0.4 oz), it has a grayish green back, white throat, and whitish yellow belly. Two white wing bars traverse the upper portion of the wing. A slight eye ring common among flycatchers is often absent in the southwestern willow flycatcher (Peterson 1990; Udvardy and Farrand 1994).

A neotropical migratory species, the southwestern willow flycatcher represents one of the four currently recognized willow flycatcher subspecies (Unitt 1987). Migration occurs in preparation for winter, when the flycatcher leaves its breeding grounds in the southwestern United States for warmer climates in Mexico, Central America, or northern South America (Farrand 1988). The San Pedro River Basin lies at the southern extreme of its potential breeding range (Unitt 1987).

Flycatcher habitat consists of dense riparian vegetation along streams, rivers, and wetlands (figure 12.1). Vegetation composition varies by location. Often vegetation is dominated by a dense growth of willows with an overstory of cottonwoods, tamarisk, or other large trees. The key characteristic appears to be the presence of dense vegetation throughout all vegetation layers (Peterson 1990; Udvardy and Farrand 1994; Sheridan Stone, personal communication).

Most breeding habitat is close to water or saturated soil. Large rivers, small streams, springs, or marshes all represent adequate water sources for the willow flycatcher. In some instances water sources may dry up in the later parts of the breeding season. The presence of water is important for the willow flycatcher, but ultimately, the limiting factor appears to be a high water table. A high water table encourages dense growth of riparian vegetation, which is a key feature of breeding habitat.

Recent decline in numbers has caused the southwestern willow

Photo 12.2 ■ Southwest willow flycatcher

Photo 12.3 ■ Southwest willow flycatcher habitat

flycatcher to be given endangered status by the USFWS (USFWS 1995). Causes of habitat loss include urban growth, expansion of agriculture, loss of groundwater, stream channelization, and livestock grazing. Urban growth and agricultural expansion result in the removal of riparian vegetation. Stream channelization and groundwater loss reduce the amount and extent of groundwater available for uptake by riparian plant communities. Livestock trample vegetation and bring a host of introduced species with them. One introduced species—the brown-headed cowbird,

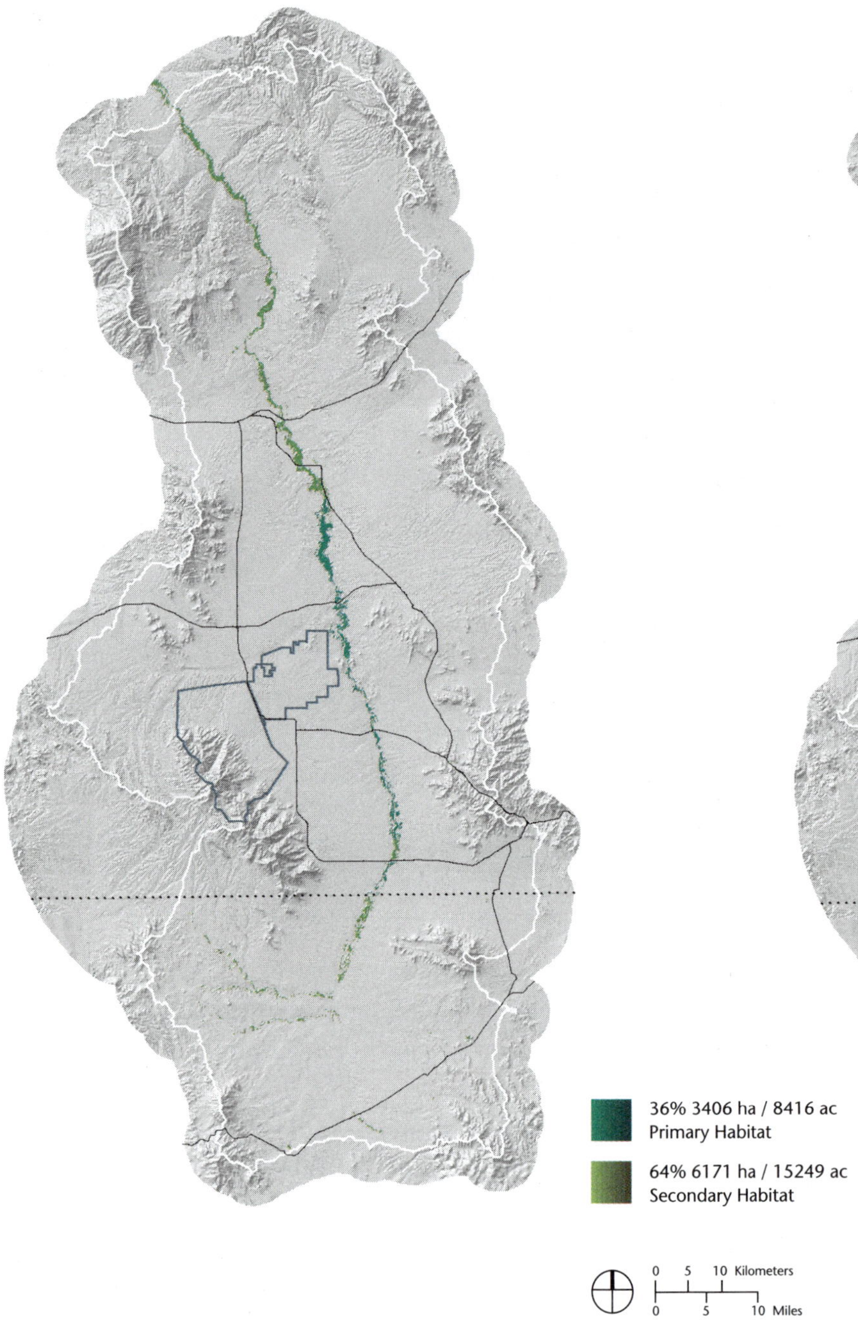
36% 3406 ha / 8416 ac
Primary Habitat
64% 6171 ha / 15249 ac
Secondary Habitat
0 5 10 Kilometers
0 5 10 Miles

Figure 12.1 ■ Southwestern willow flycatcher potential habitat, 2000

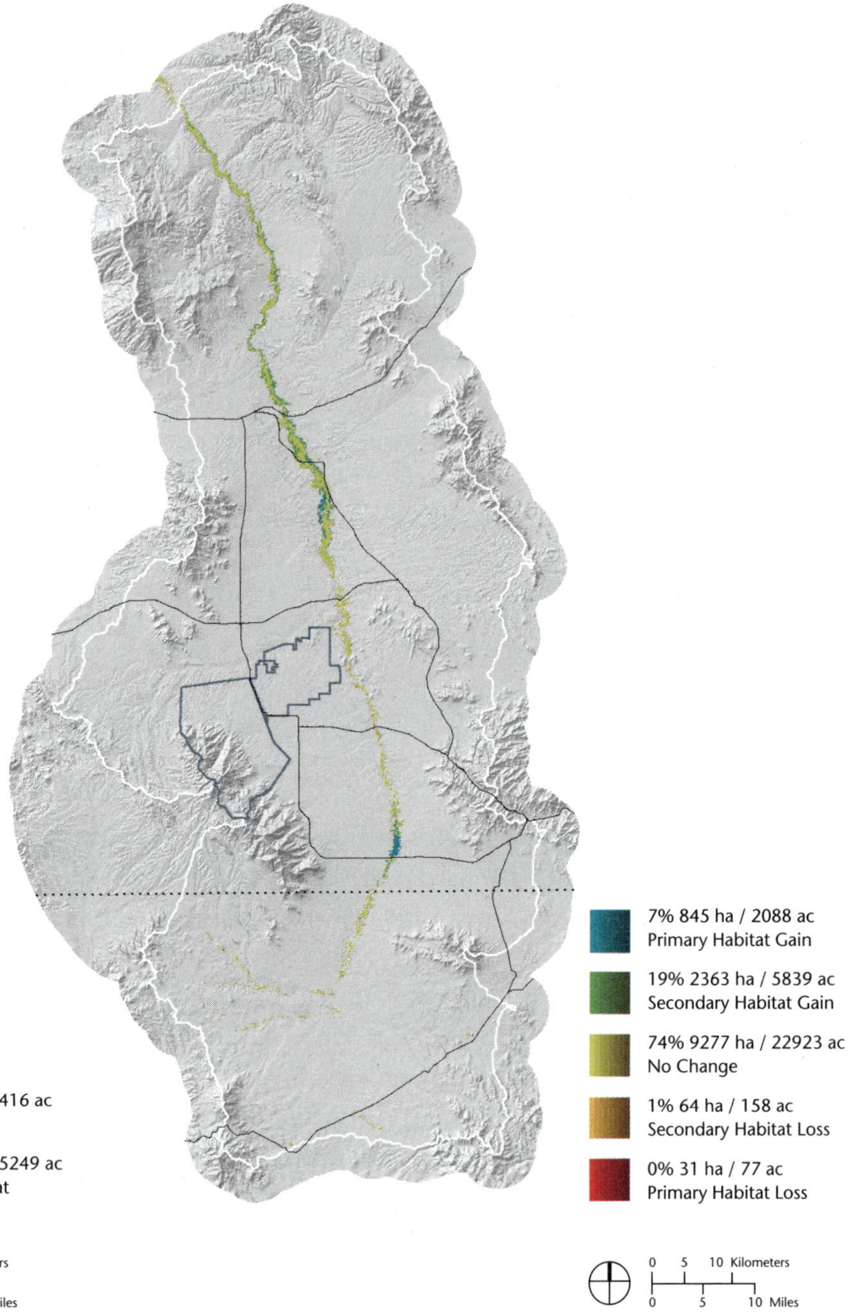
7% 845 ha / 2088 ac
Primary Habitat Gain
19% 2363 ha / 5839 ac
Secondary Habitat Gain
74% 9277 ha / 22923 ac
No Change
1% 64 ha / 158 ac
Secondary Habitat Loss
0% 31 ha / 77 ac
Primary Habitat Loss
0 5 10 Kilometers
0 5 10 Miles

Figure 12.2a ■ PLANS,
Southwestern willow flycatcher habitat impacts, 2000–2020

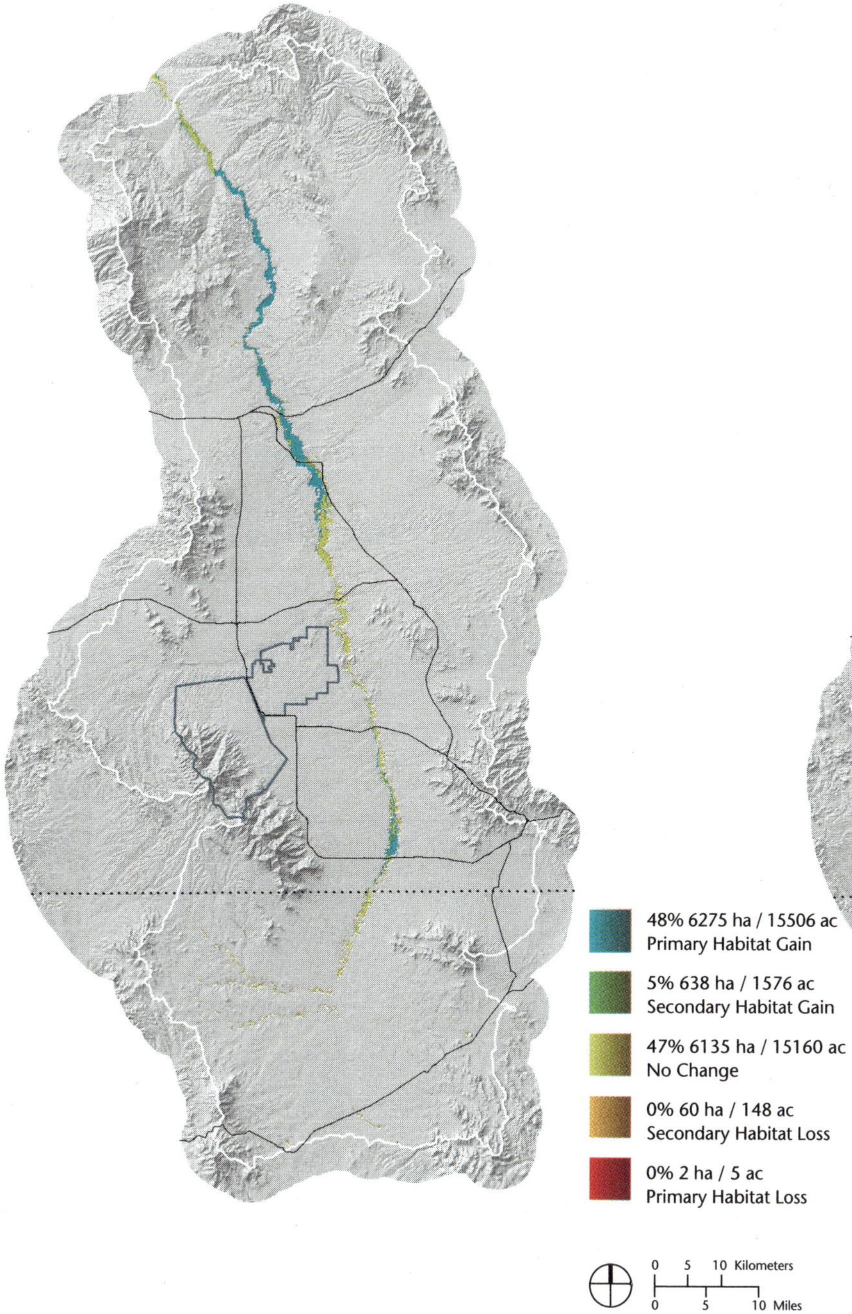
48% 6275 ha / 15506 ac
Primary Habitat Gain
5% 638 ha / 1576 ac
Secondary Habitat Gain
47% 6135 ha / 15160 ac
No Change
0% 60 ha / 148 ac
Secondary Habitat Loss
0% 2 ha / 5 ac
Primary Habitat Loss
0 5 10 Kilometers
0 5 10 Miles

Figure 12.2b ■ CONSTRAINED,
Southwestern willow flycatcher habitat impacts, 2000–2020

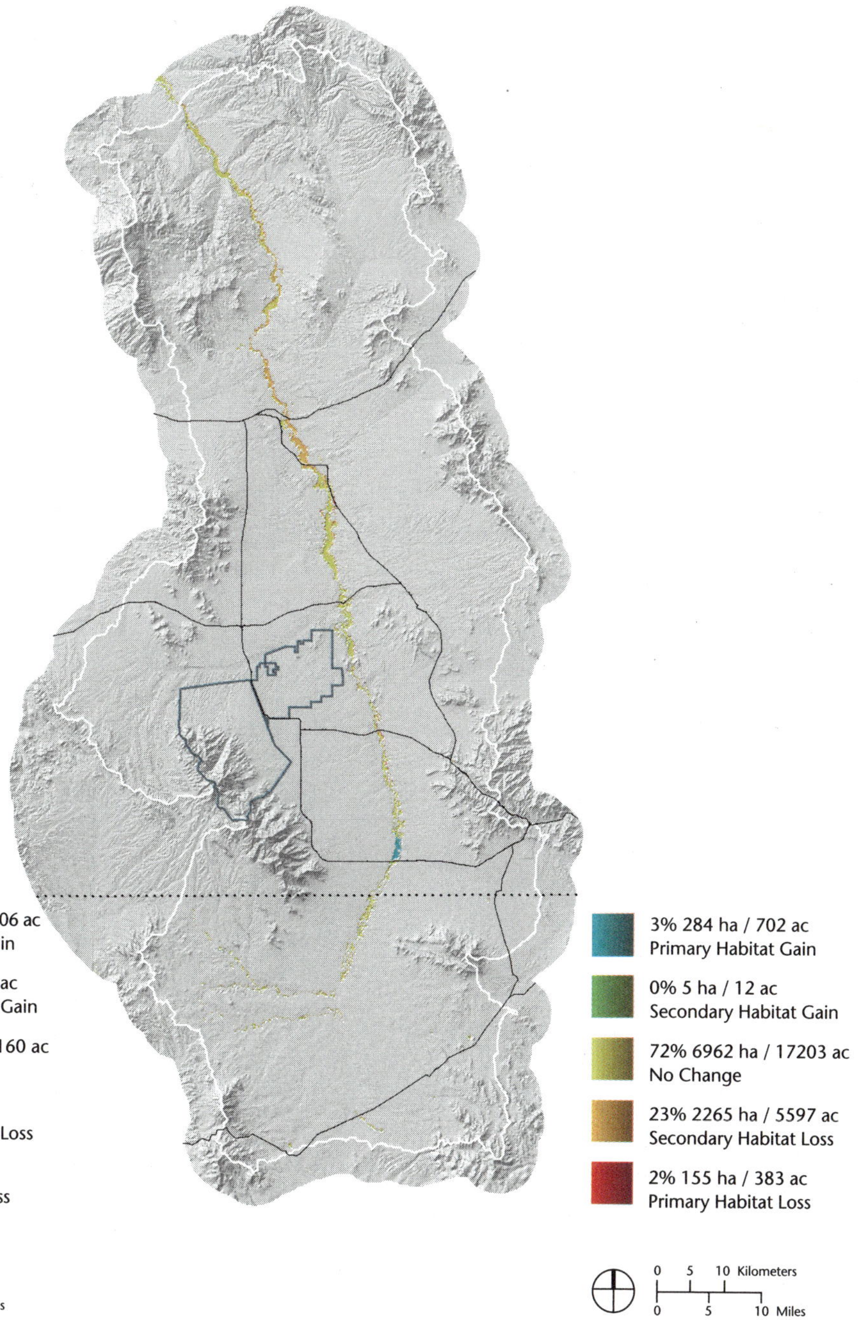
3% 284 ha / 702 ac
Primary Habitat Gain
0% 5 ha / 12 ac
Secondary Habitat Gain
72% 6962 ha / 17203 ac
No Change
23% 2265 ha / 5597 ac
Secondary Habitat Loss
2% 155 ha / 383 ac
Primary Habitat Loss
0 5 10 Kilometers
0 5 10 Miles

Figure 12.3c ■ OPEN,
Southwestern willow flycatcher habitat impacts, 2000–2020

Table 12.1 Southwestern willow flycatcher habitat: Impacts, 2000–2020

	change in primary and seconday habitat / ha
Baseline 2000	9,577
Plans	3,113
Plans 1	2,663
Plans 2	2,852
Plans 3	6,352
Constrained	6,852
Constrained 1	6,812
Constrained 2	6,819
Open	-2,130
Open 1	-1,985
Open 2	-2,146

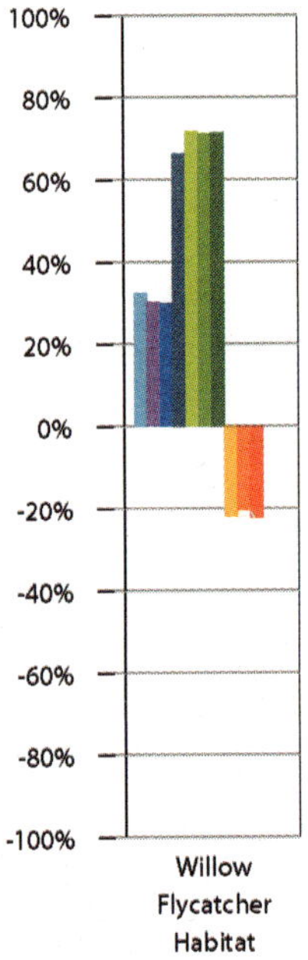
100%
80%
60%
40%
20%
0%
-20%
-40%
-60%
-80%
-100%
Willow Flycatcher Habitat

Relative impacts

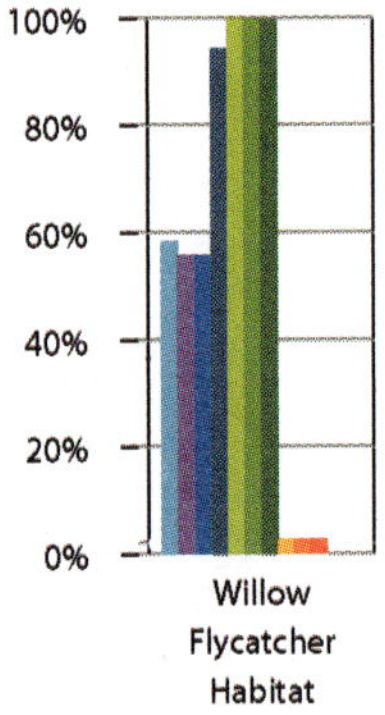
100%
80%
60%
40%
20%
0%
Willow Flycatcher Habitat

Percent impacts

Molothrus aeneus—is associated with the introduction of cattle into an area. It practices nest parasitism by laying its eggs in the nests of the flycatchers. The larger cowbird nestlings displace the baby flycatchers. Competition for food often results in the death of the smaller flycatcher nestlings (Whitfield and Enos 1996; Sogge et al. 1997).

Primary habitat for the southwestern willow flycatcher consists of riparian areas greater than 1 km (.62 mi) from areas that are being grazed. Secondary habitat includes riparian areas within 1 km of potentially grazed locales. The removal of grazing from locations close to riparian vegetation causes an increase in primary habitat. New habitat may be created by an increase in the groundwater level within the San Pedro River floodplain so that riparian vegetation can be expected to replace the existing desert scrub communities. Increased grazing or lowering of the groundwater levels results in loss of willow flycatcher habitat.

Groundwater levels change under all the scenarios and influence the amount of riparian vegetation available for flycatcher habitat (figure 12.2a–c and table 12.1). The OPEN scenario results in a 20 percent decrease in riparian vegetation. Under the OPEN scenarios, loss occurs immediately north of the San Pedro Riparian National Conservation Area and extends beyond Interstate Highway 10. The proposed extension of the conservation area creates a gain in habitat around the Palominas bridge on Arizona Highway 92. The gain is a result of the removal of grazing and an increased groundwater level caused by the removal of agricultural activity and its associated pumping in the immediate area. There is little variation in willow flycatcher habitat among the OPEN scenarios.

The PLANS scenarios result in willow flycatcher habitat increases of from 30 percent to 66 percent. In most cases, this improvement results from rises in groundwater levels caused by the removal of agricultural activity and wells within 1.6 km (1 mi) of the San Pedro River and the subsequent expansion of riparian vegetation into the San Pedro River floodplain. Removal of grazing from all public lands and from the proposed extensions of the conservation area to the north and the south results in an increase of potential primary habitat available under the PLANS 3 alternative future.

The CONSTRAINED scenarios result in the largest expansion of potential willow flycatcher habitat, with potential increases of more than 70 percent. About half the increase comes from the expansion of riparian vegetation caused by a rise in groundwater levels. Fewer homes and the elimination of agricultural land and wells in and near the riparian area result in raised groundwater levels. Removal of grazing from all state lands and from the expanded conservation area to the north and south cause secondary habitat to improve and become primary habitat. This change greatly increases the amount of potential primary habitat available directly north of the current San Pedro Riparian National Conservation Area.

Northern Goshawk Potential Habitat

The northern goshawk, *Accipiter gentilis,* is one of the largest raptors in Arizona. Females are slightly larger than their male counterparts, weighing an average of 1.1 kg (2.4 lb). Males weigh .86 kg (1.9 lb) on average. Wingspan ranges from 97 to 114 cm (38 to 45 in.). Adults have a conspicuous white stripe above the eye. The rest of the head is mostly black and the tail is gray with black bars. In flight, the underside is white-gray with a series of black bands on the belly (Wheeler and Clark 1995; Peterson 1990).

The northern goshawk forages in forested areas. Its body allows for quick flight among the trees so that unsuspecting prey may be taken in a rapid dash. Relatively short wings and a long tail increase the maneuverability of the goshawk in flight among the trees. Prey includes small mammals and birds that inhabit forested areas (Snyder and Snyder 1998; Peterson 1990).

Northern goshawks may be found in mountainous areas in the West from Alaska south to northern Mexico. They rarely breed at elevations below 1830 m (6000 ft). The lowest nest spotted by Snyder and Snyder (1998) was at an elevation of 1500 m (4900 ft) in an oak. Breeding sites consist of large trees characteristic of older growth. Northern goshawks prefer to nest in large conifers, but have been known to use large oak trees. Nesting trees tend to be in relatively open locations where the birds have few obstructions to flight. Nests are large conspicuous structures generally located on the lower branches of trees. Protection of the nest is fierce. Human activity should be minimized around active nests (Snyder and Snyder 1998).

A goshawk may range over large areas in a day, to feed and to defend its territory against other raptors, including other goshawks. The area of home range averages 648 ha (1614 ac) (Crocker-Bedford 1990).

Potential habitat is located in mountainous parts of the study area (figure 12.3). Areas dominated by conifers and oaks at

Photo 12.4 ■ Northern goshawk

Photo 12.5 ■ Northern goshawk habitat

Table 12.2 Northern goshawk habitat: Impacts, 2000–2020

	change in habitat / ha
Baseline 2000	146,185
Plans	0
Plans 1	0
Plans 2	0
Plans 3	0
Constrained	84
Constrained 1	80
Constrained 2	80
Open	-67
Open 1	-511
Open 2	-14

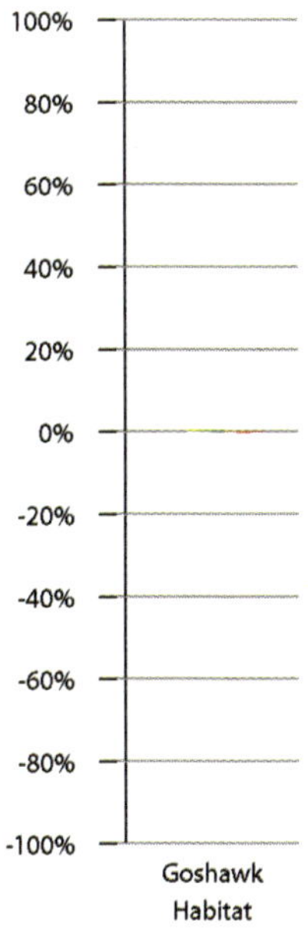
100%
80%
60%
40%
20%
0%
-20%
-40%
-60%
-80%
-100%
Goshawk Habitat

Relative impacts

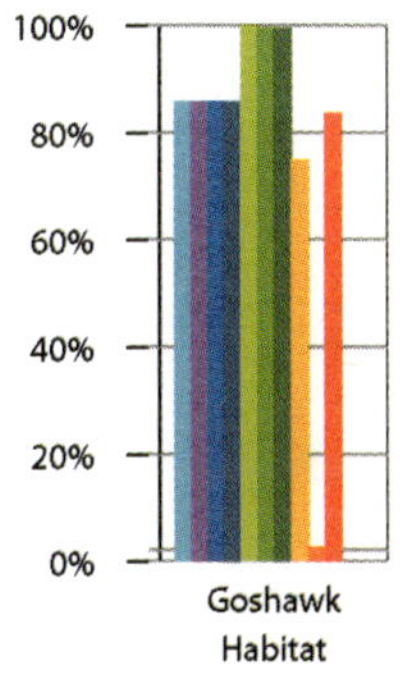
100%
80%
60%
40%
20%
0%
Goshawk Habitat

Percent impacts

elevations above 1830 m (6000 ft) are identified as primary habitat. Areas dominated by oaks at elevations from 1500 to 1830 m (4900 to 6000 ft) constitute secondary habitat. Minimum habitat area must comprise a single home range of 648 hectares (1614 ac) to be considered viable. Destruction or modification of these habitat areas affects the survival of the goshawk.

All of the alternative futures indicate little development in mountain areas. Thus, very little goshawk habitat modification occurs (figure 12.4a-c and table 12.2). The OPEN scenarios result in a loss of less than 1 percent of primary and secondary habitat. Less than 1 percent of habitat area is gained under the CONSTRAINED scenarios. The PLANS scenarios cause no change to goshawk habitat. These results show very little difference among the scenarios in impacts on goshawk habitat. Habitat losses are the result of development in the lower elevation oak vegetation communities. Gains occur where high elevation agricultural lands are retired and allowed to revert to forest plant species.

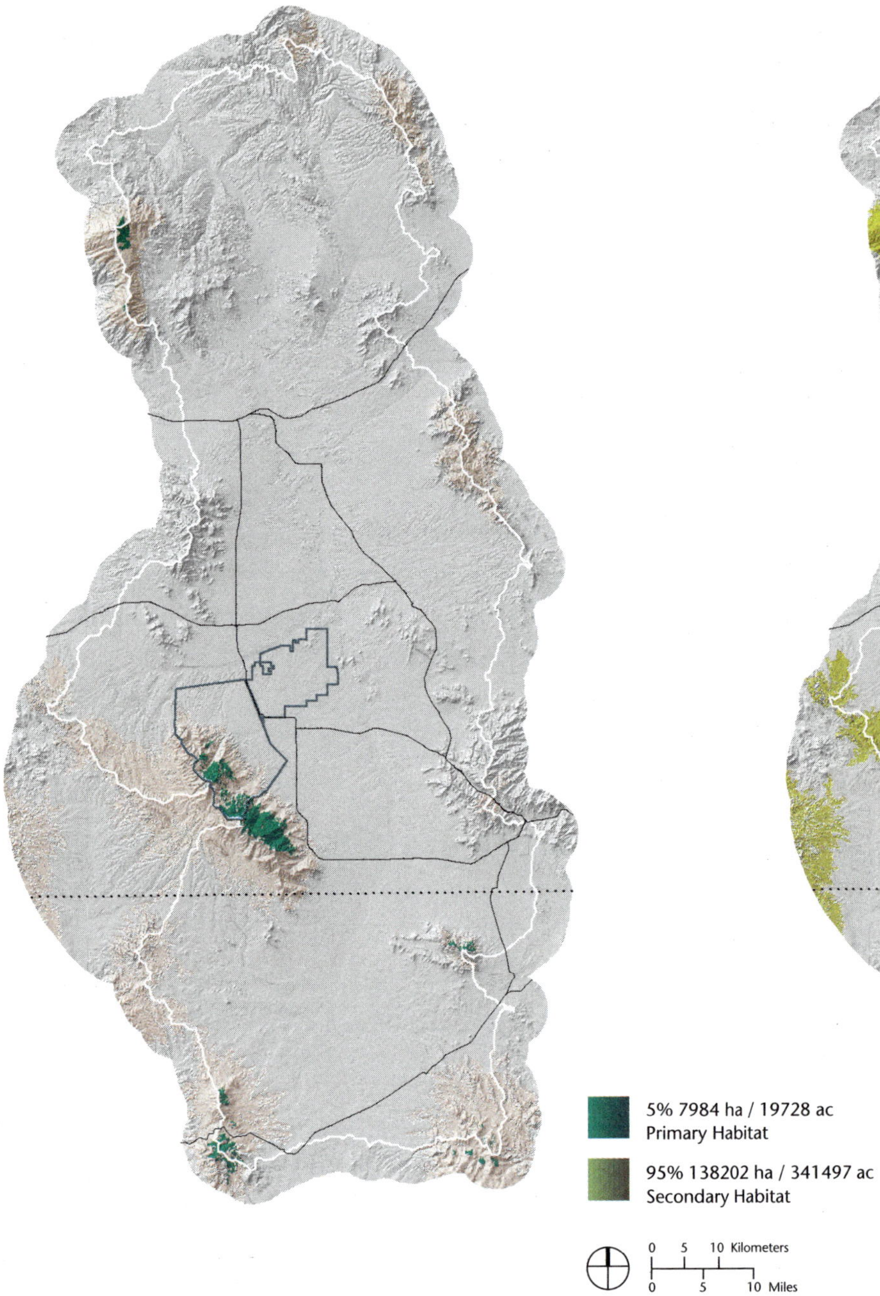
5% 7984 ha / 19728 ac
Primary Habitat
95% 138202 ha / 341497 ac
Secondary Habitat
0 5 10 Kilometers
0 5 10 Miles

Figure 12.3 ■ Northern goshawk potential habitat, 2000

100% 146185 ha / 361223 ac
No Change
0 5 10 Kilometers
0 5 10 Miles

**Figure 12.4a ■ PLANS,
Northern goshawk potential habitat impacts, 2000–2020**

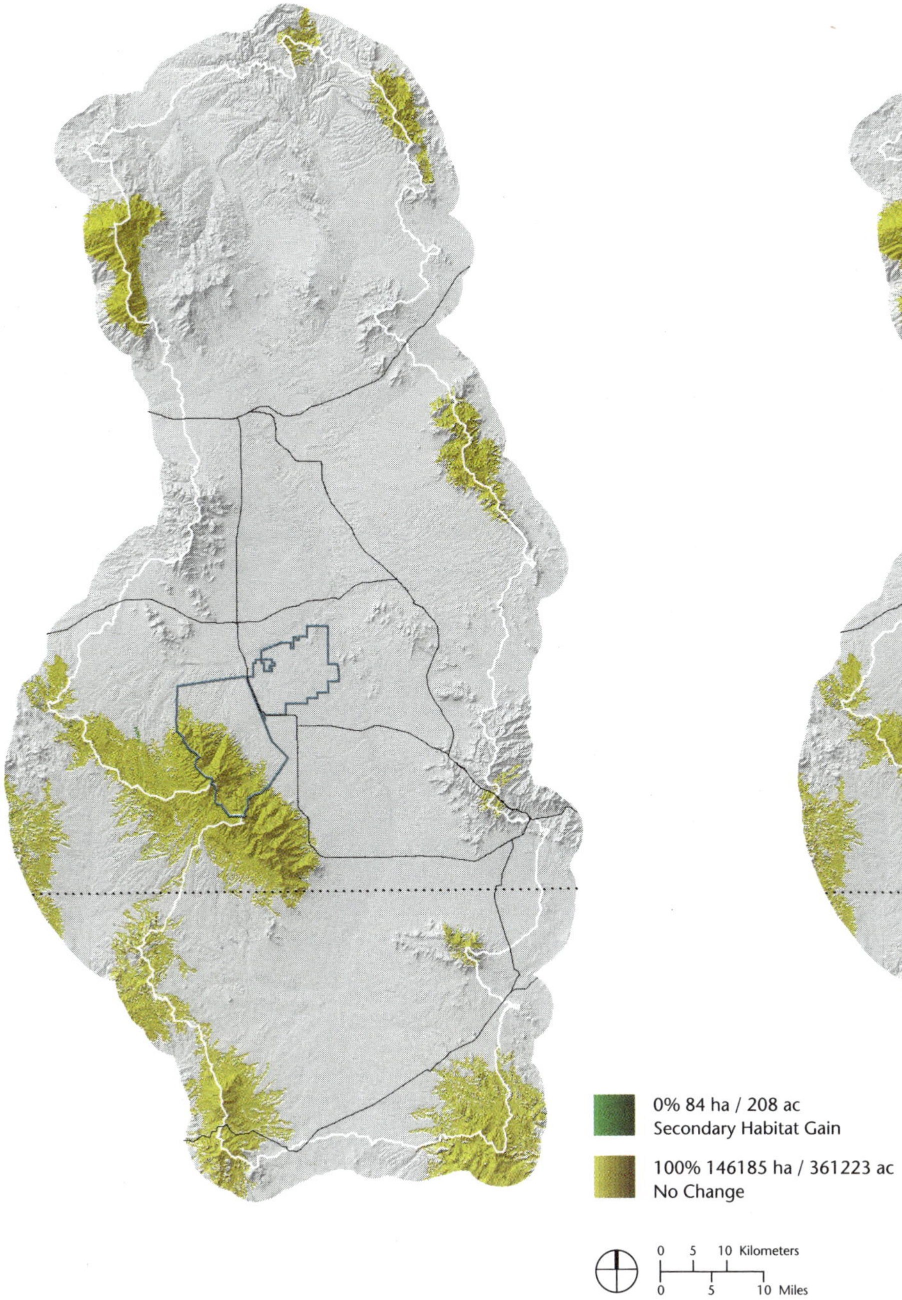
0% 84 ha / 208 ac
Secondary Habitat Gain
100% 146185 ha / 361223 ac
No Change
0 5 10 Kilometers
0 5 10 Miles

Figure 12.4b ■ CONSTRAINED,
Northern goshawk potential habitat impacts, 2000–2020

100% 146119 ha / 361060 ac
No Change
0% 67 ha / 166 ac
Secondary Habitat Loss
0 5 10 Kilometers
0 5 10 Miles

Figure 12.4c ■ OPEN,
Northern goshawk potential habitat impacts, 2000–2020

Gila Monster Potential Habitat

The Gila monster, *Heloderma suspectum,* represents one of only two venomous lizards in the world. Unlike snakes that strike and inject their venom through fangs, the Gila monster uses its immense jaws to hold and chew, thereby causing venom to enter the victim through injuries caused by gnawing. The venom produces a painful wound. If enough venom is absorbed death may ensue (Stoops and Wright 1993).

Large for a North American lizard, the Gila monster ranges in length from 22 to 35 cm (9 to 14 in.). Thick bodied, with a short thick tail and magnificent coloration, the Gila monster catches the eye of any observer. Its black body is marked with stripes or large spots that may be colored pink, orange, or yellow. A forked tongue and a sinuous walk give a sinister ambiance to this lizard (Stebbins 1985).

Found from southwestern Utah to Sonora, the Gila monster inhabits a diverse range of vegetative communities within the Mojave, Sonoran, and Chihuahuan deserts. It prefers desert scrub, grasses, and occasionally oak woodlands. Exposed gravelly and sandy soils in foothills provide an excellent substrate for burrows. Stream banks and arroyos are ideal locations. Burrows or areas under rocks are used for protection from the elements and for hibernation (Stebbins 1985).

Hibernation occurs in the winter, when fat reserves stored in the tail and abdomen provide nourishment until warmer weather. In the spring, the Gila monster emerges and begins its quest for food (Beck 1990; Bogert and Del Campo 1956). Prey consists of a variety of items found at ground level. The Gila monster feeds on the eggs of ground-nesting birds and other reptiles, although small mammals, insects, carrion, and even other reptiles are consumed. Feeding occurs at night and during the early evening hours. Activity varies in accordance with the temperature. Very high temperatures are avoided (Bogert and Del Campo 1956).

Photo 12.6 ■ Gila monster

Photo 12.7 ■ Gila monster habitat

Table 12.3 Gila monster habitat: Impacts, 2000–2020

	change in habitat / ha
Baseline 2000	208,993
Plans	791
Plans 1	547
Plans 2	801
Plans 3	967
Constrained	1,664
Constrained 1	1,209
Constrained 2	1,209
Open	-2,437
Open 1	-2,637
Open 2	-2,545

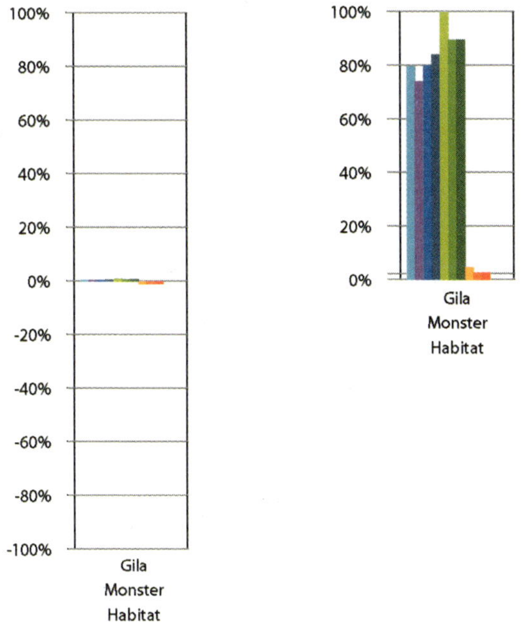
100%
80%
60%
40%
20%
0%
-20%
-40%
-60%
-80%
-100%
Gila Monster Habitat
100%
80%
60%
40%
20%
0%
Gila Monster Habitat

Relative impacts

Percent impacts

Opportunity appears the key to a meal. A Gila monster's home range is typically around 1 sq km (.4 sq mi) in area (Beck 1990).

Potential habitat consists of desert scrub communities close to moderately sloping areas (figure 12.5). Most Gila monster habitat is located along the edge of the foothills. Removal or alteration of desert foothill locations reduces habitat. Although Gila monsters have been seen in other locations, the foothills provide the best opportunities for shelter. An adequate number of shelter locations is paramount to their survival.

Very little development along the foothills within desert scrub communities occurs in the alternative futures. Most of the Gila monster habitat is located north of Interstate Highway 10, where little development is predicted to occur. Impact on Gila monster habitat is light, with less than 2 percent of the total habitat changing (figure 12.6a–c and table 12.3). The OPEN scenarios result in a little over 1 percent decrease in available habitat. The CONSTRAINED and PLANS scenarios cause less than a 1 percent increase in habitat. Losses in habitat are due to development in the desert scrub communities along the foothills. Gains are the result of vegetation transition, mostly from the change of grassland into desert scrub.

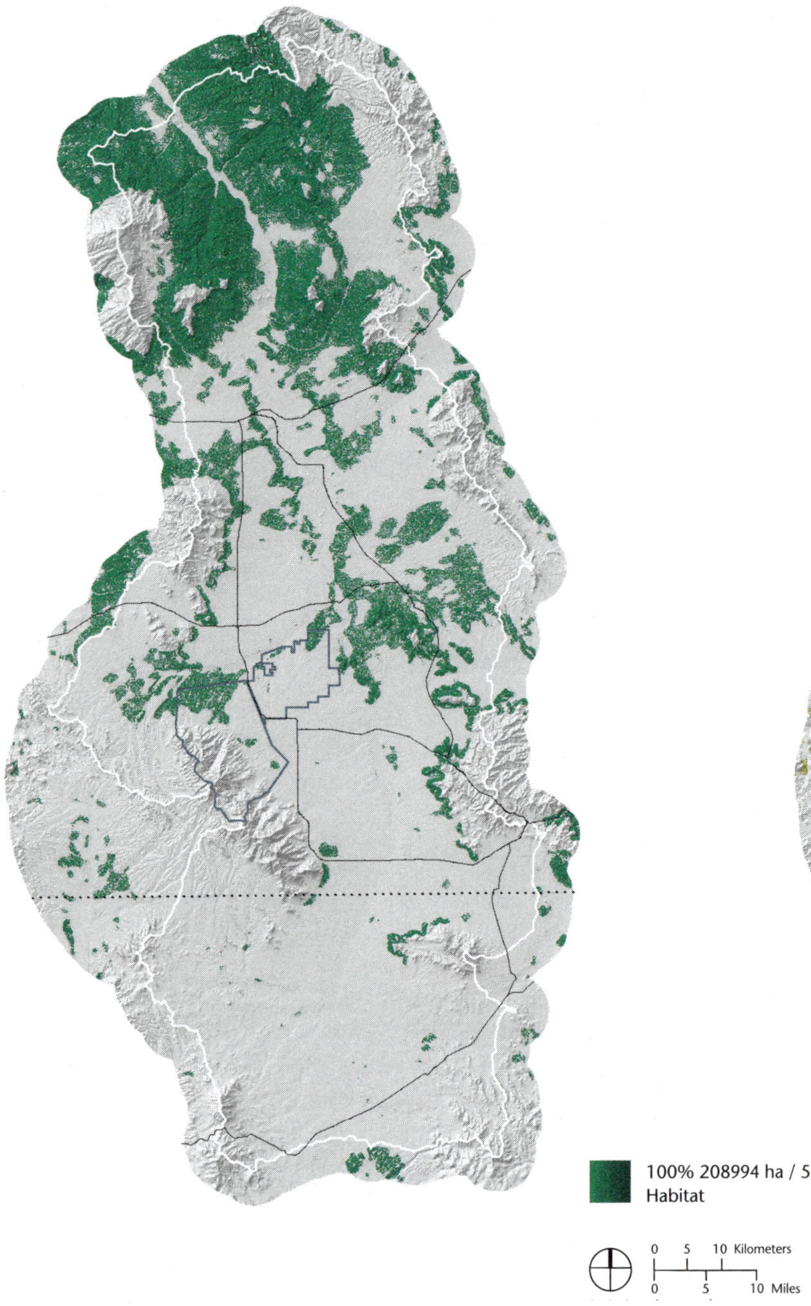
100% 208994 ha / 516424 ac
Habitat
0 5 10 Kilometers
0 5 10 Miles

Figure 12.5 ■ Gila monster potential habitat, 2000

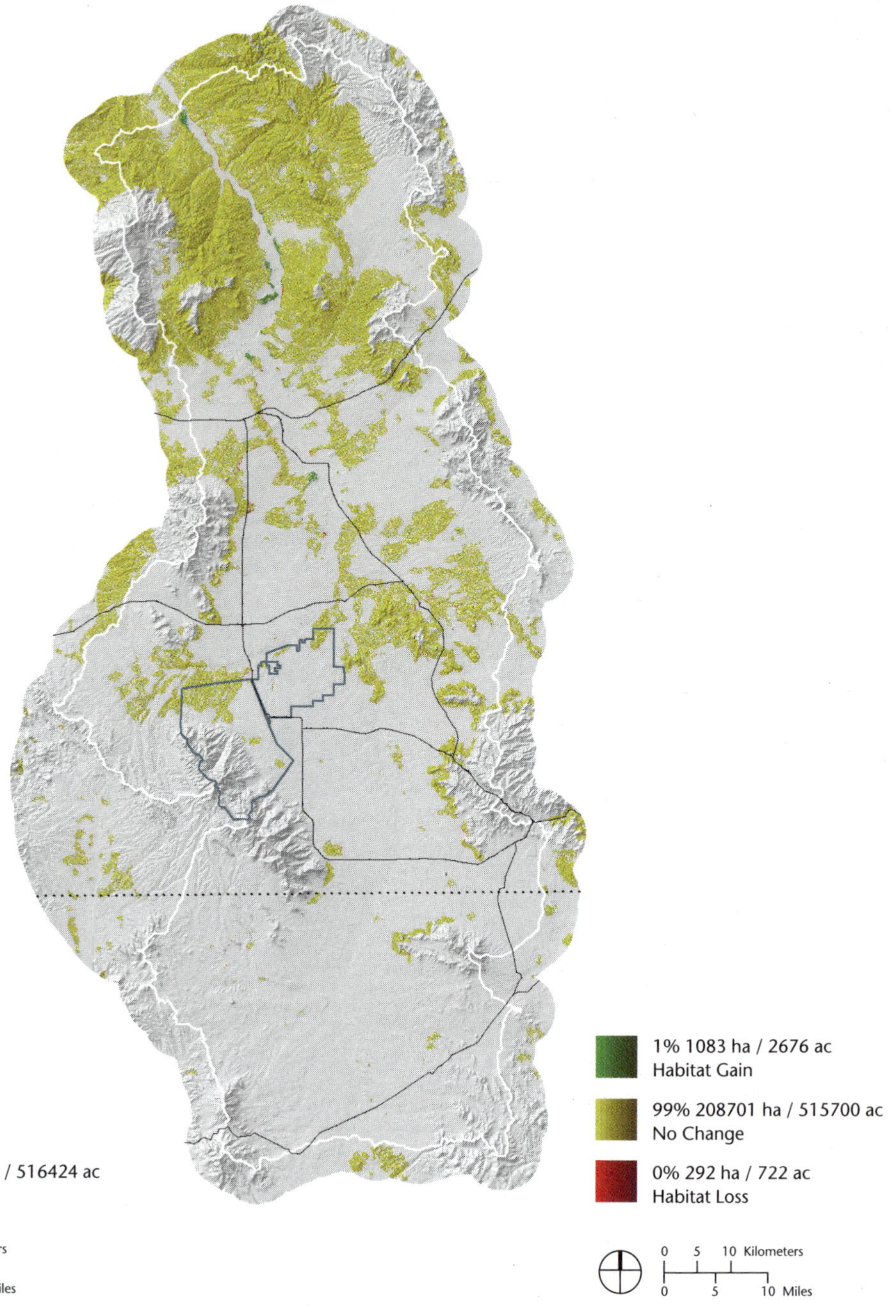
1% 1083 ha / 2676 ac
Habitat Gain
99% 208701 ha / 515700 ac
No Change
0% 292 ha / 722 ac
Habitat Loss
0 5 10 Kilometers
0 5 10 Miles

Figure 12.6a ■ PLANS,
Gila monster habitat impacts, 2000–2020

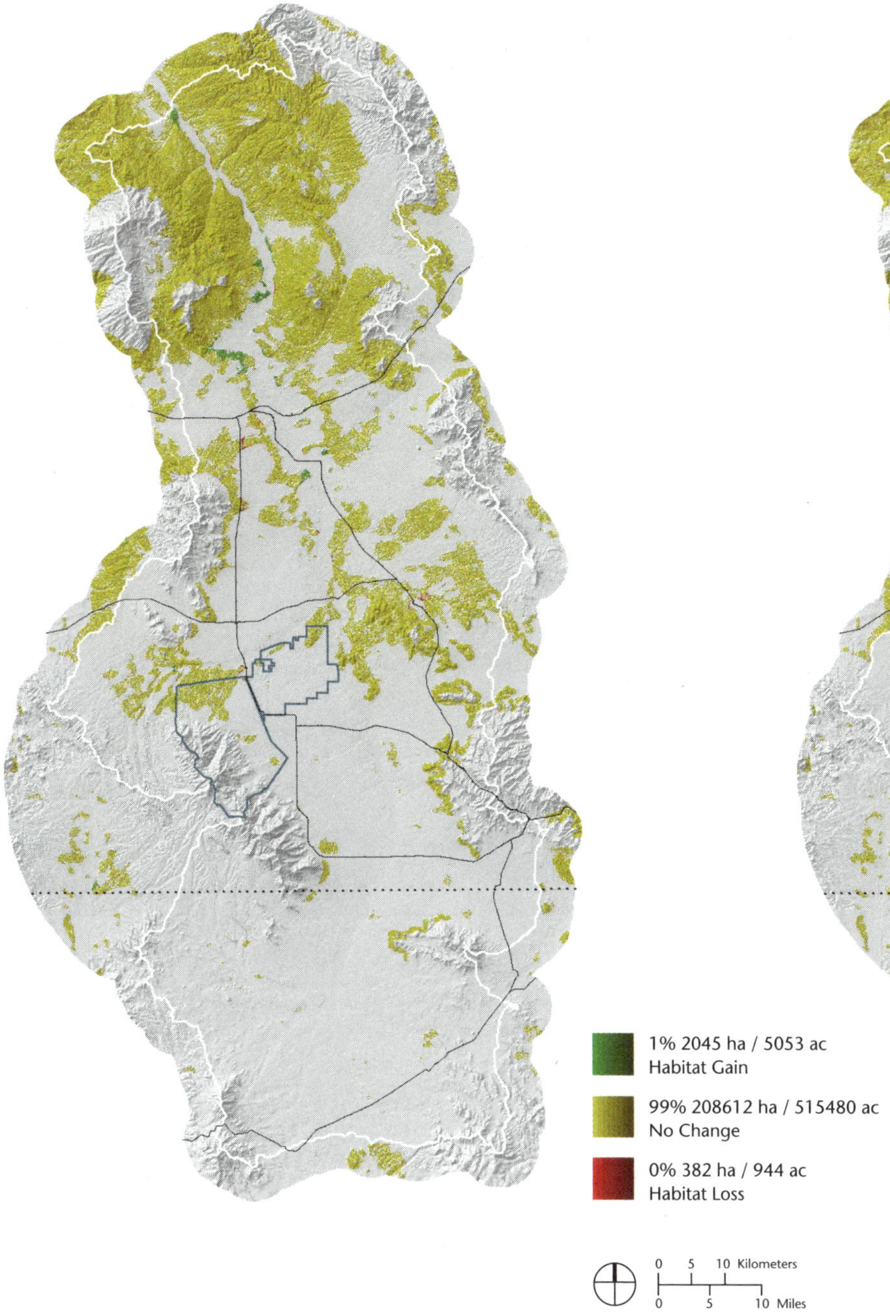
1% 2045 ha / 5053 ac
Habitat Gain
99% 208612 ha / 515480 ac
No Change
0% 382 ha / 944 ac
Habitat Loss
0 5 10 Kilometers
0 5 10 Miles

Figure 12.6b ■ CONSTRAINED, Gila monster habitat impacts, 2000–2020

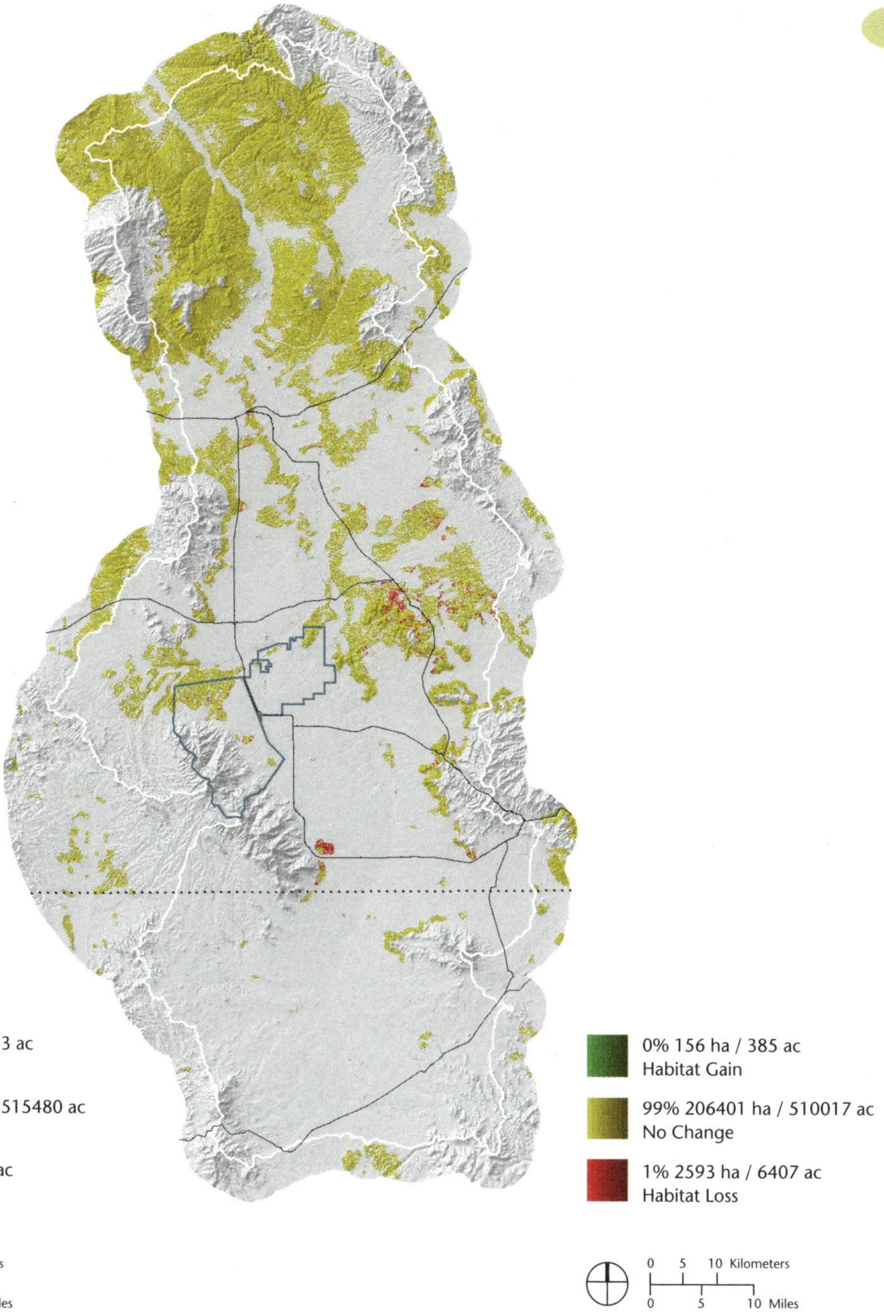
0% 156 ha / 385 ac
Habitat Gain
99% 206401 ha / 510017 ac
No Change
1% 2593 ha / 6407 ac
Habitat Loss
0 5 10 Kilometers
0 5 10 Miles

Figure 12.6c ■ OPEN, Gila monster habitat impacts, 2000–2020

Beaver Potential Habitat

The beaver, *Castor canadensis,* is a large rodent that lives near perennial water sources. It weighs from 13.5 to 27 kg (30 to 60 lb). Dark brown waterproof fur, and a thick fatty layer just under the skin provide the needed insulation for swimming in cold water. The large scaly, paddle-shaped tail is used to slap the water to warn of danger. Its chisel-shaped front teeth grow continually. They are used to fell riparian trees so the nutrient-rich bark and leaves may be eaten. Without the wear caused by gnawing on trees, the teeth would lengthen and penetrate the upper and lower jaw (Burt and Grossenheider 1980).

Freshwater streams, lakes, or canals provide the water necessary for beaver habitat. Typically, beaver habitat contains a number of riparian tree species along the banks (figure 12.7). Beavers build dams and lodges. Often, lodges are replaced by holes dug in the banks of streams and lakes (Findley 1987).

Beaver dams typically are about 1.5 m (5 ft) in height and usually more than 3 m (10 ft) wide at the base. Dams create a widened body of water and an increased depth so that a lodge may be constructed. Lodges are reached by swimming, which helps limit disturbance by other animals. Dams are made of branches, stones, and mud packed together to form a wall. In many cases, several dams are built to distribute the pressure of flowing water and protect the downstream dam from breaching. Dams often increase the local groundwater level, creating small wetlands. Eventually the pond behind the dam is filled by sediment and must be abandoned. The abandoned dam site becomes a meadow (Apple et al. 1984; Barnes and Mallik 1997).

Historically, the beaver could be found throughout the San Pedro River Basin. Their beautiful fur resulted in their being extirpated from the river system. Recently, the Bureau of Land Management began to reintroduce beaver into the river, ultimately intending to release ten animals. The newly introduced animals constructed four dams along the river system, with the largest 1 m (3 ft) high and 25 m (82 ft) across. (Parnell 2000).

To ensure the survival of the beaver, water must remain in the San Pedro River. The potential habitat model identifies locations along the stream where water flows most of the year. The model assumes that dams built in the stream corridor are a maximum of 2 m (6.3 ft) in height. The resulting pond creates additional beaver habitat. Beavers depend on the presence of water in the

Photo 12.8 ■ Beaver

Photo 12.9 ■ Beaver habitat

stream, and on the availability of sites suitable for dams and ponds.

The predicted length of river with free flowing water in the alternative futures is changed by the policy choices in each of the scenarios (figures 12.8a–c and table 12.4).

More than half the current beaver habitat is lost under the OPEN scenarios. There is no gain in habitat anywhere along the river. The sole remaining portion of habitat is located within the San Pedro River National Conservation Area. There is little difference in beaver potential habitat among the OPEN scenarios.

The PLANS scenarios create alternative futures with less than 10 percent loss in beaver habitat. Under PLANS, habitat is lost just north and south of the conservation area; however, habitat is gained north of Interstate Highway 10. The reduction of potential habitat appears to result from loss of groundwater that recharges the river in Mexico and in the Sierra Vista area. The removal of agriculture and its associated pumping in the U.S. portion of the study area increases flow in the river at locations considerably downstream (north) of the areas where pumping and agriculture are removed. Potential beaver habitat increases in downstream areas where the stream flow is improved. Little variation, less than 5 percent, exists among the PLANS scenarios.

The CONSTRAINED scenarios result in increased potential beaver habitat. New habitat is added north of the conservation area. Under the CONSTRAINED alternative future, little or no loss of existing habitat occurs. Among the CONSTRAINED scenarios, there is little variation.

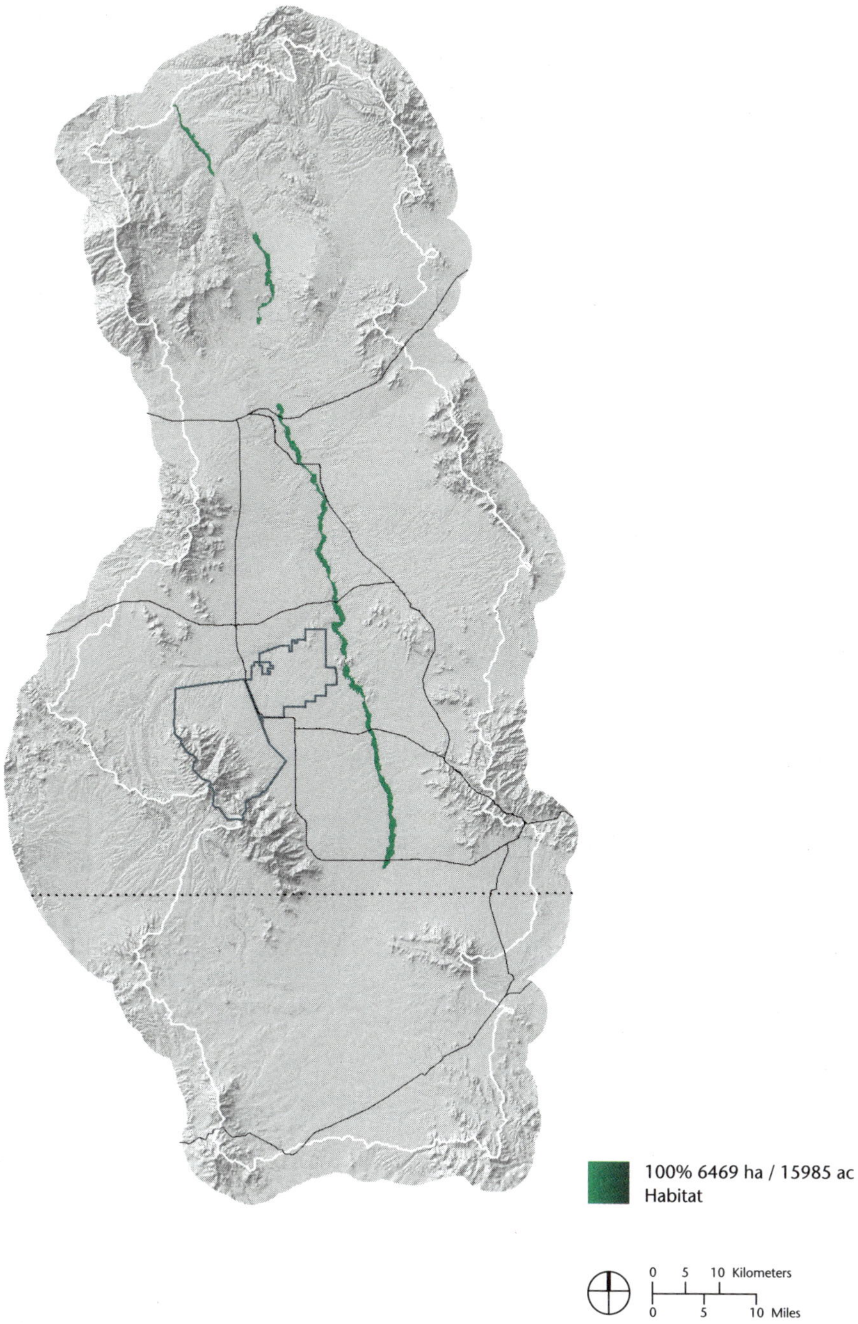
100% 6469 ha / 15985 ac
Habitat
0 5 10 Kilometers
0 5 10 Miles

Figure 12.7 ■ Beaver potential habitat, 2000

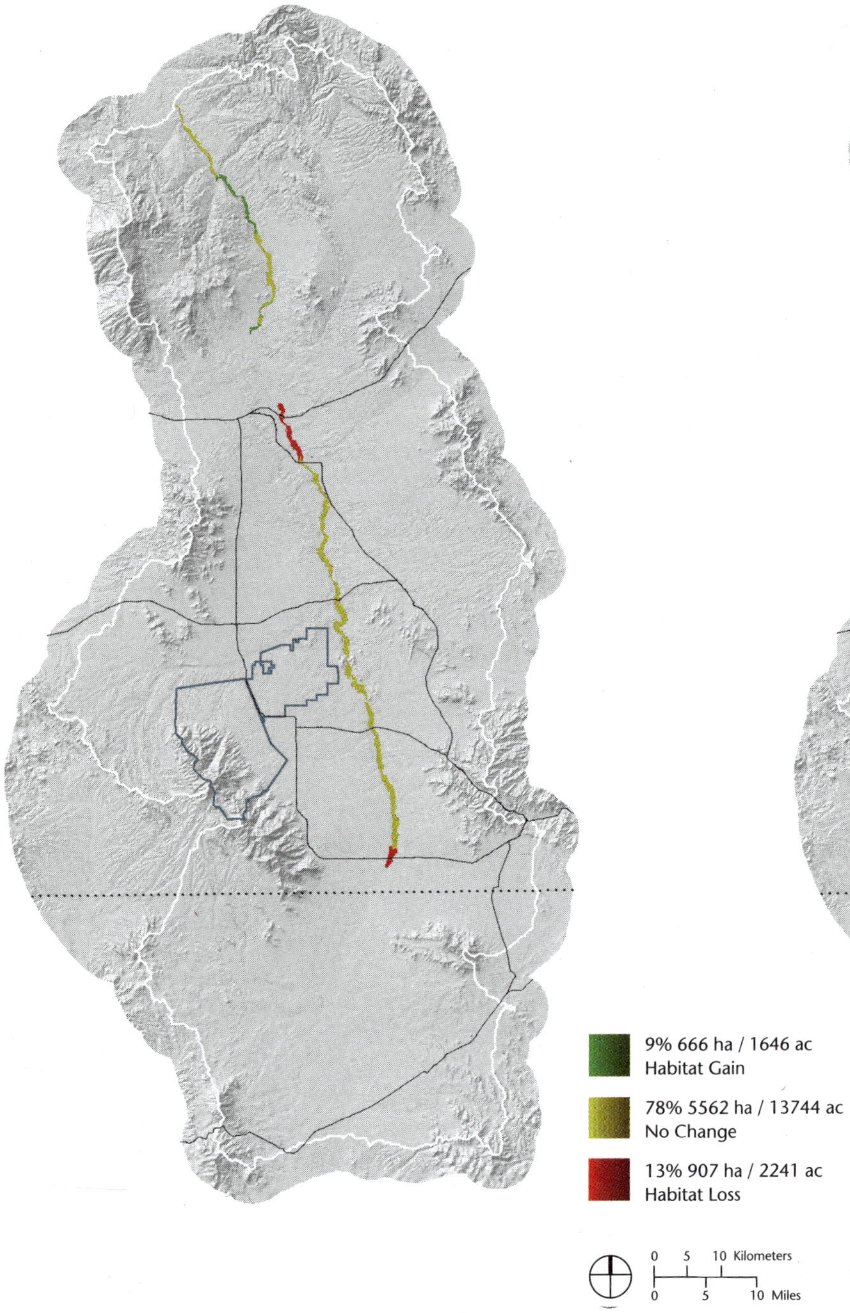
9% 666 ha / 1646 ac
Habitat Gain
78% 5562 ha / 13744 ac
No Change
13% 907 ha / 2241 ac
Habitat Loss
0 5 10 Kilometers
0 5 10 Miles

Figure 12.8a ■ PLANS, Beaver habitat impacts, 2000–2020

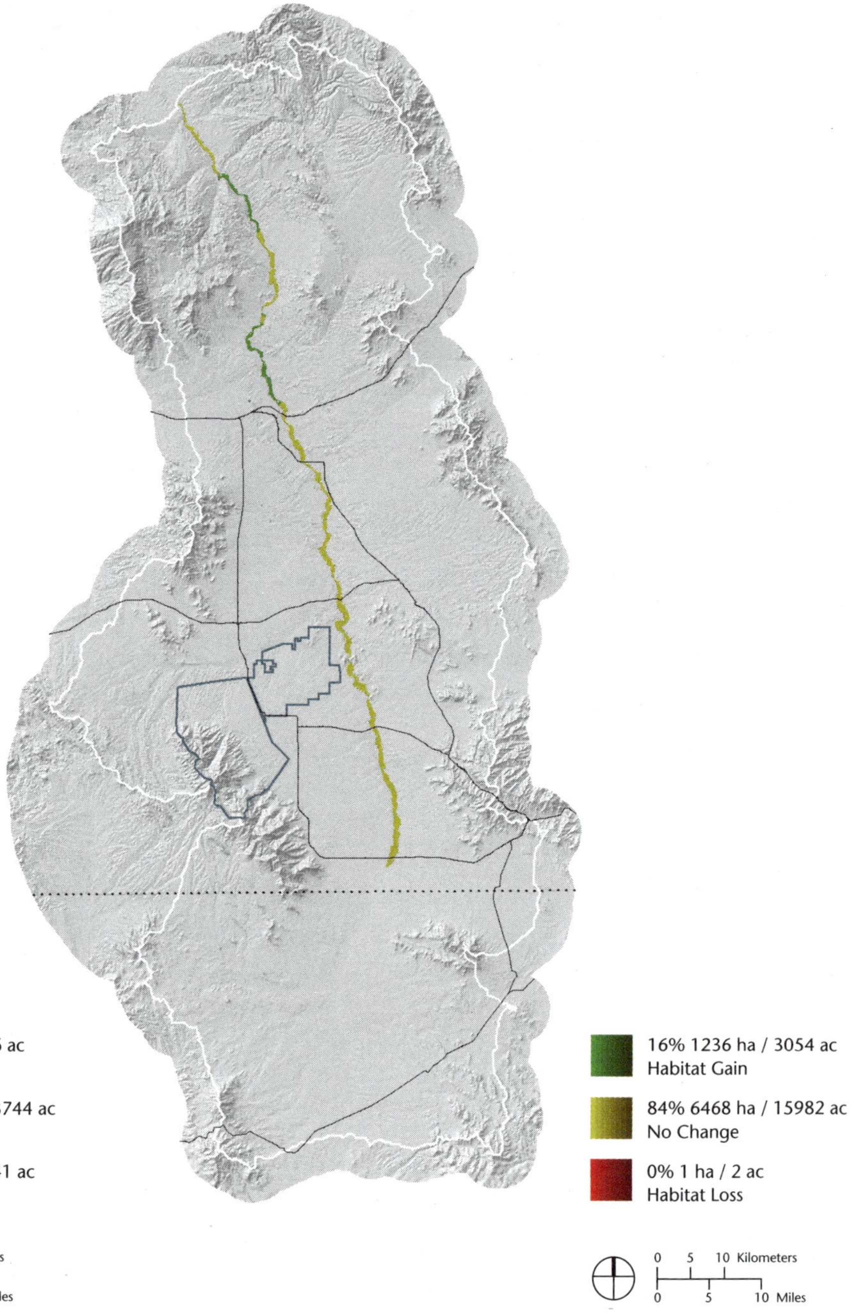
16% 1236 ha / 3054 ac
Habitat Gain
84% 6468 ha / 15982 ac
No Change
0% 1 ha / 2 ac
Habitat Loss
0 5 10 Kilometers
0 5 10 Miles

Figure 12.8b ■ CONSTRAINED, Beaver habitat impacts, 2000–2020

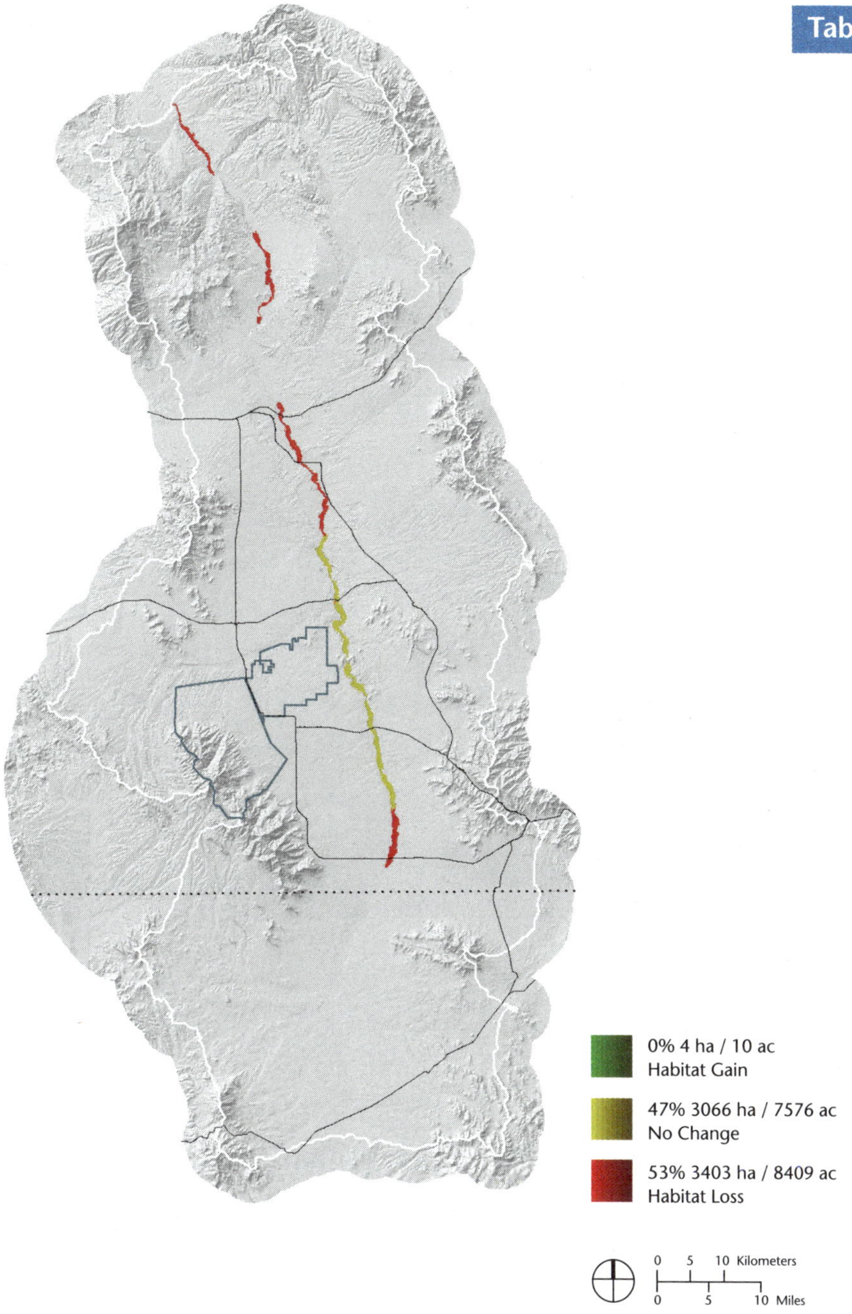
0% 4 ha / 10 ac
Habitat Gain
47% 3066 ha / 7576 ac
No Change
53% 3403 ha / 8409 ac
Habitat Loss
0 5 10 Kilometers
0 5 10 Miles

Figure 12.8c ■ OPEN, Beaver habitat impacts, 2000–2020

Table 12.4 Beaver habitat: Impacts, 2000–2020

	change in habitat / ha
Baseline 2000	6,469
Plans	-241
Plans 1	-374
Plans 2	-530
Plans 3	-251
Constrained	1,235
Constrained 1	1,352
Constrained 2	1,235
Open	-3,399
Open 1	-3,353
Open 2	-3,451

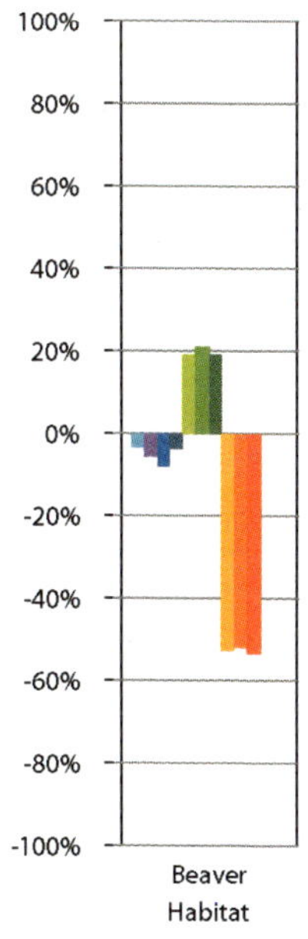
100%
80%
60%
40%
20%
0%
-20%
-40%
-60%
-80%
-100%
Beaver Habitat

Relative impacts

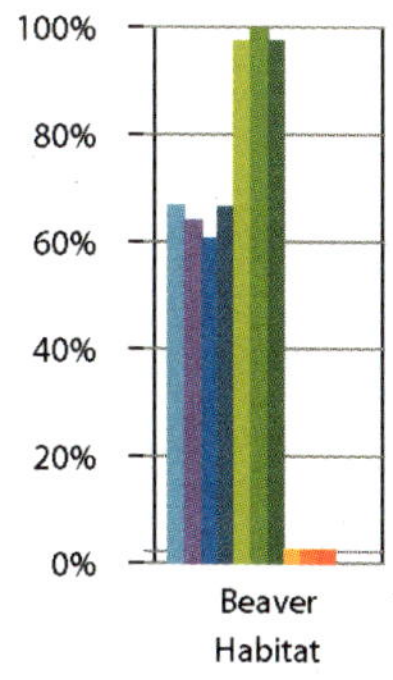
100%
80%
60%
40%
20%
0%
Beaver Habitat

Percent impacts

Pronghorn Potential Habitat

The pronghorn, *Antilocapra americana,* is the fastest animal in the Western Hemisphere, attaining speeds of 64 km per hour (40 mph). Unlike cheetahs and other sprint animals, the pronghorn has the ability to run for prolonged periods at a fast pace. Another characteristic found only in the pronghorn is horn shedding (Burt and Grossenheider 1980).

Slender in appearance, the pronghorn has a body shape similar to deer. Its weight ranges between 33.7 and 58.5 kg (75 to 130 lb), with a height of 1 m (3 ft). Its fur is pale tan with a white underbelly. Males have a black patch on the nose and on the back of the neck. Horns may reach a length of 50 cm (20 in.) (Burt and Grossenheider 1980).

Traditionally inhabiting the plains or deserts, the pronghorn may be found individually or in small bands in summer and in larger herds in winter months. Open flat plains and deserts are well suited to animals that rely on speed and keen eyesight for survival. As winter begins, the herds form initially as harems defended by a dominant male. Herds and individuals range over large areas of land. Home range size varies from 938 to 3733 ha (2317 to 9220 ac), averaging 2259 ha (5579 ac) (Clemente et al. 1995).

The pronghorn is a browser and eats a variety of plants. Shrubs, forbs, and grasses may be grazed based on their abundance in an area. Pronghorn are known to selectively feed on the plant species that provide the most nourishment in a given season. In times of drought, often they seek out areas close to riparian vegetation (USFWS 1998).

Surface water is not necessary for survival of pronghorn. Succulent vegetation can meet their daily requirement for water. Potential habitat is not affected by distance to water (Monson 1968).

The pronghorn inhabits the western arid region from southern Canada to northern Mexico. Five subspecies are identified. Of these, three are listed as endangered by the USFWS. The subspecies inhabiting the western portion of the study area around Sonoita is the Sonoran pronghorn, *A. a. sonoriensis,* listed as endangered in 1967. Many recovery plans have been made to return the Sonoran pronghorn to its historic range. According to these plans, the Sonoran pronghorn was found from the Sonoita grasslands in Arizona westward to the southern tip of California, and as far south as Hermosillo, Mexico. The plans note that the edges of the historic range are approximate and that the pronghorn may have inhabited additional areas of similar habitat characteristics. Because

Photo 12.10 ■ Pronghorn

Photo 12.9 ■ Pronghorn habitat

of this uncertainty, potential pronghorn habitat is extended into the San Pedro River watershed (USFWS 1998).

Pronghorn are currently known to occur in the grassland areas surrounding Sonoita. Potential habitat is based on the abundance of large grassland areas (figure 12.9). The abundance of grass is measured as a function of the amount of grassland within a pronghorn's home range area. Primary habitat is defined as locations where 66 percent of the land cover is comprised of grassland (Wood 1989). Secondary habitat is defined as locations where 33 percent of the land cover is grassland.

In the recent past, grassland vegetation communities have been declining and are being replaced by an upland mesquite vegetation community. The alternative futures predict a continuation of this trend and a decline in potential pronghorn habitat (figure 12.10a–c and table 12.5). Most of the loss is from secondary habitat. Most areas with the densest grassland vegetation are outside the San Pedro River Basin.

The OPEN scenarios cause the greatest reduction in potential pronghorn habitat. Most of the loss may be attributed to the current trend of grasslands to revert into upland mesquite at lower elevations. A secondary cause of grassland decline and subsequent pronghorn habitat loss is the suppression of fire. Under the OPEN scenarios, no fire management plan is included. Without fire, grasslands eventually revert into desert scrub in bajadas regions. (Bajadas are gently sloping plains ranging in elevation from 1380 to 1680 m [4500 to 5500 ft] typically dominated by grasslands that emanate from the base of mountains.) There is little difference among the OPEN scenarios.

Within the PLANS and CONSTRAINED scenarios, potential pronghorn habitat loss is roughly the same. Fire management plans allow for controlled burns in the bajadas region of the study area, and grasslands are maintained. At lower elevations, the current trend of grassland conversion to upland mesquite continues, and pronghorn habitat declines. There is little variation among the PLANS and CONSTRAINED alternative futures.

Table 12.5 Pronghorn habitat: Impacts, 2000–2020

	change in habitat / ha
Baseline 2000	253,802
Plans	-22,546
Plans 1	-22,866
Plans 2	-22,827
Plans 3	-22,456
Constrained	-21,757
Constrained 1	-21,950
Constrained 2	-21,950
Open	-32,306
Open 1	-30,613
Open 2	-30,717

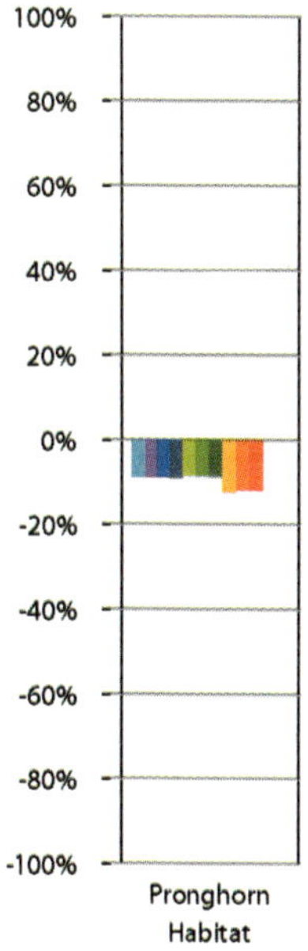
100%
80%
60%
40%
20%
0%
-20%
-40%
-60%
-80%
-100%
Pronghorn Habitat

Relative impacts

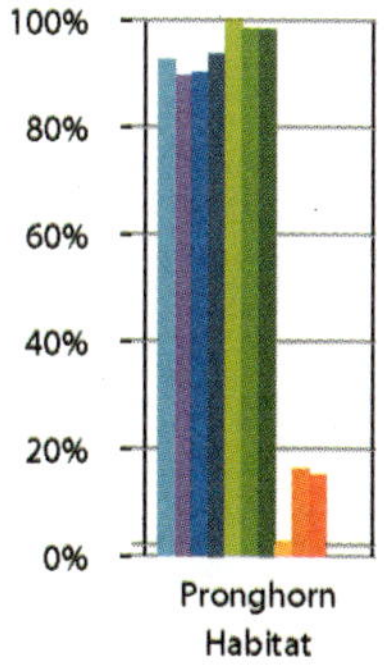
100%
80%
60%
40%
20%
0%
Pronghorn Habitat

Percent impacts

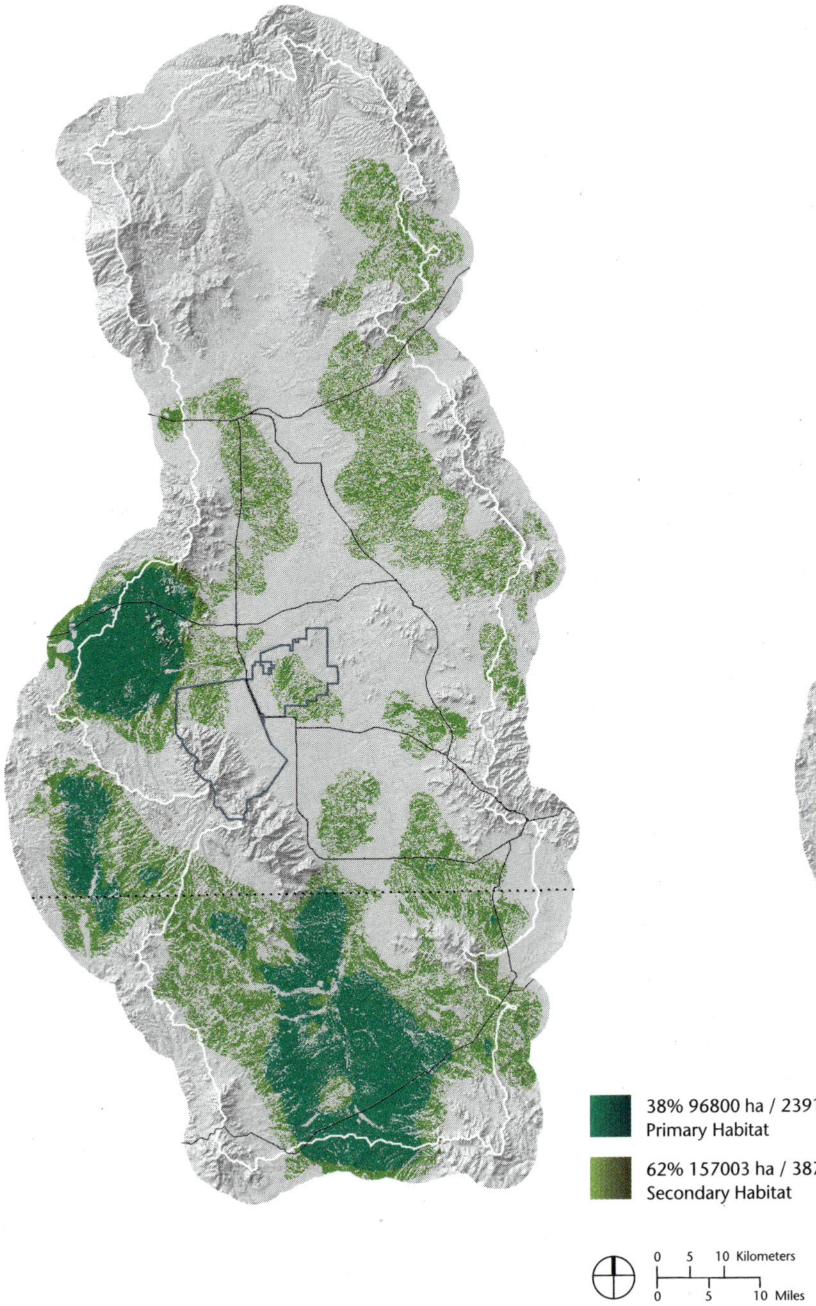
38% 96800 ha / 239193 ac
Primary Habitat
62% 157003 ha / 387954 ac
Secondary Habitat
0 5 10 Kilometers
0 5 10 Miles

Figure 12.9 ■ Pronghorn potential habitat, 2000

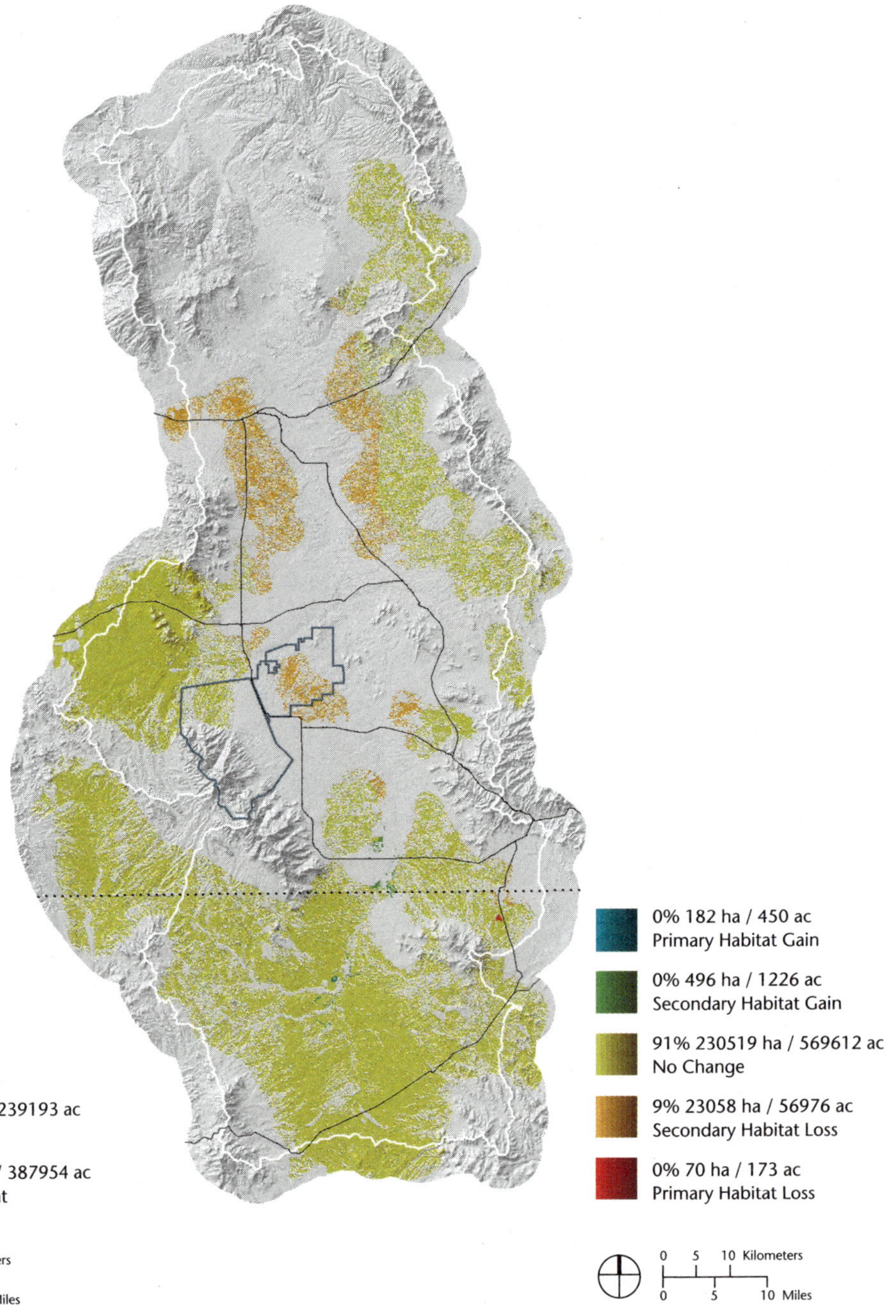
0% 182 ha / 450 ac
Primary Habitat Gain
0% 496 ha / 1226 ac
Secondary Habitat Gain
91% 230519 ha / 569612 ac
No Change
9% 23058 ha / 56976 ac
Secondary Habitat Loss
0% 70 ha / 173 ac
Primary Habitat Loss
0 5 10 Kilometers
0 5 10 Miles

Figure 12.10a ■ PLANS, Pronghorn habitat impacts, 2000–2020

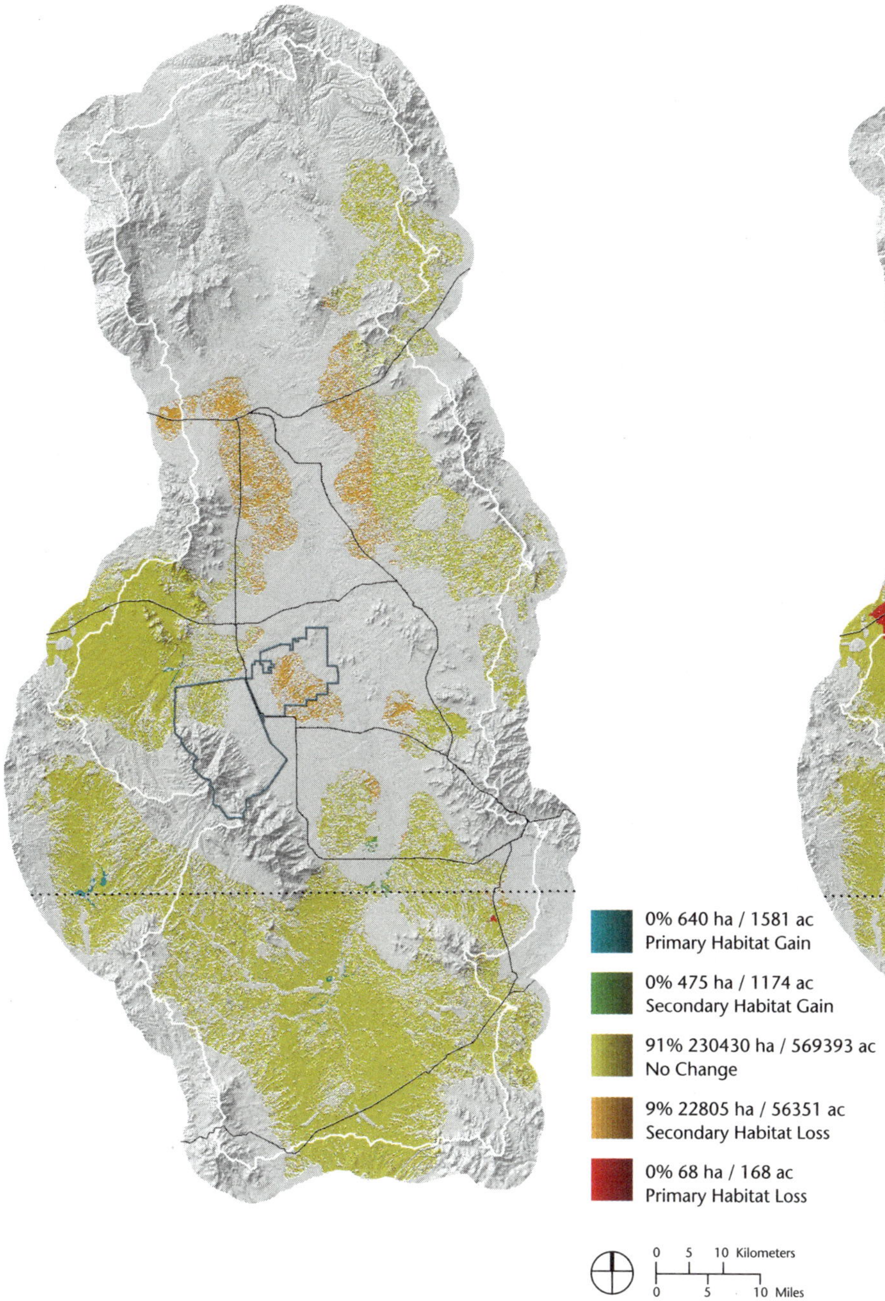
0% 640 ha / 1581 ac
Primary Habitat Gain
0% 475 ha / 1174 ac
Secondary Habitat Gain
91% 230430 ha / 569393 ac
No Change
9% 22805 ha / 56351 ac
Secondary Habitat Loss
0% 68 ha / 168 ac
Primary Habitat Loss
0 5 10 Kilometers
0 5 10 Miles

Figure 12.10b ■ CONSTRAINED, Pronghorn habitat impacts, 2000–2020

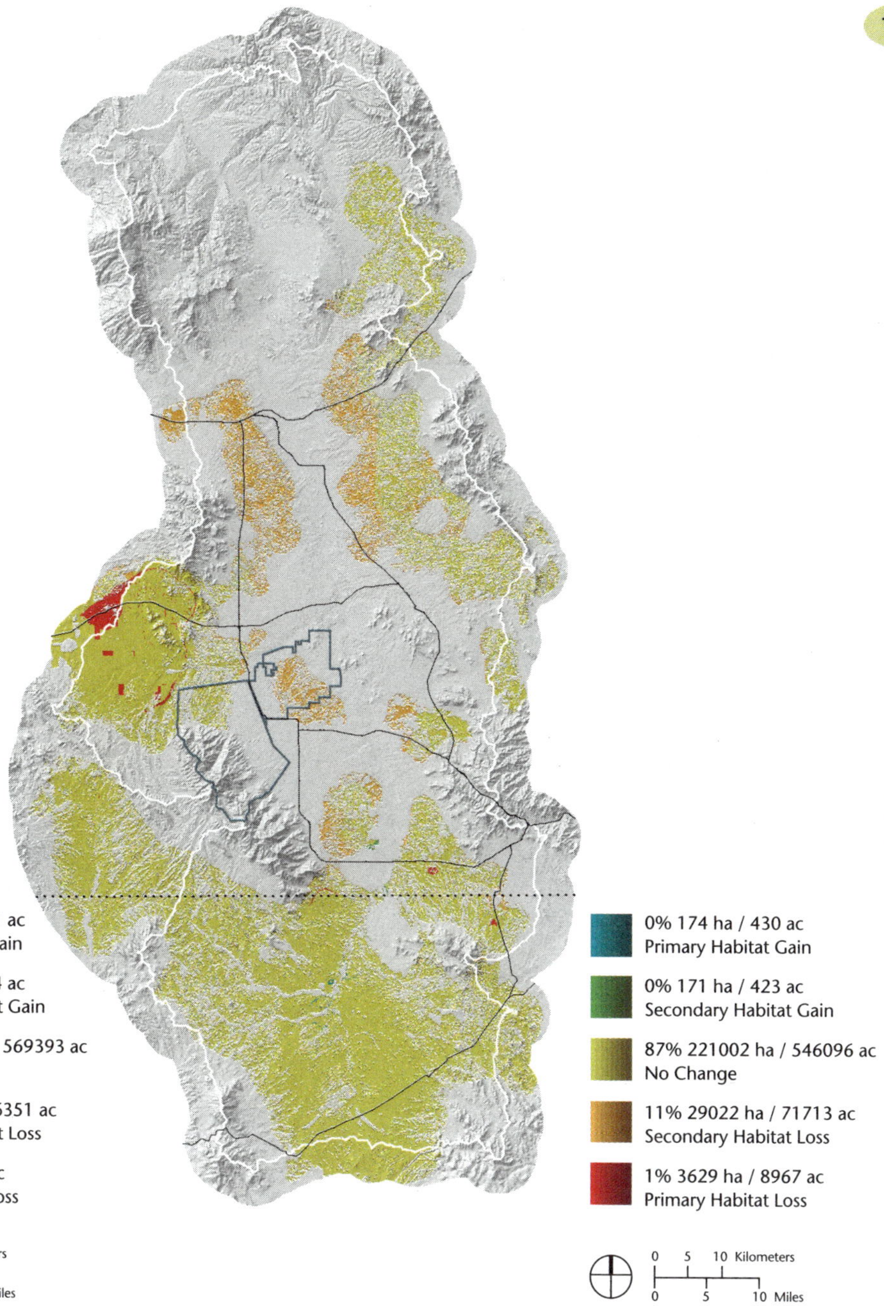
0% 174 ha / 430 ac
Primary Habitat Gain
0% 171 ha / 423 ac
Secondary Habitat Gain
87% 221002 ha / 546096 ac
No Change
11% 29022 ha / 71713 ac
Secondary Habitat Loss
1% 3629 ha / 8967 ac
Primary Habitat Loss
0 5 10 Kilometers
0 5 10 Miles

Figure 12.10c ■ OPEN, Pronghorn habitat impacts, 20002020

Jaguar Potential Habitat

The jaguar, *Panthera onca,* is the largest cat native to the Western Hemisphere, ranging in weight from 68 to 100 kg (150 to 225 lb). Its fur is cinnamon-buff in color with black spots over its entire body. Spots on the back and sides form a rosette pattern consisting of a black ring with a small black spot in the center. Its belly is white with black spots. Approximately 2 m (6.5 ft) in length, with a muscular build and short strong limbs, the jaguar is a formidable predator (Burt and Grossenheider 1980).

Jaguar habitat is diverse and varies with location. At the southern and northern edges of their range, they inhabit more arid areas that include oak-pine woodlands and riparian corridors. In arid locales they appear to prefer low mountain areas. Highly adaptable to a variety of vegetation communities, the jaguar's potential habitat appears to be related to their prey base (Oliveira 1994).

A large carnivore, the jaguar feeds on a variety of prey, which consists of peccaries and other large mammals, turtles, and fish. Livestock may be taken, creating a problem for ranchers. Along the U.S./Mexico border, javelina and deer are mainstays of their diet. As an ambush predator, the jaguar requires adequate cover. When hunting, its uniquely patterned fur provides excellent camouflage. The jaguar may stalk prey or hide and wait for the opportunity to pounce from an area of dense cover. The jaguar kills with a massive bite to the head, its large incisors penetrating the skull of its prey. Other large cats usually kill through strangulation of their prey. A jaguar kill is relatively easy to recognize (Arizona Game and Fish 1999; Taber et al 1997).

Territorial by nature, the jaguar is solitary except during times of breeding. Breeding can occur throughout the year with litter size ranging from one to four cubs. The cubs stay by the mother for two years, and maturity is reached in three to four years (Hoogesteign and Mondolfi 1992).

Jaguars must range over large areas. Their average home range

Photo 12.12 ■ Jaguar

Photo 12.13 ■ Jaguar habitat

is 54.3 sq km (21 sq mi) during the dry season. Dry season area requirements are used in the potential habitat model because of the arid conditions of the study region. Daily movements within this range vary in accordance with the abundance of prey species. Typical jaguar habitat, driven by the habitat requirements of prey species, consists of a mosaic of large trees consisting of conifers, oaks, or cottonwoods surrounded by or interwoven within relatively open areas. Forest areas serve as cover from which the jaguar may pounce and catch its prey, while open areas provide foraging areas where prey may be located. The jaguar will carry its prey up to 185 m (200 yd) to a tree for consumption (Hoogesteign and Mondolfi 1992; Crawshaw and Quigley 1991).

The large habitat area required by individual jaguars creates difficulties. Most potential habitat exists within the lower elevations of mountainous areas (figure 12.11). Elevations above 2000 m (6560 ft) are less favorable for habitation. A single montane area is not sufficient to guarantee the survival of the species. Adequate lowland corridors through which jaguars may move between mountain ranges in safety are essential. Free movement through large areas is required for breeding. With the presence of people in the lowlands, movement corridors are disrupted, and jaguars are seen as a threat. Ranchers know that jaguars take livestock and traditionally have shot jaguars on sight. A change of attitude toward the jaguar, especially in Mexico, must come if the species is to survive (Hoogesteign and Mondolfi 1992).

Although the jaguar was placed on the list of endangered species in August 1997, there is little or no sign of its presence in Arizona. It is believed that with proper care and a management strategy that allows large carnivores to move throughout the region, the jaguar may return. Regardless of the presence or absence of the jaguar, its apparent disappearance from the region emphasizes the need to consider mountain habitats and the associated movement corridors between them (Robinson 1999).

Potential jaguar habitat includes two parts, cover habitat and feeding habitat. All potential habitat is below 2000 m (6560 ft) in elevation. Cover habitat contains large trees to allow the jaguar to consume its prey in peace and sufficient density of vegetation to provide cover. Feeding habitat includes areas of open vegetation close to cover habitat. Feeding habitat must be within 185 m (202 yd.) of cover habitat. The combined area of feeding and cover habitat must exceed 54.3 sq km (21 sq mi) for a single individual to survive. Smaller areas are eliminated as potential habitat.

The various scenarios create a range of effects on jaguar potential habitat (figure 12.12a–c and table 12.6).

The PLANS scenarios cause small increases in potential jaguar habitat. Most of the expansion is due to localized increases in groundwater levels north of Saint David. Higher groundwater levels increase the extent of riparian vegetation along the San Pedro River and extend the potential jaguar habitat. Very little difference exists among the PLANS alternative futures.

The CONSTRAINED scenarios all create small increases in potential jaguar habitat, similar to those under PLANS scenarios. The only difference between PLANS and CONSTRAINED appears to be in amount. Again, rising groundwater levels increase the amount of riparian vegetation, resulting in more habitat. Habitat increases are most abundant north of Saint David. There is little difference among the CONSTRAINED alternative futures.

The greatest loss of potential jaguar habitat occurs under the OPEN scenarios, with minor differences among the variations. Under the OPEN alternative future, vegetation loss fragments cover habitat, eliminating much of the potential jaguar habitat. Cover habitat north of Saint David is lost because of losses of riparian vegetation. Decreasing groundwater levels cause riparian trees to die, resulting in the loss of cover habitat and adjacent feeding habitat.

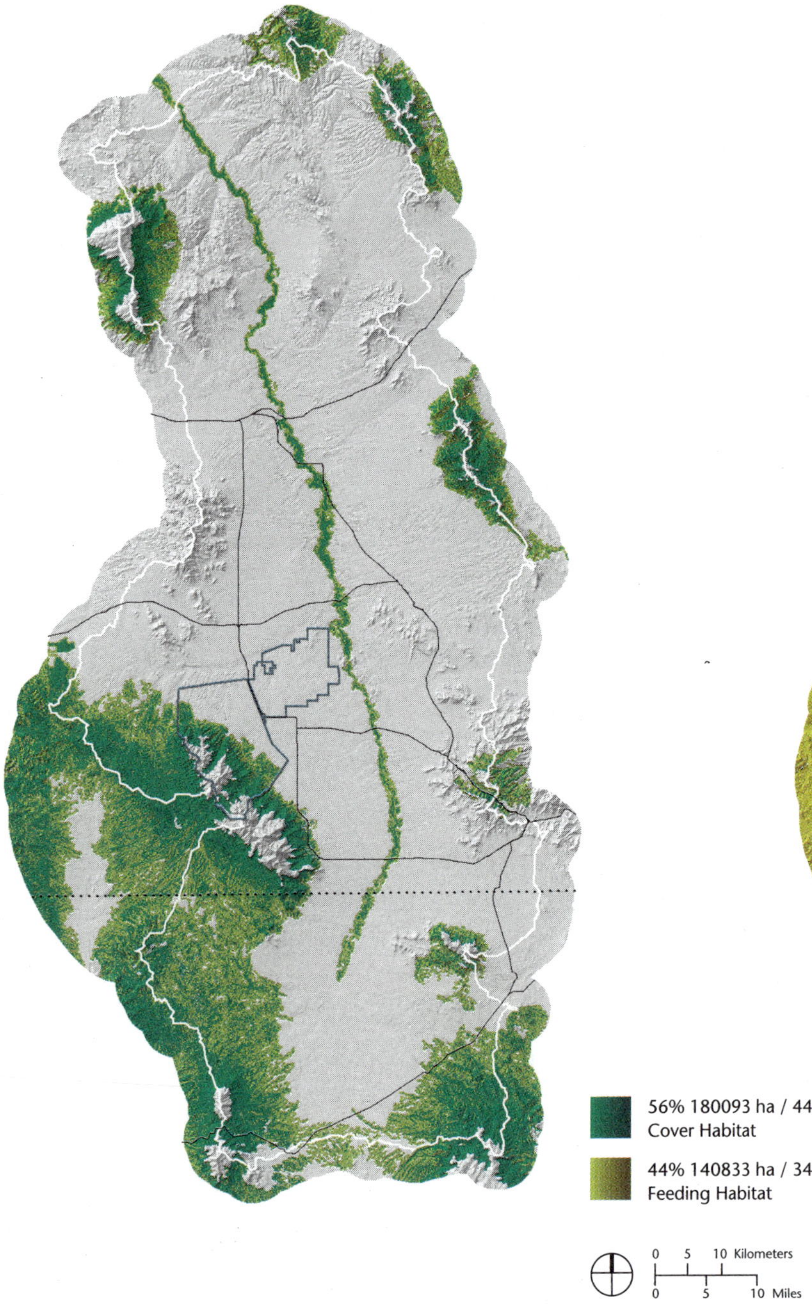
56% 180093 ha / 445010 ac
Cover Habitat
44% 140833 ha / 347998 ac
Feeding Habitat
0 5 10 Kilometers
0 5 10 Miles

Figure 12.11 ■ Jaguar potential habitat, 2000

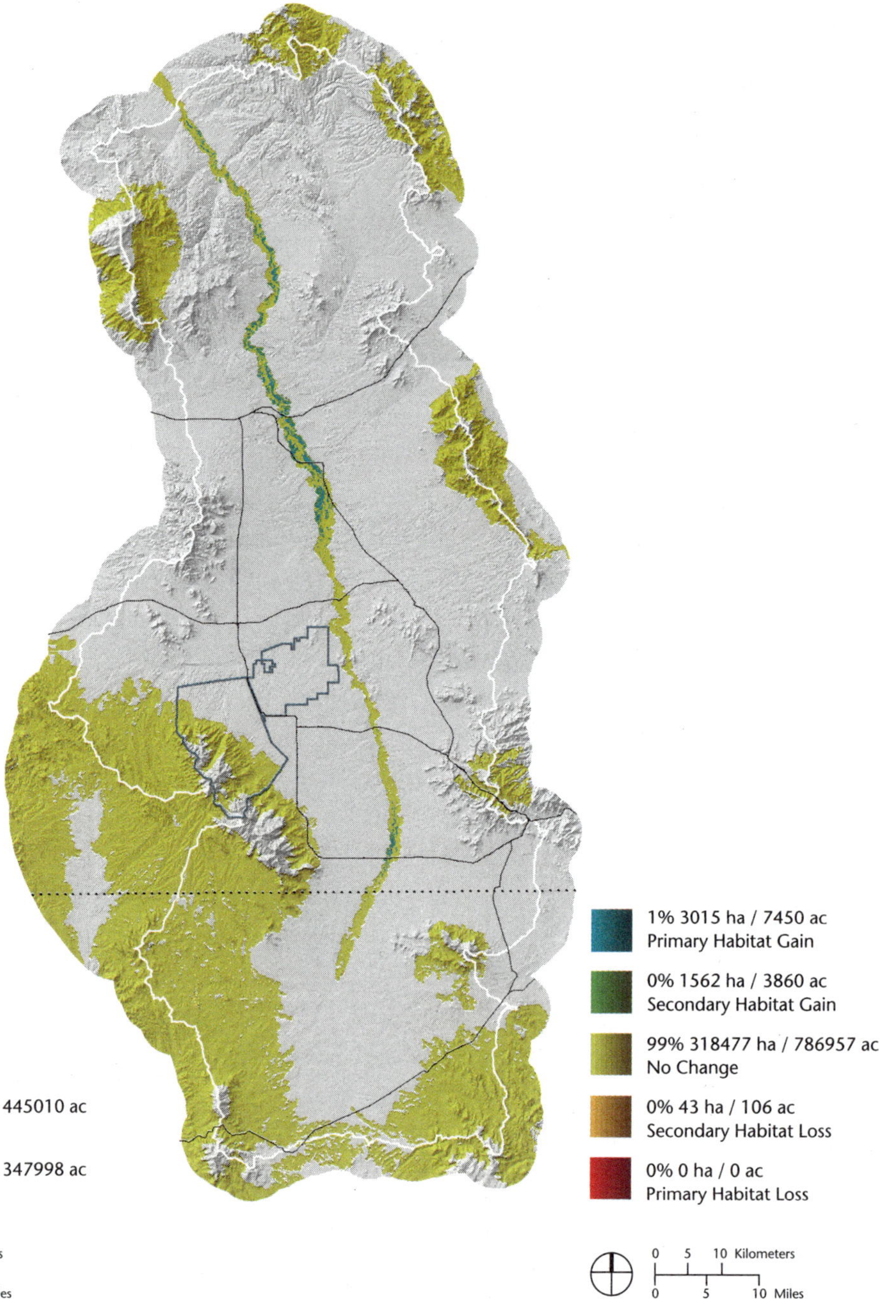
1% 3015 ha / 7450 ac
Primary Habitat Gain
0% 1562 ha / 3860 ac
Secondary Habitat Gain
99% 318477 ha / 786957 ac
No Change
0% 43 ha / 106 ac
Secondary Habitat Loss
0% 0 ha / 0 ac
Primary Habitat Loss
0 5 10 Kilometers
0 5 10 Miles

Figure 12.12a ■ PLANS,
Jaguar habitat impacts, 2000–2020

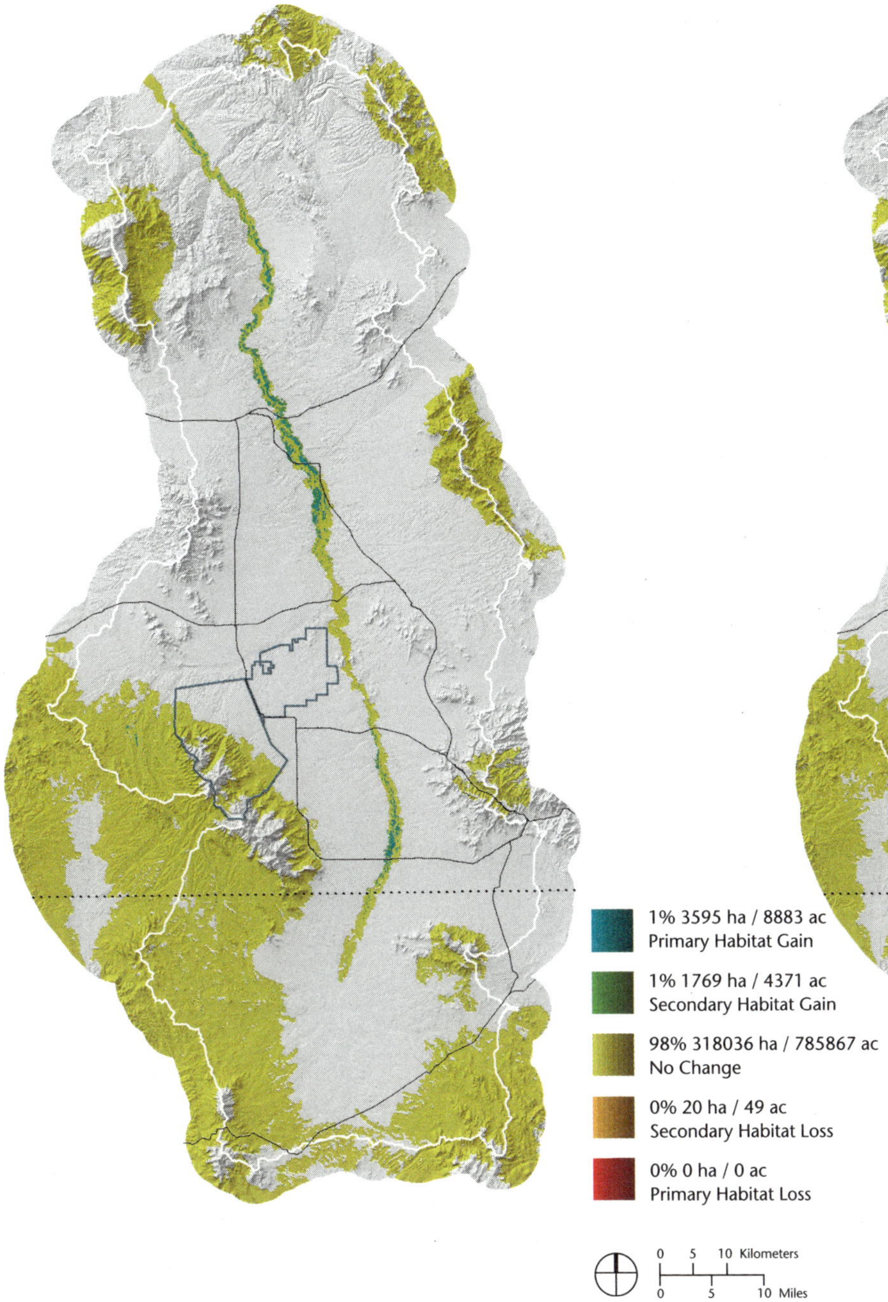
1% 3595 ha / 8883 ac
Primary Habitat Gain
1% 1769 ha / 4371 ac
Secondary Habitat Gain
98% 318036 ha / 785867 ac
No Change
0% 20 ha / 49 ac
Secondary Habitat Loss
0% 0 ha / 0 ac
Primary Habitat Loss
0 5 10 Kilometers
0 5 10 Miles

Figure 12.12b ■ CONSTRAINED, Jaguar habitat impacts, 2000–2020

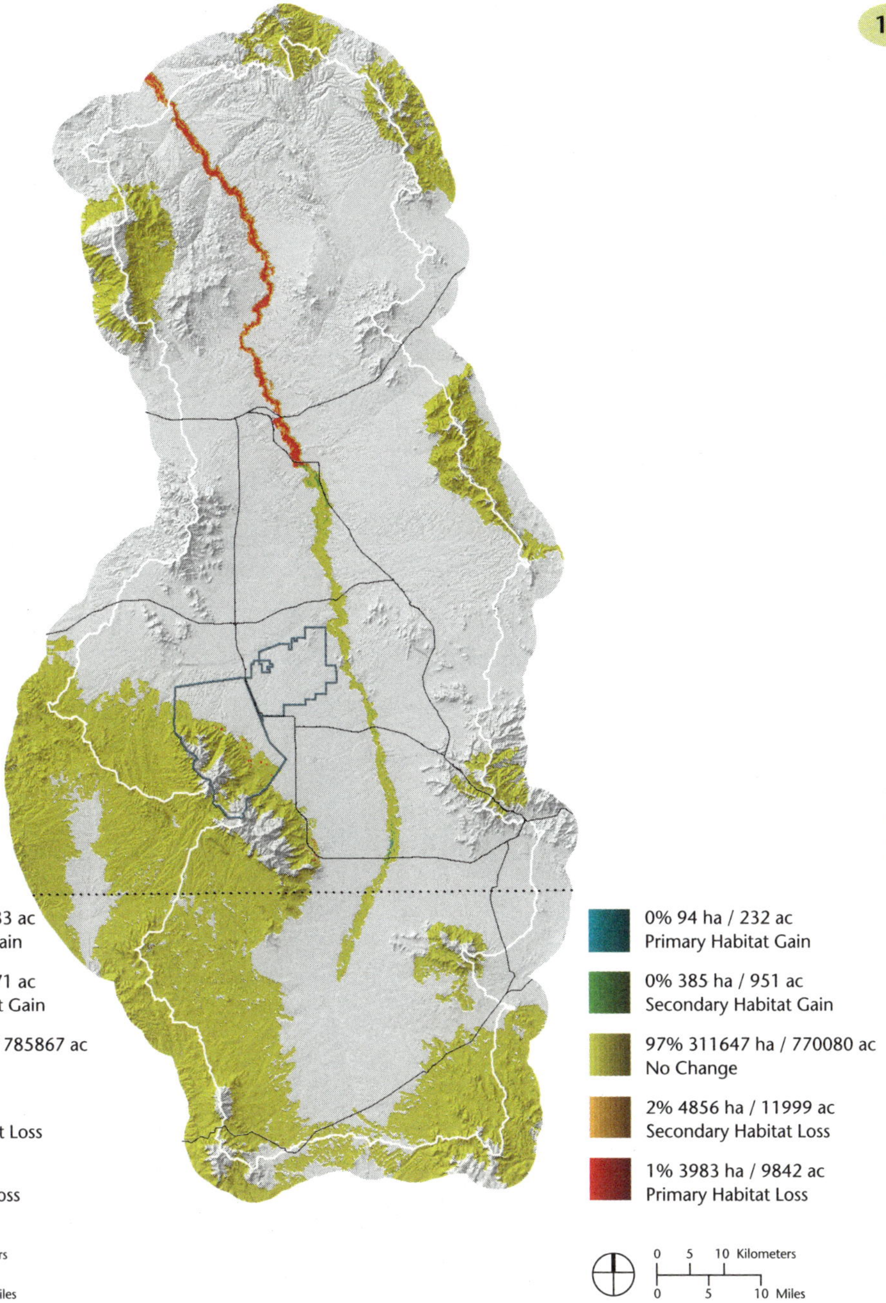
0% 94 ha / 232 ac
Primary Habitat Gain
0% 385 ha / 951 ac
Secondary Habitat Gain
97% 311647 ha / 770080 ac
No Change
2% 4856 ha / 11999 ac
Secondary Habitat Loss
1% 3983 ha / 9842 ac
Primary Habitat Loss
0 5 10 Kilometers
0 5 10 Miles

Figure 12.12c ■ OPEN, Jaguar habitat impacts, 2000–2020

Table 12.6 Jaguar habitat: Impacts, 2000–2020

	change in habitat / ha
Baseline 2000	320,926
Plans	4,534
Plans 1	4,225
Plans 2	3,946
Plans 3	4,629
Constrained	5,344
Constrained 1	5,282
Constrained 2	5,291
Open	-8,360
Open 1	-9.444
Open 2	-8,481

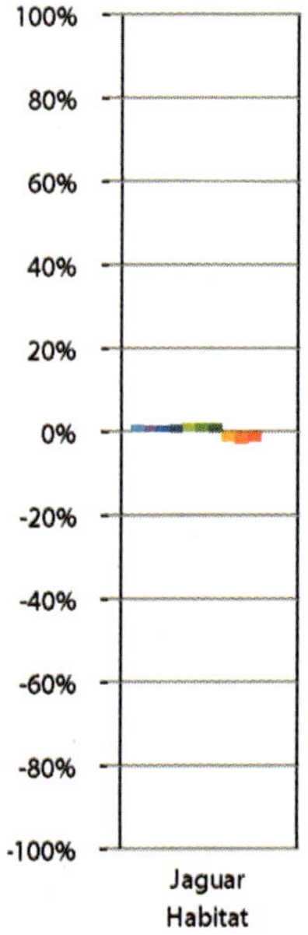
100%
80%
60%
40%
20%
0%
-20%
-40%
-60%
-80%
-100%
Jaguar Habitat

Relative impacts

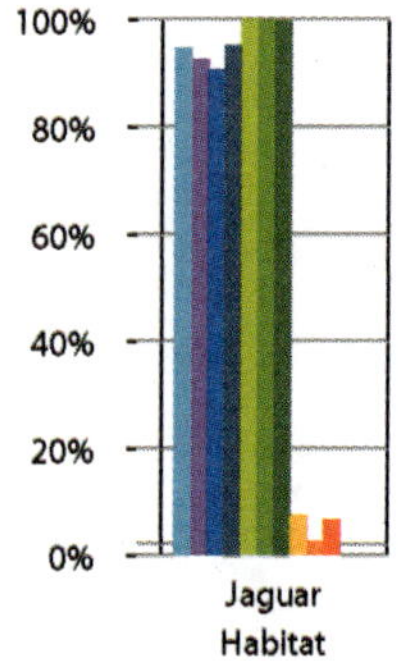
100%
80%
60%
40%
20%
0%
Jaguar Habitat

Percent impacts

CHAPTER 13

Threatened and Endangered Species Potential Habitat

The Endangered Species Act of 1973 protects species whose numbers have been so depleted that they are in danger of extinction. Although species may be classified as either threatened or endangered, the same protection is extended to both categories. Endangered status denotes a relatively higher level of threat of extinction than threatened status. Individuals may propose the listing of species, based on research. Once placed on the list, species are given all the protections defined in the Act.

Seven species found within the San Pedro River Basin are listed as threatened or endangered by the U.S. Fish and Wildlife Service (USFWS) (Arizona Department of Game and Fish 1998). Habitat requirements and locations vary by species. Most of the listed species inhabit areas similar to ciñegas, small areas of wetland conditions where the water table is high enough for the ground to remain damp or slightly submerged throughout the year. The seven species and their dominant habitat association are listed in table 13.1.

Of the seven, the lesser long-nosed bat is not considered in this study because of difficulties in modeling its habitat. Agave is essential to its survival. Agave plants are widely scattered in arid environments. Identifying agaves in a grassland, oak, desert scrub, or other vegetative communities is nearly impossible using satel-

Photo 13.1 ■ San Pedro riparian corridor

Table 13.1 Threatened and endangered species

Common Name	Scientific Name	Dominant Habitat
Sonoran tiger salamander	*Ambystoma tigrinum stebbinsi*	Ponds, Cienegas
Desert pupfish	*Cyprinodon macularius macularius*	Small water bodies, *Cienegas*
Southwestern willow flycatcher	*Empidonax traillii extimus*	Riparian
Lesser long-nosed bat	*Leptonycteris curasoae yerbabuenae*	Caves, Agave
Huachuca water umbel	*Lilaeopsis schaffneriana var recurva*	Cienegas
Madrean ladies'-tresses	*Spiranthes delitescens*	Cienegas
Mexican spotted owl	*Strix occidentalis lucida*	Forest

Table 13.2 Threatened and endangered species habitat: Impacts, 2000–2020

	change in primary and seconday habitat / ha
Baseline 2000	136,329
Plans	1,175
Plans 1	1,045
Plans 2	993
Plans 3	1,210
Constrained	1,464
Constrained 1	1,453
Constrained 2	1,460
Open	-3,185
Open 1	-3,334
Open 2	-3,281

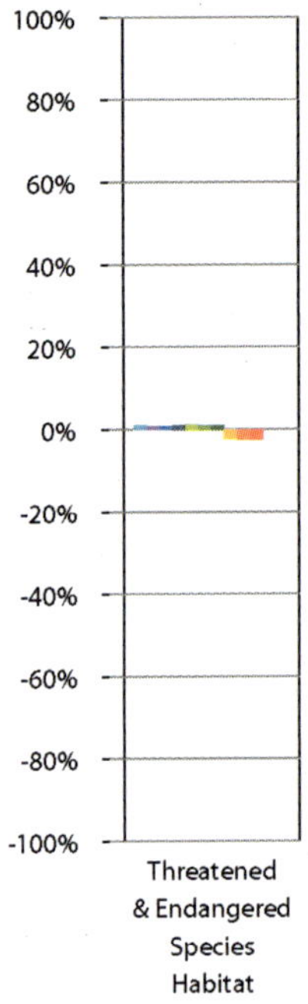
100%
80%
60%
40%
20%
0%
-20%
-40%
-60%
-80%
-100%
Threatened & Endangered Species Habitat

Relative impacts

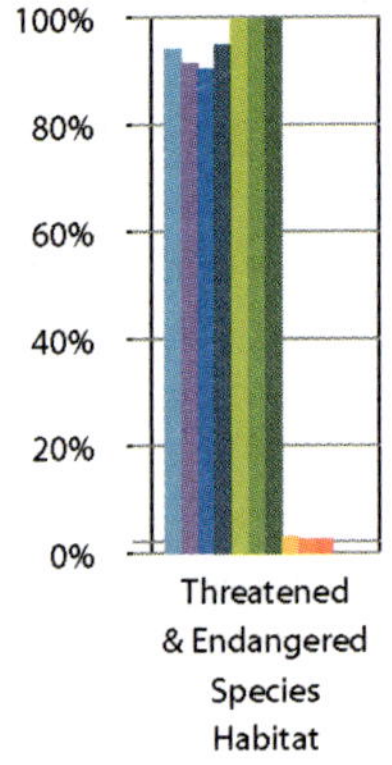
100%
80%
60%
40%
20%
0%
Threatened & Endangered Species Habitat

Percent impacts

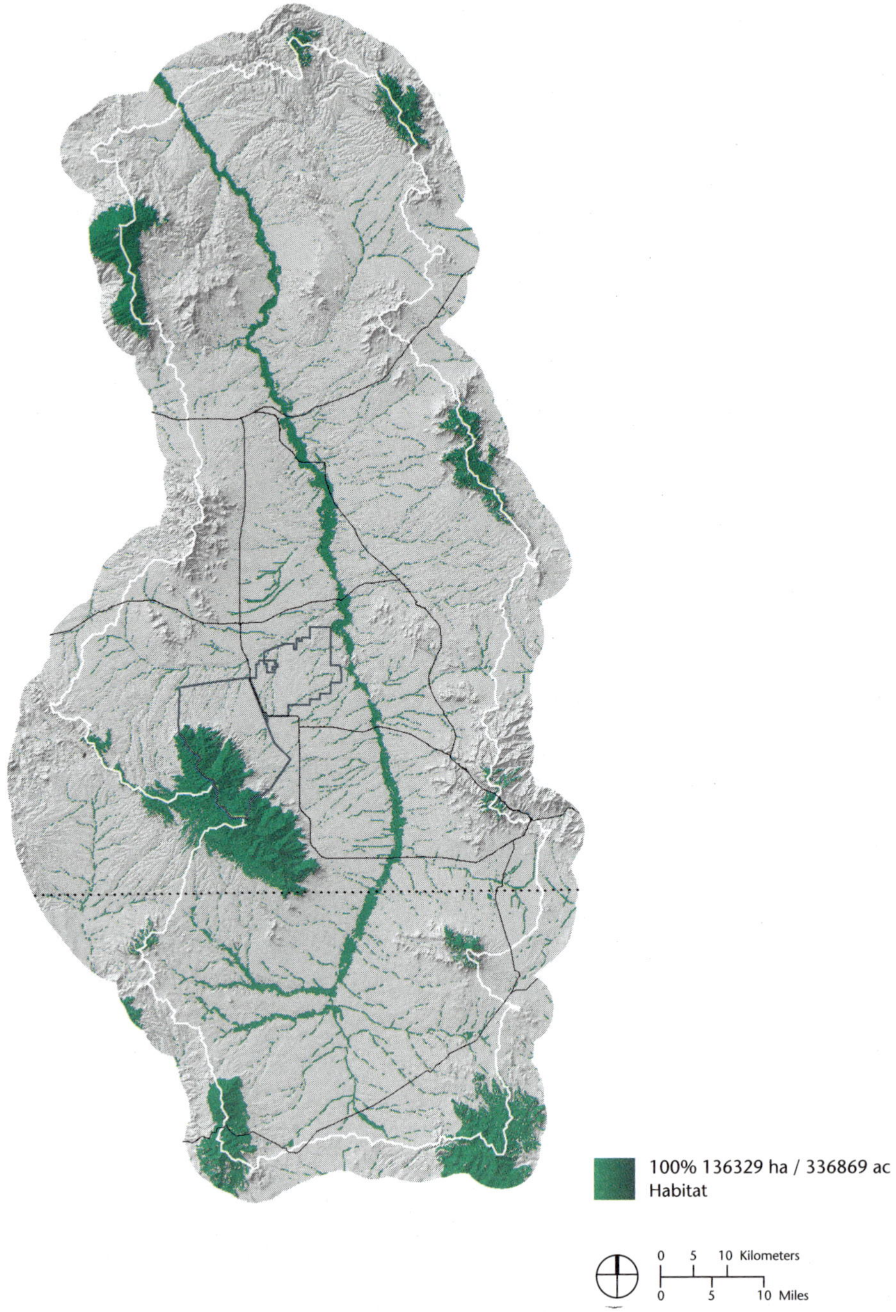
100% 136329 ha / 336869 ac
Habitat
0 5 10 Kilometers
0 5 10 Miles

Figure 13.1 ■ Threatened and endangered species potential habitat, 2000

lite-based sensors. Similarly, caves can only be located by ground surveys (USFWS 1997b).

The remaining six threatened and endangered species found in the Upper San Pedro River Basin are considered. The Sonoran tiger salamander is found along watercourses in the Huachuca Mountains and, like most salamanders, requires standing water (USFWS 1997a.). The desert pupfish occurs in shallow water of springs, streams, and marshes below 1525 m (5000 ft) (USFWS 2000). Southwestern willow flycatchers inhabit riparian areas with a dense understory of vegetation (Peterson 1990). Huachuca water umbels prefer ciñega habitats within the elevation ranges of 1067 to 1980 m (3500 to 6500 ft) (USFWS 1999). Canelo Hills ladies' tresses occupy bright areas within ciñegas (Sheviak 1990). The Mexican spotted owl lives in forested areas above 1677 m (5500 ft) and is the only species listed as threatened in the study area (Karalus and Eckert 1974).

Threatened and endangered species' potential habitat is identified in three parts and subsequently aggregated into a single measure (figure 13.1). First, potential habitat for the southwestern willow flycatcher is transformed into a single value map by combining primary and secondary habitat. Next, Mexican spotted owl habitat is defined as forested areas above 1677 m (5500 ft), and located. Last, potential and existing flat ciñega or pond-forming areas are identified along the major watercourses and arroyos. These areas represent potential habitat for the remaining four species. The three potential habitat types are aggregated to identify potential habitat for threatened and endangered species.

Mapping these species reveals the rarity of their potential habitats. Through conservation, further decline and eventual extinction may be avoided. Before addressing the impacts of the alternative futures on potential habitat for threatened and endangered species, it should be noted that under all the scenarios, the policy is to protect endangered species habitat. This means that little change should be anticipated.

Under the PLANS and CONSTRAINED scenarios, there are small gains of potential habitat in the northern part of the San Pedro River corridor (figure 13.2a–c and table 13.2). Gains are a consequence of increased groundwater levels causing riparian vegetation to flourish. Small losses do occur throughout the basin caused by housing development. There is little difference among the PLANS and CONSTRAINED alternative futures.

The OPEN alternative futures anticipate a loss of habitat from the Saint David area northward to just beyond Interstate Highway 10. Most of the loss is a consequence of a drop in groundwater level affecting riparian habitats along the San Pedro River. There are other small losses throughout the basin caused by housing development eliminating potential ciñega or pond-forming locations. There is little difference among the OPEN alternative futures.

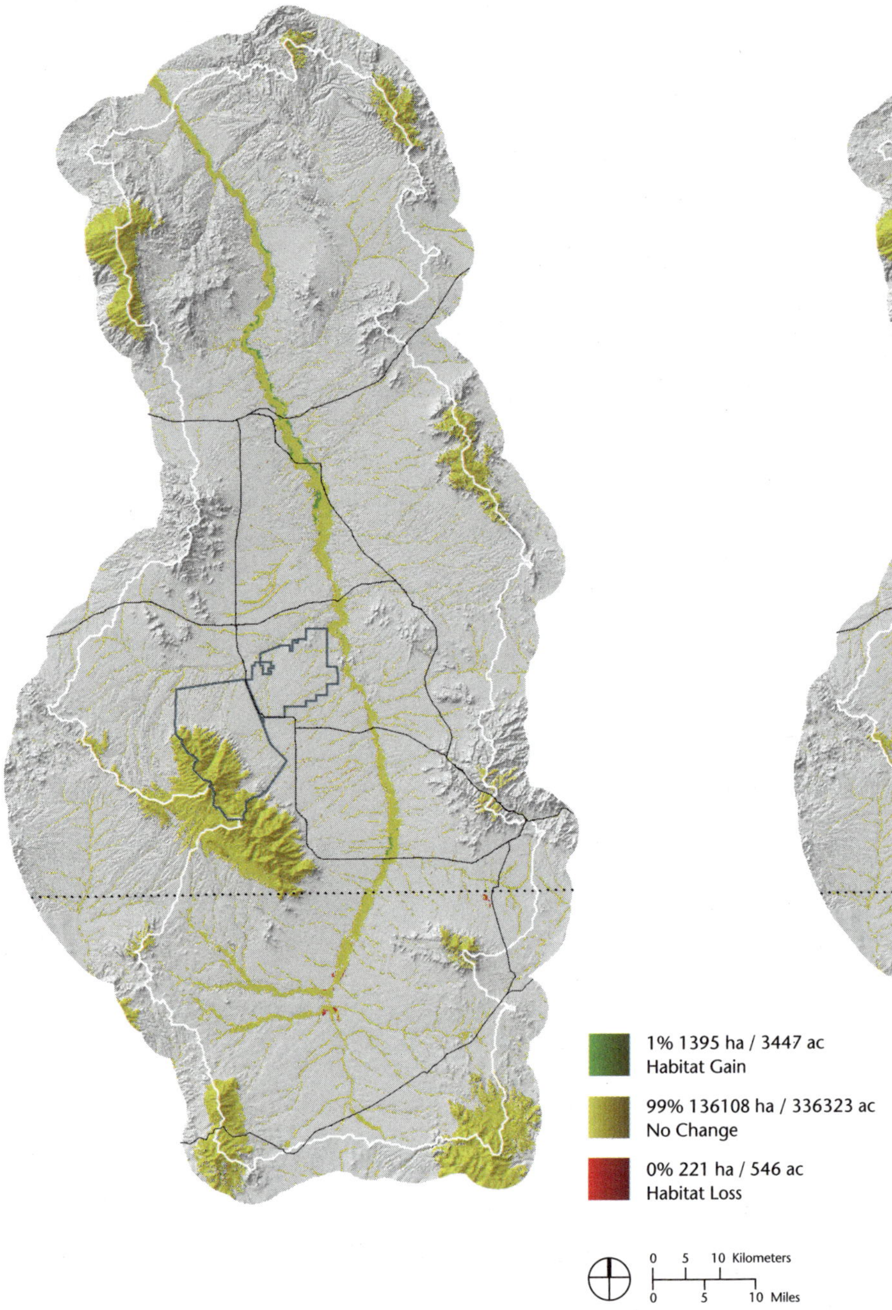
1% 1395 ha / 3447 ac
Habitat Gain
99% 136108 ha / 336323 ac
No Change
0% 221 ha / 546 ac
Habitat Loss
0 5 10 Kilometers
0 5 10 Miles

Figure 13.2a ■ PLANS,
Threatened and endangered species habitat impacts, 2000–2020

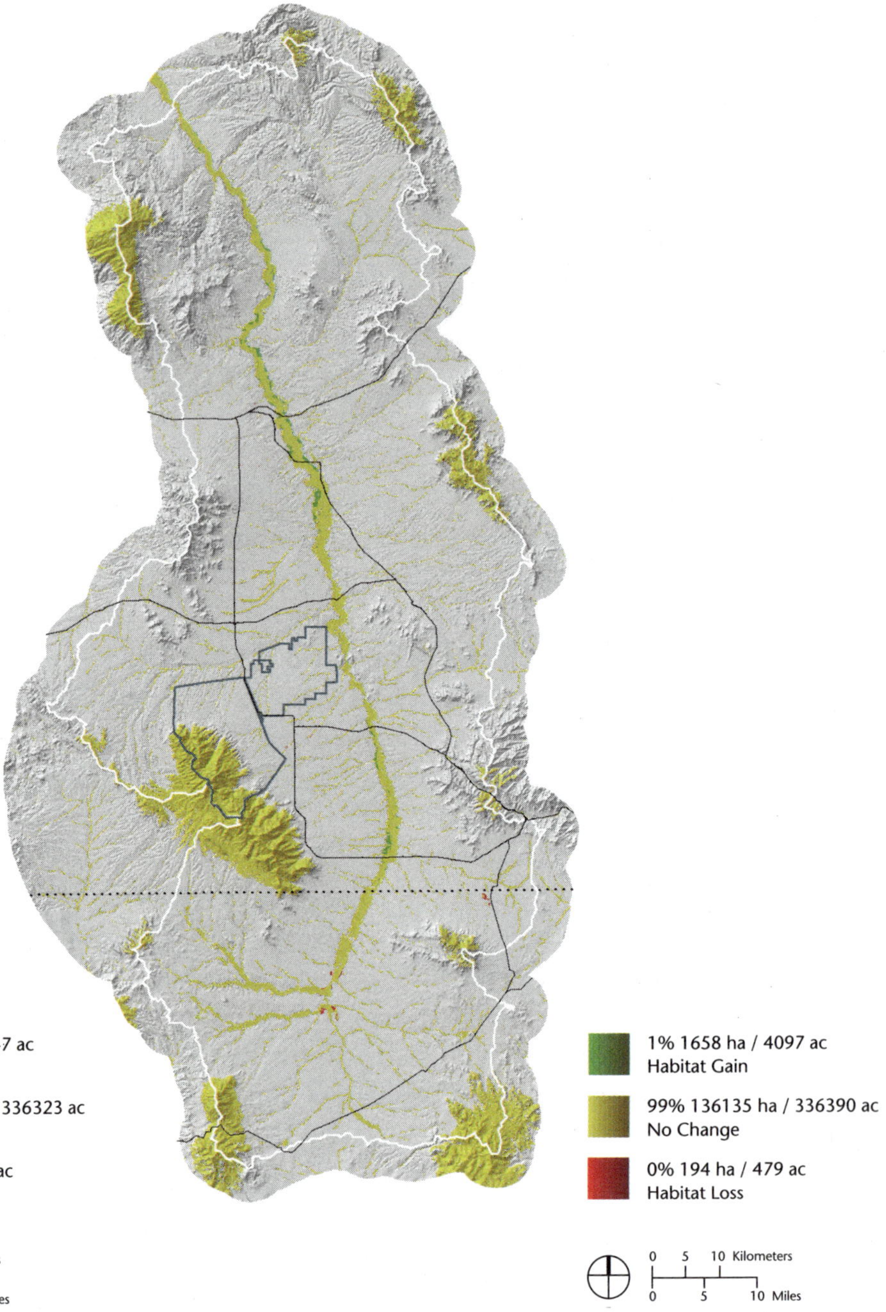
1% 1658 ha / 4097 ac
Habitat Gain
99% 136135 ha / 336390 ac
No Change
0% 194 ha / 479 ac
Habitat Loss
0 5 10 Kilometers
0 5 10 Miles

Figure 13.2b ■ OPEN,
Threatened and endangered species habitat impacts, 2000–2020

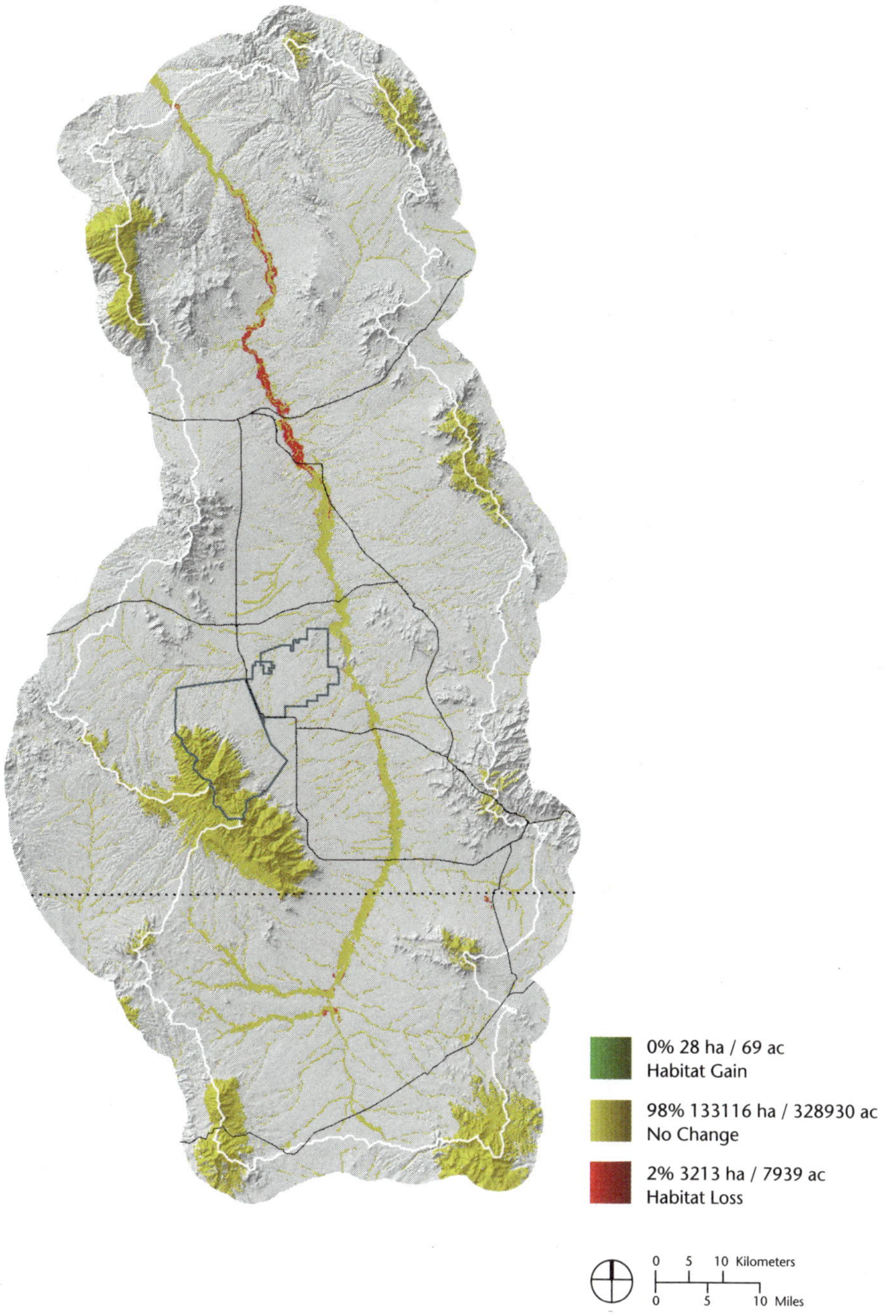
0% 28 ha / 69 ac
Habitat Gain
98% 133116 ha / 328930 ac
No Change
2% 3213 ha / 7939 ac
Habitat Loss
0 5 10 Kilometers
0 5 10 Miles

Figure 13.2c ■ CONSTRAINED,
Threatened and endangered species habitat impacts, 2000–2020

CHAPTER 14

The Vertebrate Species Richness and GAP Species Models

Species richness is a concept used to assess biodiversity. It relies on the distribution of all resident terrestrial vertebrates (amphibians, reptiles, birds, and mammals). A conservation strategy based solely on species richness would protect much of the biodiversity of a region, but would not necessarily protect every species.

Terrestrial Vertebrate Species Richness

The terrestrial vertebrate species richness model uses a large number of species to give an indication of levels of diversity and the impacts of future change, even though the information on some species may be limited. The model assumes that although information is limited, the overall trend in species richness can be predicted and that minor errors caused by lack of information may be overcome through use of a large number of species.

Using vegetation, land cover, and topographic information, a Wildlife Habitat Relations (WHR) model identifies areas in which a given species can potentially live. The Arizona vegetation classification for species modeling, obtained from the Arizona GAP Analysis Program, provides the basis for species distributions (Bennett et al., unpublished). This vegetation classification describes plant communities by location and composition (Brown et al. 1979). The level of detail of the vegetation classification system exceeded that of the mapped land cover/land use in this

Photo 14.1 ■ Mixed landscape of oak woodland and grassland

Photo 14.2 ■ Riparian habitat

Photo 14.3 ■ Coniferous woodland with meadow

study. However, the Arizona vegetation classification uses 100 ha (247 ac) as the minimum spatial mapping unit. This is much larger than the .09 ha (.22 ac) minimum mapping unit used in this study. The number of vegetation classes located in the study region and present in the Arizona GAP vegetation map was fewer than in the land use/land cover map created for this study.

The species-specific WHR models for the study area were taken from the Arizona WHR GAP Analysis models (Kunzmann n.d.). In the study area, a total of 389 terrestrial vertebrate species, including 215 birds, 90 mammals, 67 reptiles, and 17 amphibians, were identified using the existing GAP distributions. Because work on the GAP program was not yet complete, additional information was taken from Peterson *Field Guides* (Peterson 1990; Stebbins 1985; Burt and Grossenheider 1980).

Each species' potential habitat is identified and located. Potential habitat is identified using four components: land cover, water, land form, and area. The land cover inhabited by each species was extracted from the Arizona GAP WHR vegetation classification and adapted to the land use/land cover map categories. Distance to water is an important habitat factor for a variety of species in arid regions. The required distances are determined on a species by species basis. In some instances, proximity to mountains or hills is required to identify a species habitat. Slope was used to locate mountain and hill land forms. Finally, area requirements for each species were determined. Any patch of potential habitat too small to comprise a single home range was eliminated species by species. Home range sizes were determined using equations that calculated the area required by each species based on its weight (Belovsky and Slade 1979; Bassett 2001).

The vertebrate species richness model overlays the distributions of all 389 species and creates a spatially explicit depiction of terrestrial vertebrate species richness (figure 14.1). The highest richness value in the study area is 235 species. The areas of higher value are found in the San Pedro riparian corridor and along the

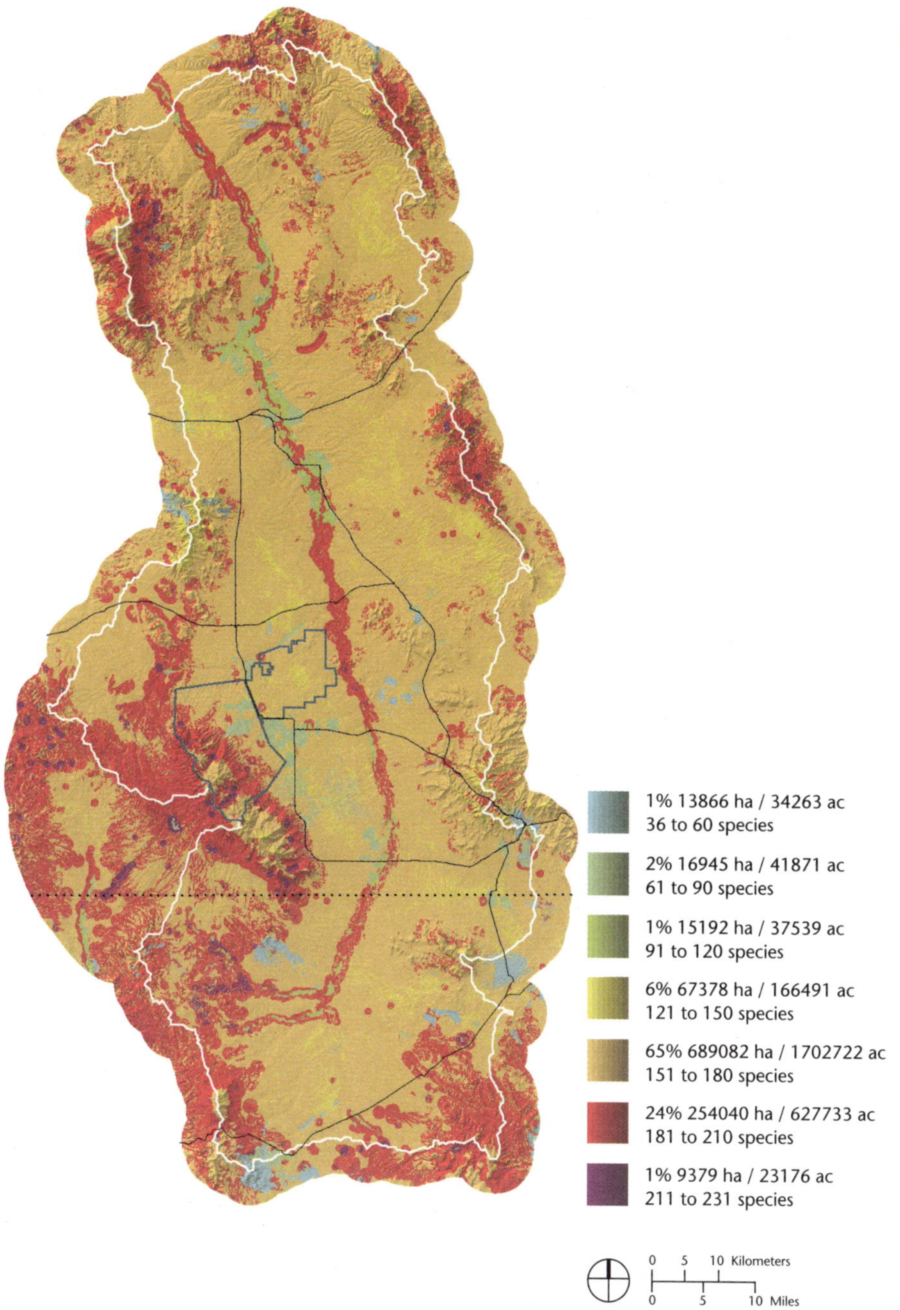
1% 13866 ha / 34263 ac
36 to 60 species
2% 16945 ha / 41871 ac
61 to 90 species
1% 15192 ha / 37539 ac
91 to 120 species
6% 67378 ha / 166491 ac
121 to 150 species
65% 689082 ha / 1702722 ac
151 to 180 species
24% 254040 ha / 627733 ac
181 to 210 species
1% 9379 ha / 23176 ac
211 to 231 species
0 5 10 Kilometers
0 5 10 Miles

Figure 14.1 ■ Vertebrate species richness, 2000

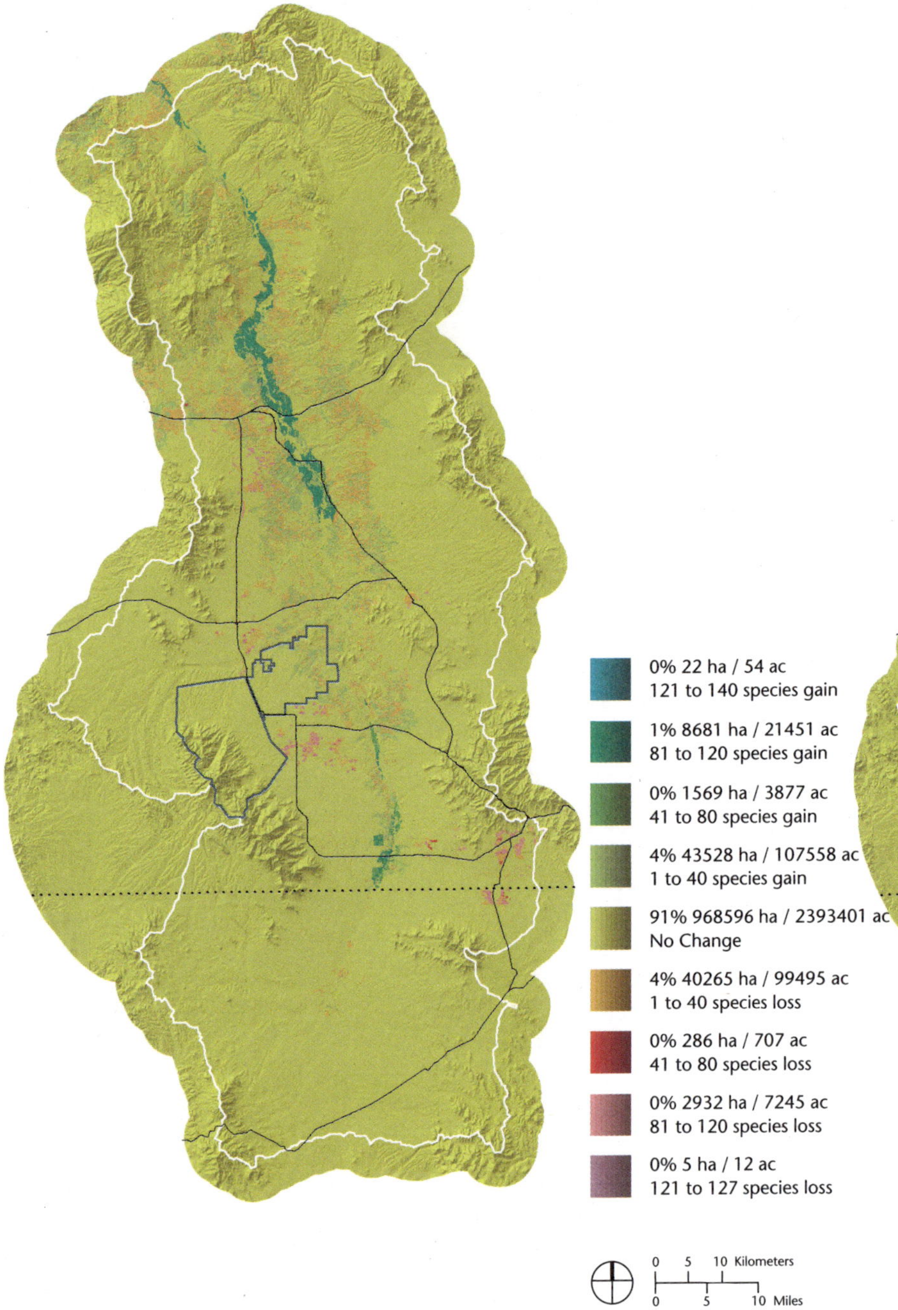
0% 22 ha / 54 ac
121 to 140 species gain
1% 8681 ha / 21451 ac
81 to 120 species gain
0% 1569 ha / 3877 ac
41 to 80 species gain
4% 43528 ha / 107558 ac
1 to 40 species gain
91% 968596 ha / 2393401 ac
No Change
4% 40265 ha / 99495 ac
1 to 40 species loss
0% 286 ha / 707 ac
41 to 80 species loss
0% 2932 ha / 7245 ac
81 to 120 species loss
0% 5 ha / 12 ac
121 to 127 species loss
0 5 10 Kilometers
0 5 10 Miles

Figure 14.2a ■ PLANS,
Vertebrate species richness impacts, 2000–2020

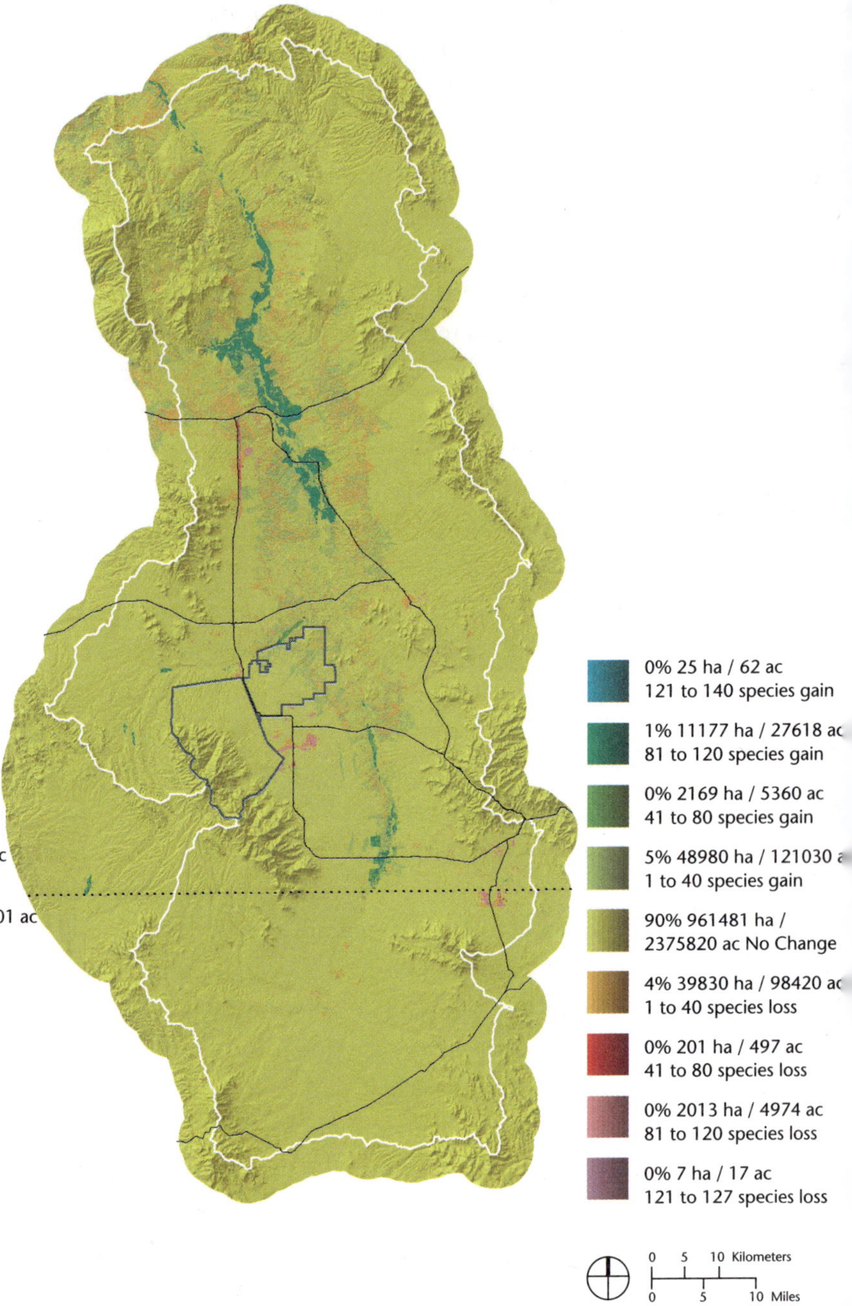
0% 25 ha / 62 ac
121 to 140 species gain
1% 11177 ha / 27618 ac
81 to 120 species gain
0% 2169 ha / 5360 ac
41 to 80 species gain
5% 48980 ha / 121030
1 to 40 species gain
90% 961481 ha /
2375820 ac No Change
4% 39830 ha / 98420 ac
1 to 40 species loss
0% 201 ha / 497 ac
41 to 80 species loss
0% 2013 ha / 4974 ac
81 to 120 species loss
0% 7 ha / 17 ac
121 to 127 species loss
0 5 10 Kilometers
0 5 10 Miles

Figure 14.2b ■ CONSTRAINED,
Vertebrate species richness impacts, 2000–2020

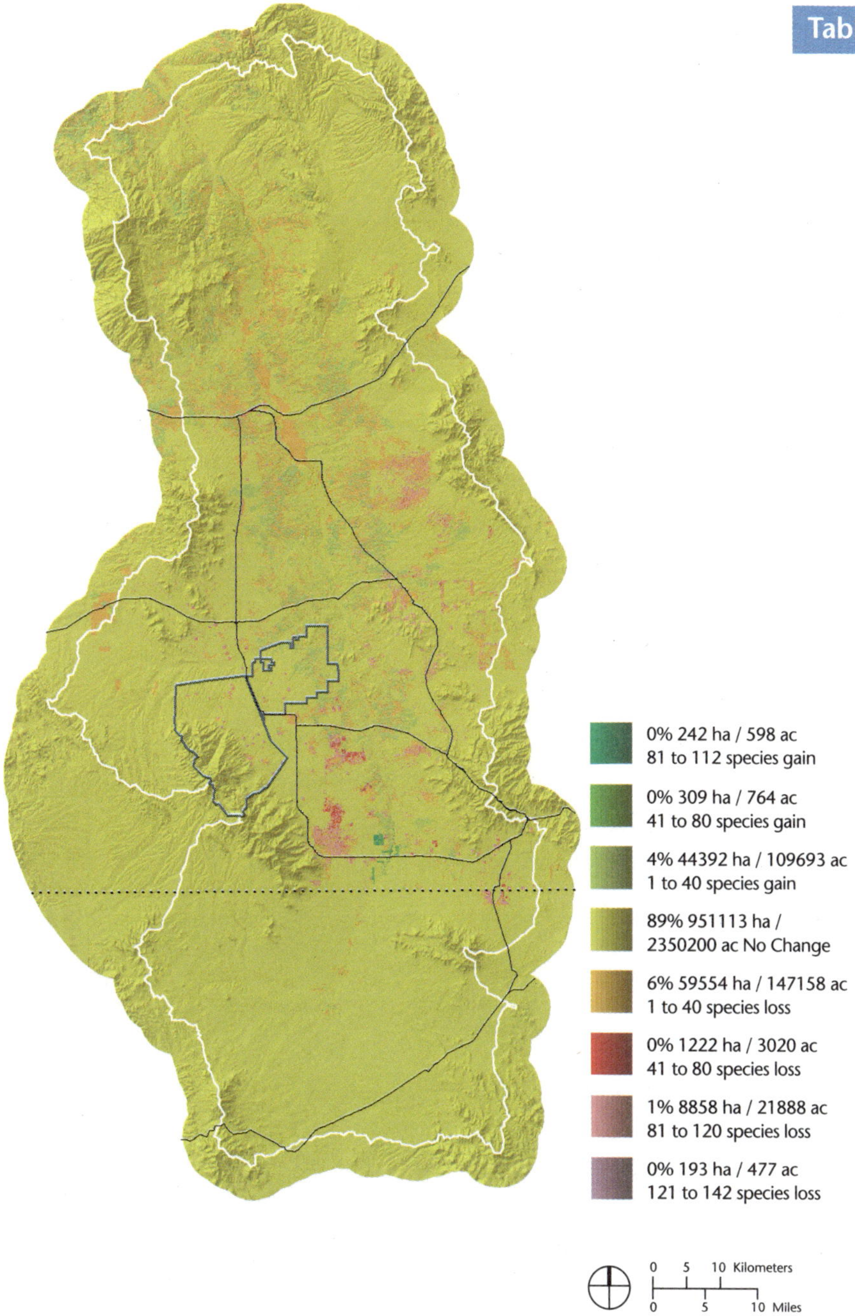
0% 242 ha / 598 ac
81 to 112 species gain
0% 309 ha / 764 ac
41 to 80 species gain
4% 44392 ha / 109693 ac
1 to 40 species gain
89% 951113 ha /
2350200 ac No Change
6% 59554 ha / 147158 ac
1 to 40 species loss
0% 1222 ha / 3020 ac
41 to 80 species loss
1% 8858 ha / 21888 ac
81 to 120 species loss
0% 193 ha / 477 ac
121 to 142 species loss
0 5 10 Kilometers
0 5 10 Miles

Figure 14.2c ■ OPEN,
Vertebrate species richness impacts, 2000–2020

Table 14.1 Vertebrate species: Impacts, 2000–2020

	change in average number of vertebrate species app. per cell
Baseline 2000	167.69 avg
Plans	0.56
Plans 1	0.37
Plans 2	0.51
Plans 3	0.61
Constrained	0.93
Constrained 1	0.90
Constrained 2	0.90
Open	-1.04
Open 1	-1.15
Open 2	-0.94

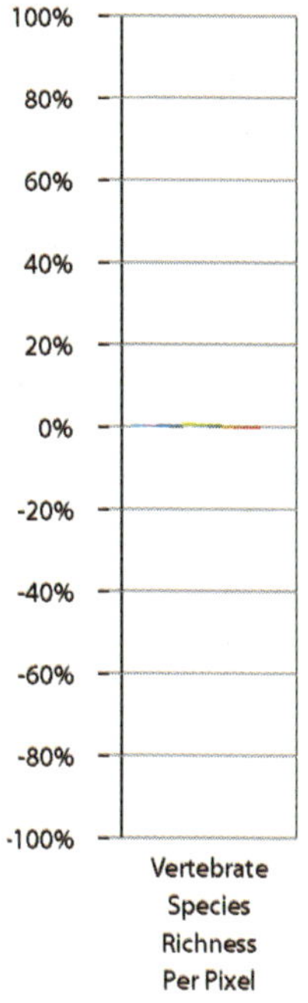
100%
80%
60%
40%
20%
0%
-20%
-40%
-60%
-80%
-100%
Vertebrate Species Richness Per Pixel

Relative impacts

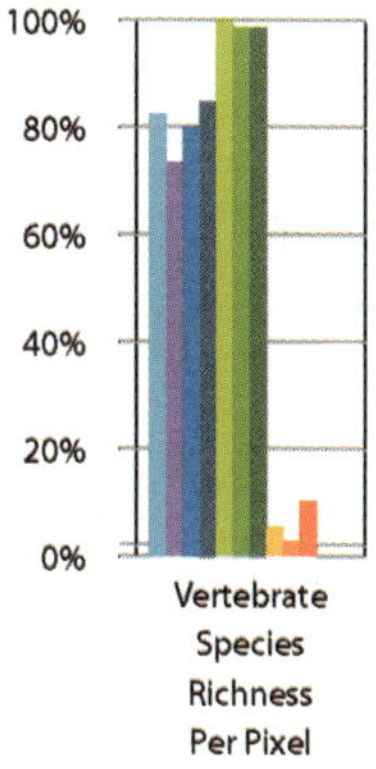
100%
80%
60%
40%
20%
0%
Vertebrate Species Richness Per Pixel

Percent impacts

lower mountain elevations. It is important to note that this map overestimates actual vertebrate species richness because it is based on individual species maps of potential habitat, not on observed occurrences. This map serves as the basis for subsequent analyses estimating the relative change in species richness under the various alternative futures.

The alternative futures for the Upper San Pedro River Basin cause little change in overall species richness (figure 14.2a–c and table 14.1). In relation to the size of the study area, the areas of development are small.

The PLANS and CONSTRAINED scenarios result in an increase in overall species richness. Under both groups of alternative futures, groundwater levels near the river increase, resulting in more flow in the river and an increase in the abundance of riparian vegetation. The potential habitat for individual species improves near the river. In the PLANS alternative futures, the overall increase is less than in the CONSTRAINED alternative futures. There is little difference among the variations within the scenarios.

The OPEN scenarios all cause reductions in species richness. Most of the reduction is a result of the lowering of groundwater levels. With less groundwater, riparian vegetation and streamflows suffer. Most of the diversity in the region is located within the riparian area, where any loss would cause a severe reduction in species numbers. Most of the loss is along the San Pedro River. It represents loss of the rarest naturally occurring habitat in the basin, the riparian vegetation communities.

GAP Species Models

GAP analysis is a policy-oriented methodology to analyze species richness. GAP analysis looks at the protection afforded each terrestrial vertebrate specie. The method identifies the amount of potential habitat within existing or proposed protected areas that are managed according to a management plan for biodiversity (Edwards et al. 1993). Areas with active management plans are considered to be stable environments (figure 14.3).

The GAP species model uses two types of spatial information. A map of existing protected areas identifies locations where active management plans for biodiversity exist. Maps of individual species distributions provide information on geographical extent of habitats. The distribution maps are developed by the species richness model. Each of the 389 species distributions is applied to the study area to identify "GAP species," those that do not have sufficient protected habitat.

The model overlays the map of protected areas with each species distribution map. Those species that lack enough area to comprise a single home range are considered to be underprotected and are identified as GAP species. The area of their habitats that lie outside protected areas are GAP locations. Not all the land area

Photo 14.4 ■ San Pedro River National Conservation Area

identified as GAP locations must be protected, but protection of some portion of the GAP species distribution is necessary to ensure long-term survival. Identifying species and areas that lack protection can help guide the choice of future conservation areas.

Currently, four species account for the GAP locations: the eared trogon (*Euptilotis neoxenus*), the Ramsey Canyon leopard frog (*Rana subaquavocalis*), the Sonoran whipsnake (*Masticophis bilineatus*), and the Yaqui black-headed snake (*Tantilla yaquia*). In general, protection of the GAP species requires management and protection of the middle elevations or foothills areas and of the northernmost riparian parts of the study area. The GAP locations include a variety of vegetation types.

Differences among the alternative futures are due to the location of future conservation areas (figure 14.4a–c and table 14.2). There are no new GAP species or locations created by any of the scenarios. This is expected because none of the scenarios reduces the amount of protected land.

Under the OPEN 2 and PLANS 2 alternative futures, there is no reduction in GAP species. These two scenarios extend the current San Pedro Riparian National Conservation Area from the Palominas bridge to the Mexican border. Increasing the extent of the conservation area to the south does not provide sufficient habitat for the GAP species.

The PLANS, PLANS 2, OPEN, and OPEN 1 alternative futures reduce the number of GAP species by two. The eared trogon and Yaqui black-headed snake are protected by the expansion of the San Pedro Riparian National Conservation Area northward to Cascabel. The expansion protects riparian habitat at lower elevations adjacent to high sloping areas.

The PLANS 3 and all the CONSTRAINED alternative futures reduce the number GAP species. Additional conservation areas in the Mexican portion of the study area account for this improvement. The expansion provides protection for three of the GAP species, leaving only the Ramsey Canyon leopard frog unprotected. This frog requires high elevation riparian vegetation. Ramsey Canyon leopard frog habitat is difficult to develop, so although it remains a GAP species, the actual threat to its habitat is limited.

Table 14.2 GAP species: Impacts, 2000–2020

	Number of GAP species
Baseline 2000	4
Plans	2
Plans 1	2
Plans 2	4
Plans 3	1
Constrained	1
Constrained 1	1
Constrained 2	1
Open	2
Open 1	2
Open 2	4

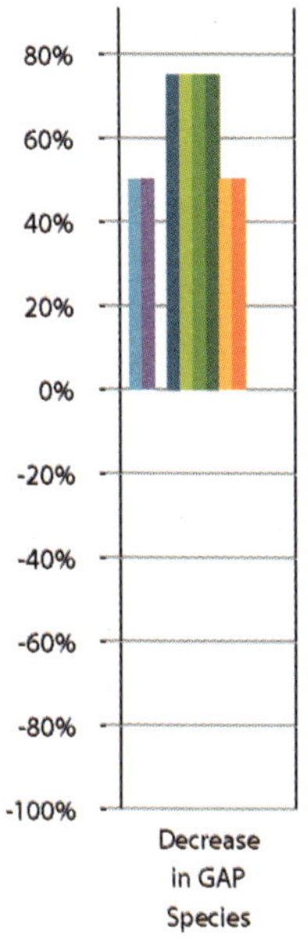
80%
60%
40%
20%
0%
-20%
-40%
-60%
-80%
-100%
Decrease in GAP Species

Relative impacts

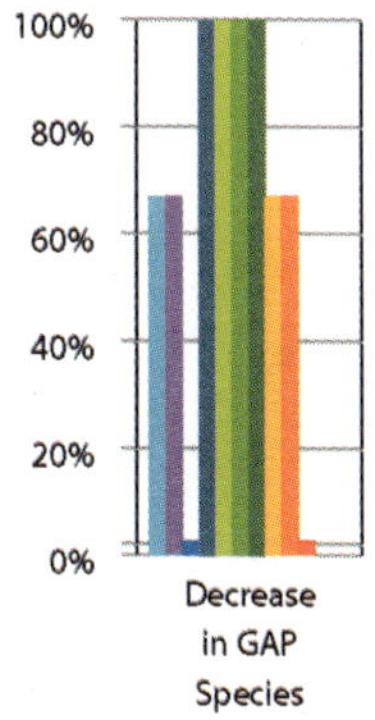
100%
80%
60%
40%
20%
0%
Decrease in GAP Species

Percent impacts

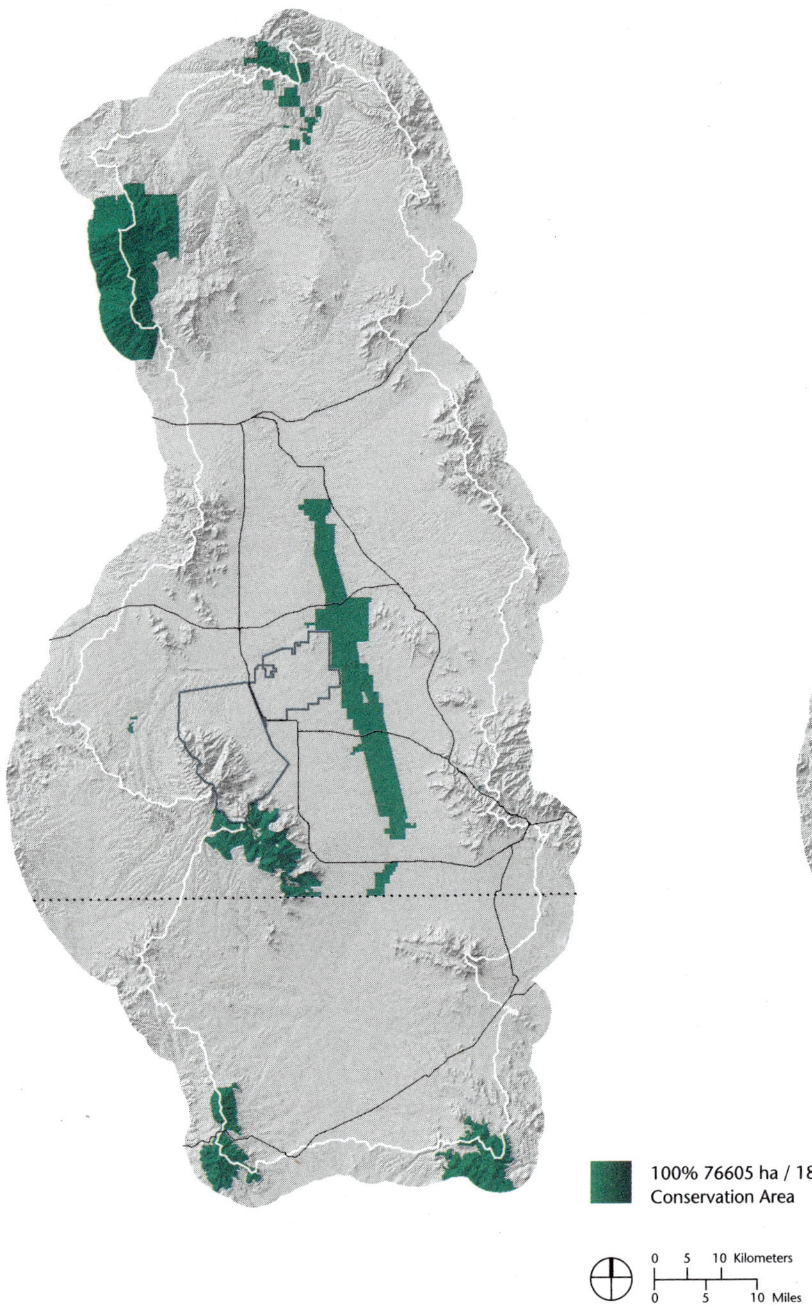
100% 76605 ha / 189291 ac
Conservation Area
0 5 10 Kilometers
0 5 10 Miles

Figure 14.3 ■ Wildlife reserves, 2000

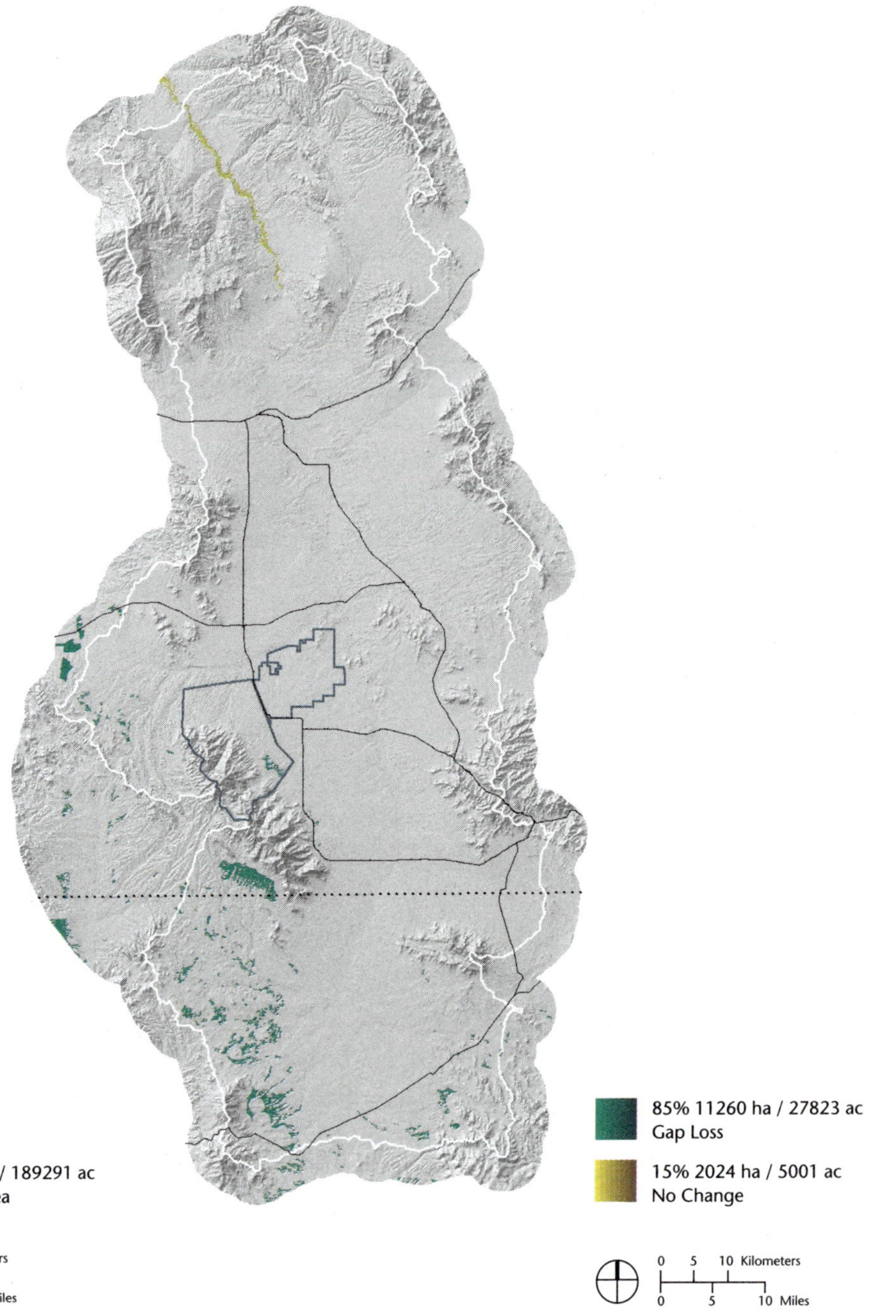
85% 11260 ha / 27823 ac
Gap Loss
15% 2024 ha / 5001 ac
No Change
0 5 10 Kilometers
0 5 10 Miles

Figure 14.4a ■ PLANS,
GAP Species potential habitat impacts, 2000–2020

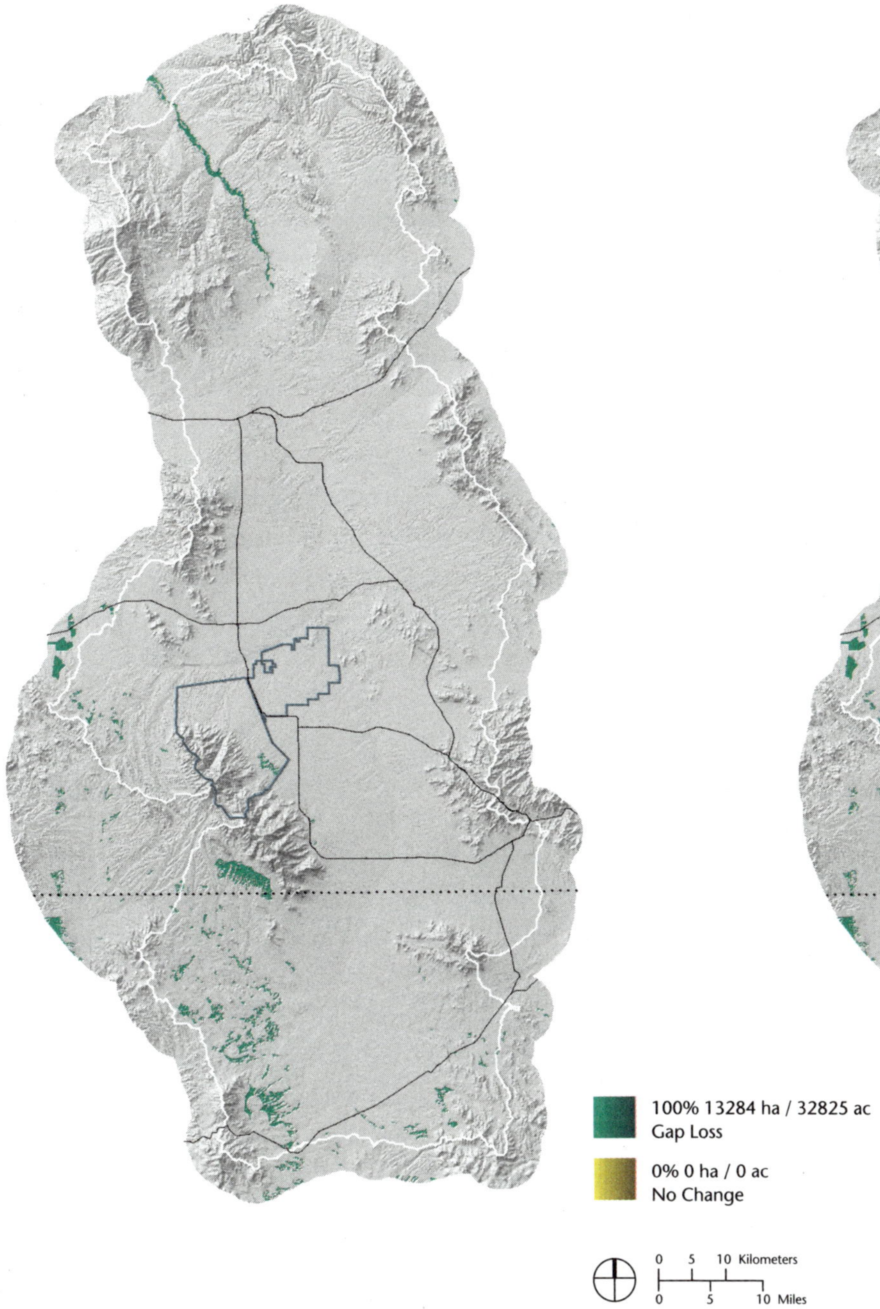
100% 13284 ha / 32825 ac
Gap Loss
0% 0 ha / 0 ac
No Change
0 5 10 Kilometers
0 5 10 Miles

Figure 14.4b ■ CONSTRAINED, GAP Species potential habitat impacts, 2000–2020

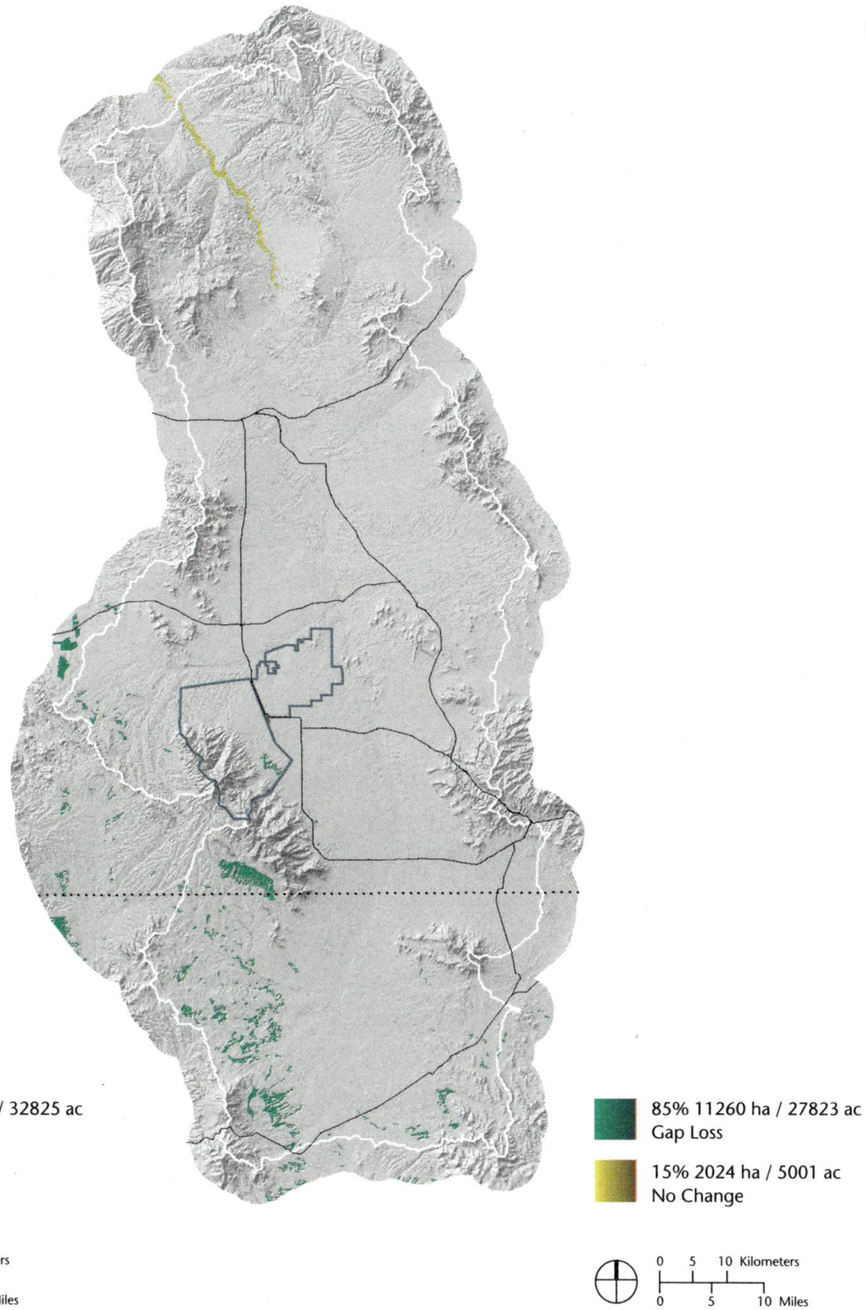
85% 11260 ha / 27823 ac
Gap Loss
15% 2024 ha / 5001 ac
No Change
0 5 10 Kilometers
0 5 10 Miles

Figure 14.4c ■ OPEN, GAP Species potential habitat impacts, 2000–2020

CHAPTER 15

The Visual Preference Model

The aim of the visual preference model is to identify areas of scenic attractiveness in terms of the preferences expressed by residents of the San Pedro region and to evaluate how these areas of scenic attractiveness might change in the future. The visual model closely follows the U.S. Forest Service methodology (USFS 1995), which combines preference with visual exposure to determine the overall visual value of the area.

Visual preference was determined by using a photographic survey. Forty photographs representing different landscape elements were shown to fourteen individuals currently living in southeastern Arizona. The forty photographs illustrated the major vegetation communities, land forms, and built elements within the study area. Participants expressed their preferences by sorting the photographs into three groups: most attractive, neutral, and least attractive (figure 15.1). Land uses and land cover types in the foreground of photographs that were judged to be attractive include forest, oak, riparian, mesquite, northern desert scrub, agriculture, water, and golf courses. Land uses/land cover judged to be unattractive include urban, rural, and exurban residential development; mines; industry; and commerce.

Dominant attractive aspects of the larger background landscape include mountain views and views of mixed types of natural vegetation without visible development. Vegetation types such as riparian, oak, saguaro cactus, and coniferous forest are also positive elements. Least attractive elements included all the built areas and mines. The presence of a negative element in the foreground of an otherwise attractive setting generally resulted in low attractiveness.

Visual exposure is a measure of the area that can be seen radially from any point in the study area, based on the 30 m (98.5 ft) grid of the geographic information system. For determining the visual value of each location, the foreground viewshed radius is limited to 800 m (0.5 mi), which represents the maximum distance from which most landscape elements can be identified. This distance is based on the preference research and on-site investigations. For example, a building on top of a hill and seen for approximately 800 m (0.5 mi) in all directions would lower the visual preference when seen from any visible point in the nearby area. Conversely, a mountain seen from across the valley adds positive visual preference. The background portion of each viewshed is considered to extend to the surrounding mountains.

There are two distance-defined evaluations that are combined into the summary evaluation: foreground and background. Because the overall landscape of the San Pedro region is positively valued, in cases where both positively and negatively preferred elements are within a view, the negative will be most noticed and will override the positive elements. Table 15.1 gives examples of the elements typical of the several classes of attractiveness. Figure 15.2 shows the visual preference as seen from all locations in the study area.

Each alternative future will change the spatial pattern of land use and land cover. Assuming that judgments about the attractiveness of the region's landscapes remain constant, the visual preference model evaluates each alternative future in terms of its visual impacts (figure 15.3a–c and table 15.2).

The visual attractiveness of the Upper San Pedro River Basin will decline substantially in all of the alternative futures. The CONSTRAINED scenarios result in less decline than the others. The

Table 15.1 Attractiveness of typical visual elements

Attractiveness	Foreground Elements	Background Elements
Least attractive	Commercial strip	With no or one mountain range, or a non-diverse natural or a developed view
Less attractive	Suburban residential	With two or more mountain ranges or a non-diverse natural or a developed view
Neutral	Desert scrub	With no or one mountain range or a non-diverse natural or developed view
More attractive	Mixed vegetation types	With two or more mountain ranges or a diverse natural view
Most attractive	Riparian vegetation	With two or more mountain ranges and a diverse natural view

Table 15.2 Visual preference: Impacts, 2000–2020

	change in average visual value of views by cell	decline in positive visual value ha
Baseline 2000	3.63	570,862
Plans	-0.06	49,078
Plans 1	-0.07	54,871
Plans 2	-0.07	49,790
Plans 3	-0.05	43,851
Constrained	-0.05	49,220
Constrained 1	-0.05	50,652
Constrained 2	-0.06	50,870
Open	-0.13	79,983
Open 1	-0.13	84,106
Open 2	-0.10	66,485

OPEN scenarios cause the most dramatic decline because development and consequent changes in vegetation are most widespread.

There is almost no place from which the view will be improved, and less attractive views will be seen from most stretches of the region's major roads, particularly those in Arizona. In addition, most currently existing residential areas will experience less attractive views. Decline in visual attractiveness is the most widespread of any of the impacts assessed in this research, regardless of scenario. One consequence is likely to be a generally held perception that the region is declining at an accelerated rate, perhaps faster than the actual rate of decline as described by other measures.

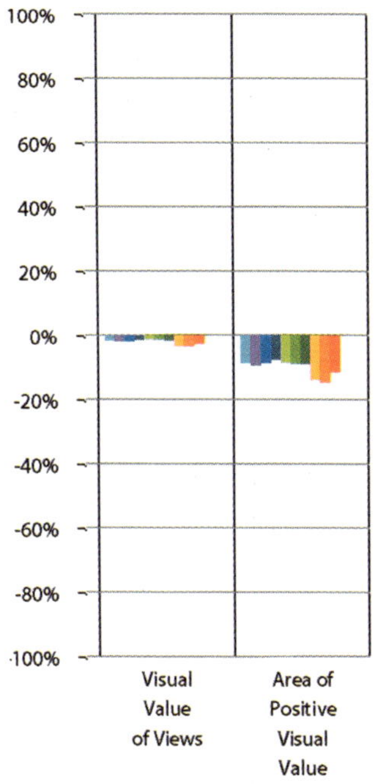
100%
80%
60%
40%
20%
0%
-20%
-40%
-60%
-80%
-100%
Visual Value of Views
Area of Positive Visual Value

Relative impacts

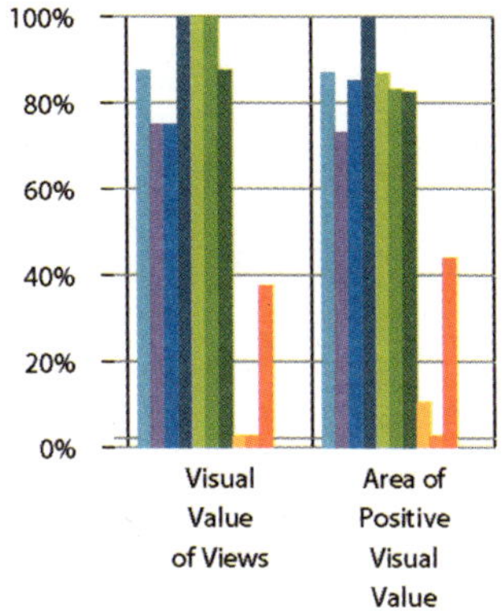
100%
80%
60%
40%
20%
0%
Visual Value of Views
Area of Positive Visual Value

Percent impacts

1 (1.071)
2 (1.071)
3 (1.071)
4 (1.214)
5 (1.214)
6 (1.286)
7 (1.286)
8 (1.286)
9 (1.357)
10 (1.429)
11 (1.429)
12 (1.429)
13 (1.429)
14 (1.571)
15 (1.786)
16 (1.857)
17 (1.857)
18 (1.929)
19 (2.000)
20 (2.000)

Figure 15.1 ■ Visual preference survey rankings

21 (2.071)
22 (2.143)
23 (2.143)
24 (2.143)
25 (2.214)
26 (2.214)
27 (2.286)
28 (2.357)
29 (2.357)
30 (2.429)
31 (2.429)
32 (2.500)
33 (2.571)
34 (2.643)
35 (2.643)
36 (2.643)
37 (2.786)
38 (2.786)
39 (2.929)
40 (2.929)

Figure 15.1 ■ Visual preference survey rankings, continued

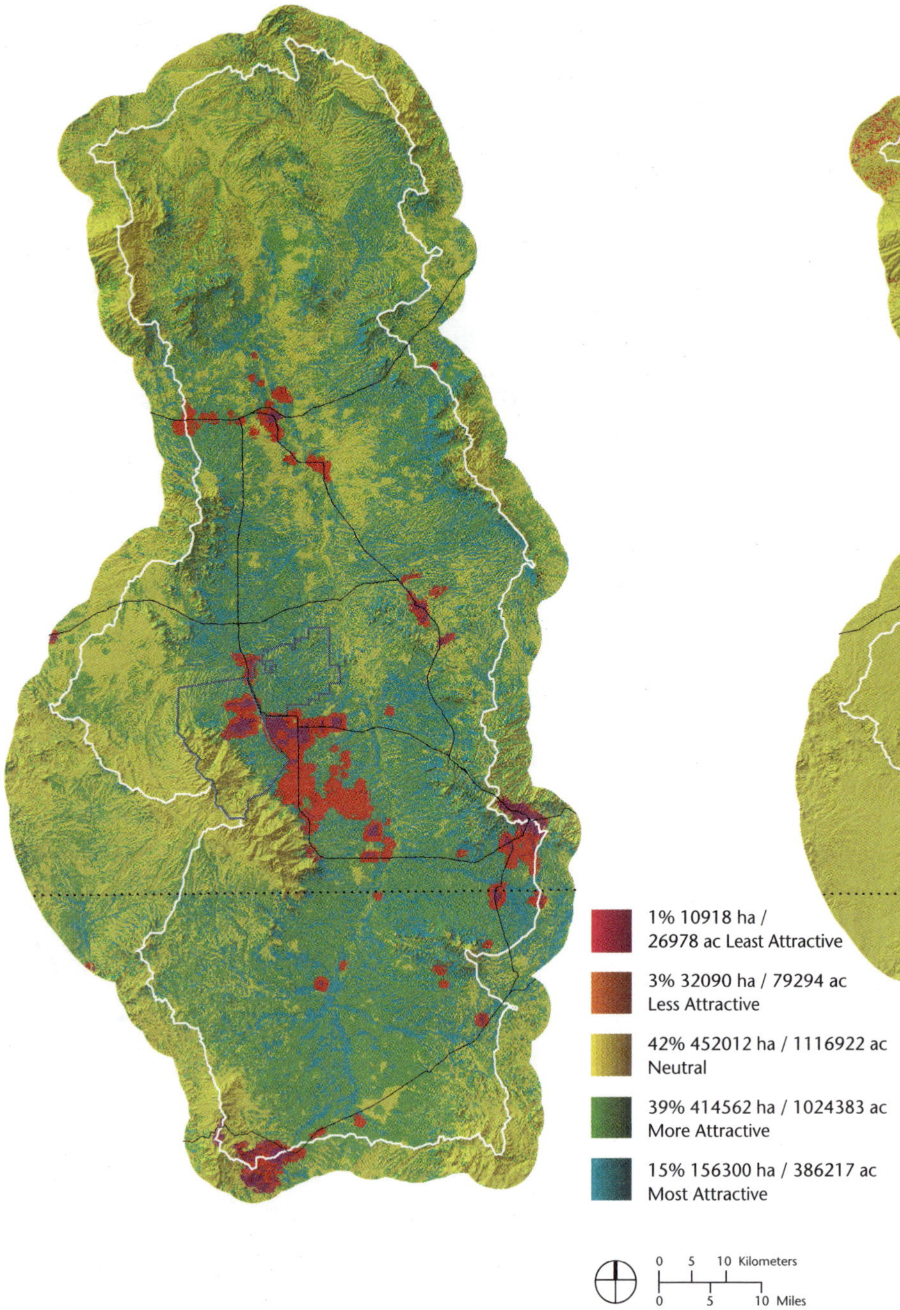
1% 10918 ha / 26978 ac Least Attractive
3% 32090 ha / 79294 ac Less Attractive
42% 452012 ha / 1116922 ac Neutral
39% 414562 ha / 1024383 ac More Attractive
15% 156300 ha / 386217 ac Most Attractive
0 5 10 Kilometers
0 5 10 Miles

Figure 15.2 ■ Visual preference, 2000

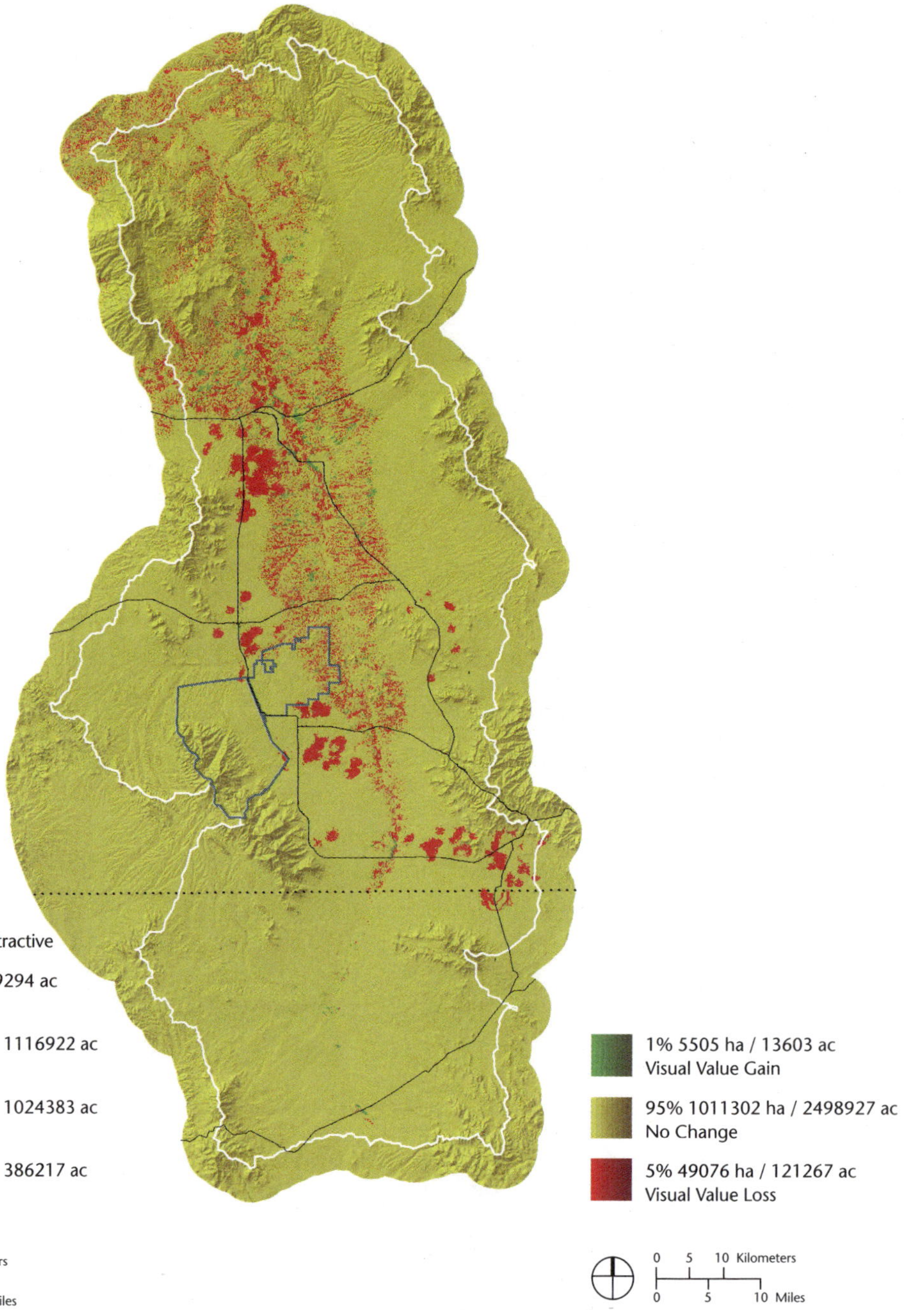
1% 5505 ha / 13603 ac Visual Value Gain
95% 1011302 ha / 2498927 ac No Change
5% 49076 ha / 121267 ac Visual Value Loss
0 5 10 Kilometers
0 5 10 Miles

Figure 15.3a ■ PLANS, Visual preference impacts, 2000–2020

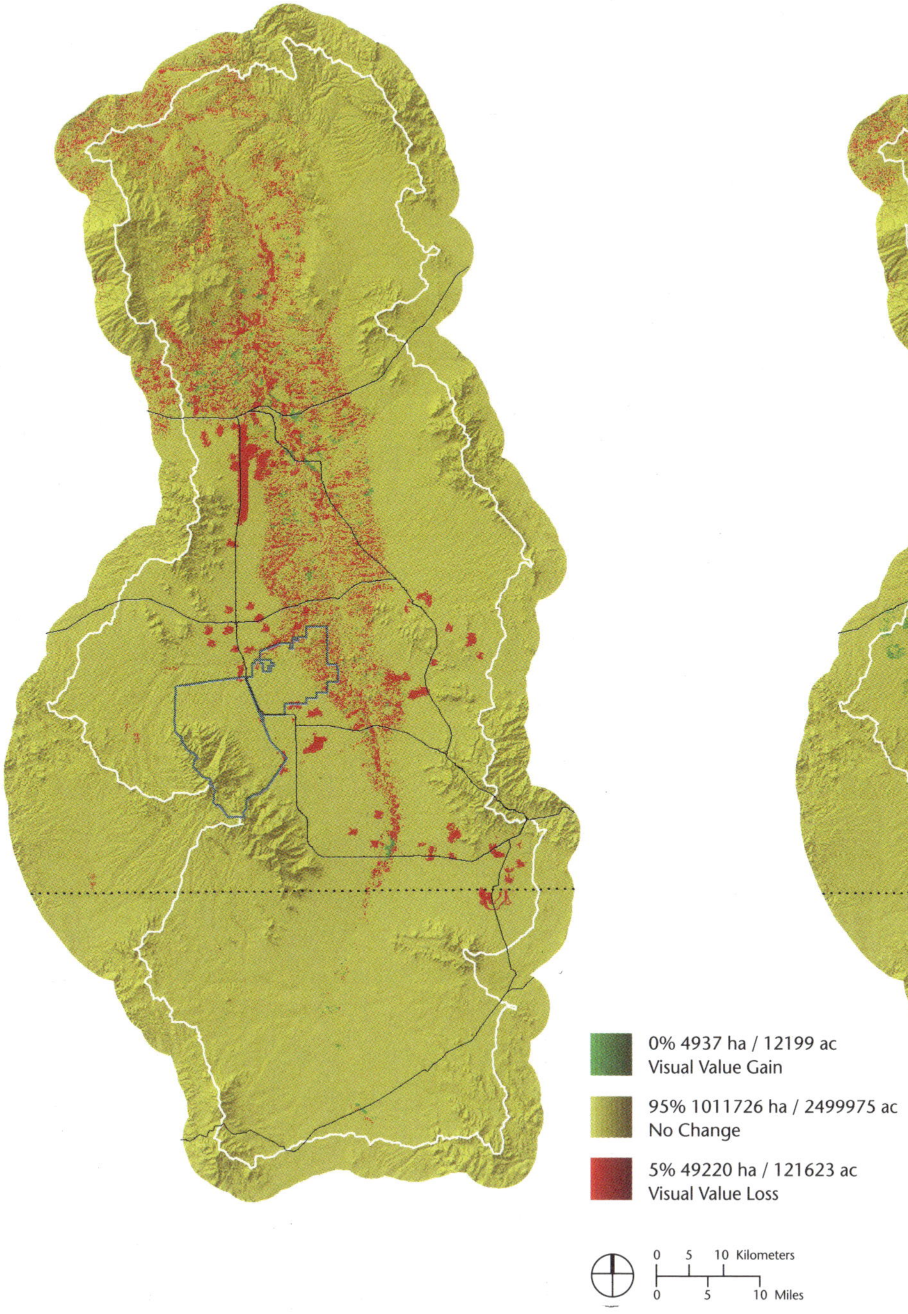
0% 4937 ha / 12199 ac
Visual Value Gain
95% 1011726 ha / 2499975 ac
No Change
5% 49220 ha / 121623 ac
Visual Value Loss
0 5 10 Kilometers
0 5 10 Miles

Figure 15.3b ■ CONSTRAINED, Visual preference impacts, 2000–2020

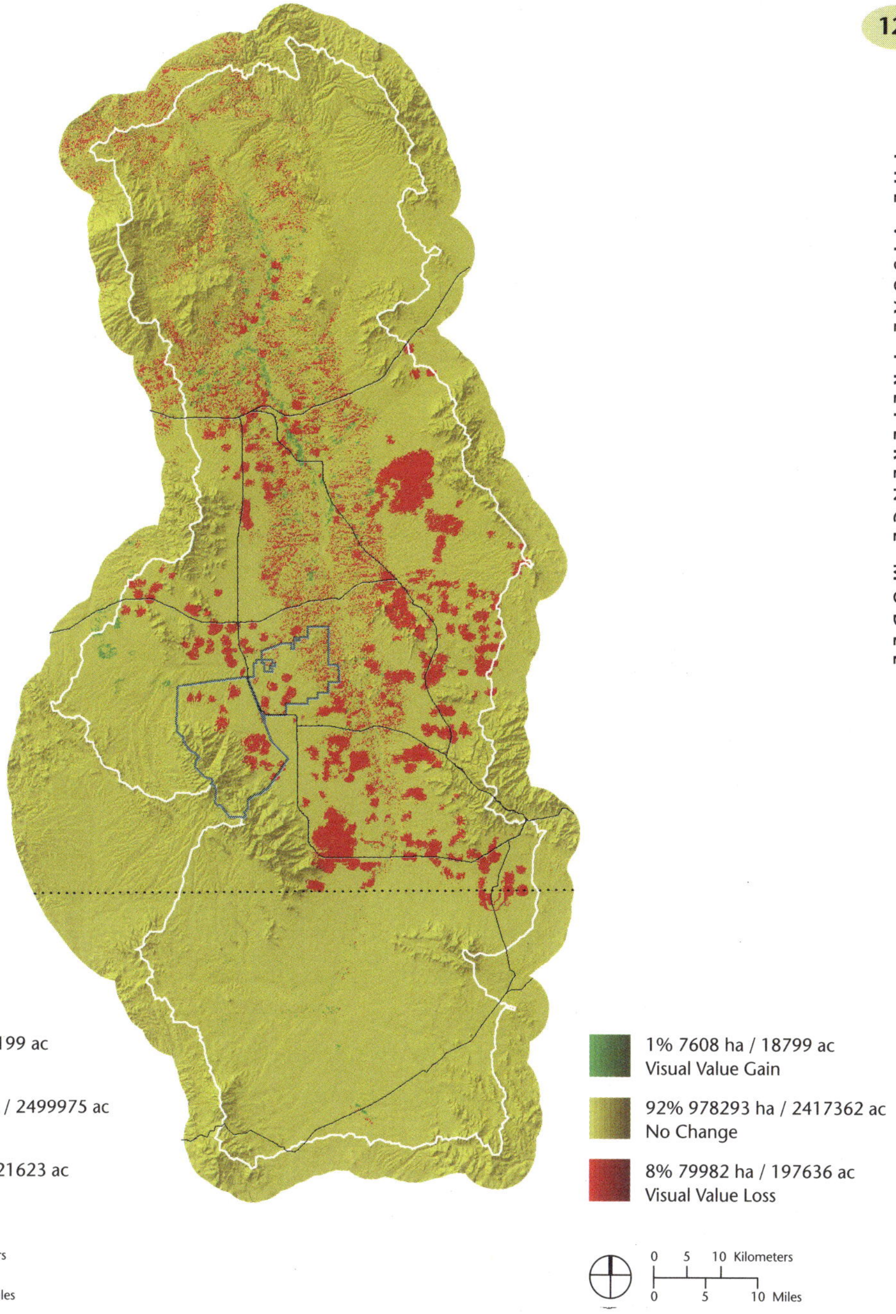
1% 7608 ha / 18799 ac
Visual Value Gain
92% 978293 ha / 2417362 ac
No Change
8% 79982 ha / 197636 ac
Visual Value Loss
0 5 10 Kilometers
0 5 10 Miles

Figure 15.3c ■ OPEN, Visual preference impacts, 2000–2020

CHAPTER 16

Summary of Impacts

Applying the process models to the alternative futures for 2020 and comparing the results with the reference period 2000 yields impact assessments. Table 16.1 shows the impacts of the ten alternative futures to 2020. Impacts are summarized graphically in two different ways: by percent change relative to baseline conditions, and by percent ranking within the range of the ten alternative futures. For all but the residential attractiveness ratings, percent change measures are expressed relative to baseline conditions in 2000. Because data limitations prevented the calculation of residential attractiveness indices for 2000, these are expressed relative to the PLANS scenario in 2020.

Urbanization and agriculture are the major environmental stresses affecting the San Pedro River Basin. Direct impacts on hydrology and habitat are caused by activities such as grading, paving, plowing, grazing, irrigation, and water use. Indirect effects include modified hydrology, fire suppression, and vegetation change. Indirect effects may remain unnoticed by the casual observer, but their cumulative effects can be as detrimental to biodiversity as the direct impacts. Both direct and indirect impacts are assessed, and each impact assessment reveals one aspect of how an alternative future is predicted to change the landscape.

In general, the three OPEN alternative futures have the greatest attractiveness to development. They provide the largest area of developable land from which to choose, resulting in lower land prices and lower housing costs. The OPEN alternative futures have the greatest negative impact on groundwater storage and recharge, substantially increasing drying of the San Pedro River, increasing vegetation loss, and reducing all of the measures of potential wildlife habitat and visual quality. The OPEN alternative futures result in a diffuse pattern of development and the least environmentally sustainable set of alternative futures.

The three CONSTRAINED alternative futures, which direct most future development into existing developed areas, cause substantial reduction in attractiveness for developers. These alternative futures assume changes in current development practice and are dependent on changes in the nature of the housing market. They have the lowest negative hydrological impacts, providing for reduced loss of groundwater, improvements in river flow, and increased riparian vegetation. The CONSTRAINED alternative futures also result in least loss and greatest gains in habitat and in the least harmful impacts on visual quality.

The four PLANS alternative futures are between those of the OPEN and CONSTRAINED alternative futures, but they are closer to the CONSTRAINED alternative futures in impacts. The PLANS alternative futures are attractive to developers, except when urban development is limited to areas within current sewer service areas. They result in reduced loss of groundwater, but the water table continues to lower. The PLANS alternative futures cause impacts that generally represent a slow decline in several important hydrological, ecological, and visual qualities of the region.

The hydrological model is used to simulate the effects of pumping in the alternative futures. Comparing the model's results for each alternative future in 2020 with conditions in 2000 shows the effects of various policy choices and assumptions on the hydrological system in 2020. The OPEN scenarios produce a continued increase in pumping and consequently an increase in the rate of groundwater storage loss. Capture from both the river and from evapotranspiration also increases, as stream flows are diminished and evapotranspiration is reduced. The PLANS and

CONSTRAINED scenarios produce some increase in evapotranspiration from 2000 conditions and reductions in stream capture. All of these effects are caused by the reduction of groundwater pumping. However, although the rate of loss from groundwater storage is reduced, there is no indication of storage replenishment. Groundwater is still being lost from storage, only at a slower rate in the PLANS and in the CONSTRAINED alternative futures.

The CONSTRAINED and PLANS scenarios produce less loss of stream flow than do the OPEN scenarios. All the OPEN scenarios produce increases in dry reaches of the San Pedro River. Stream flows in some of the CONSTRAINED and PLANS alternative futures increase in many areas because of the reduction of evapotranspiration resulting from management of cottonwood, willow, and mesquite trees and the removal of irrigated agriculture.

In all the alternative futures, the effects of changes in patterns of land use and land policies on vegetation and on habitat in the region of the Upper San Pedro River Basin will be significant and dramatic. Increasing urbanization within the uplands, especially near Sierra Vista and Cananea, will result in a decrease in the extent of grassland. However, changes in development policies, fire management practice, retirement of agricultural water rights, and management of riparian vegetation can result in dramatic improvement to both upland and riparian vegetation.

The comparative pattern of impacts in which the OPEN alternative futures have considerably more harmful impacts than do the PLANS and CONSTRAINED alternative futures is seen throughout all the habitat-related measures. They are most pronounced for those species that depend on riparian habitat, such as the flycatcher and the beaver, and on species richness, much of which is accounted for by riparian species. Visual impacts follow the same pattern, and the OPEN alternative futures show significant declines in visual preference all along the edges of the San Pedro Valley in Arizona and along most major roads and urban areas because of sprawling lower density development.

Table 16.1 Summary of impacts, 2000–2020

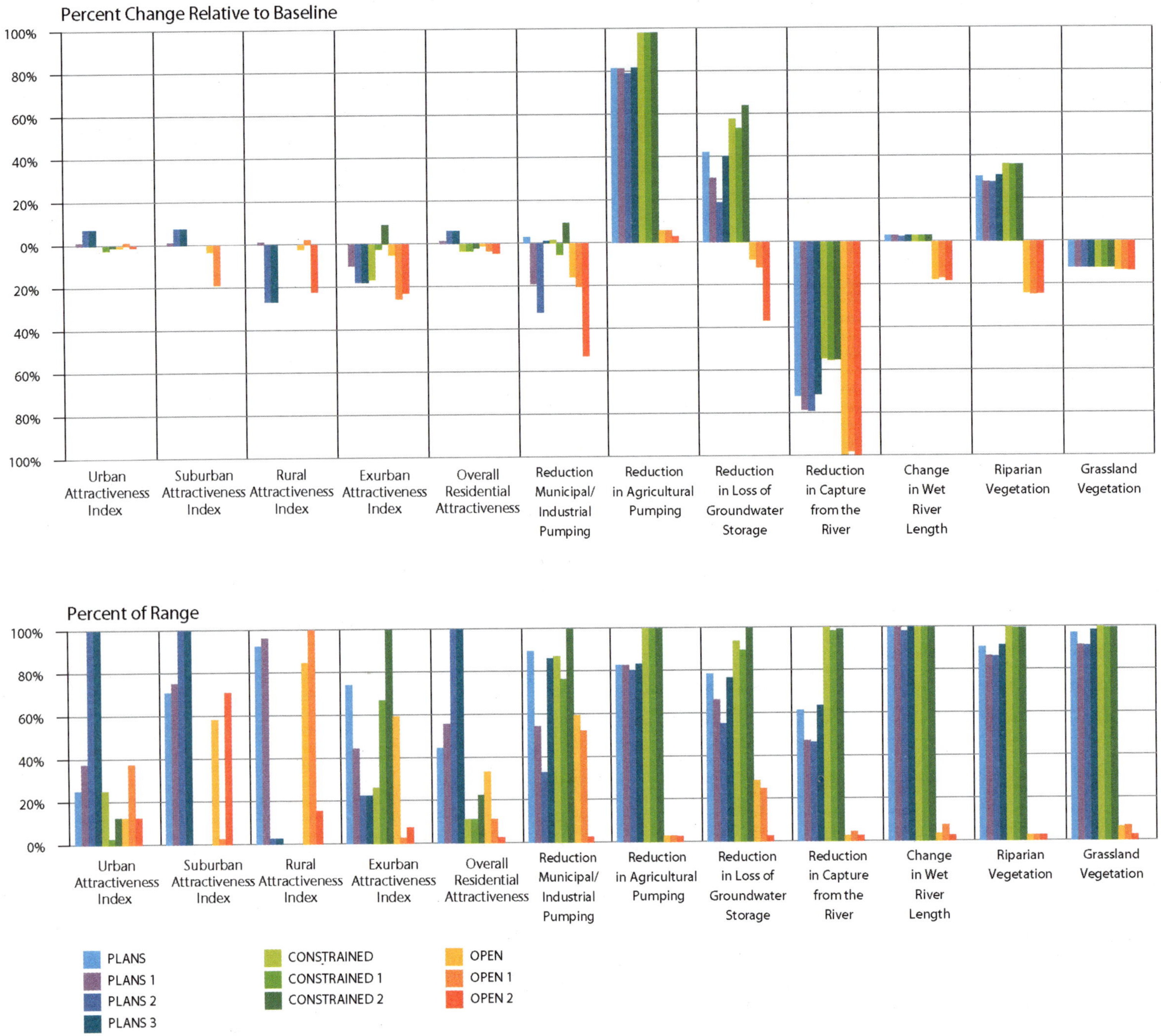
Percent Change Relative to Baseline
100%
80%
60%
40%
20%
0%
20%
40%
60%
80%
100%
Urban Attractiveness Index
Suburban Attractiveness Index
Rural Attractiveness Index
Exurban Attractiveness Index
Overall Residential Attractiveness
Reduction Municipal/ Industrial Pumping
Reduction in Agricultural Pumping
Reduction in Loss of Groundwater Storage
Reduction in Capture from the River
Change in Wet River Length
Riparian Vegetation
Grassland Vegetation
Percent of Range
100%
80%
60%
40%
20%
0%
Urban Attractiveness Index
Suburban Attractiveness Index
Rural Attractiveness Index
Exurban Attractiveness Index
Overall Residential Attractiveness
Reduction Municipal/ Industrial Pumping
Reduction in Agricultural Pumping
Reduction in Loss of Groundwater Storage
Reduction in Capture from the River
Change in Wet River Length
Riparian Vegetation
Grassland Vegetation
PLANS
PLANS 1
PLANS 2
PLANS 3
CONSTRAINED
CONSTRAINED 1
CONSTRAINED 2
OPEN
OPEN 1
OPEN 2

Table 16.1 Summary of impacts, 2000–2020, continued

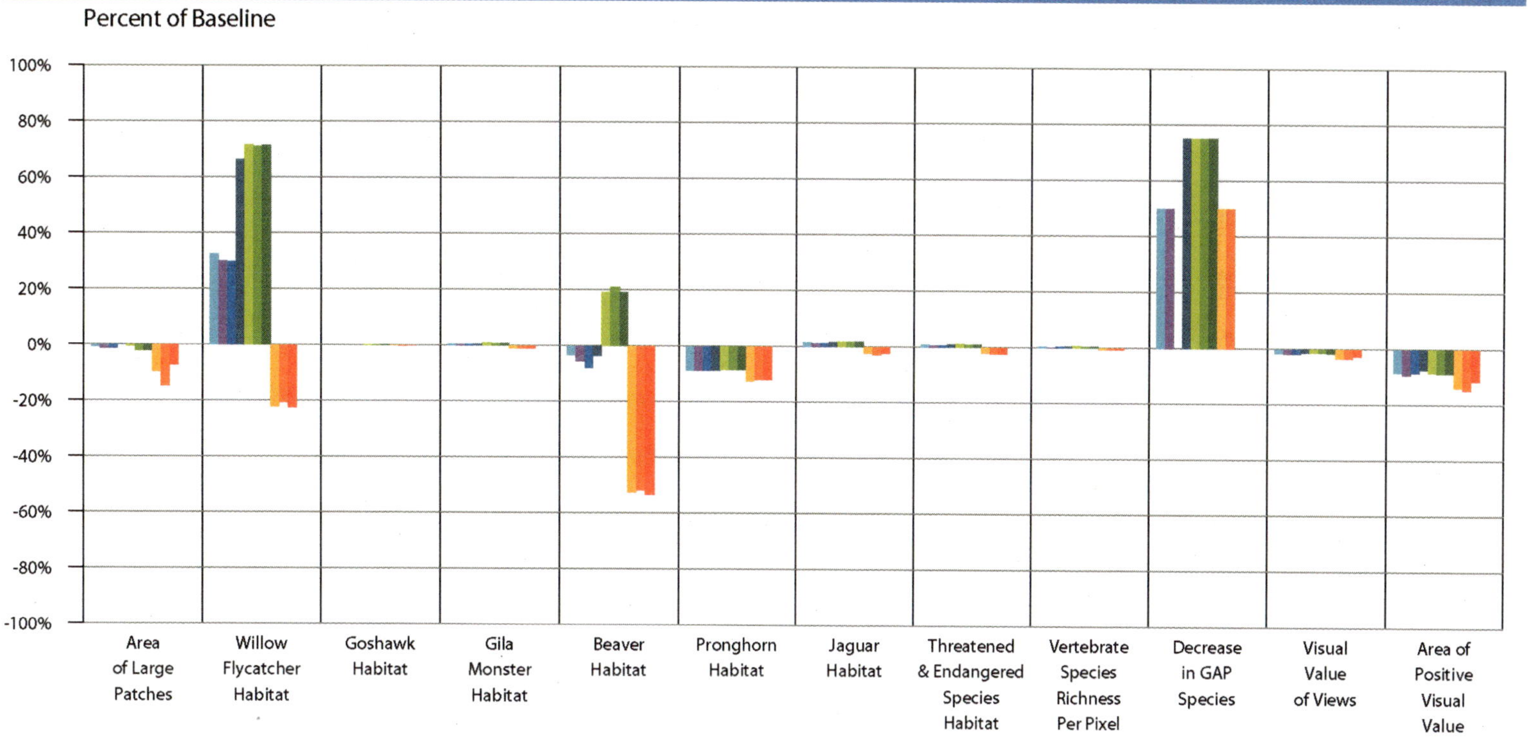
Percent of Baseline
100%
80%
60%
40%
20%
0%
-20%
-40%
-60%
-80%
-100%
Area of Large Patches
Willow Flycatcher Habitat
Goshawk Habitat
Gila Monster Habitat
Beaver Habitat
Pronghorn Habitat
Jaguar Habitat
Threatened & Endangered Species Habitat
Vertebrate Species Richness Per Pixel
Decrease in GAP Species
Visual Value of Views
Area of Positive Visual Value

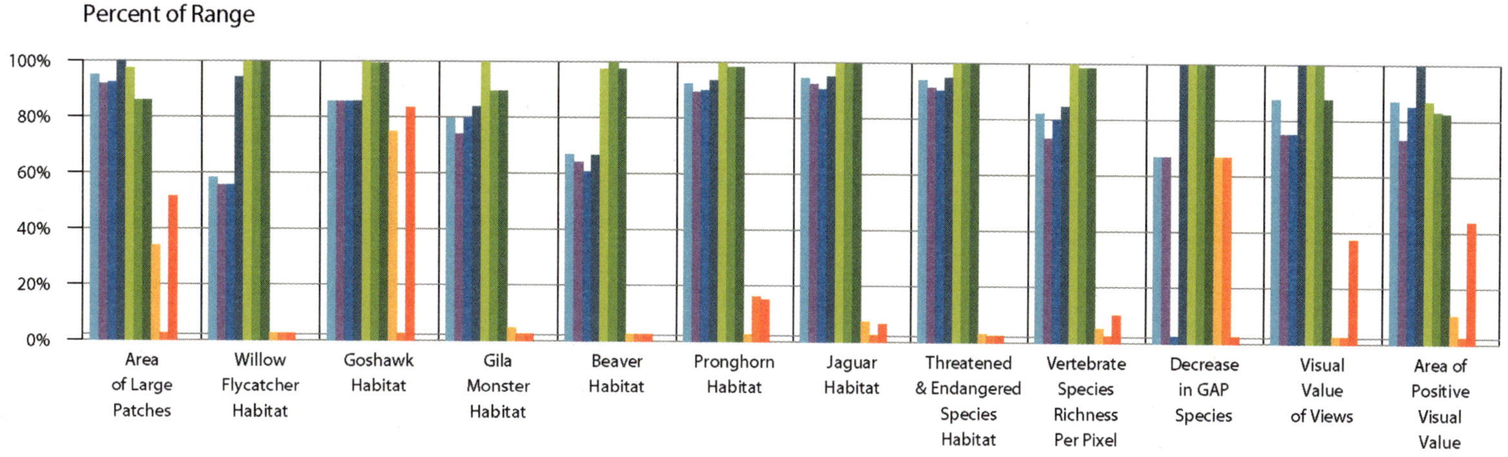
Percent of Range
100%
80%
60%
40%
20%
0%
Area of Large Patches
Willow Flycatcher Habitat
Goshawk Habitat
Gila Monster Habitat
Beaver Habitat
Pronghorn Habitat
Jaguar Habitat
Threatened & Endangered Species Habitat
Vertebrate Species Richness Per Pixel
Decrease in GAP Species
Visual Value of Views
Area of Positive Visual Value

CHAPTER 17

Testing the Alternative Futures

The impacts caused by variations in specific assumptions and policies within the scenarios are tested by comparison of selected alternative futures. Eleven tests of sensitivity to key policy choices were conducted. In all cases, the impact assessments are made from a regional perspective and are shown in the summary tables of impacts throughout the chapter. There are locally varied impacts, which are shown in the accompanying maps.

Test 1: What is the widest range of environmental impacts that might be expected by 2020? What is the variance between the scenario that is most development/least conservation oriented and the one that is least development/most conservation?

The OPEN 2 scenario creates the alternative future resulting from the policies that most favor housing development. The CONSTRAINED 2 scenario creates the alternative future that most favors conservation. The CONSTRAINED 2 scenario has the smallest population increase, and OPEN 2 has the largest. Table 17.1 shows their summary impacts.

When the groundwater model is used to simulate the effects on pumping of these two scenarios, positive and negative effects on the hydrologic system become most apparent (figure 17.1a and b).

The OPEN 2 scenario produces a continued increase in pumping from present amounts and consequently produces an increase in the rate of groundwater storage loss. The OPEN 2 scenario shows the greatest lowering of groundwater levels throughout the basin. The continued use of large-scale agricultural irrigation in Arizona continues to reduce groundwater levels near the San Pedro River, and increasing population creates demand that causes dramatic lowering of the groundwater around urbanized areas. The CONSTRAINED 2 scenario shows a continued but slower lowering of groundwater levels near urbanized areas. However, groundwater levels increase near the San Pedro River.

Streamflows in the San Pedro River are diminished, and evapotranspiration is reduced in OPEN 2. The CONSTRAINED 2 scenario produces some increase of evapotranspiration from 2000 conditions as well as some increases in streamflow. These effects are the result of reduction in groundwater pumping. However, although the rate of loss from groundwater storage is reduced, there is no indication that groundwater supply is being replenished. Water is still being lost from groundwater storage, only at a slower rate. In

CONSTRAINED 2, water flows in the San Pedro River increase in many areas as a result of the cessation of irrigated agriculture and the reduction in evapotranspiration by selective removal of cottonwood, willow, and mesquite trees. The cumulative effect can be seen in figure 17.2a and b.

Much of the landscape ecological pattern is protected by public ownership. However, extensive rural and exurban residential development in OPEN 2 will diminish the ecological value of almost all of the lower mountain slopes bordering the San Pedro valley in Arizona. Several important arroyo corridors will be lost to development. The CONSTRAINED 2 scenario will cause much less impact, which will be mainly concentrated near Interstate Highway 10 (figure 17.3a and b). In CONSTRAINED 2, increases in streamflow and changes in vegetation cause gains in habitat for the willow flycatcher and the beaver and provide a movement corridor for the jaguar. There are few changes to goshawk, Gila monster, and pronghorn habitats. This contrasts strongly with the substantial losses seen in the OPEN 2 alternative future. The OPEN 2 scenario shows a sharp decline in species richness in the area between Interstate Highway 10 and the Mexican border, whereas CONSTRAINED 2 shows a smaller loss.

There are major differences in visual impact (figure 17.4a and b). In CONSTRAINED 2, there are several areas of concentrated decline in visual preference because of development. There is a major zone of decline along Arizona Highway 90 between Interstate Highway 10 and the entrance to Kartchner Caverns State Park. In OPEN 2, almost all of the currently developed areas and all of the lower mountain slopes decline in visual preference because of additional development. In both scenarios, the transformation of extensive grasslands to mesquite causes a decline in visual preference and results in a loss of long-distance views as the trees grow and eliminate the sense of wide open spaces.

Given the above findings, it is interesting to note that the PLANS scenario results in an alternative future that much more closely resembles the pattern of impact results from CONSTRAINED 2 than from OPEN 2. The reflection of current conservation oriented plans and policies in PLANS might be effective in balancing the interests of conservation and development, but only if fully implemented both in Arizona and in Sonora.

Table 17.1 OPEN 2 and CONSTRAINED 2

Scenario	Baseline 2000	CONSTRAINED 2	OPEN 2
Urban Attractiveness Index	8.3	8.2	8.2
Suburban Attractiveness Index	9.1	N/A	9.1
Rural Attractiveness Index	9.0	N/A	7.0
Exurban Attractiveness Index	7.8	8.5	6.0
Overall Residential Attractiveness	8.4	8.2	8.0
Municipal/Industrial Pumping (m^3/day)	94,614	-9,000	+49,975
Agricultural Pumping (m^3/day)	113,153	-110,859	-3,294
Loss of Groundwater Storage (m^3/day)	-131,494	-47,515	-179,707
Capture from the River (m^3/day)	38,279	+21,050	+38,267
Wet River Length (Km)	180	185	147
Riparian Vegetation (ha)	9,618	+3,444	-2,348
Grassland Vegetation (ha)	372,041	-46,056	-50,731
Area of Large Patches (ha)	687,983	-15,503	-49,991
Willow Flycatcher Habitat (ha)	9,577	+6,819	-2,146
Goshawk Habitat (ha)	146,185	+80	-14
Gila Monster Habitat (ha)	208,993	+1,209	-2,545
Beaver Habitat (ha)	6,469	+1,235	-3,451
Pronghorn Habitat (ha)	253,802	-21,950	-30,717
Jaguar Habitat (ha)	320,926	+5,291	-8,481
Threatened & Endangered Species Habitat (ha)	136,329	+1,460	-3,281
Vertebrate Species Richness Per Pixel	168	+.9	-.94
GAP Species	4	+3	0
Visual Value of Views	4	-.06	-.1
Area of Positive Visual Value	570,862	-50,870	-66,485

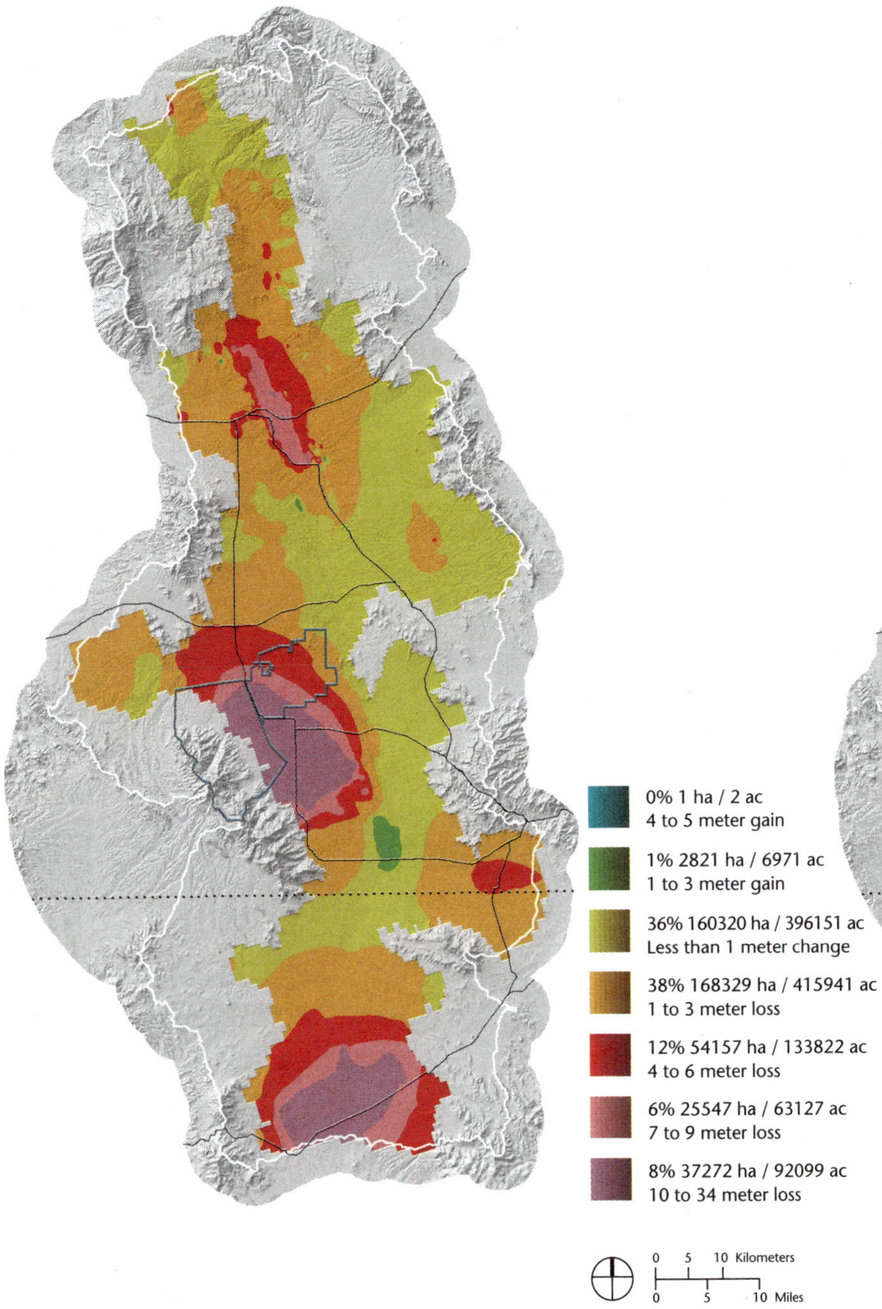
0% 1 ha / 2 ac
4 to 5 meter gain
1% 2821 ha / 6971 ac
1 to 3 meter gain
36% 160320 ha / 396151 ac
Less than 1 meter change
38% 168329 ha / 415941 ac
1 to 3 meter loss
12% 54157 ha / 133822 ac
4 to 6 meter loss
6% 25547 ha / 63127 ac
7 to 9 meter loss
8% 37272 ha / 92099 ac
10 to 34 meter loss
0 5 10 Kilometers
0 5 10 Miles

Figure 17.1a ■ OPEN 2, Groundwater impacts, 2000–2020

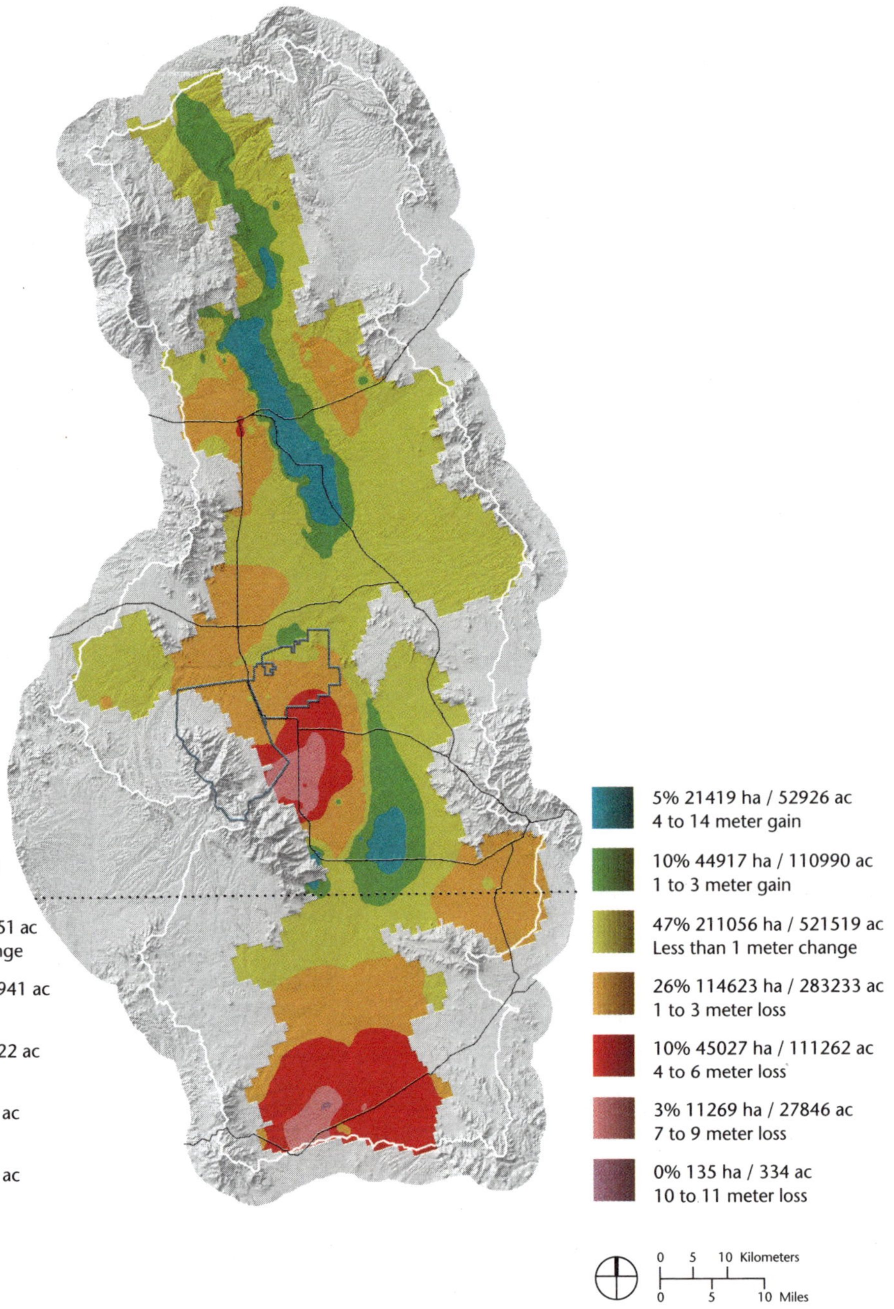
5% 21419 ha / 52926 ac
4 to 14 meter gain
10% 44917 ha / 110990 ac
1 to 3 meter gain
47% 211056 ha / 521519 ac
Less than 1 meter change
26% 114623 ha / 283233 ac
1 to 3 meter loss
10% 45027 ha / 111262 ac
4 to 6 meter loss
3% 11269 ha / 27846 ac
7 to 9 meter loss
0% 135 ha / 334 ac
10 to 11 meter loss
0 5 10 Kilometers
0 5 10 Miles

Figure 17.1b ■ CONSTRAINED 2, Groundwater impacts, 2000–2020

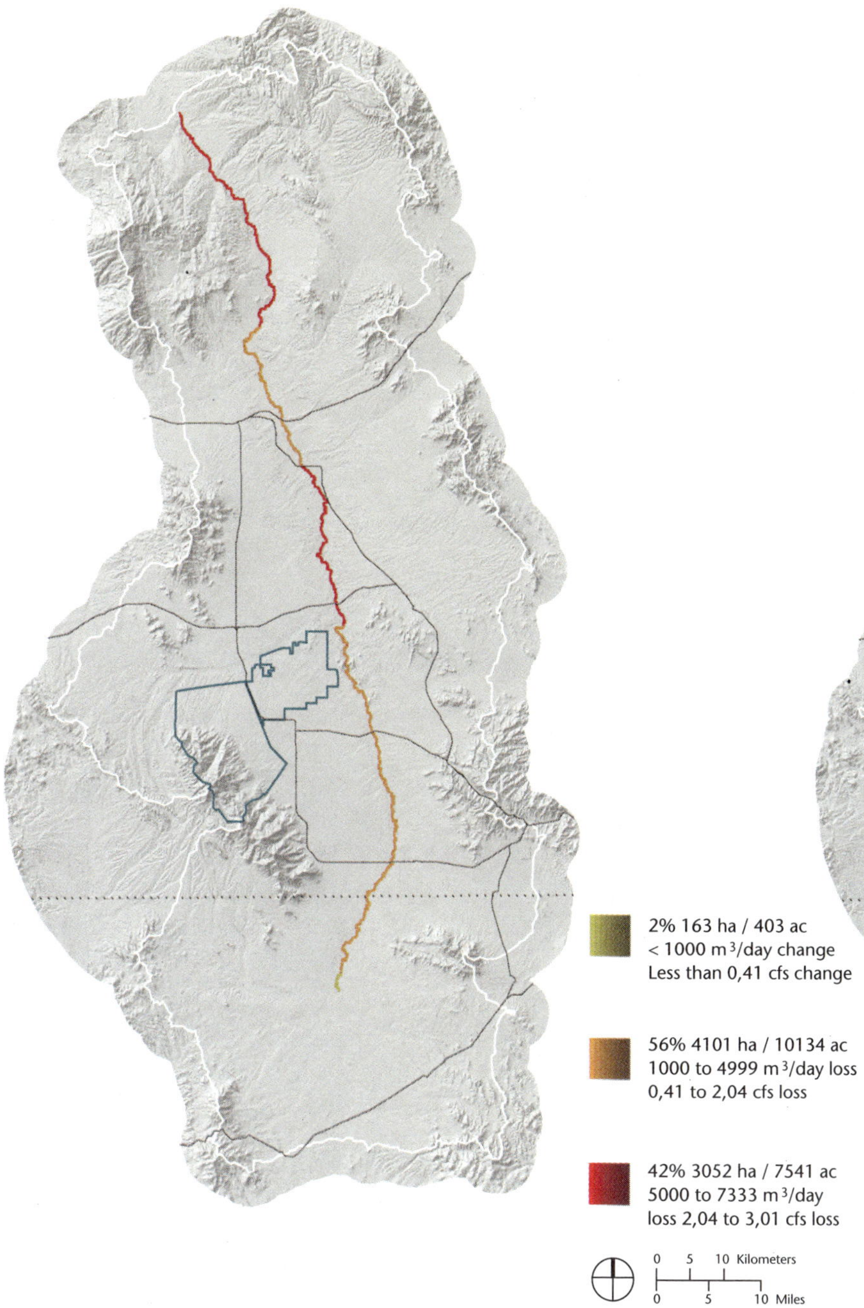
2% 163 ha / 403 ac
< 1000 m³/day change
Less than 0,41 cfs change
56% 4101 ha / 10134 ac
1000 to 4999 m³/day loss
0,41 to 2,04 cfs loss
42% 3052 ha / 7541 ac
5000 to 7333 m³/day
loss 2,04 to 3,01 cfs loss
0 5 10 Kilometers
0 5 10 Miles

Figure 17.2a ■ OPEN 2, Streamflow impacts, 2000–2020

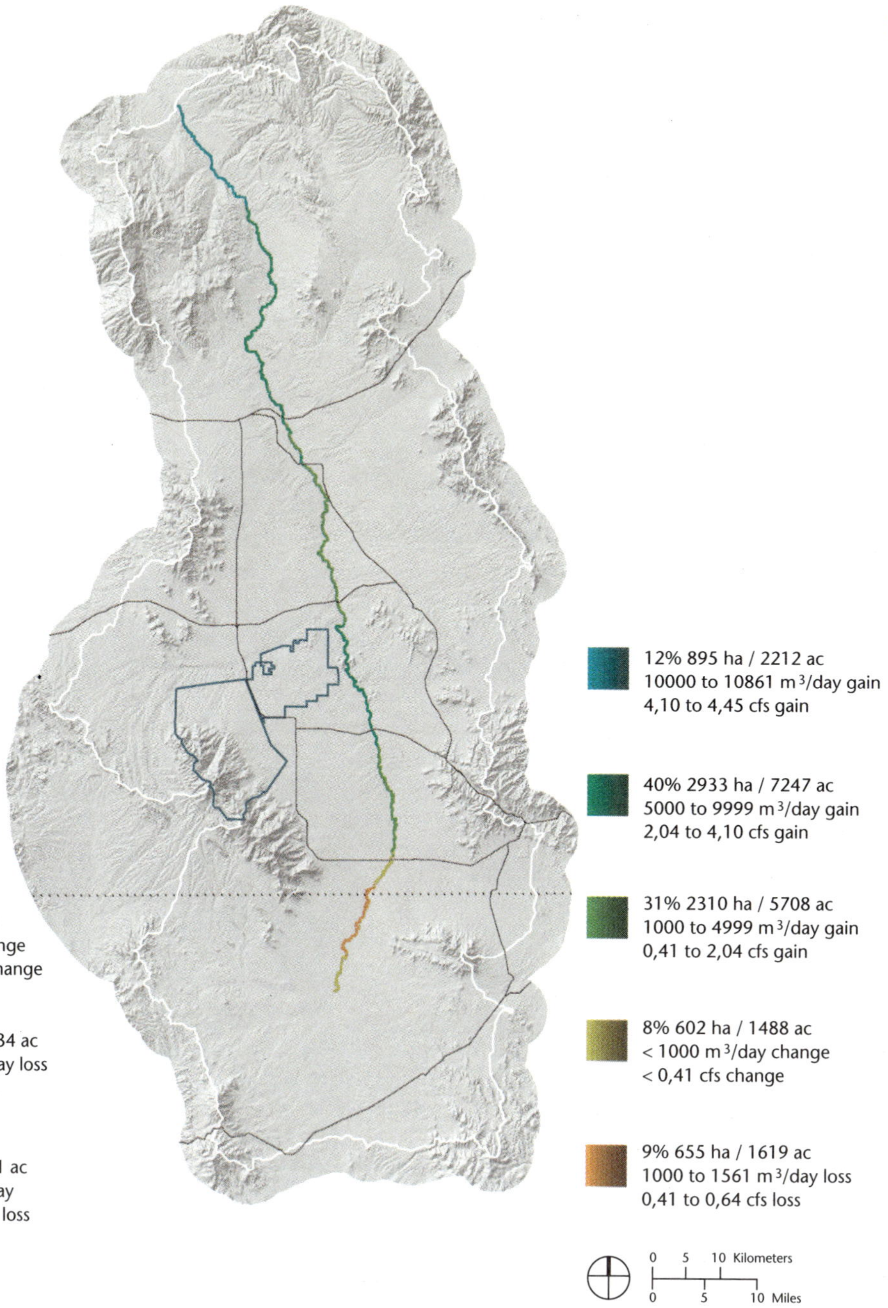
12% 895 ha / 2212 ac
10000 to 10861 m³/day gain
4,10 to 4,45 cfs gain
40% 2933 ha / 7247 ac
5000 to 9999 m³/day gain
2,04 to 4,10 cfs gain
31% 2310 ha / 5708 ac
1000 to 4999 m³/day gain
0,41 to 2,04 cfs gain
8% 602 ha / 1488 ac
< 1000 m³/day change
< 0,41 cfs change
9% 655 ha / 1619 ac
1000 to 1561 m³/day loss
0,41 to 0,64 cfs loss
0 5 10 Kilometers
0 5 10 Miles

Figure 17.2b ■ CONSTRAINED 2, Streamflow impacts, 2000–2020

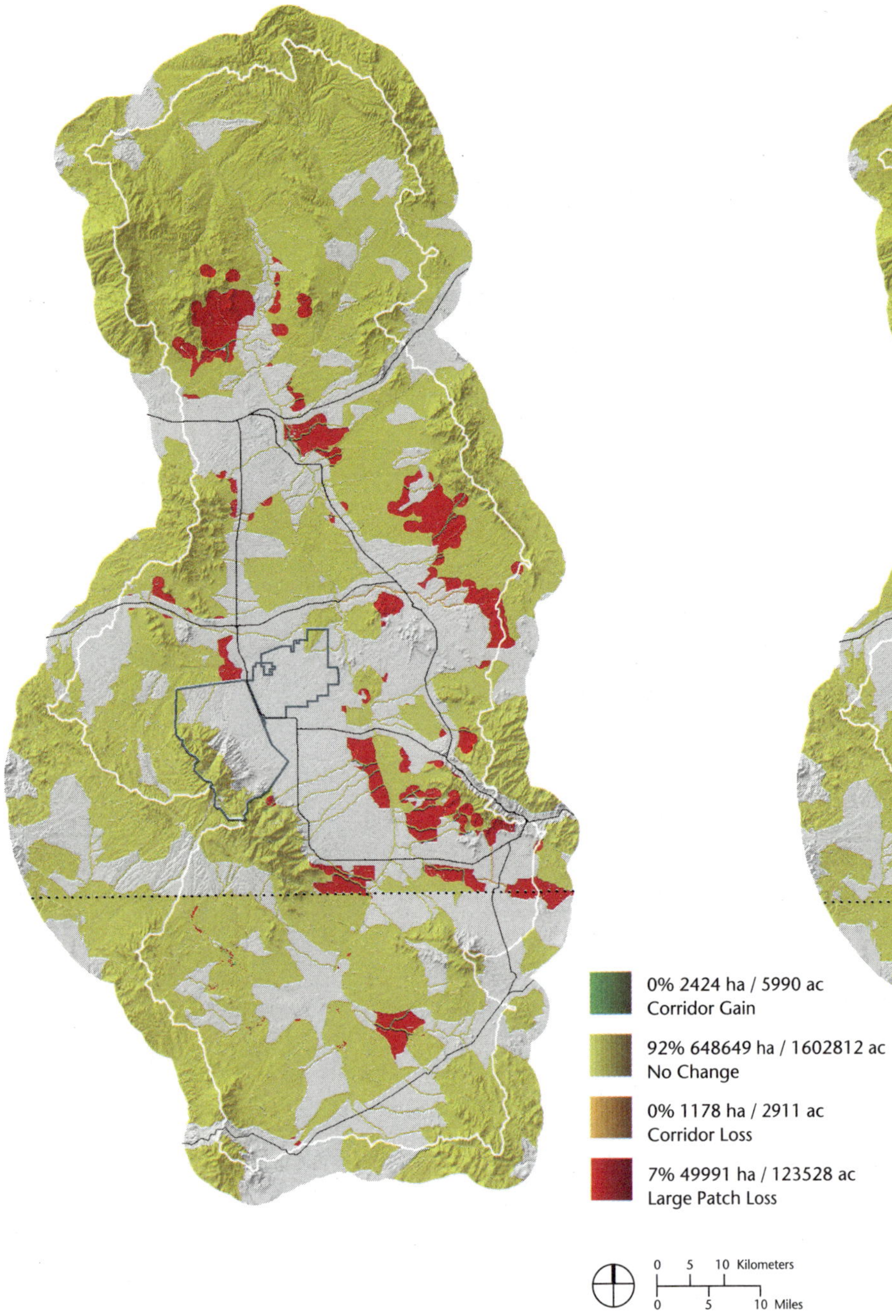
0% 2424 ha / 5990 ac
Corridor Gain
92% 648649 ha / 1602812 ac
No Change
0% 1178 ha / 2911 ac
Corridor Loss
7% 49991 ha / 123528 ac
Large Patch Loss
0 5 10 Kilometers
0 5 10 Miles

Figure 17.3a ■ OPEN 2,
Landscape ecological pattern impacts, 2000–2020

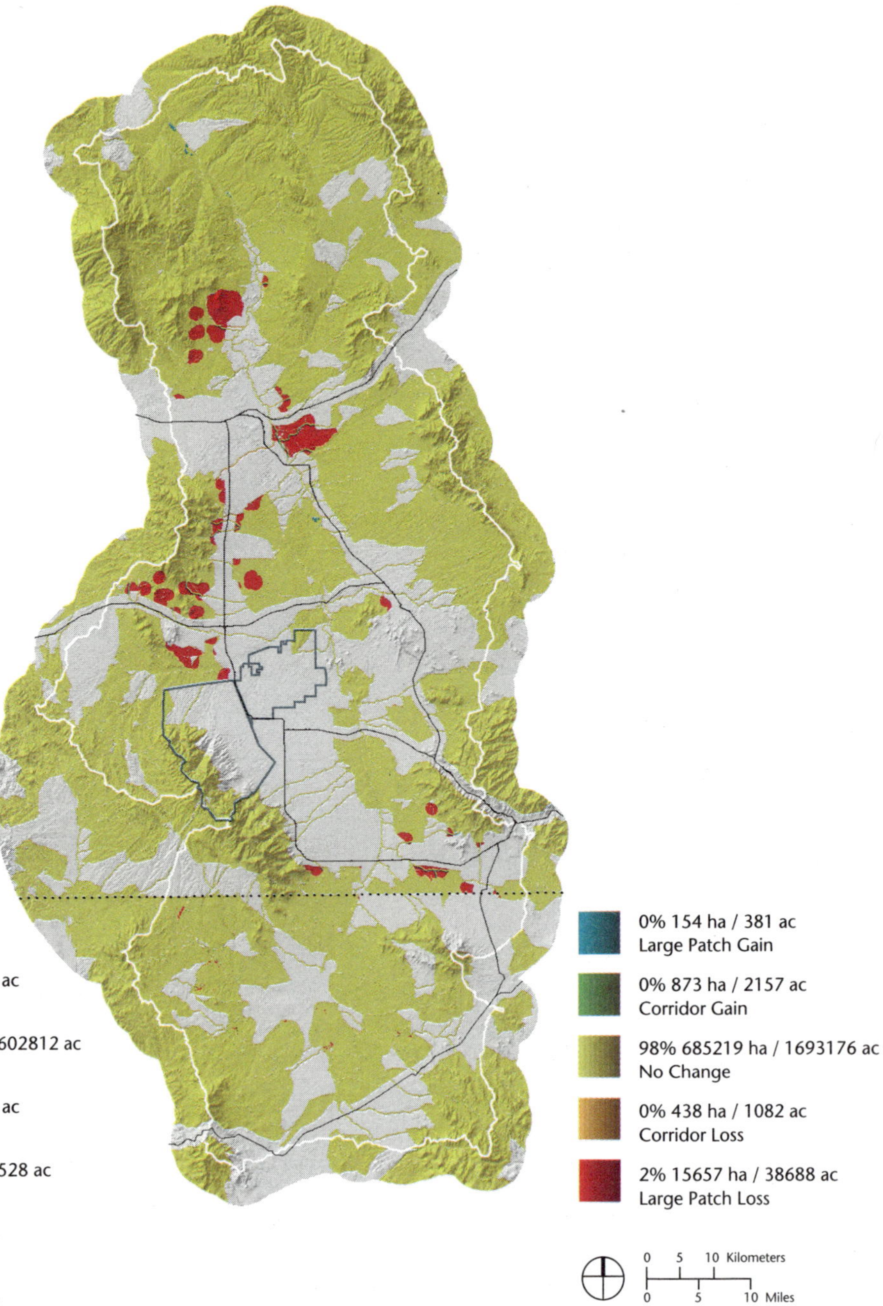
0% 154 ha / 381 ac
Large Patch Gain
0% 873 ha / 2157 ac
Corridor Gain
98% 685219 ha / 1693176 ac
No Change
0% 438 ha / 1082 ac
Corridor Loss
2% 15657 ha / 38688 ac
Large Patch Loss
0 5 10 Kilometers
0 5 10 Miles

Figure 17.3b ■ CONSTRAINED 2,
Landscape ecological pattern impacts, 2000–2020

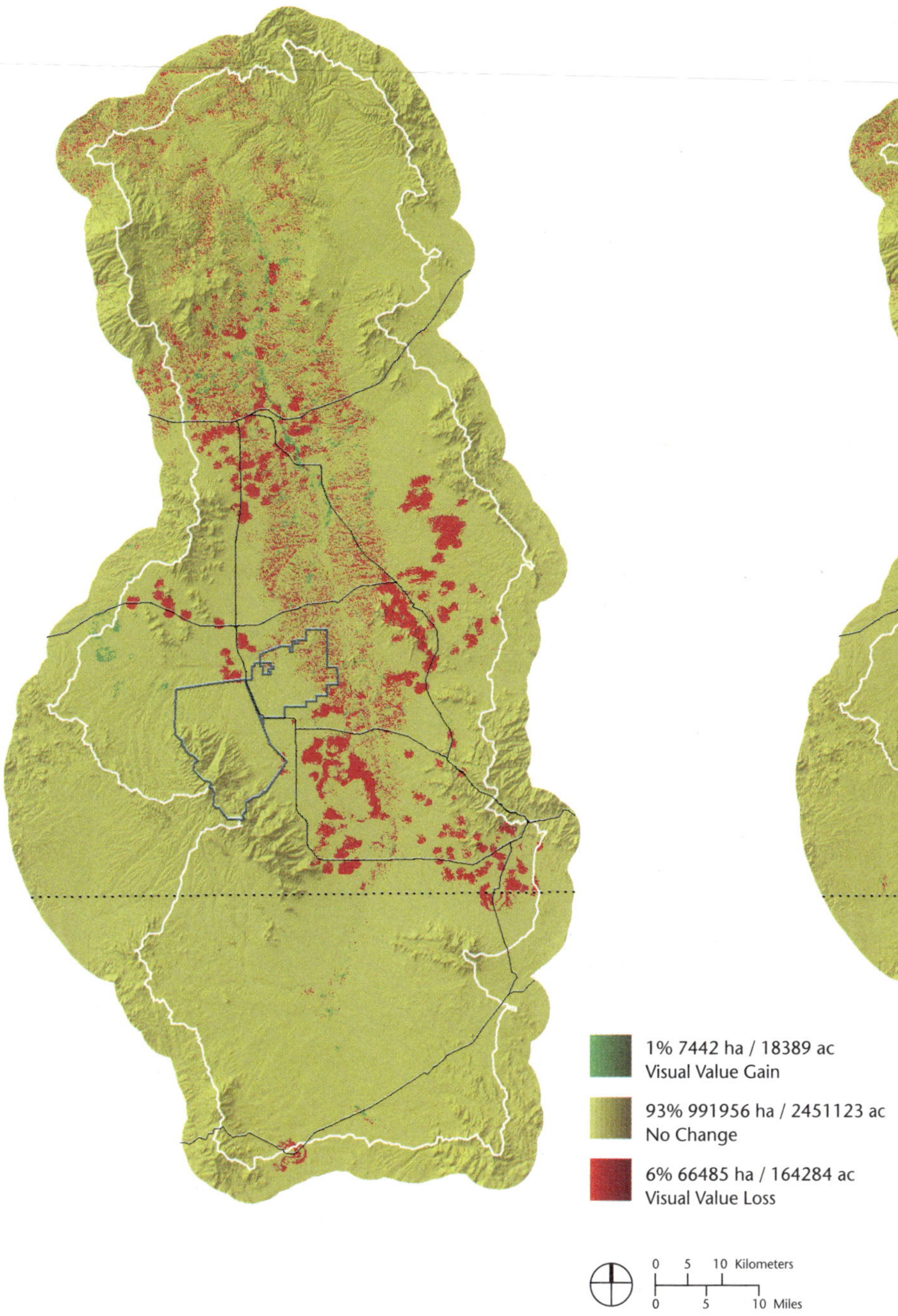
1% 7442 ha / 18389 ac
Visual Value Gain
93% 991956 ha / 2451123 ac
No Change
6% 66485 ha / 164284 ac
Visual Value Loss
0 5 10 Kilometers
0 5 10 Miles

Figure 17.4a ■ OPEN 2, Visual preference impacts, 2000–2020

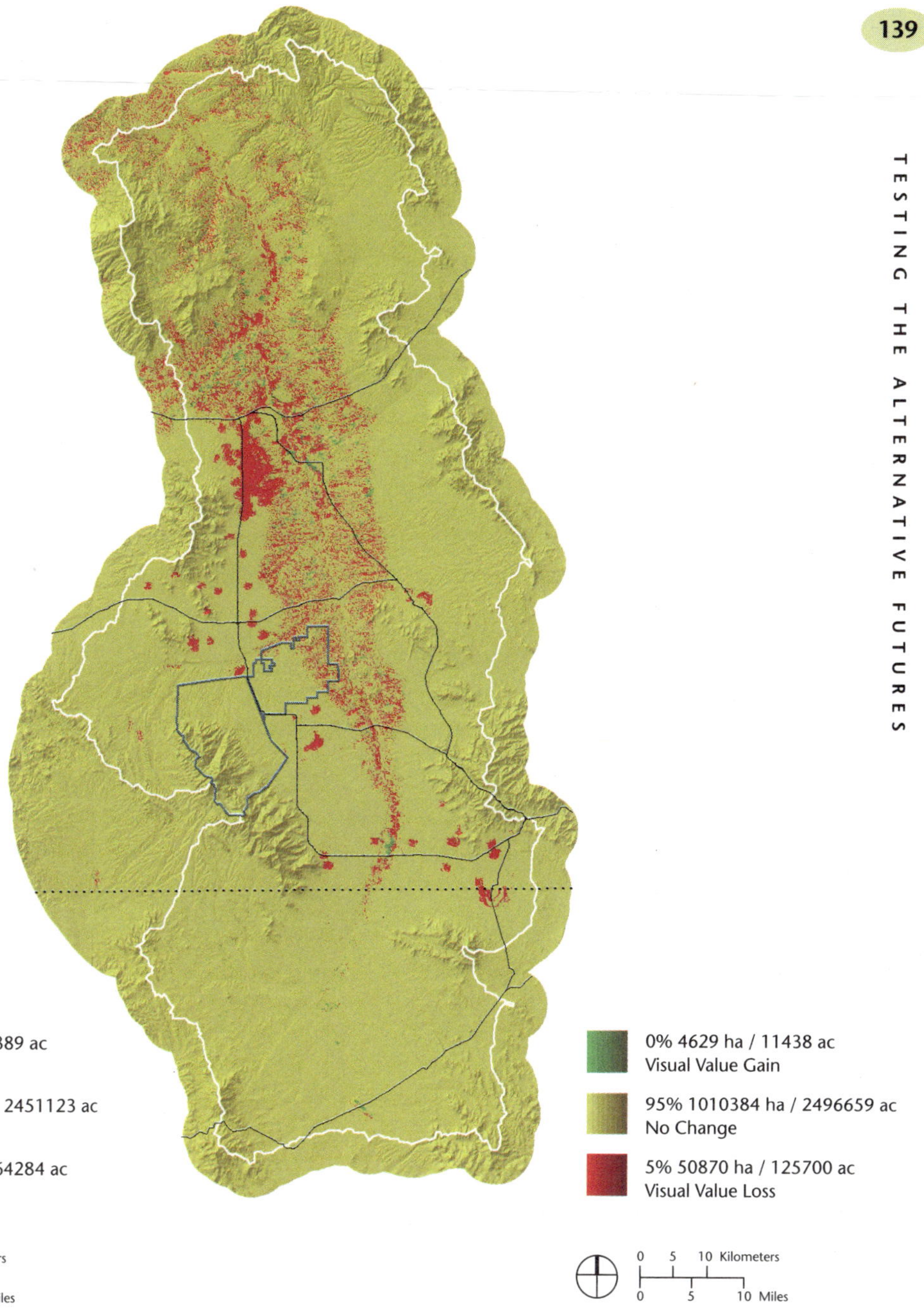
0% 4629 ha / 11438 ac
Visual Value Gain
95% 1010384 ha / 2496659 ac
No Change
5% 50870 ha / 125700 ac
Visual Value Loss
0 5 10 Kilometers
0 5 10 Miles

Figure 17.4b ■ CONSTRAINED 2, Visual preference impacts, 2000–2020

Test 2: What are the impacts on future conditions in Arizona and Sonora if the current population forecast for the Arizona portion of the study area is doubled?

The PLANS scenario is based on the current policies and population forecasts both in Arizona and Sonora. The forecast population growth in Arizona is doubled in PLANS 1. (As a result, the PLANS 1 alternative future shows the same outcome as extending the PLANS scenario an additional 20 years into the future to 2040, assuming an unchanged rate of population growth.) Table 17.2 shows their summary impacts.

The most significant regional difference in impact is on groundwater. Despite the policy assumption of reduced municipal and industrial water demand per capita, the increased population in PLANS 1 overwhelms the assumed water savings resulting from the scenario policies in PLANS, and the groundwater level continues its accelerated decline in the areas around Sierra Vista, Bisbee, and Cananea (figure 17.5a and b). In both PLANS and PLANS 1, policies that retire water rights for agricultural irrigation have beneficial environmental impacts to the south and north of the present SPRNCA. These benefits are seen in improved streamflow and vegetation and in the habitat assessments that include the riparian area. There are other differences, in that PLANS 1 always results in greater decline than PLANS, because of its larger population in Arizona. These differences are not considered to be regionally significant.

Table 17.2 PLANS AND PLANS 1

Summary of Impacts: 2000–2020

Scenario	Baseline 2000	PLANS	PLANS 1
Urban Attractiveness Index	8.3	8.3	8.4
Suburban Attractiveness Index	9.1	9.1	9.2
Rural Attractiveness Index	9.0	9.0	9.1
Exurban Attractiveness Index	7.8	7.8	7.0
Overall Residential Attractiveness	8.4	8.4	8.5
Reduction Municipal/Industrial Pumping (m^3/day)	94,614	-2,759	+17,941
Reduction in Agricultural Pumping (m^3/day)	113,153	-92,190	-92,190
Reduction in Loss of Groundwater Storage (m^3/day)	-131,494	-76,133	-92,058
Reduction in Capture from the River (m^3/day)	38,279	+27,634	+30,087
Change in Wet River Length (Km)	180	+185	+185
Riparian Vegetation (ha)	9,618	+2,920	+2,669
Grassland Vegetation (ha)	372,041	-46,161	-46,421
Area of Large Patches (ha)	687,983	-6,466	-9,632
Willow Flycatcher Habitat (ha)	9,577	+3,113	+2,863
Goshawk Habitat (ha)	146,185	0	0
Gila Monster Habitat (ha)	208,993	+791	+547
Beaver Habitat (ha)	6,469	-241	-374
Pronghorn Habitat (ha)	253,802	-22,546	-22,866
Jaguar Habitat (ha)	320,926	+4,534	+4,225
Threatened & Endangered Species Habitat (ha)	136,329	+1,175	+1,045
Vertebrate Species Richness Per Pixel	168	+.6	+.4
Decrease in GAP Species	4	+2	+2
Visual Value of Views	3.63	-0.06	-0.07
Area of Positive Visual Value	570,862	-49,076	-54,671

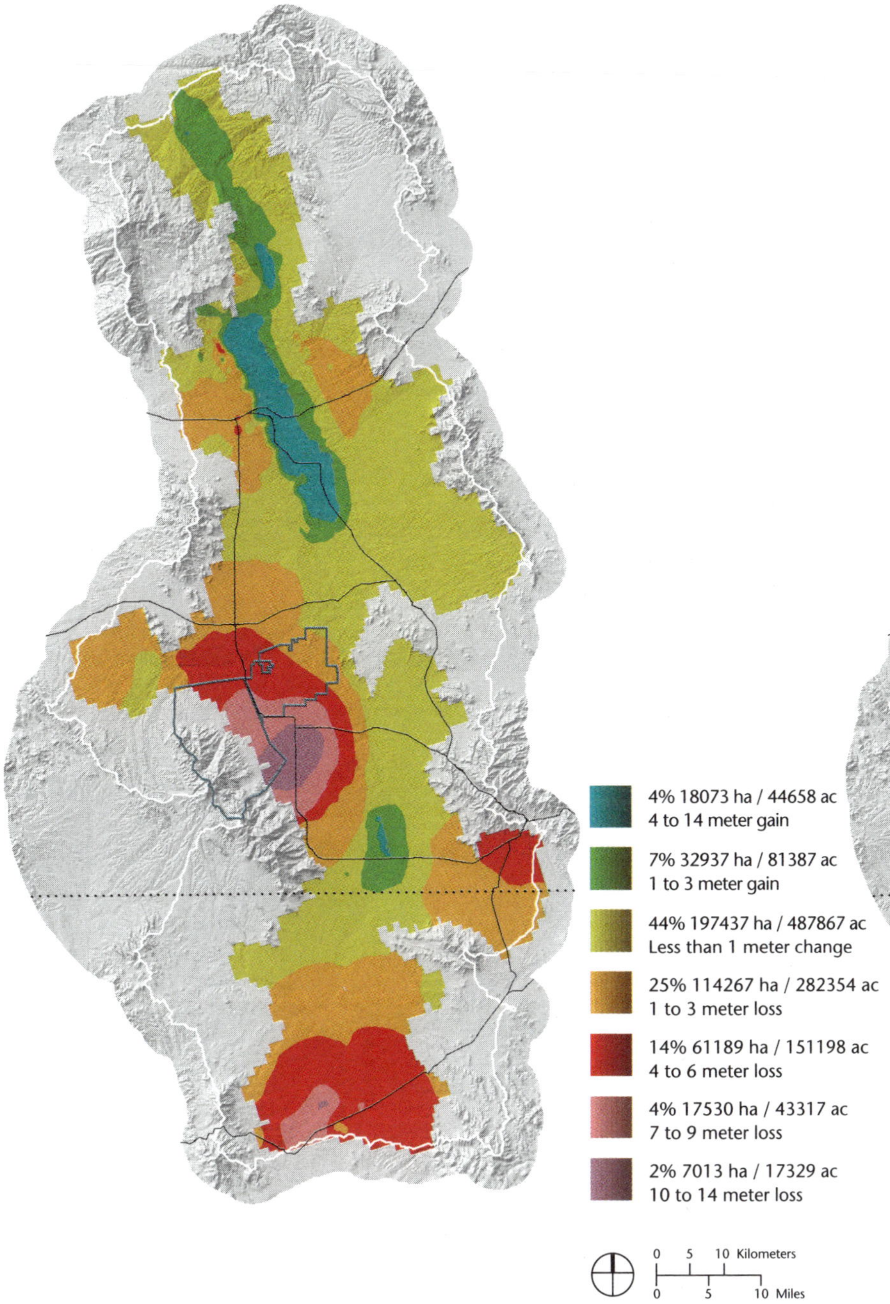
4% 18073 ha / 44658 ac
4 to 14 meter gain
7% 32937 ha / 81387 ac
1 to 3 meter gain
44% 197437 ha / 487867 ac
Less than 1 meter change
25% 114267 ha / 282354 ac
1 to 3 meter loss
14% 61189 ha / 151198 ac
4 to 6 meter loss
4% 17530 ha / 43317 ac
7 to 9 meter loss
2% 7013 ha / 17329 ac
10 to 14 meter loss
0 5 10 Kilometers
0 5 10 Miles

Figure 17.5a ■ PLANS, Groundwater impacts, 2000–2020

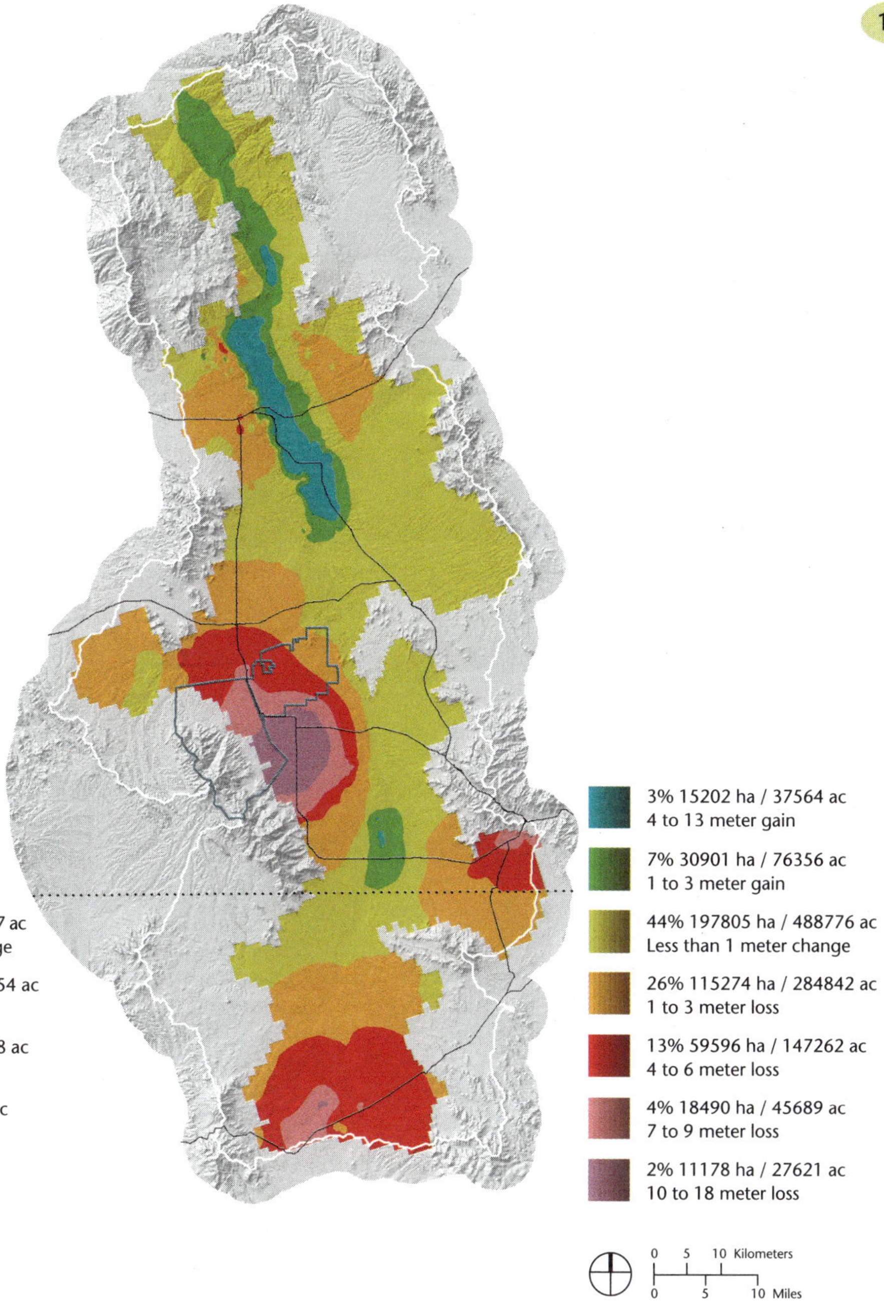
3% 15202 ha / 37564 ac
4 to 13 meter gain
7% 30901 ha / 76356 ac
1 to 3 meter gain
44% 197805 ha / 488776 ac
Less than 1 meter change
26% 115274 ha / 284842 ac
1 to 3 meter loss
13% 59596 ha / 147262 ac
4 to 6 meter loss
4% 18490 ha / 45689 ac
7 to 9 meter loss
2% 11178 ha / 27621 ac
10 to 18 meter loss
0 5 10 Kilometers
0 5 10 Miles

Figure 17.5b ■ PLANS 1, Groundwater impacts, 2000–2020

Test 3: What are the impacts on future conditions in Arizona and in Sonora if there is unexpectedly rapid growth in Sonora?

The PLANS scenario is based on current policies and forecasts in Arizona and in Sonora, whereas in PLANS 2, there is accelerated growth in Sonora and the doubling of Cananea's population and its associated mining industry and of Naco and its agricultural area. Their summary impacts are shown in table 17.3.

Because of increased groundwater pumping and water use in Cananea, there is an accelerated rate of lowering of the water table in Sonora. Many of the environmental impacts are felt in Sonora, especially near the development areas of Cananea and Naco (figure 17.6a and b). There are some impacts in Arizona, but these are minor when compared to the impacts in Arizona caused by the water-related policies and plans in the Arizona portion of the river basin.

Table 17.3 PLANS AND PLANS 2

Summary of Impacts: 2000–2020

Scenario	Baseline 2000	PLANS	PLANS 2
Urban Attractiveness Index	8.3	8.3	8.9
Suburban Attractiveness Index	9.1	9.1	9.8
Rural Attractiveness Index	9.0	9.0	6.6
Exurban Attractiveness Index	7.8	7.8	6.4
Overall Residential Attractiveness	8.4	8.4	8.9
Reduction Municipal/Industrial Pumping (m^3/day)	94,614	-2,759	+30,737
Reduction in Agricultural Pumping (m^3/day)	113,153	-92,190	-89,496
Reduction in Loss of Groundwater Storage (m^3/day)	-131,494	-76,133	-106,991
Reduction in Capture from the River (m^3/day)	38,279	+27,634	+30,218
Change in Wet River Length (Km)	180	+185	+184
Riparian Vegetation (ha)	9,618	+2,920	+2,659
Grassland Vegetation (ha)	372,041	-46,161	-46,437
Area of Large Patches (ha)	687,983	-6,466	-9,302
Willow Flycatcher Habitat (ha)	9,577	+3,113	+2,852
Goshawk Habitat (ha)	146,185	0	0
Gila Monster Habitat (ha)	208,993	+791	+801
Beaver Habitat (ha)	6,469	-241	-530
Pronghorn Habitat (ha)	253,802	-22,546	-22,827
Jaguar Habitat (ha)	320,926	+4,534	+3,946
Threatened & Endangered Species Habitat (ha)	136,329	+1,175	+993
Vertebrate Species Richness Per Pixel	168	+.6	+.5
Decrease in GAP Species	4	+2	+
Visual Value of Views	3.63	-0.06	-0.07
Area of Positive Visual Value	570,862	-49,076	-49,790

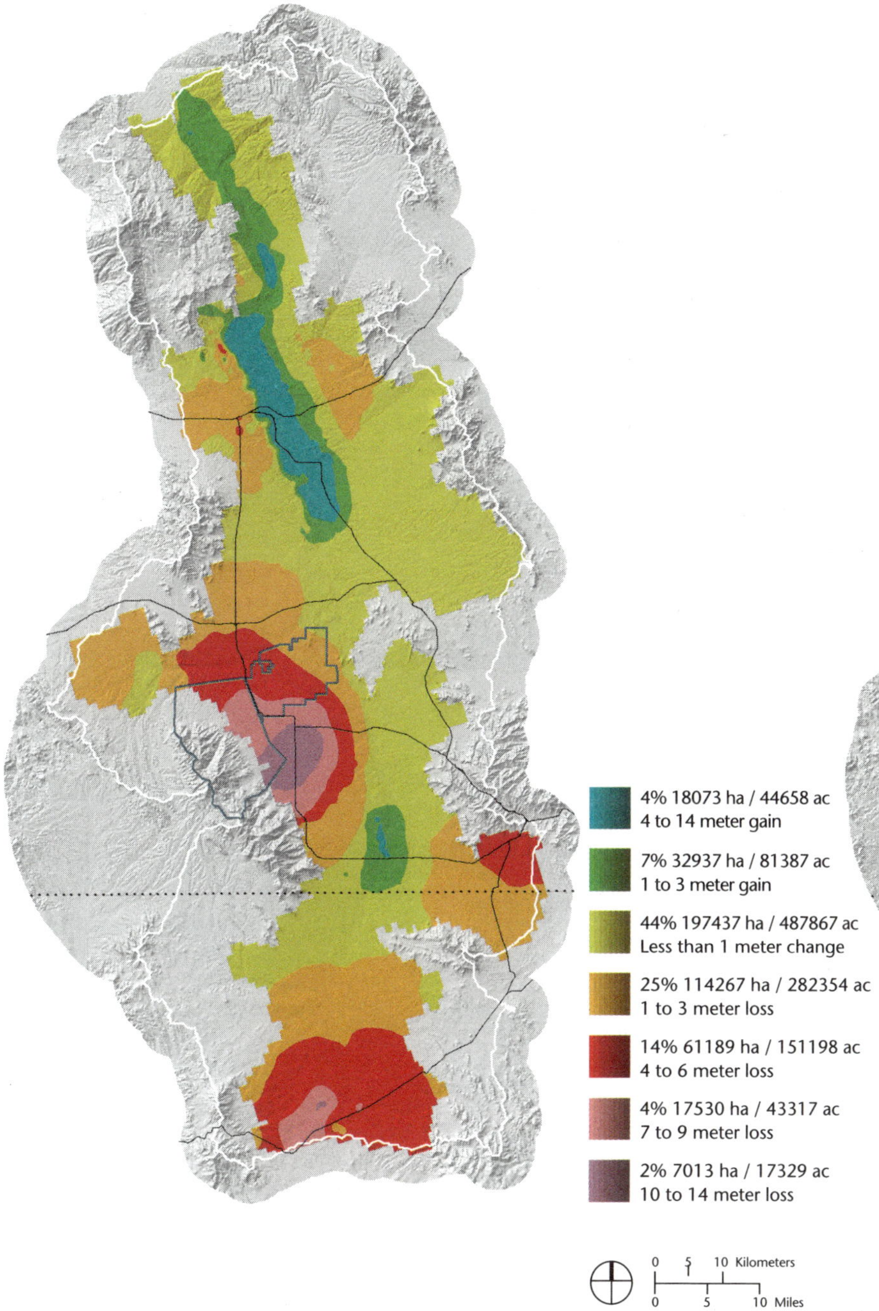
4% 18073 ha / 44658 ac
4 to 14 meter gain
7% 32937 ha / 81387 ac
1 to 3 meter gain
44% 197437 ha / 487867 ac
Less than 1 meter change
25% 114267 ha / 282354 ac
1 to 3 meter loss
14% 61189 ha / 151198 ac
4 to 6 meter loss
4% 17530 ha / 43317 ac
7 to 9 meter loss
2% 7013 ha / 17329 ac
10 to 14 meter loss
0 5 10 Kilometers
0 5 10 Miles

Figure 17.6a ■ PLANS, Groundwater impacts, 2000–2020

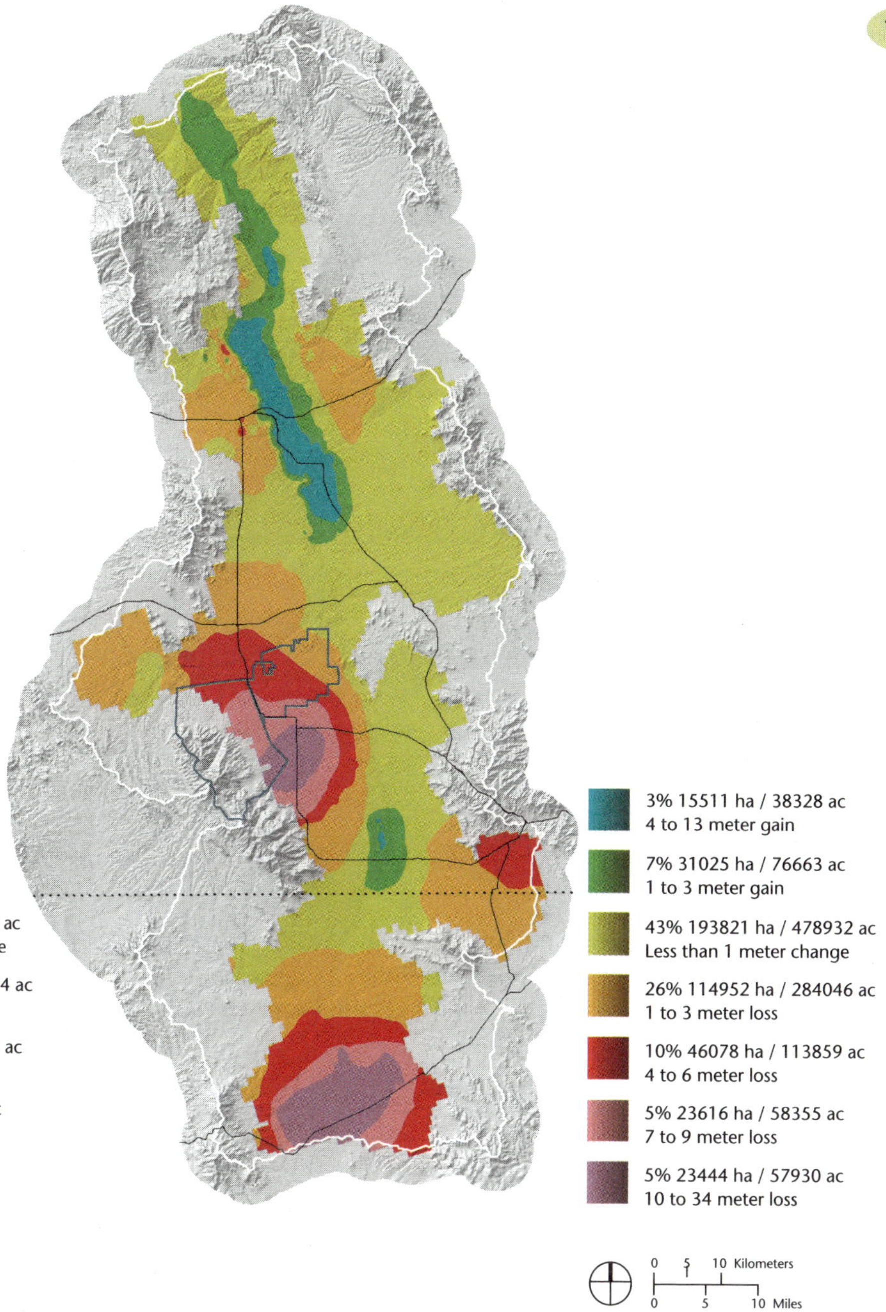
3% 15511 ha / 38328 ac
4 to 13 meter gain
7% 31025 ha / 76663 ac
1 to 3 meter gain
43% 193821 ha / 478932 ac
Less than 1 meter change
26% 114952 ha / 284046 ac
1 to 3 meter loss
10% 46078 ha / 113859 ac
4 to 6 meter loss
5% 23616 ha / 58355 ac
7 to 9 meter loss
5% 23444 ha / 57930 ac
10 to 34 meter loss
0 5 10 Kilometers
0 5 10 Miles

Figure 17.6b ■ PLANS 2, Groundwater impacts, 2000–2020

Test 4: What are the impacts of strict enforcement of policies that guide future development in Arizona into development zones around existing urban areas?

Current plans and population assumptions for Arizona and Sonora as reflected in PLANS are compared with policies that guide Arizona's future development into four zones: Sierra Vista, Benson, Tombstone, and Bisbee, as reflected in PLANS 3. Growth is attracted into the zones mainly by the provision of infrastructure capacity in advance of development, but development outside the four zones is not prohibited. The problem of compensation for landowners' development rights is not addressed. Their summary impacts are seen in table 17.4.

The policy to create development zones has hydrologic and other environmental advantages for the region, but it will have local disadvantages as well. It improves attractiveness for urban and suburban development because of available infrastructure, but it reduces the attractiveness of rural and exurban development. Groundwater and streamflow declines are slowed, except in areas near Sierra Vista and Bisbee. Regionally significant impacts of the PLANS 3 alternative future include a doubling of the increase in willow flycatcher habitat when compared to the PLANS alternative future (figure 17.7a and b).

The PLANS 3 scenario also produces the least overall decline in regional visual preference of all the alternative futures. However, areas of decline are concentrated around Bisbee and Sierra Vista.

Table 17.4 PLANS AND PLANS 3

Summary of Impacts: 2000–2020

Scenario	Baseline 2000	PLANS	PLANS 3
Urban Attractiveness Index	8.3	8.3	8.9
Suburban Attractiveness Index	9.1	9.1	9.8
Rural Attractiveness Index	9.0	9.0	6.6
Exurban Attractiveness Index	7.8	7.8	6.4
Overall Residential Attractiveness	8.4	8.4	8.9
Reduction Municipal/Industrial Pumping (m^3/day)	94,614	-2,759	-816
Reduction in Agricultural Pumping (m^3/day)	113,153	-92,190	-92,533
Reduction in Loss of Groundwater Storage (m^3/day)	-131,494	-76,133	-78,735
Reduction in Capture from the River (m^3/day)	38,279	27,634	27,259
Change in Wet River Length (Km)	180	185	185
Riparian Vegetation (ha)	9,618	2,920	2,967
Grassland Vegetation (ha)	372,041	-46,161	-46,103
Area of Large Patches (ha)	687,983	-6,466	-1,601
Willow Flycatcher Habitat (ha)	9,577	3,113	6,352
Goshawk Habitat (ha)	146,185	0	0
Gila Monster Habitat (ha)	208,993	791	967
Beaver Habitat (ha)	6,469	-241	-251
Pronghorn Habitat (ha)	253,802	-22,546	-22,456
Jaguar Habitat (ha)	320,926	4,534	4,629
Threatened & Endangered Species Habitat (ha)	136,329	1,175	1,210
Vertebrate Species Richness Per Pixel	168	1	1
Decrease in GAP Species	4	2	3
Visual Value of Views	4	0	0
Area of Positive Visual Value	570,862	-49,076	-43,851

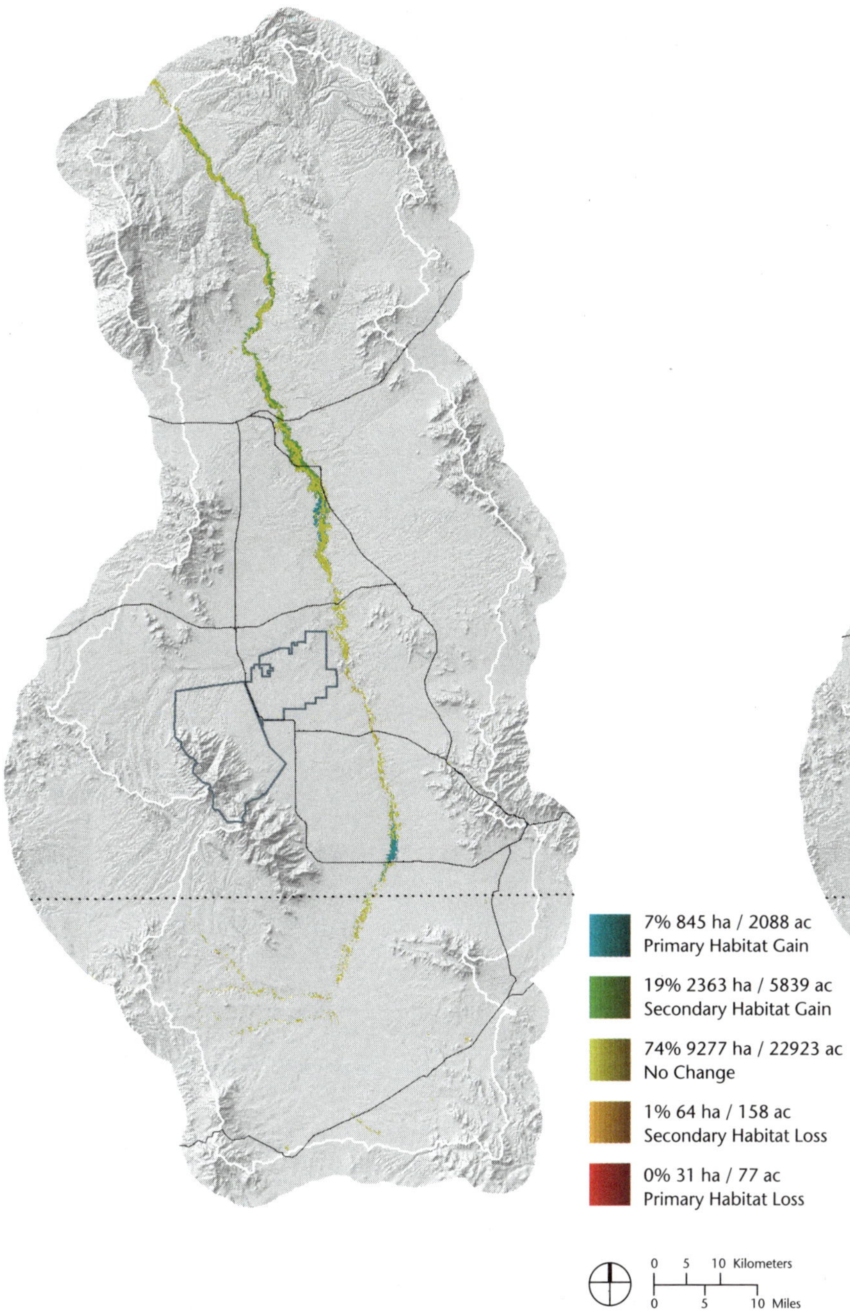
7% 845 ha / 2088 ac
Primary Habitat Gain
19% 2363 ha / 5839 ac
Secondary Habitat Gain
74% 9277 ha / 22923 ac
No Change
1% 64 ha / 158 ac
Secondary Habitat Loss
0% 31 ha / 77 ac
Primary Habitat Loss
0 5 10 Kilometers
0 5 10 Miles

Figure 17.7a ■ PLANS, Southwestern willow flycatcher potential habitat impacts, 2000–2020

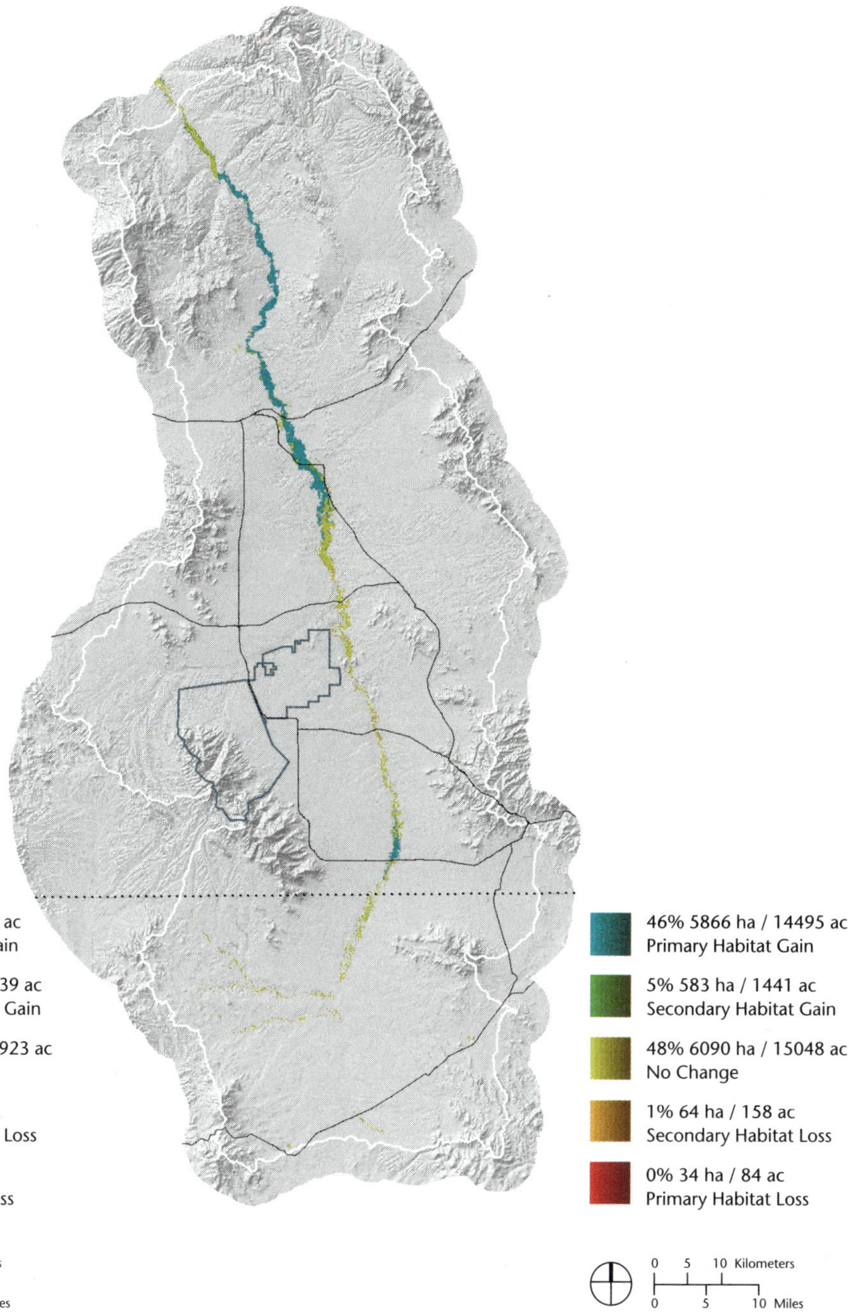
46% 5866 ha / 14495 ac
Primary Habitat Gain
5% 583 ha / 1441 ac
Secondary Habitat Gain
48% 6090 ha / 15048 ac
No Change
1% 64 ha / 158 ac
Secondary Habitat Loss
0% 34 ha / 84 ac
Primary Habitat Loss
0 5 10 Kilometers
0 5 10 Miles

Figure 17.7b ■ PLANS 3, Southwestern willow flycatcher potential habitat impacts, 2000–2020

Test 5: In a policy climate that favors development and is less focused on conservation, what are the impacts of accelerated growth in population and development in Arizona and in Sonora?

The OPEN scenario assumes a relaxation of development controls and a high population growth rate in Arizona. In OPEN 2, on-base population of Fort Huachuca doubles, and in addition, Sonora experiences high growth with the doubling of Cananea and Naco. Their summary impacts are shown in table 17.5.

As anticipated, OPEN 2 produces by far the highest impact on regional hydrology, with the most rapid rate of depletion of groundwater (figure 17.8a and b). This is due mainly to increases in municipal and industrial water use. The largest depletion is in the vicinity of Cananea and is caused by both mining and population growth. There is a small expansion in the extent of the cone of depression in the groundwater near Sierra Vista. In both OPEN and OPEN 2 alternative futures, there is major decline in water flows in the San Pedro River, with related harmful effects on riparian habitats. Both have serious negative impacts on the landscape ecological pattern (figure 17.9a and b), particularly along lower mountain slopes, and on species richness and visual preference.

Table 17.5 OPEN AND OPEN 2

Summary of Impacts: 2000–2020

Scenario	Baseline 2000	OPEN	OPEN 2
Urban Attractiveness Index	8.3	8.2	8.2
Suburban Attractiveness Index	9.1	8.8	9.1
Rural Attractiveness Index	9.0	8.8	7.0
Exurban Attractiveness Index	7.8	7.4	6.0
Overall Residential Attractiveness	8.4	8.3	8.0
Reduction Municipal/Industrial Pumping (m^3/day)	94,614	15,083	49,975
Reduction in Agricultural Pumping (m^3/day)	113,153	-6,382	-3,294
Reduction in Loss of Groundwater Storage (m^3/day)	-131,494	-142,102	-179,707
Reduction in Capture from the River (m^3/day)	38,279	38,098	38,267
Change in Wet River Length (Km)	180	148	147
Riparian Vegetation (ha)	9,618	-2,334	-2,348
Grassland Vegetation (ha)	372,041	-50,434	-50,731
Area of Large Patches (ha)	687,983	-67,486	-49,991
Willow Flycatcher Habitat (ha)	9,577	-2,130	-2,146
Goshawk Habitat (ha)	146,185	-67	-14
Gila Monster Habitat (ha)	208,993	-2,437	-2,545
Beaver Habitat (ha)	6,469	-3,399	-3,451
Pronghorn Habitat (ha)	253,802	-32,306	-30,717
Jaguar Habitat (ha)	320,926	-8,360	-8,481
Threatened & Endangered Species Habitat (ha)	136,329	-3,185	-3,281
Vertebrate Species Richness Per Pixel	168	-1	-1
Decrease in GAP Species	4	2	0
Visual Value of Views	4	0	0
Area of Positive Visual Value	570,862	-79,983	-66,485

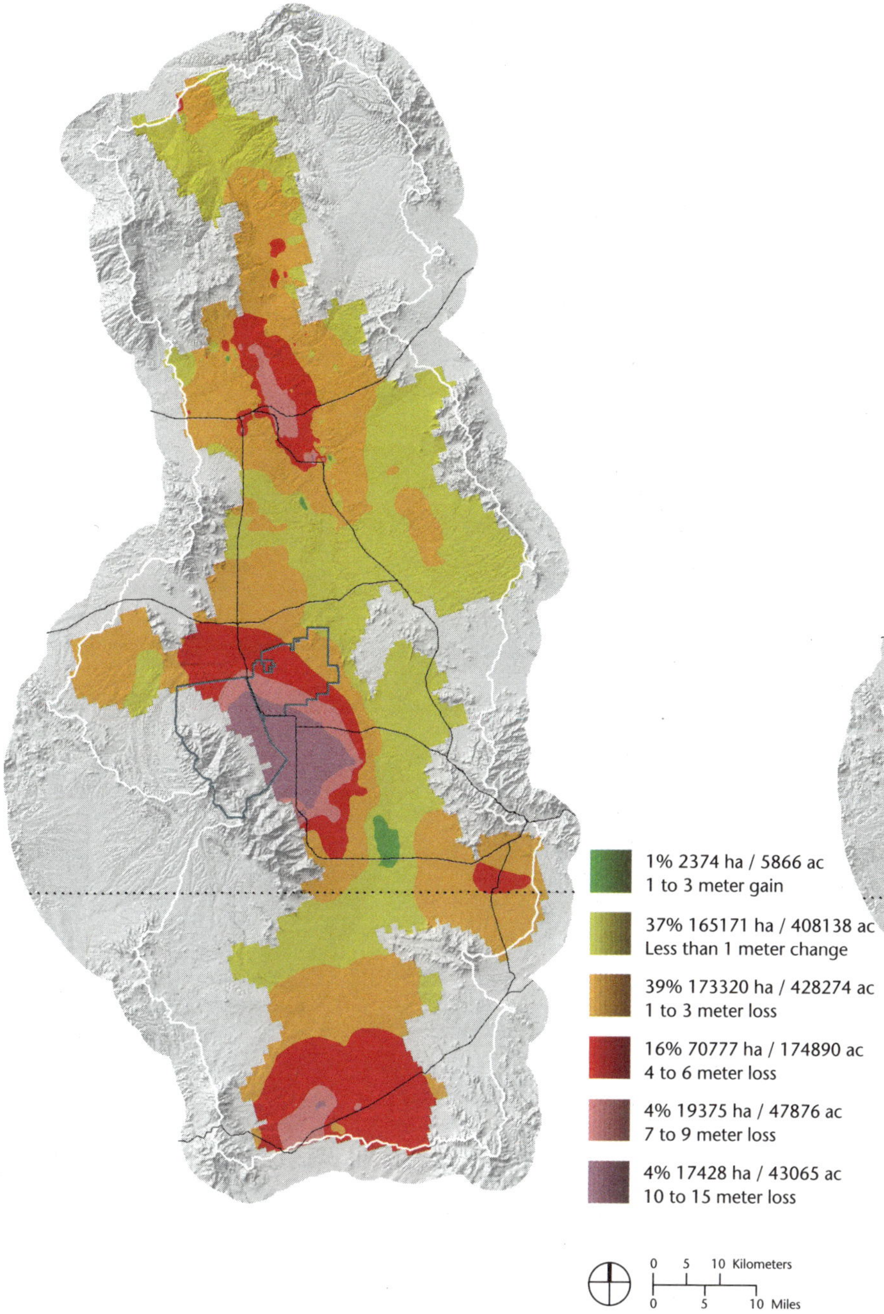
1% 2374 ha / 5866 ac
1 to 3 meter gain
37% 165171 ha / 408138 ac
Less than 1 meter change
39% 173320 ha / 428274 ac
1 to 3 meter loss
16% 70777 ha / 174890 ac
4 to 6 meter loss
4% 19375 ha / 47876 ac
7 to 9 meter loss
4% 17428 ha / 43065 ac
10 to 15 meter loss
0 5 10 Kilometers
0 5 10 Miles

Figure 17.8a ■ OPEN, Groundwater impacts, 2000–2020

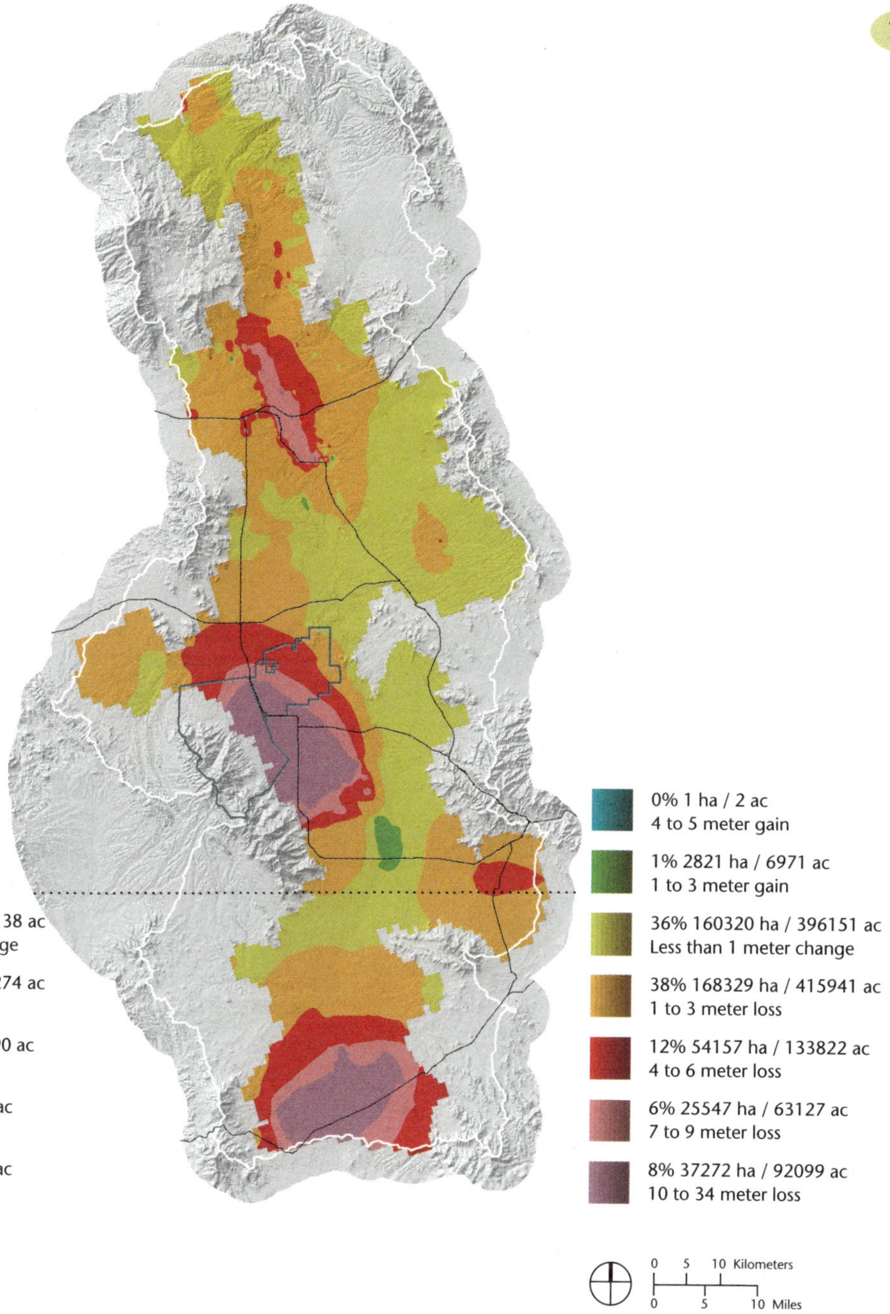
0% 1 ha / 2 ac
4 to 5 meter gain
1% 2821 ha / 6971 ac
1 to 3 meter gain
36% 160320 ha / 396151 ac
Less than 1 meter change
38% 168329 ha / 415941 ac
1 to 3 meter loss
12% 54157 ha / 133822 ac
4 to 6 meter loss
6% 25547 ha / 63127 ac
7 to 9 meter loss
8% 37272 ha / 92099 ac
10 to 34 meter loss
0 5 10 Kilometers
0 5 10 Miles

Figure 17.8b ■ OPEN 2, Groundwater impacts, 2000–2020

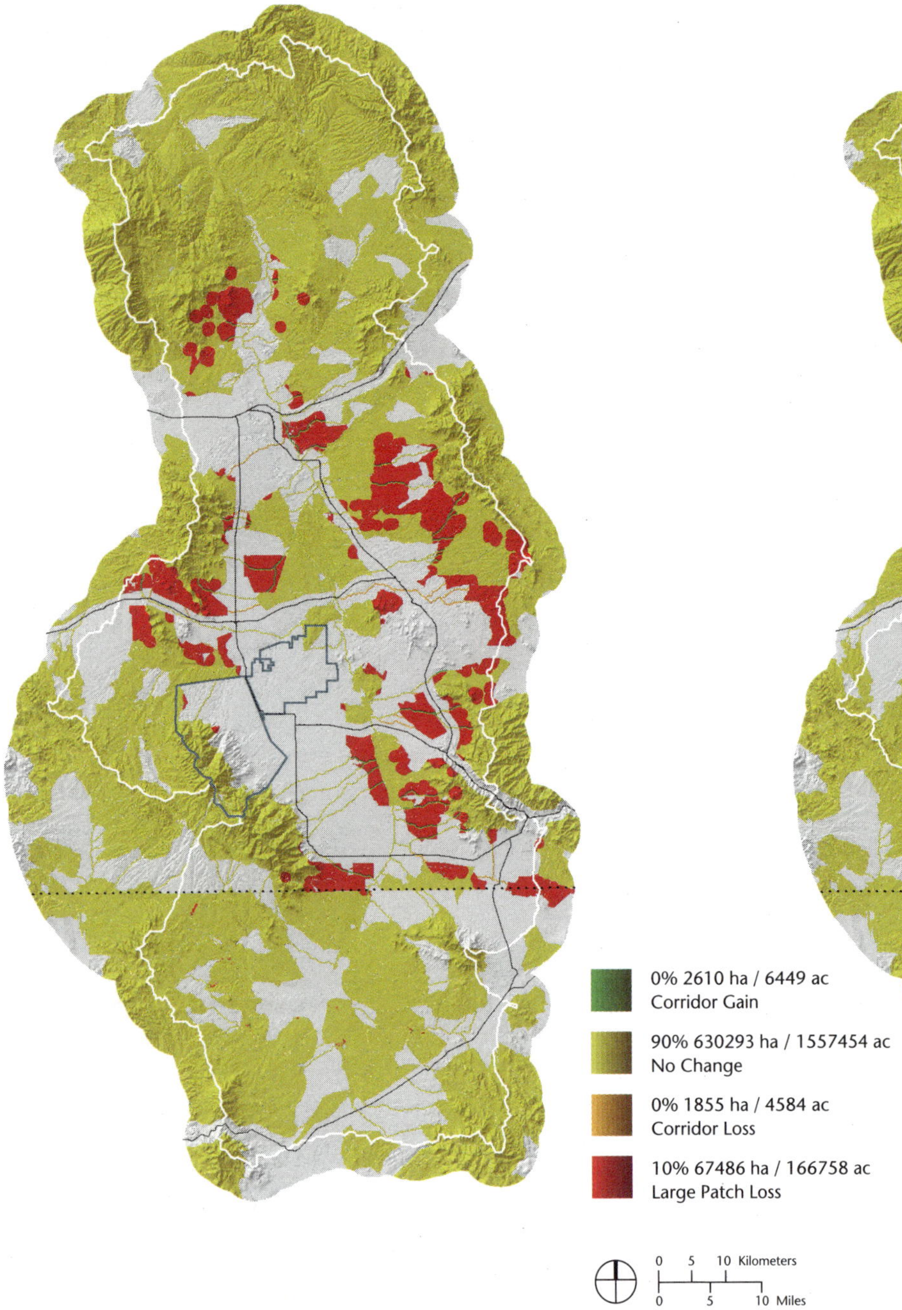
0% 2610 ha / 6449 ac
Corridor Gain
90% 630293 ha / 1557454 ac
No Change
0% 1855 ha / 4584 ac
Corridor Loss
10% 67486 ha / 166758 ac
Large Patch Loss
0 5 10 Kilometers
0 5 10 Miles

Figure 17.9a ■ OPEN,
Landscape ecological pattern impacts, 2000–2020

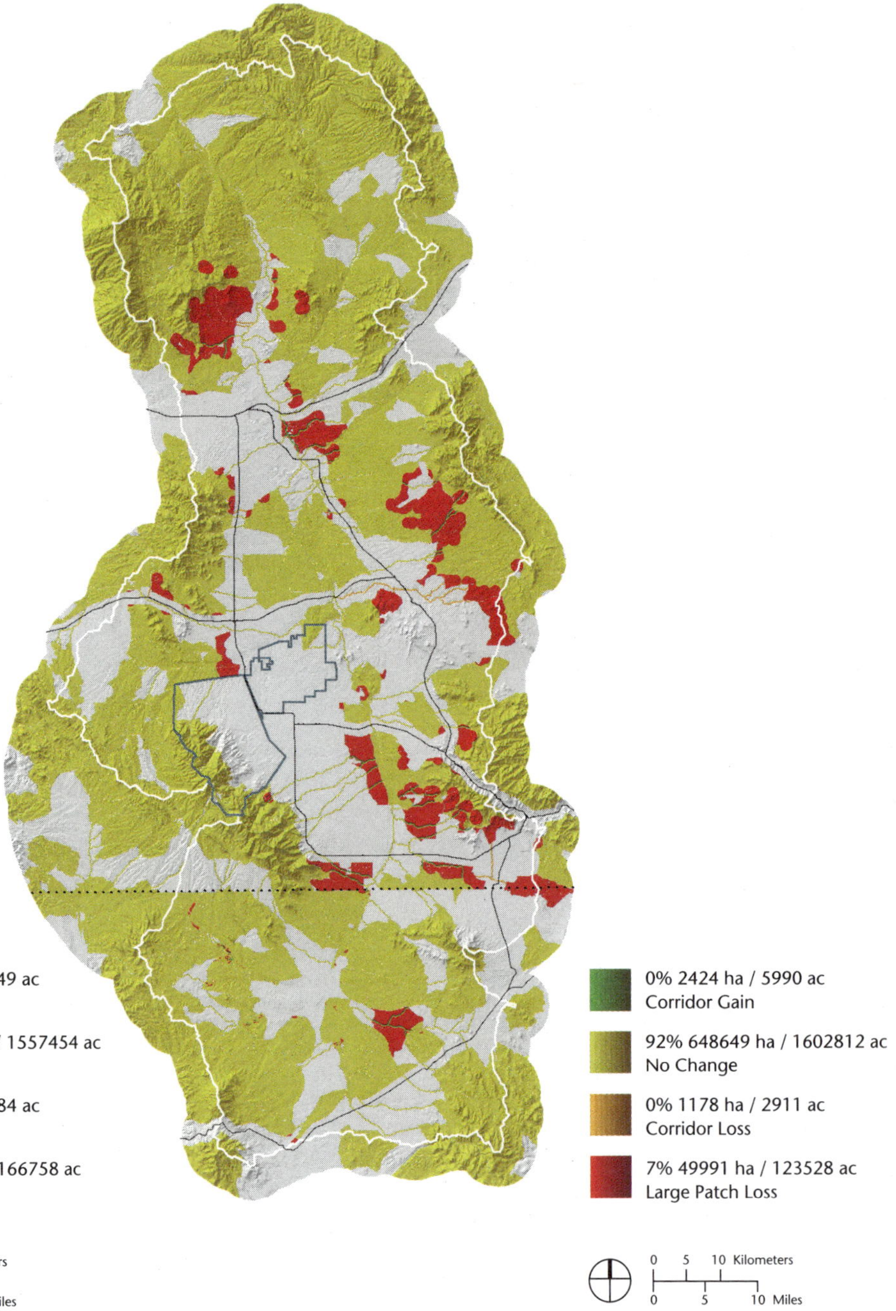
0% 2424 ha / 5990 ac
Corridor Gain
92% 648649 ha / 1602812 ac
No Change
0% 1178 ha / 2911 ac
Corridor Loss
7% 49991 ha / 123528 ac
Large Patch Loss
0 5 10 Kilometers
0 5 10 Miles

Figure 17.9b ■ OPEN 2,
Landscape ecological pattern impacts, 2000–2020

Test 6: In a scenario that constrains development for assumed environmental benefits, what are the impacts of doubling Fort Huachuca's on-base population?

The CONSTRAINED scenario has the lowest population forecast, is more restrictive on the location of future development and on several water-use policies, and is the most expansive in conservation in Arizona. In Sonora, it maintains current plans and policies. In CONSTRAINED 1 these plans and policies continue, but the on-base population of Fort Huachuca is doubled. This test estimates the largest relative (negative) impact of Fort Huachuca encompassed within the alternatives futures. Table 17.6 shows their summary impacts.

Impacts on development attractiveness and on environmental assessments are insignificant, except for impacts on groundwater (figure 17.10a and b). The level of the water table will be affected locally around Sierra Vista, where the zone of decline forecast to exceed 10 m (32 ft) will double in area. It is important to note that Fort Huachuca's proposed gray water treatment plant and the resulting aquifer recharge are not considered in the CONSTRAINED alternative futures.

Under the assumptions of the CONSTRAINED scenarios, the impacts of the groundwater changes near Sierra Vista will not extend to the riparian zone of the San Pedro River by 2020.

Photo 17.1 ■ Housing, Fort Huachuca

Table 17.6 CONSTRAINED AND CONSTRAINED 1

Summary of Impacts: 2000–2020

Scenario	Baseline 2000	CONSTRAINED	CONSTRAINED 1
Urban Attractiveness Index	8.3	8.3	8.1
Suburban Attractiveness Index	9.1	N/A	N/A
Rural Attractiveness Index	9.0	N/A	N/A
Exurban Attractiveness Index	7.8	6.5	7.6
Overall Residential Attractiveness	8.4	8.1	8.1
Reduction Municipal/Industrial Pumping (m^3/day)	94,614	-1,370	5,140
Reduction in Agricultural Pumping (m^3/day)	113,153	-110,859	-110,859
Reduction in Loss of Groundwater Storage (m^3/day)	-131,494	-55,726	-61,493
Reduction in Capture from the River (m^3/day)	38,279	20,901	21,185
Change in Wet River Length (Km)	180	185	185
Riparian Vegetation (ha)	9,618	3,477	3,438
Grassland Vegetation (ha)	372,041	-46,016	-46,056
Area of Large Patches (ha)	687,983	-4,232	-15,503
Willow Flycatcher Habitat (ha)	9,577	6,852	6,812
Goshawk Habitat (ha)	146,185	84	80
Gila Monster Habitat (ha)	208,993	1,664	1,209
Beaver Habitat (ha)	6,469	1,235	1,352
Pronghorn Habitat (ha)	253,802	-21,757	-21,950
Jaguar Habitat (ha)	320,926	5,344	5,282
Threatened & Endangered Species Habitat (ha)	136,329	1,464	1,453
Vertebrate Species Richness Per Pixel	168	1	1
Decrease in GAP Species	4	3	3
Visual Value of Views	4	0	0
Area of Positive Visual Value	570,862	-49,220	-50,652

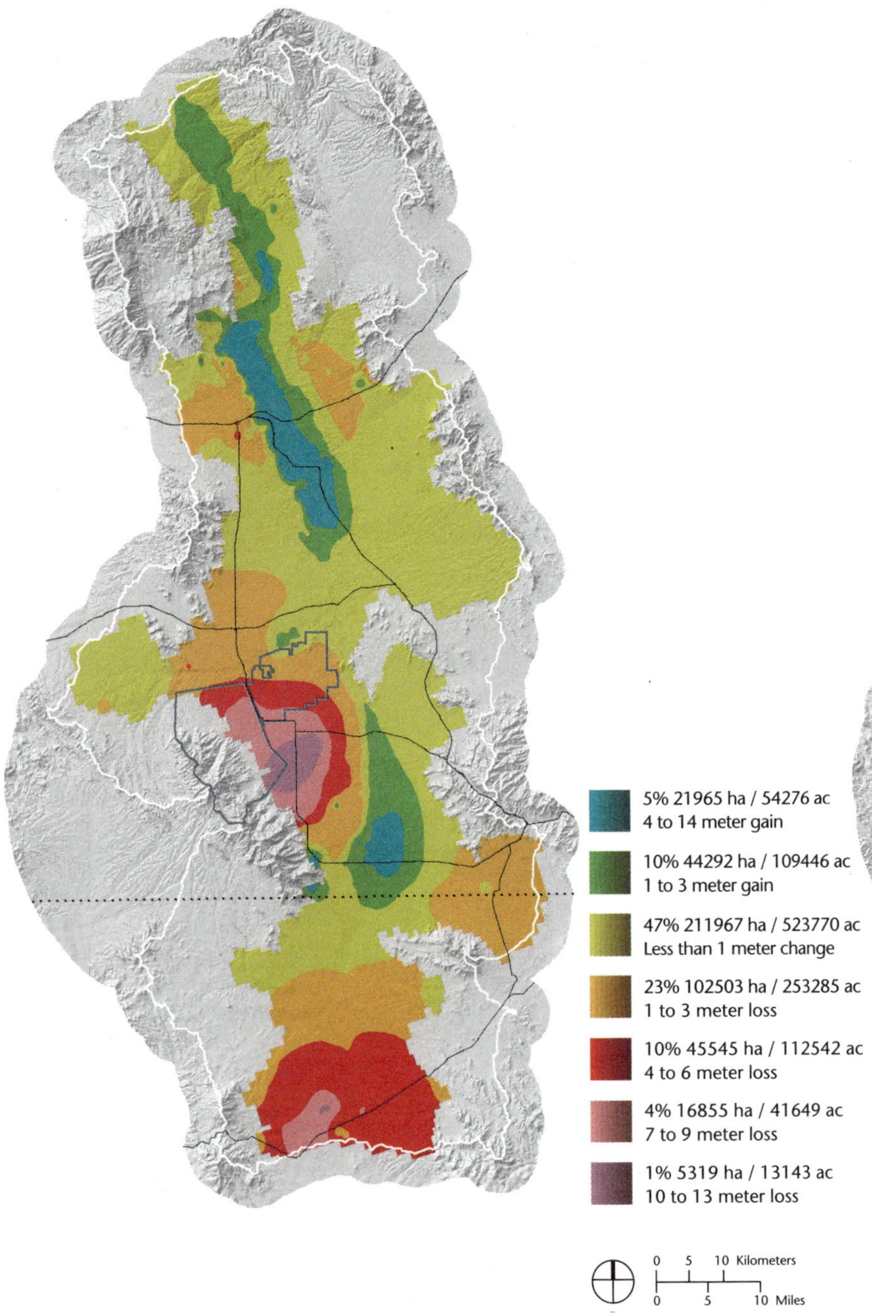
5% 21965 ha / 54276 ac
4 to 14 meter gain
10% 44292 ha / 109446 ac
1 to 3 meter gain
47% 211967 ha / 523770 ac
Less than 1 meter change
23% 102503 ha / 253285 ac
1 to 3 meter loss
10% 45545 ha / 112542 ac
4 to 6 meter loss
4% 16855 ha / 41649 ac
7 to 9 meter loss
1% 5319 ha / 13143 ac
10 to 13 meter loss
0 5 10 Kilometers
0 5 10 Miles

Figure 17.10a ■ CONSTRAINED, Groundwater impacts, 2000–2020

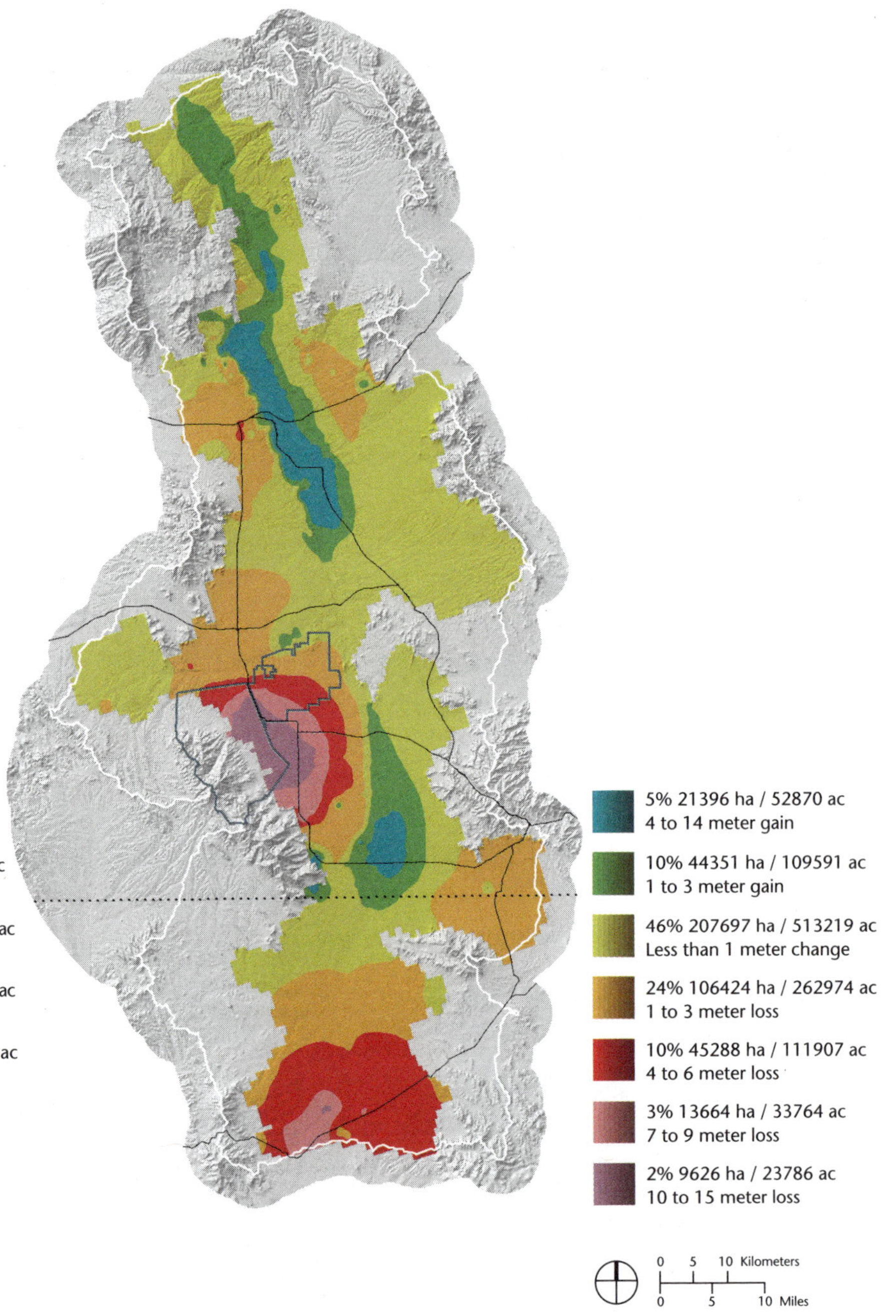
5% 21396 ha / 52870 ac
4 to 14 meter gain
10% 44351 ha / 109591 ac
1 to 3 meter gain
46% 207697 ha / 513219 ac
Less than 1 meter change
24% 106424 ha / 262974 ac
1 to 3 meter loss
10% 45288 ha / 111907 ac
4 to 6 meter loss
3% 13664 ha / 33764 ac
7 to 9 meter loss
2% 9626 ha / 23786 ac
10 to 15 meter loss
0 5 10 Kilometers
0 5 10 Miles

Figure 17.10b ■ CONSTRAINED 1, Groundwater impacts, 2000–2020

Test 7: In the most development-constraining and conservation-favoring scenario, what are the impacts of closing Fort Huachuca?

The CONSTRAINED alternative future is based on the most conservation-oriented plans and policies in Arizona and Sonora. In CONSTRAINED 2, Fort Huachuca is closed and its land is divided between conservation and development. Their summary impacts are seen in table 17.7.

Because it has the lowest forecast population, CONSTRAINED 2 is expected to have the lowest impact on hydrology and habitats (figure 17.11a and b). It increases attractiveness for development because of desirable new sites within the Fort Huachuca property. Although, as expected, it has the lowest hydrological impacts, CONSTRAINED 2 continues to cause lowering of the water table near Sierra Vista. However, this decline is the smallest seen in any of the alternative futures; only CONSTRAINED 2 shows no increase in the area of decline in groundwater of over 10 m (32 ft).

There are no other regionally significant differences between the two alternative futures.

Table 17.7 CONSTRAINED AND CONSTRAINED 2

Summary of Impacts: 2000–2020

Scenario	Baseline 2000	CONSTRAINED	CONSTRAINED 2
Urban Attractiveness Index	8.3	8.3	8.2
Suburban Attractiveness Index	9.1	N/A	N/A
Rural Attractiveness Index	9.0	N/A	N/A
Exurban Attractiveness Index	7.8	6.5	8.5
Overall Residential Attractiveness	8.4	8.1	8.2
Reduction Municipal/Industrial Pumping (m^3/day)	94,614	-1,370	-9,000
Reduction in Agricultural Pumping (m^3/day)	113,153	-110,859	-110,859
Reduction in Loss of Groundwater Storage (m^3/day)	-131,494	-55,726	-47,515
Reduction in Capture from the River (m^3/day)	38,279	20,901	21,050
Change in Wet River Length (Km)	180	185	185
Riparian Vegetation (ha)	9,618	3,477	3,444
Grassland Vegetation (ha)	372,041	-46,016	-46,056
Area of Large Patches (ha)	687,983	-4,232	-15,503
Willow Flycatcher Habitat (ha)	9,577	6,852	6,819
Goshawk Habitat (ha)	146,185	84	80
Gila Monster Habitat (ha)	208,993	1,664	1,209
Beaver Habitat (ha)	6,469	1,235	1,235
Pronghorn Habitat (ha)	253,802	-21,757	-21,950
Jaguar Habitat (ha)	320,926	5,344	5,291
Threatened & Endangered Species Habitat (ha)	136,329	1,464	1,460
Vertebrate Species Richness Per Pixel	168	1	1
Decrease in GAP Species	4	3	3
Visual Value of Views	4	0	0
Area of Positive Visual Value	570,862	-49,220	-50,870

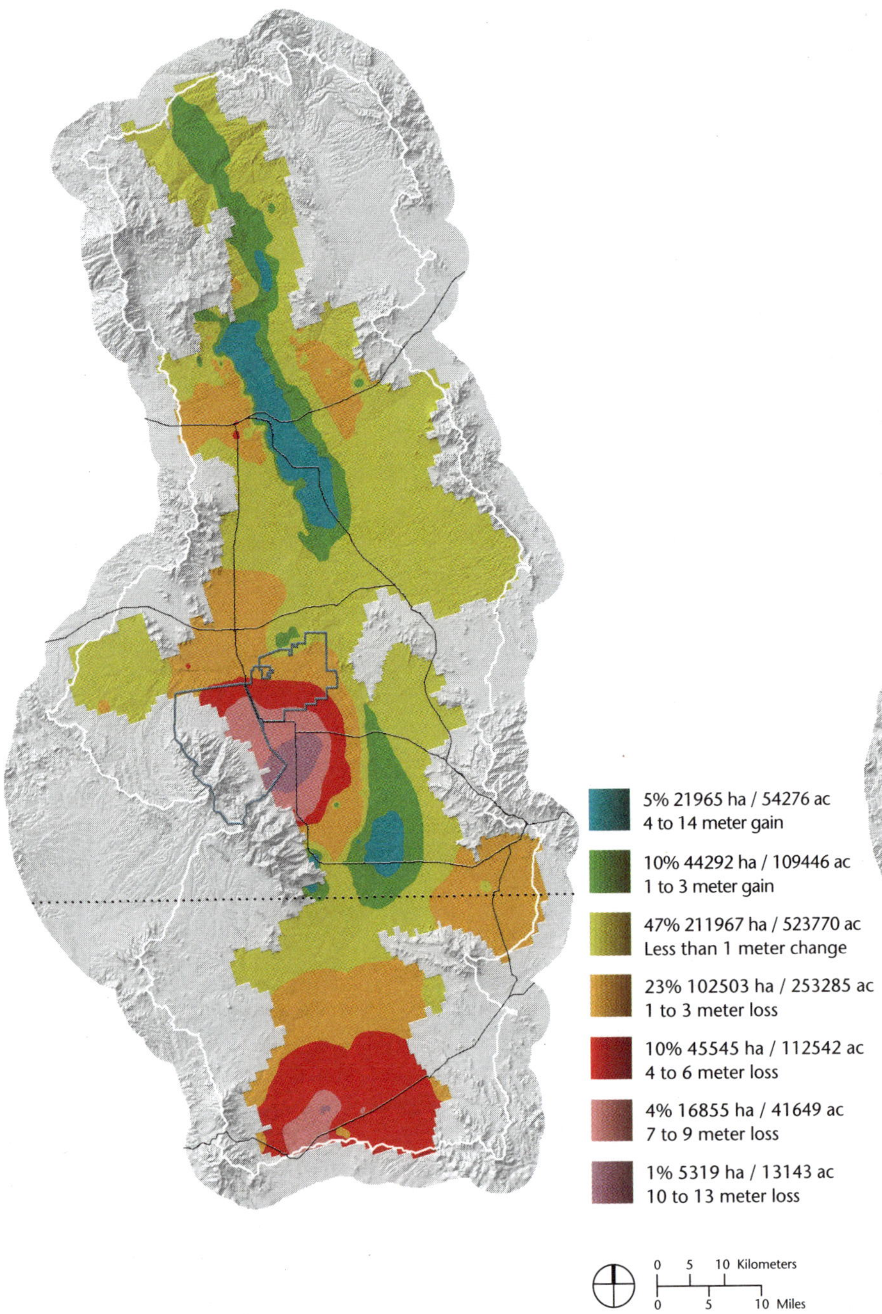
5% 21965 ha / 54276 ac
4 to 14 meter gain
10% 44292 ha / 109446 ac
1 to 3 meter gain
47% 211967 ha / 523770 ac
Less than 1 meter change
23% 102503 ha / 253285 ac
1 to 3 meter loss
10% 45545 ha / 112542 ac
4 to 6 meter loss
4% 16855 ha / 41649 ac
7 to 9 meter loss
1% 5319 ha / 13143 ac
10 to 13 meter loss
0 5 10 Kilometers
0 5 10 Miles

Figure 17.11a ■ CONSTRAINED, Groundwater impacts, 2000–2020

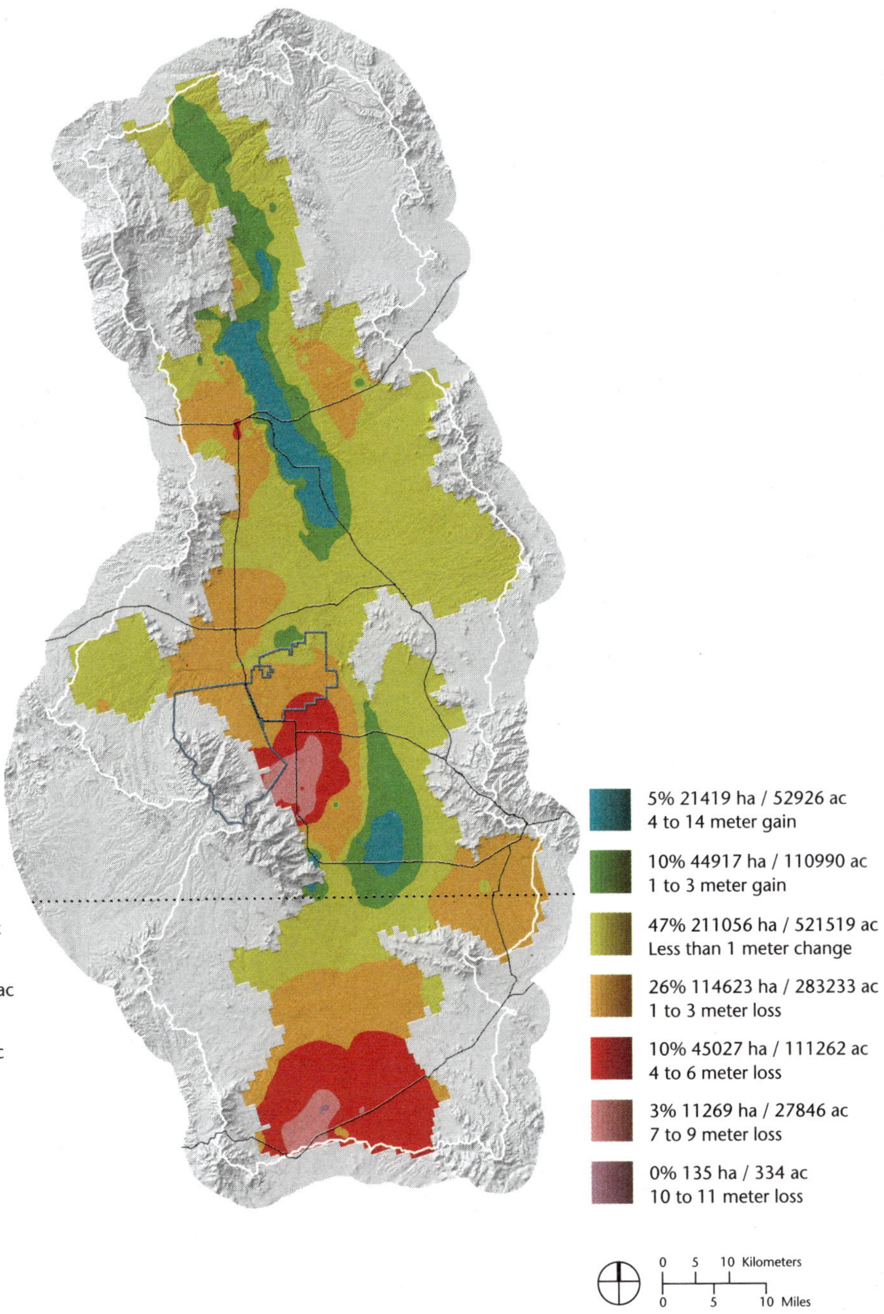
5% 21419 ha / 52926 ac
4 to 14 meter gain
10% 44917 ha / 110990 ac
1 to 3 meter gain
47% 211056 ha / 521519 ac
Less than 1 meter change
26% 114623 ha / 283233 ac
1 to 3 meter loss
10% 45027 ha / 111262 ac
4 to 6 meter loss
3% 11269 ha / 27846 ac
7 to 9 meter loss
0% 135 ha / 334 ac
10 to 11 meter loss
0 5 10 Kilometers
0 5 10 Miles

Figure 17.11b ■ CONSTRAINED 2, Groundwater impacts, 2000–2020

Test 8: What are the impacts of closing Fort Huachuca in an environment of accelerated and less constrained growth in Arizona and one that favors rural and exurban development?

In Arizona, the OPEN scenario has the highest population forecast, fewer constraints on development than do current plans and policies and a lowered emphasis on conservation. In Sonora, it follows current forecasts and policies. Within this set of assumptions, OPEN 1 closes Fort Huachuca and divides its land between conservation and development. The minimum exurban lot size is 16.2 ha (40 ac). Table 17.8 shows their summary impacts.

The OPEN 1 scenario shows the effect of accelerated sprawl. The OPEN 1 scenario increases attractiveness for development because of the increase in available land, but for suburban and exurban residential types, attractiveness decreases because increased demand and larger lot sizes use up the best available land at a faster rate. The OPEN 1 scenario attempts to control wildcat development by allowing rural development only on 16.2 ha (40 ac) parcels, rather than at the present effective density of 3.2 ha (8 ac) per home. The OPEN 1 scenario assumes the same number of new rural homes as the OPEN scenario, but because of the increase in parcel size, the resulting exurban land demand requires five times more area than in the OPEN scenario. Because much less desirable exurban land must be used to provide the larger area, the average attractiveness score for exurban land drops from 7.4 to 5.8 in the OPEN 1 alternative future.

Differences in groundwater impact are insignificant. However, in OPEN 1, there are more serious losses in streamflow in the San Pedro River north of Interstate Highway 10. Most significant are the impacts in OPEN 1 caused by a greater spread of low-density housing types along the lower slopes of the mountains in Arizona. This widespread development causes the greatest damage to the landscape ecological pattern, with the greatest loss of large natural patches, along with declines in species richness (figure 17.12a and b). The OPEN 1 scenario also produces the greatest decline in visual preference of all the alternative futures.

The effects of closing Fort Huachuca in the OPEN 1 scenario are overwhelmed by the impacts of the policies that favor greater low-density rural and exurban development.

Table 17.8 OPEN AND OPEN 1

Summary of Impacts: 2000–2020

Scenario	Baseline 2000	OPEN	OPEN 1
UUrban Attractiveness Index	8.3	8.2	8.4
Suburban Attractiveness Index	9.1	8.8	7.4
Rural Attractiveness Index	9.0	8.8	9.2
Exurban Attractiveness Index	7.8	7.4	5.8
Overall Residential Attractiveness	8.4	8.3	8.1
Reduction Municipal/Industrial Pumping (m^3/day)	94,614	15,083	19,213
Reduction in Agricultural Pumping (m^3/day)	113,153	-6,382	-6,382
Reduction in Loss of Groundwater Storage (m^3/day)	-131,494	-142,102	-147,114
Reduction in Capture from the River (m^3/day)	38,279	38,098	37,523
Change in Wet River Length (Km)	180	148	150
Riparian Vegetation (ha)	9,618	-2,334	-2,369
Grassland Vegetation (ha)	372,041	-50,434	-50,408
Area of Large Patches (ha)	687,983	-67,486	-101,445
Willow Flycatcher Habitat (ha)	9,577	-2,130	-1,985
Goshawk Habitat (ha)	146,185	-67	-511
Gila Monster Habitat (ha)	208,993	-2,437	-2,637
Beaver Habitat (ha)	6,469	-3,399	-3,353
Pronghorn Habitat (ha)	253,802	-32,306	-30,613
Jaguar Habitat (ha)	320,926	-8,360	-9,444
Threatened & Endangered Species Habitat (ha)	136,329	-3,185	-3,334
Vertebrate Species Richness Per Pixel	168	-1	-1
Decrease in GAP Species	4	2	2
Visual Value of Views	4	0	0
Area of Positive Visual Value	570,862	-79,983	-84,106

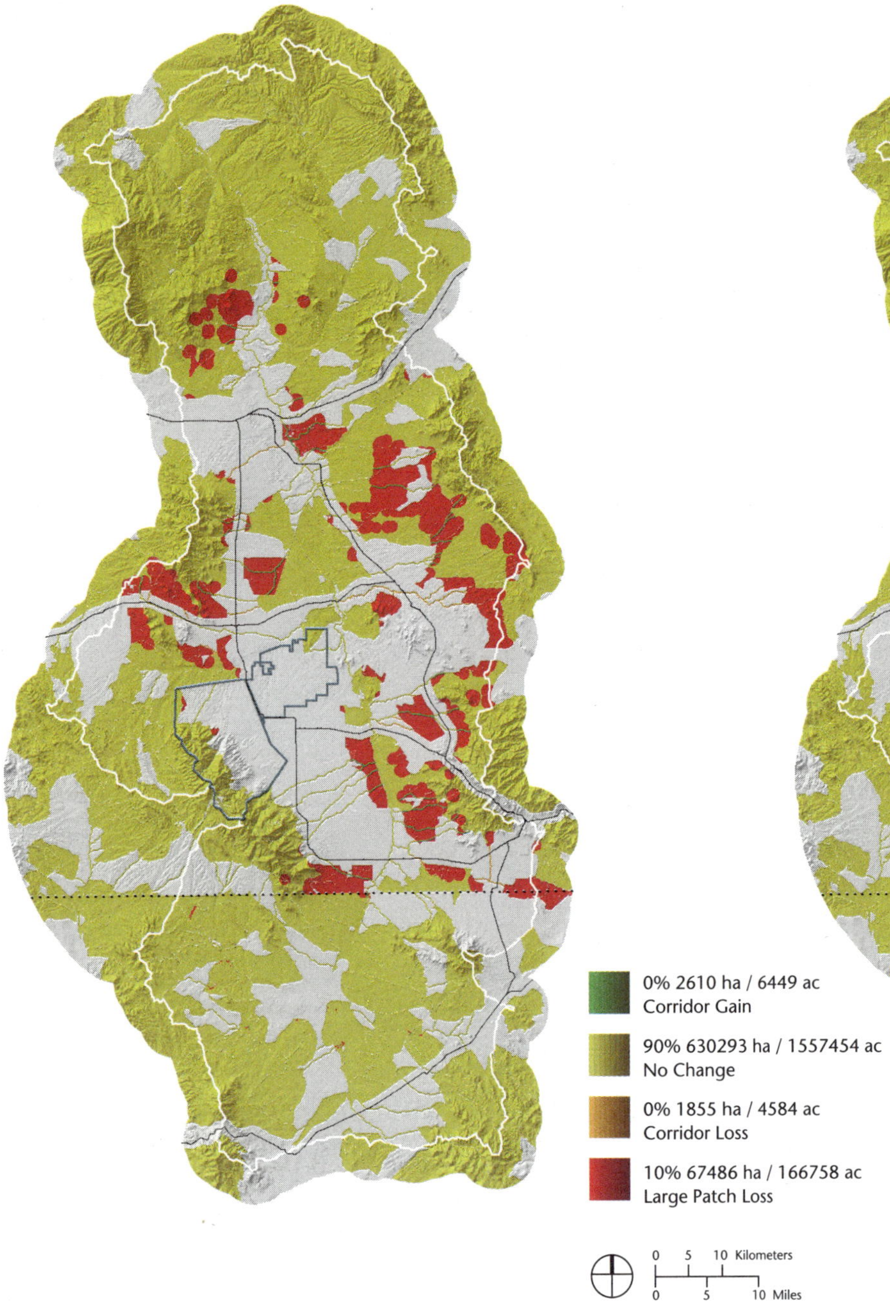
0% 2610 ha / 6449 ac
Corridor Gain
90% 630293 ha / 1557454 ac
No Change
0% 1855 ha / 4584 ac
Corridor Loss
10% 67486 ha / 166758 ac
Large Patch Loss
0 5 10 Kilometers
0 5 10 Miles

Figure 17.12a ■ OPEN,
Landscape ecological pattern impacts, 2000–2020

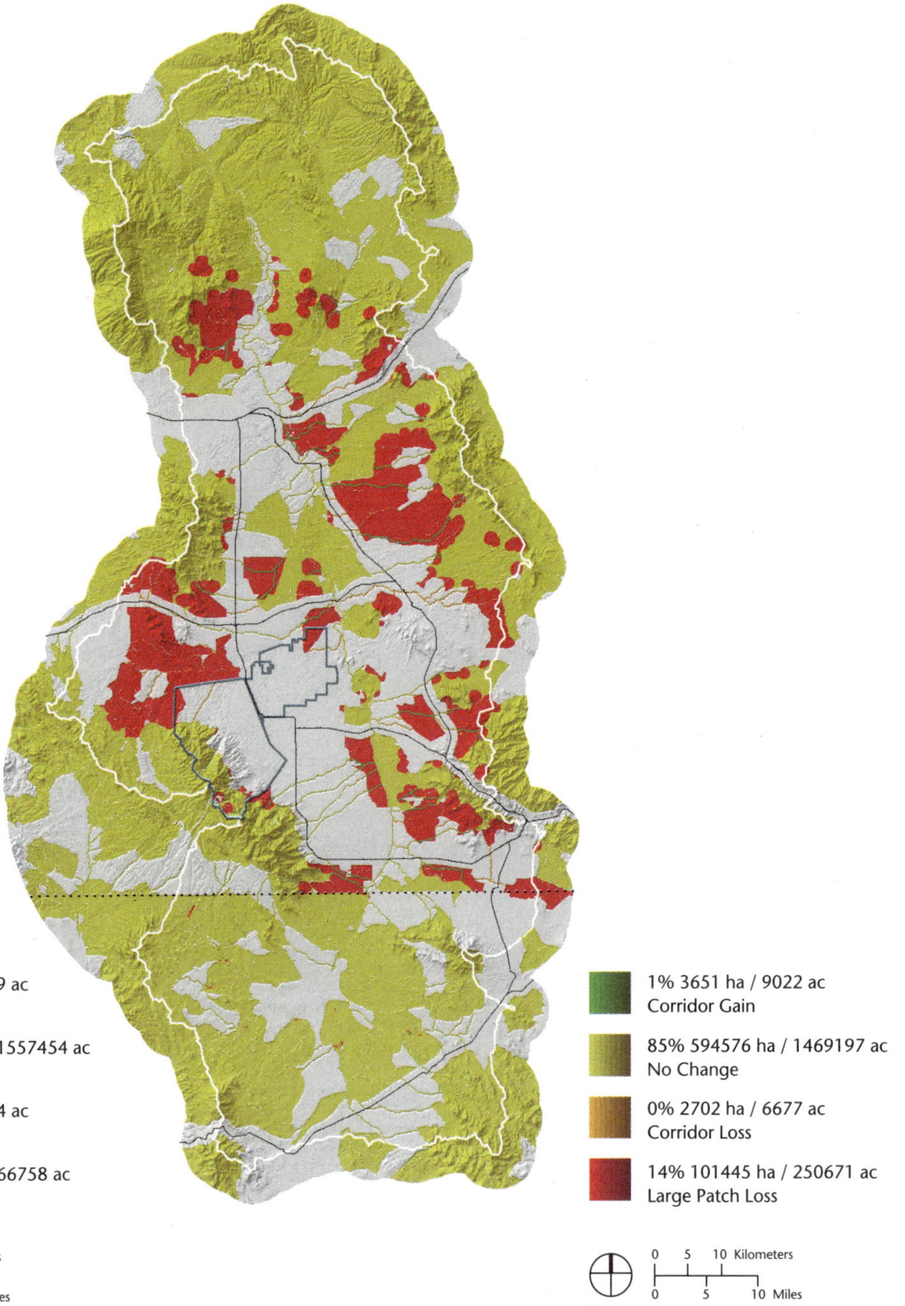
1% 3651 ha / 9022 ac
Corridor Gain
85% 594576 ha / 1469197 ac
No Change
0% 2702 ha / 6677 ac
Corridor Loss
14% 101445 ha / 250671 ac
Large Patch Loss
0 5 10 Kilometers
0 5 10 Miles

Figure 17.12b ■ OPEN 1,
Landscape ecological pattern impacts, 2000–2020

Test 9: What is the variance in impacts caused by closing Fort Huachuca or doubling its on-base population?

Fort Huachuca is assumed to be closed and its land divided between conservation and development, both in CONSTRAINED 2 and in OPEN 1. Its on-base population is doubled in CONSTRAINED 1 and in OPEN 2. Their impacts are compared in table 17.9.

The impact of closing or expanding Fort Huachuca is not easily isolated because other policy choices are incorporated into the scenarios, and secondary impacts associated with off-base employment and population changes are not assessed. However, there are some generalizations that can be made. It is important to note that while there are undoubted consequences for Sierra Vista, there are very few regionally significant environmental differences that can be attributed to Fort Huachuca. In the alternative futures that close the fort (CONSTRAINED 2 and OPEN 1), there are increases in attractiveness for development because of the increase in supply of highly attractive residential land, including, most conspicuously, the beautiful foothill sites now occupied by the fort. These two scenarios also reduce municipal pumping and cause reduced lowering of the groundwater around Sierra Vista when compared to scenarios that increase the on-base population. However, the consequences of either closing the fort or of doubling its on-base population are small when compared to the large differences in impacts caused by the set of policies and plans in the OPEN scenarios when compared with those caused by the CONSTRAINED scenarios.

Table 17.9 Efforts of Fort Huachuca

Summary of Impacts: 2000–2020

Scenario	Baseline 2000	Fort Closed		Fort Doubled	
		CONSTRAINED 2	OPEN 1	CONSTRAINED 1	OPEN 2
Urban Attractiveness Index	8.3	8.2	8.4	8.1	8.2
Suburban Attractiveness Index	9.1	N/A	7.4	N/A	9.1
Rural Attractiveness Index	9.0	N/A	9.2	N/A	7.0
Exurban Attractiveness Index	7.8	8.5	5.8	7.6	6.0
Overall Residential Attractiveness	8.4	8.2	8.1	8.1	8.0
Reduction Municipal/Industrial Pumping (m^3/day)	94,614	-9000	19,213	5,140	49,975
Reduction in Agricultural Pumping (m^3/day)	113,153	-110859	-6,382	-110,859	-3,294
Reduction in Loss of Ground-water Storage (m^3/day)	-131,494	-47515	-147,114	-61,493	-179,707
Reduction in Capture from the River (m^3/day)	38,279	21050	37,523	21,185	38,267
Change in Wet River Length (Km)	180	185.2	150	185	147
Riparian Vegetation (ha)	9,618	3444	-2,369	3,438	-2,348
Grassland Vegetation (ha)	372,041	-46056	-50,408	-46,056	-50,731
Area of Large Patches (ha)	687,983	-15502.8	-101,445	-15,503	-49,991
Willow Flycatcher Habitat (ha)	9,577	6818.58	-1,985	6,812	-2,146
Goshawk Habitat (ha)	146,185	80.28	-511	80	-14
Gila Monster Habitat (ha)	208,993	1208.61	-2,637	1,209	-2,545
Beaver Habitat (ha)	6,469	1234.98	-3,353	1,352	-3,451
Pronghorn Habitat (ha)	253,802	-21949.83	-30,613	-21,950	-30,717
Jaguar Habitat (ha)	320,926	5290.83	-9,444	5,282	-8,481
Threatened & Endangered Species Habitat (ha)	136,329	1459.89	-3,334	1,453	-3,281
Vertebrate Species Richness Per Pixel	168	0.9	-1	1	-1
Decrease in GAP Species	4	3	2	3	0
Visual Value of Views	4	-0.06	0	0	0
Area of Positive Visual Value	570,862	-50870	-84,106	-50,652	-66,485

Test 10: What differences will the relaxation of development regulations from those now in force make for the future of Sierra Vista?

The series of computer-generated aerial perspective views looking northward over the southern part of Sierra Vista illustrate several important differences between the OPEN and PLANS alternative futures.

Two views show conditions in 2000: existing land use/land cover (figure 17.13) and existing wells (figure 17.14).

Those figures are followed by paired views for comparison between the OPEN (*a* series) and PLANS (*b* series) impacts: attractiveness for suburban residential development (figure 17.15a and b); land use/land cover 2020 (figure 17.16a and b); new wells (figure 17.17a and b); change in groundwater level (figure 17.18a and b); change in streamflow in the San Pedro River (figure 17.19a and b); species richness (figure 17.20a and b); pronghorn habitat change (figure 17.21a and b); and change in visual preference (figure 17.22a and b). The outcomes of the OPEN alternative future appear on the left, and the PLANS alternative future on the right.

The PLANS alternative future shows the consequences of current plans and policies, whereas OPEN relaxes them to allow more development. When compared to PLANS, the OPEN alternative future has considerably more development along the foothills of the Huachuca Mountains and in the valley around the existing developed area. More wells will be dug, and municipal pumping at a greatly increased rate will cause much faster lowering of the groundwater. There will be harmful reductions in streamflow and consequent deterioration of vegetation in the San Pedro riparian zone. All habitat-related measures will decline and will decline over larger areas. Sierra Vista and its outskirts will decline in visual preference.

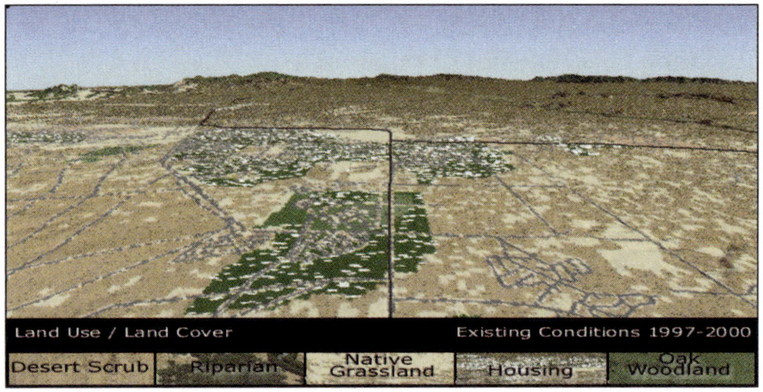
Land Use / Land Cover
Existing Conditions 1997-2000
Desert Scrub
Riparian
Native Grassland
Housing
Oak Woodland

Figure 17.13 ■ Sierra Vista aerial views land use/land cover, 2000

Wells
Current Conditions 2000

Figure 17.14 ■ Sierra Vista, Existing wells, 2000

Attractiveness to Suburban Residential Development
Highest
Least

Figure 17.15a ■ Sierra Vista OPEN, Attractiveness for suburban residential development, 2000

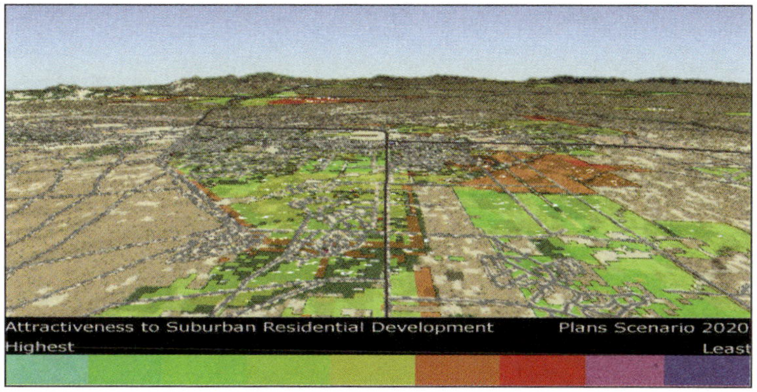
Attractiveness to Suburban Residential Development
Plans Scenario 2020
Highest
Least

Figure 17.15b ■ Sierra Vista PLANS, Attractiveness for suburban residential development, 2000

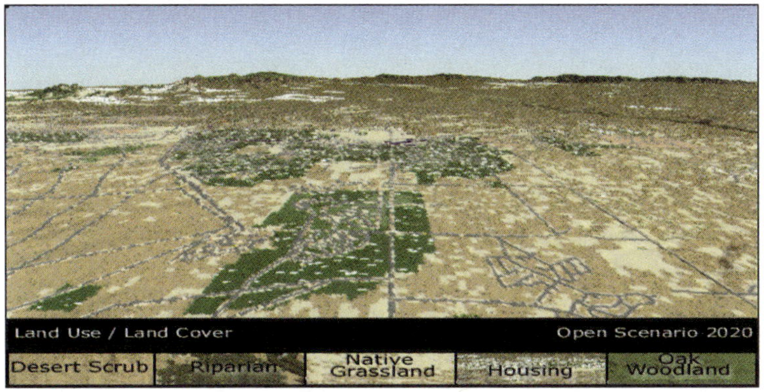
Land Use / Land Cover
Open Scenario 2020
Desert Scrub
Riparian
Native Grassland
Housing
Oak Woodland

Figure 17.16a ■ Sierra Vista OPEN, Land use/land cover, 2020

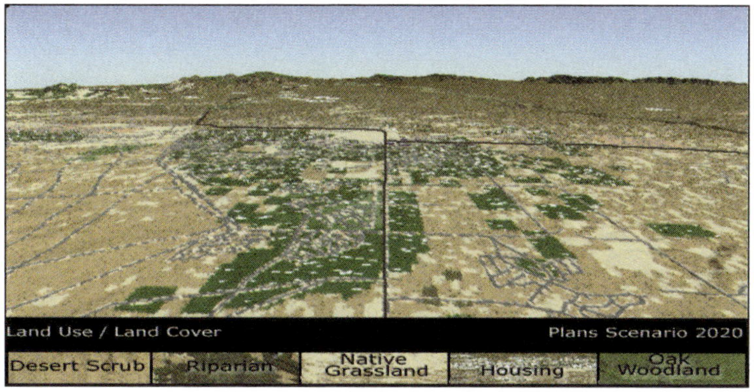
Land Use / Land Cover
Plans Scenario 2020
Desert Scrub
Riparian
Native Grassland
Housing
Oak Woodland

Figure 17.16b ■ Sierra Vista PLANS, Land use/land cover, 2020

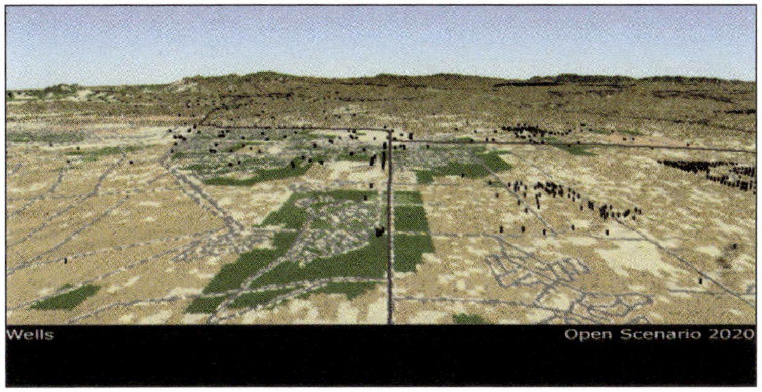
Wells
Open Scenario 2020

Figure 17.17a ■ Sierra Vista OPEN, New wells, 2000–2020

Wells
Plans Scenario 2020

Figure 17.17b ■ Sierra Vista PLANS, New wells, 2000–2020

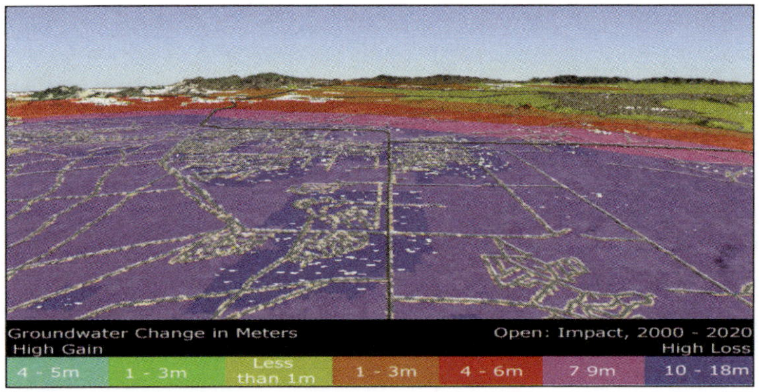
Groundwater Change in Meters
Open: Impact, 2000 - 2020
High Gain
High Loss
4 - 5m
1 - 3m
Less than 1m
1 - 3m
4 - 6m
7 9m
10 - 18m

Figure 17.18a ■ Sierra Vista OPEN, Groundwater impacts, 2000–2020

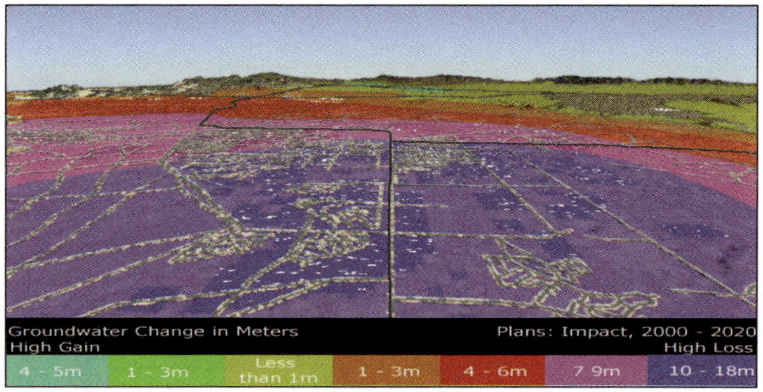
Groundwater Change in Meters
Plans: Impact, 2000 - 2020
High Gain
High Loss
4 - 5m
1 - 3m
Less than 1m
1 - 3m
4 - 6m
7 9m
10 - 18m

Figure 17.18b ■ Sierra Vista PLANS, Groundwater impacts, 2000–2020

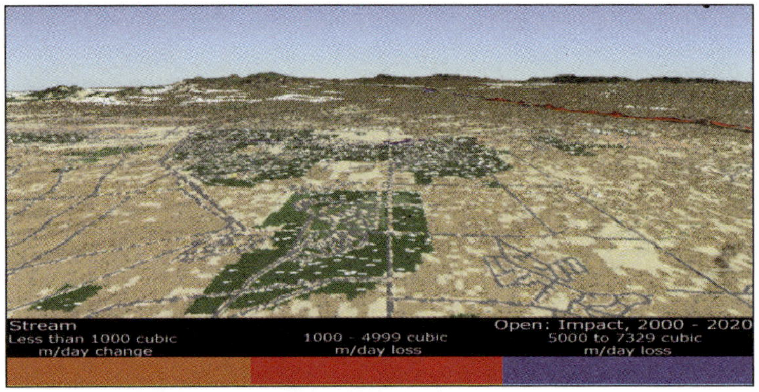
Stream
Open: Impact, 2000 - 2020
Less than 1000 cubic m/day change
1000 - 4999 cubic m/day loss
5000 to 7329 cubic m/day loss

Figure 17.19a ■ Sierra Vista OPEN, Streamflow impacts, 2000–2020

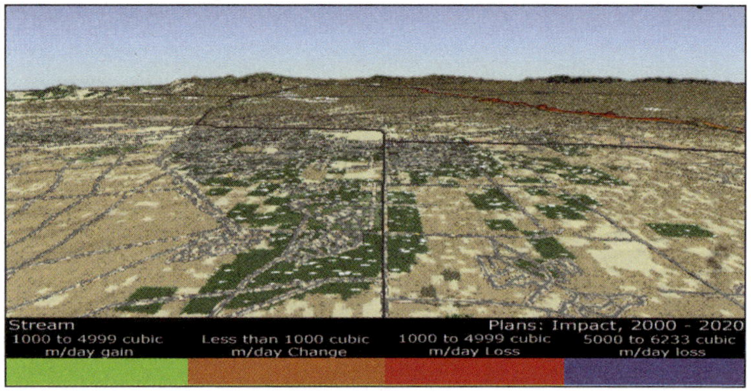
Stream
Plans: Impact, 2000 - 2020
1000 to 4999 cubic m/day gain
Less than 1000 cubic m/day Change
1000 to 4999 cubic m/day Loss
5000 to 6233 cubic m/day loss

Figure 17.19b ■ Sierra Vista PLANS, Streamflow impacts, 2000–2020

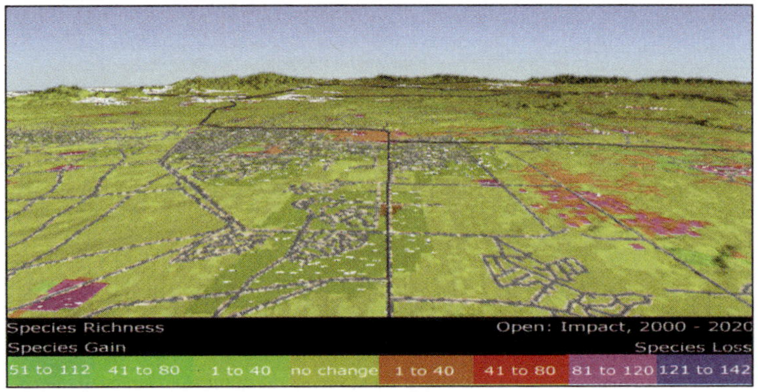
Species Richness
Open: Impact, 2000 - 2020
Species Gain
Species Loss
51 to 112
41 to 80
1 to 40
no change
1 to 40
41 to 80
81 to 120
121 to 142

Figure 17.20a ■ Sierra Vista OPEN, Species richness impacts, 2000–2020

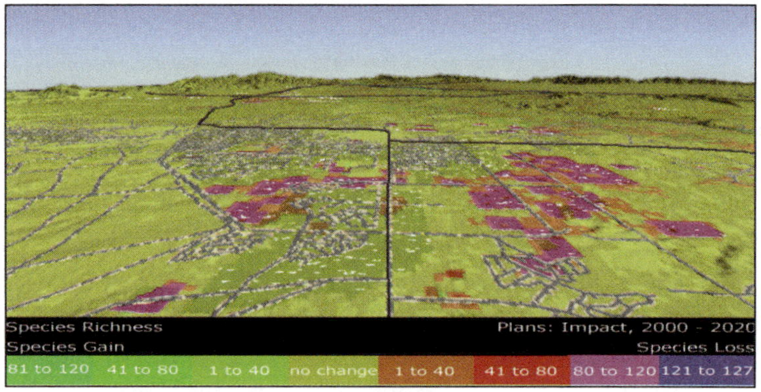
Species Richness
Plans: Impact, 2000 - 2020
Species Gain
Species Loss
81 to 120
41 to 80
1 to 40
no change
1 to 40
41 to 80
80 to 120
121 to 127

Figure 17.20b ■ Sierra Vista PLANS, Species richness impacts, 2000–2020

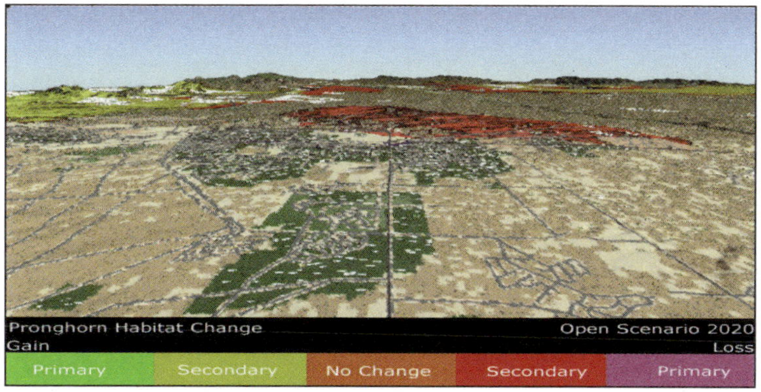
Pronghorn Habitat Change
Open Scenario 2020
Gain
Loss
Primary
Secondary
No Change
Secondary
Primary

Figure 17.21a ■ Sierra Vista OPEN, Pronghorn potential habitat impacts, 2000–2020

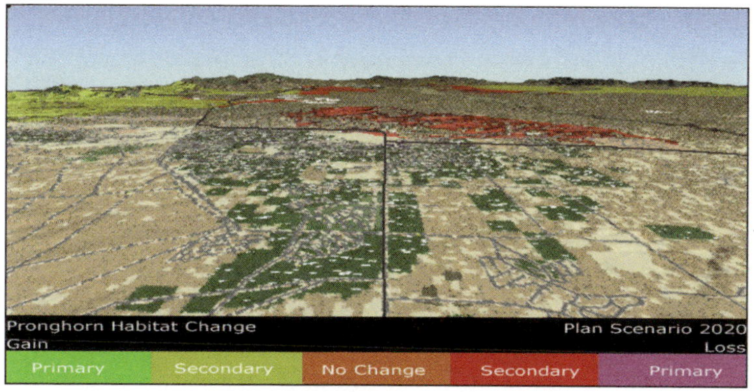
Pronghorn Habitat Change
Plan Scenario 2020
Gain
Loss
Primary
Secondary
No Change
Secondary
Primary

Figure 17.21b ■ Sierra Vista PLANS, Pronghorn potential habitat impacts, 2000–2020

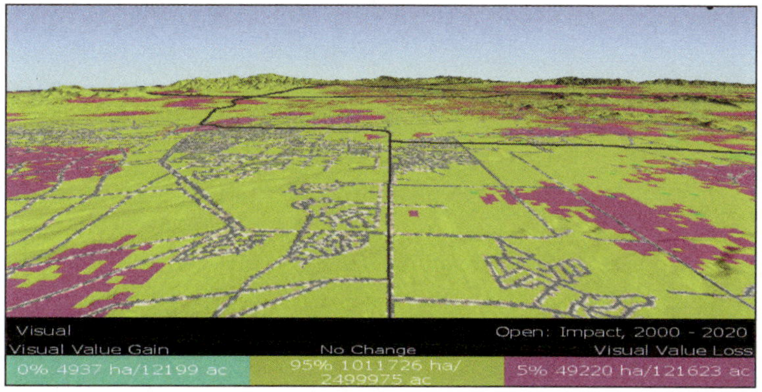
Visual
Open: Impact, 2000 - 2020
Visual Value Gain
No Change
Visual Value Loss
0% 4937 ha/12199 ac
95% 1011726 ha/ 2499975 ac
5% 49220 ha/121623 ac

Figure 17.22a ■ Sierra Vista OPEN, Visual preference impacts, 2000–2020

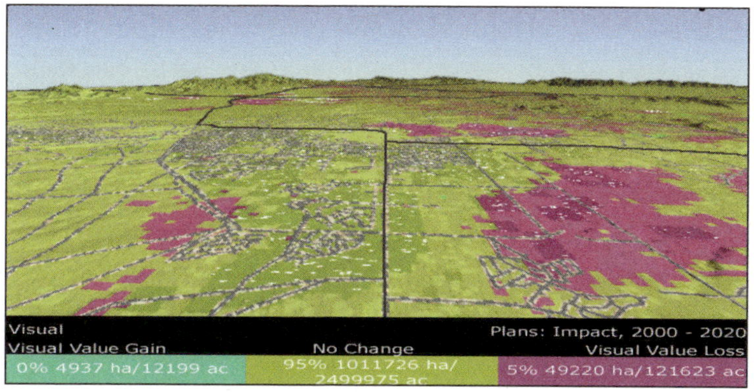
Visual
Plans: Impact, 2000 - 2020
Visual Value Gain
No Change
Visual Value Loss
0% 4937 ha/12199 ac
95% 1011726 ha/ 2499975 ac
5% 49220 ha/121623 ac

Figure 17.22b ■ Sierra Vista PLANS, Visual preference impacts, 2000–2020

Test 11: What differences will the relaxation of development regulations from those now in force make for the future of Benson?

Comparison of the OPEN alternative future with the PLANS alternative future shows the effect of relaxing development controls and of limiting additional conservation areas.

Paired aerial perspective views looking northward over Benson illustrate the comparison of the PLANS alternative future with the OPEN alternative future. Two views show conditions in 2000: existing land use/land cover (figure 17.23) and existing wells (figure 17.24). These are followed by paired views for comparison: attractiveness for suburban residential development (figure 17.25a and b); land use/land cover 2020 (figure 17.26a and b); new wells (figure 17.27a and b); change in groundwater level (figure 17.28a and b); change in streamflow in the San Pedro River (figure 17.29a and b); species richness (figure 17.30a and b); pronghorn habitat change (figure 17.31a and b); and change in visual preference (figure 17.32a and b). The outcomes of the OPEN alternative future appear on the left, and the PLANS alternative future on the right.

In the Benson area, the OPEN alternative future produces considerably more development north of Interstate Highway 10. There are significant differences in groundwater, streamflows in the San Pedro River, and species richness, especially for riparian species.

The PLANS alternative future shows a lessening of these impacts, largely because of the policies of retiring irrigated agricultural lands near Benson and upstream and of water conservation policies and subsequent slower rates of loss of groundwater in the Sierra Vista area.

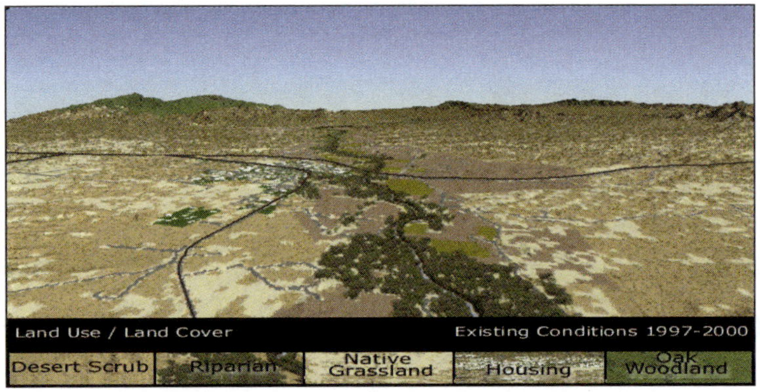
Land Use / Land Cover
Existing Conditions 1997-2000
Desert Scrub
Riparian
Native Grassland
Housing
Oak Woodland

Figure 17.23 ■ Benson aerial views, Land use/land cover, 2000

Wells
Current Conditions 2000

Figure 17.24 ■ Benson, existing wells, 2000

Attractiveness to Suburban Residential Development
Open Scenario 2020
Highest
Least

Figure 17.25a ■ Benson OPEN,
Attractiveness for suburban residential development, 2000

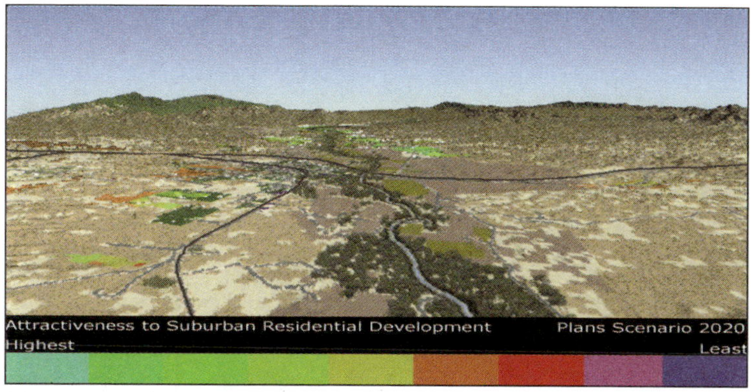
Attractiveness to Suburban Residential Development
Plans Scenario 2020
Highest
Least

Figure 17.25b ■ Benson PLANS,
Attractiveness for suburban residential development, 2000

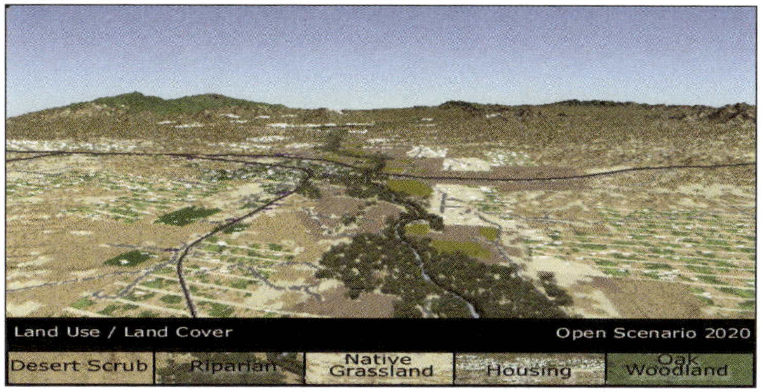
Land Use / Land Cover
Open Scenario 2020
Desert Scrub
Riparian
Native Grassland
Housing
Oak Woodland

Figure 17.26a ■ Benson OPEN, Land use/land cover, 2020

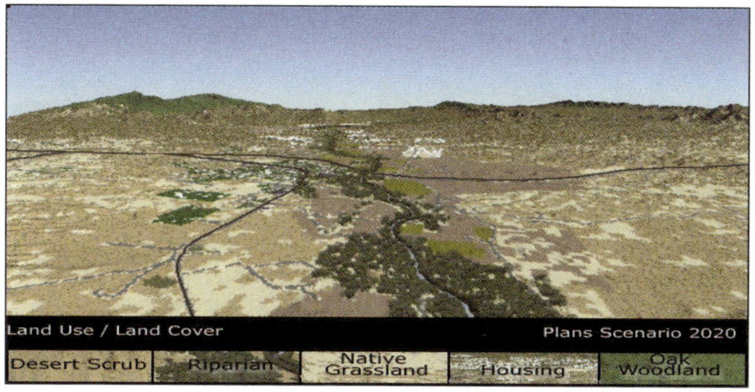
Land Use / Land Cover
Plans Scenario 2020
Desert Scrub
Riparian
Native Grassland
Housing
Oak Woodland

Figure 17.26b ■ Benson PLANS, Land use/land cover, 2020

Wells
Open Scenario 2020

Figure 17.27a ■ Benson OPEN, New wells, 2000–2020

Wells
Plans Scenario 2020

Figure 17.27b ■ Benson PLANS, New wells, 2000–2020

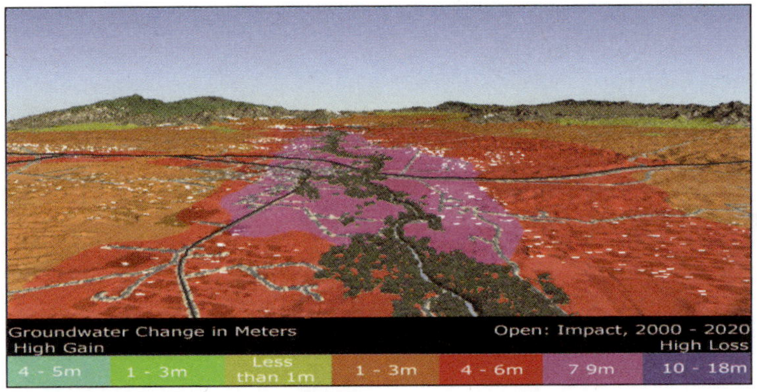
Groundwater Change in Meters
High Gain
Open: Impact, 2000 - 2020
High Loss
4 - 5m
1 - 3m
Less than 1m
1 - 3m
4 - 6m
7 9m
10 - 18m

Figure 17.28a ■ Benson OPEN, Groundwater impacts, 2000–2020

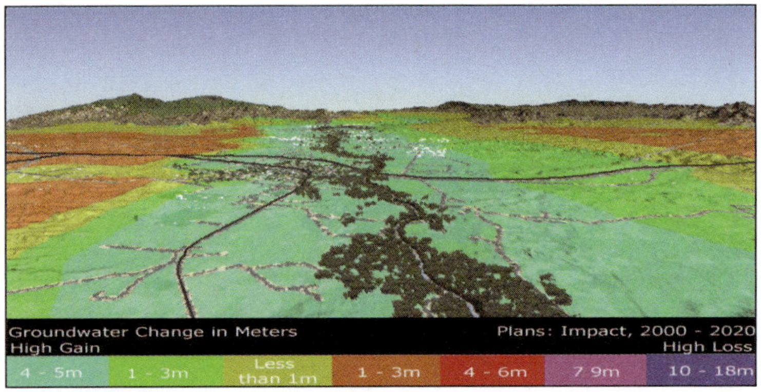
Groundwater Change in Meters
High Gain
Plans: Impact, 2000 - 2020
High Loss
4 - 5m
1 - 3m
Less than 1m
1 - 3m
4 - 6m
7 9m
10 - 18m

Figure 17.28b ■ Benson PLANS, Groundwater impacts, 2000–2020

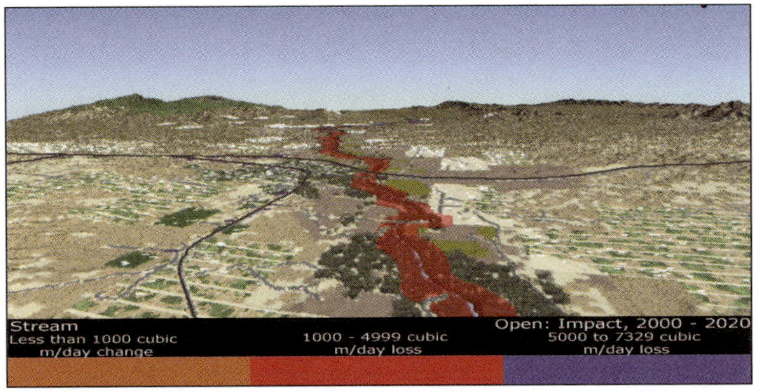
Stream
Less than 1000 cubic m/day change
1000 - 4999 cubic m/day loss
Open: Impact, 2000 - 2020
5000 to 7329 cubic m/day loss

Figure 17.29a ■ Benson OPEN, Streamflow impacts, 2000–2020

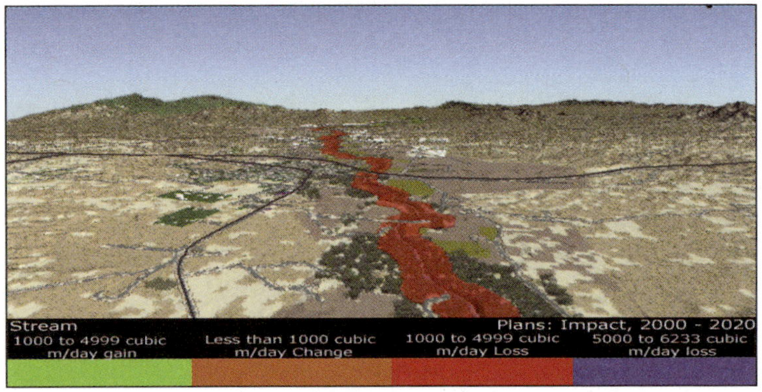
Stream
1000 to 4999 cubic m/day gain
Less than 1000 cubic m/day Change
Plans: Impact, 2000 - 2020
1000 to 4999 cubic m/day Loss
5000 to 6233 cubic m/day loss

Figure 17.29b ■ Benson PLANS, Streamflow impacts, 2000–2020

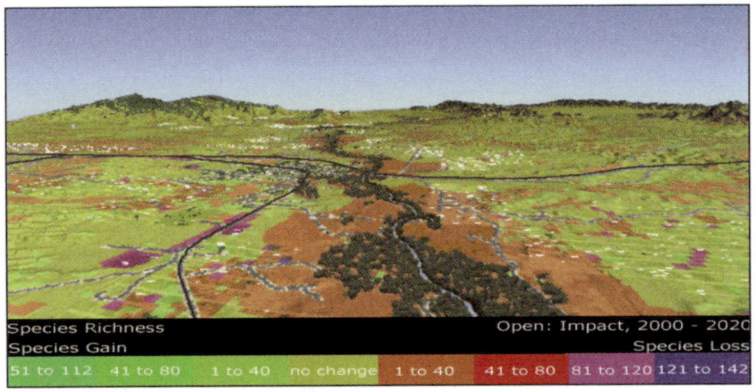
Species Richness
Species Gain
Open: Impact, 2000 - 2020
Species Loss
51 to 112
41 to 80
1 to 40
no change
1 to 40
41 to 80
81 to 120
121 to 142

Figure 17.30a ■ Benson OPEN, Species richness impacts, 2000–2020

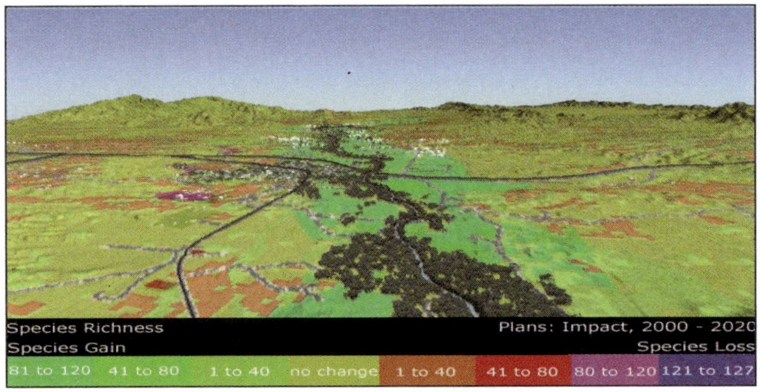
Species Richness
Species Gain
Plans: Impact, 2000 - 2020
Species Loss
81 to 120
41 to 80
1 to 40
no change
1 to 40
41 to 80
80 to 120
121 to 127

Figure 17.30b ■ Benson PLANS, Species richness impacts, 2000–2020

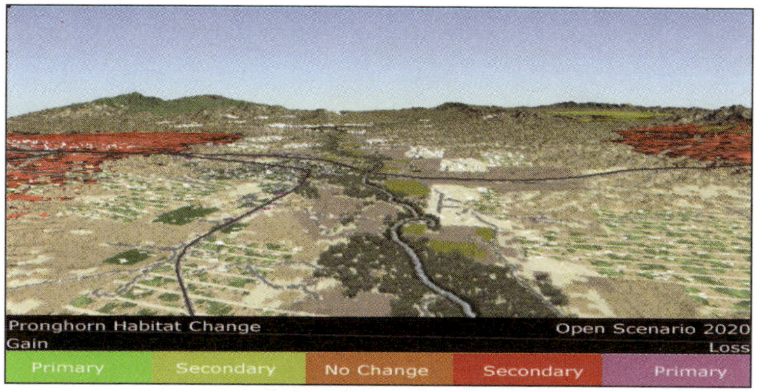
Pronghorn Habitat Change
Open Scenario 2020
Gain
Loss
Primary
Secondary
No Change
Secondary
Primary

Figure 17.31a ■ Benson OPEN,
Pronghorn potential habitat impacts, 2000–2020

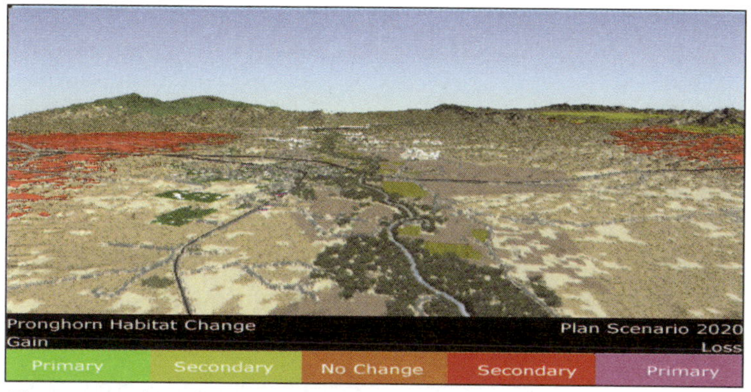
Pronghorn Habitat Change
Plan Scenario 2020
Gain
Loss
Primary
Secondary
No Change
Secondary
Primary

Figure 17.31b ■ Benson PLANS,
Pronghorn potential habitat impacts, 2000–2020

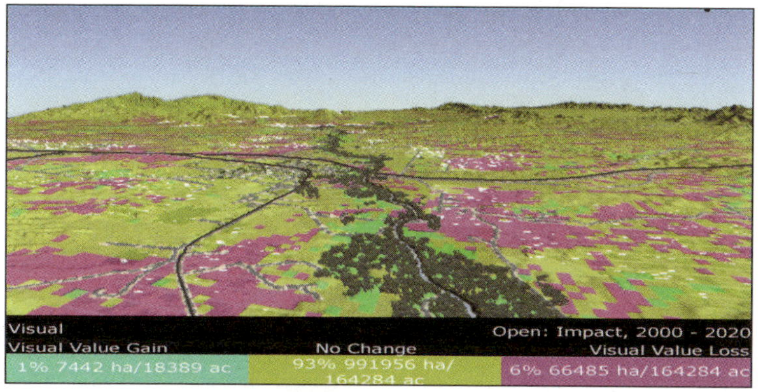
Visual
Open: Impact, 2000 - 2020
Visual Value Gain
No Change
Visual Value Loss
1% 7442 ha/18389 ac
93% 991956 ha/ 164284 ac
6% 66485 ha/164284 ac

Figure 17.32a ■ Benson OPEN,
Visual preference impacts, 2000–2020

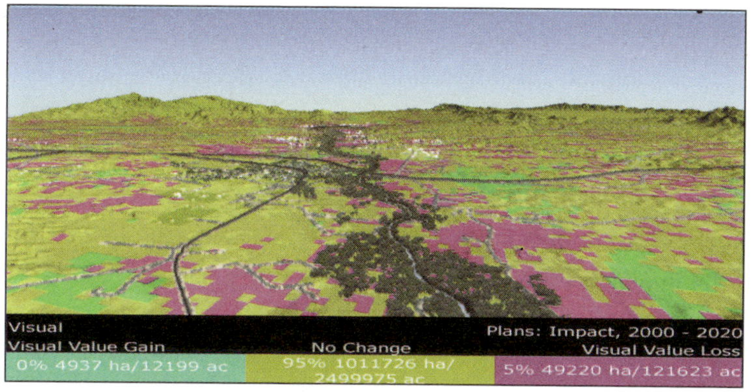
Visual
Plans: Impact, 2000 - 2020
Visual Value Gain
No Change
Visual Value Loss
0% 4937 ha/12199 ac
95% 1011726 ha/ 2499975 ac
5% 49220 ha/121623 ac

Figure 17.32b ■ Benson PLANS,
Visual preference impacts, 2000–2020

CHAPTER

18

Conclusions

The ten scenarios and their resulting alternative futures encompass a likely range of choices that are expected to influence change in the Upper San Pedro River Basin. The region is highly valued for both development and conservation. Fortunately, the region has large areas of high value for development that are not especially important for conservation purposes as well as large areas of high conservation value that have little appeal for developers. However, areas of particularly high conservation value and high development attractiveness also exist. It is in these areas where the most intense competition can be expected and where much future public debate will be focused. Direct comparison of summary development attractiveness with conservation priorities locates these critical areas.

Summary development attractiveness (figure 18.1) is based on the allocation patterns resulting from the ten scenarios. Each of

Photo 18.1 ■ Sierra Vista

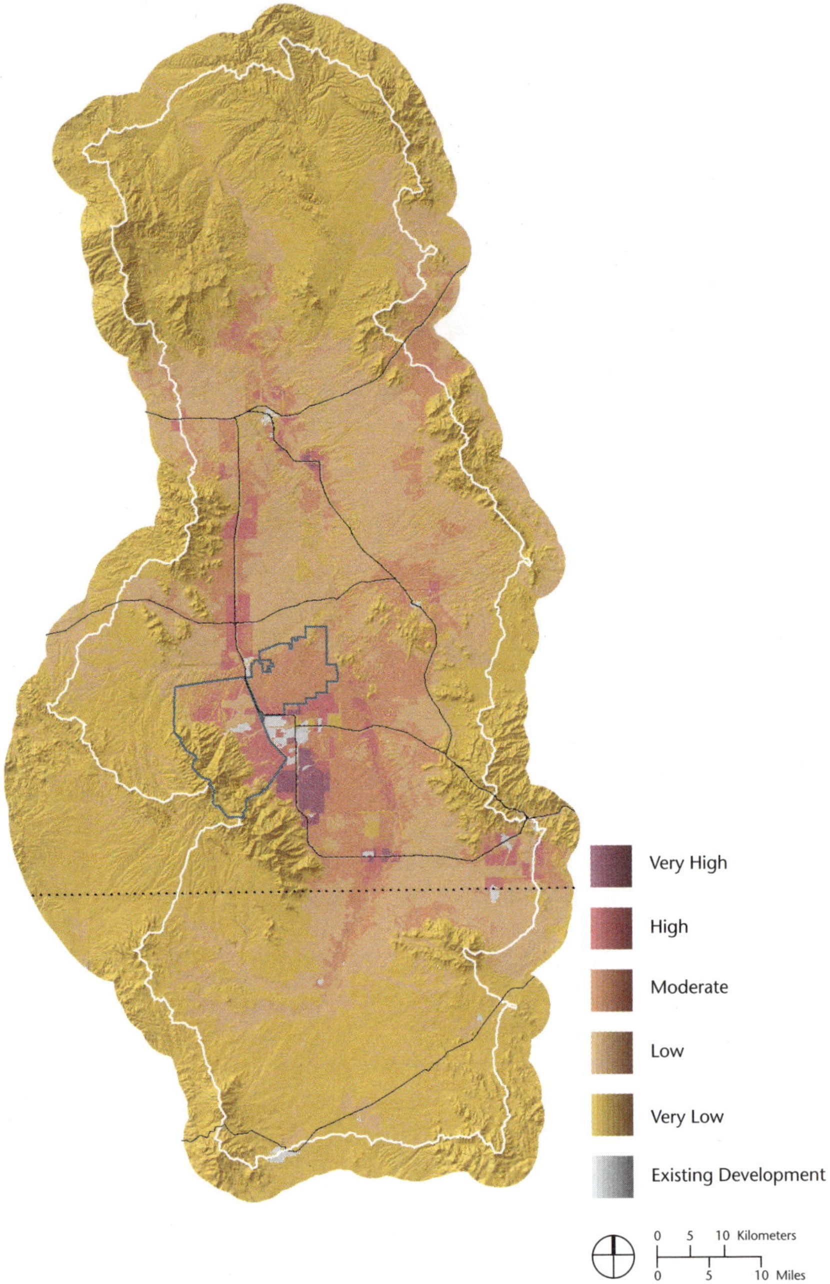
Very High
High
Moderate
Low
Very Low
Existing Development
0 5 10 Kilometers
0 5 10 Miles

Figure 18.1 ■ Summary residential development attractiveness, 2000

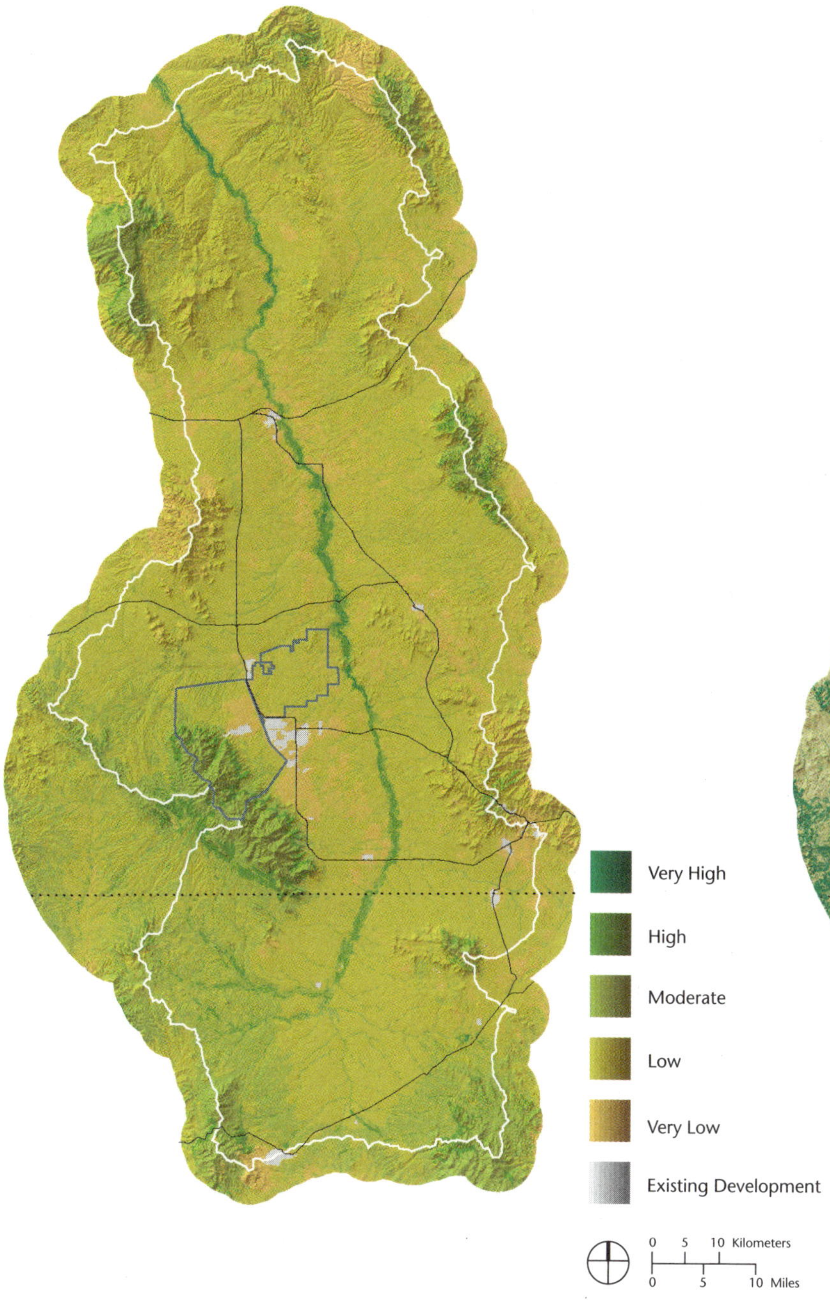
Very High
High
Moderate
Low
Very Low
Existing Development
0 5 10 Kilometers
0 5 10 Miles

Figure 18.2 ■ Summary conservation priority, 2000

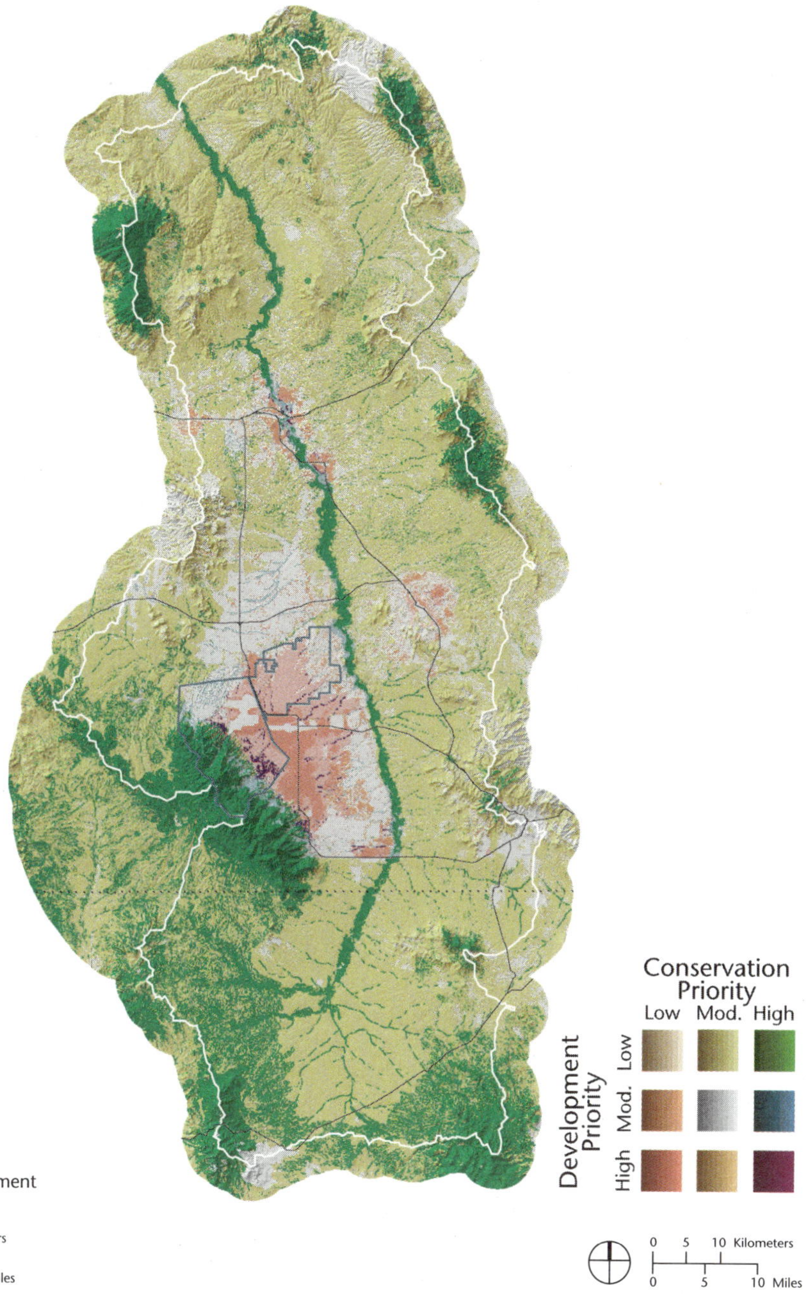
Conservation Priority
Low Mod. High
Development Priority
Low
Mod.
High
0 5 10 Kilometers
0 5 10 Miles

Figure 18.3 ■ Development/conservation competition, 2000

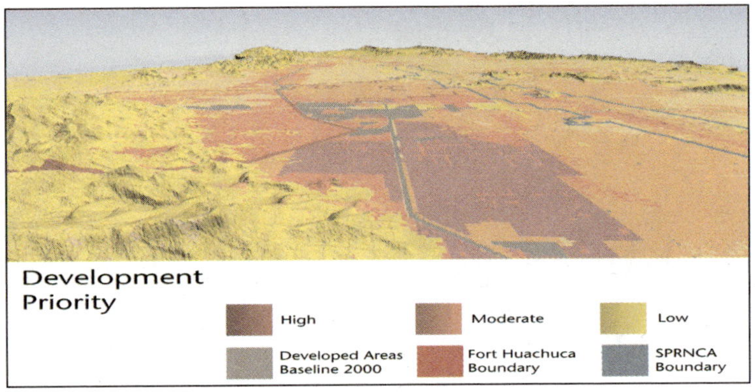
Development
Priority
High
Moderate
Low
Developed Areas
Baseline 2000
Fort Huachuca
Boundary
SPRNCA
Boundary

Figure 18.4 ■ Fort Huachuca: Summary residential development priority, 2000

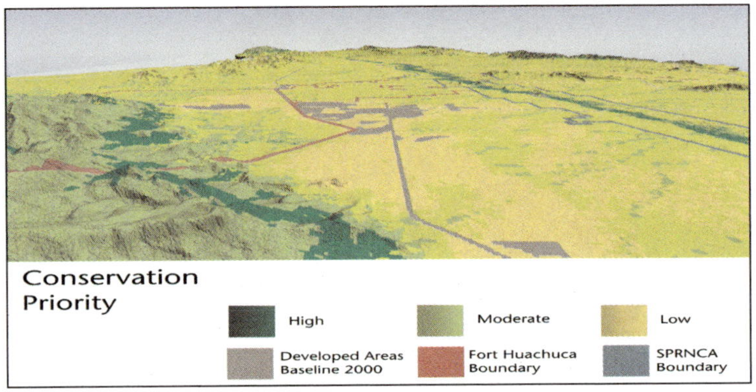
Conservation
Priority
High
Moderate
Low
Developed Areas
Baseline 2000
Fort Huachuca
Boundary
SPRNCA
Boundary

Figure 18.5 ■ Fort Huachuca: Summary conservation priority, 2000

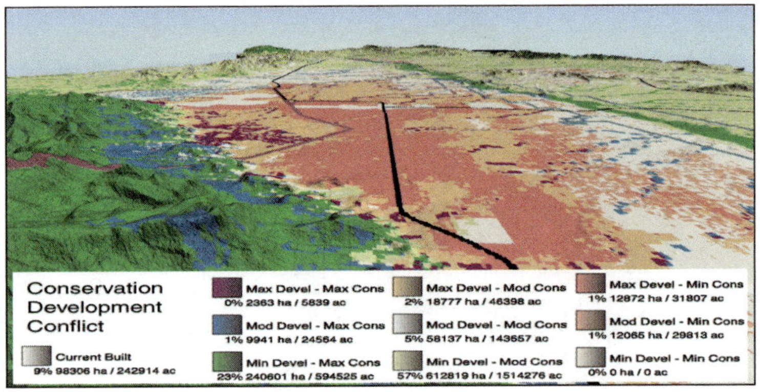
Conservation
Development
Conflict
Current Built
9% 98306 ha / 242914 ac
Max Devel - Max Cons
0% 2363 ha / 5839 ac
Mod Devel - Max Cons
1% 9941 ha / 24564 ac
Min Devel - Max Cons
23% 240601 ha / 594525 ac
Max Devel - Mod Cons
2% 18777 ha / 46398 ac
Mod Devel - Mod Cons
5% 58137 ha / 143657 ac
Min Devel - Mod Cons
57% 612819 ha / 1514276 ac
Max Devel - Min Cons
1% 12872 ha / 31807 ac
Mod Devel - Min Cons
1% 12065 ha / 29813 ac
Min Devel - Min Cons
0% 0 ha / 0 ac

Figure 18.6 ■ Fort Huachuca: Development/conservation competition, 2000

Photo 18.2 ■ Grasslands on Fort Huachuca

the attractiveness patterns for the four residential development types is weighted by its proportional allocations across all ten scenarios using simple averaging. As a result of the equal weighting, future suburban development is a major influence. Areas adjacent to and south of Sierra Vista are particularly attractive for development.

The summary evaluation of attractiveness for conservation is shown in the conservation priority map (figure 18.2). This evaluation is the result of an unweighted sum of the evaluations for all large patches and corridors from the landscape ecological pattern model, all southwest willow flycatcher potential habitat, all goshawk potential habitat, all Gila monster potential habitat, all beaver potential habitat, all pronghorn potential habitat, all jaguar potential habitat, all threatened and endangered species habitat, all locations with species richness values above 95 species (approximately 25 percent of the region), all GAP locations, and the most attractive view-types from the visual preference model. The assessment clearly shows the great importance of the San Pedro riparian corridor, the lower slopes of the mountain zones, and the pattern of arroyos that connect them.

The development/conservation competition assessment (figure 18.3) shows the spatial overlap between the priority evaluations for development and for conservation.

Most of the areas of high development priority are along the edges of existing settled areas and are not particularly desirable for conservation. Similarly, most of the areas of high conservation priority are not attractive to developers. This is largely because of current patterns of public land ownership, including Fort Huachuca and the San Pedro Riparian National Conservation Area.

However, there are some critical areas where demand for development and for conservation conflict. Foremost among these are the lower slopes of the Huachuca Mountains and the arroyos in Sierra Vista. These are areas of substantial development value as well as highest conservation priority for their critical animal habitat and movement zones.

The largest area of highest potential conflict is within Fort Huachuca. Figure 18.4 shows the summary development attractiveness, figure 18.5 shows its conservation priority, and their relationship is seen in figure 18.6. This area is largely undeveloped and has low levels of human use and substantial areas of high quality habitat. However, if the fort is closed, as is examined in some scenarios, this situation could change. Extremely attractive for residential development, large parts of the fort could become highly marketable housing. The desirability of the area can be seen in the photograph taken from the lower slopes on Fort Huachuca.

A full understanding of the maps and tables produced by the simulation of the ten scenarios into alternative futures for 2020, and of the tests of policy sensitivity, is necessary before detailed strategies for shaping the future can be chosen. There are, however, some informative generalizations that can be made from looking at the impact assessments of the ten alternative futures and the eleven tests of sensitivity to policy variations. If we consider the following to be positive impacts—slowing the decline of groundwater storage, slowing the drying up of the river, retaining

Photo 18.3 ■ San Pedro Riparian habitat

Photo 18.4 ■ Fragmentation of landscape by development

FOR SALE

Photo 18.5 ■ Chihuahua desert scrub

Photo 18.6 ■ Fort Huachuca

Photo 18.7 ■ Highway 92 with Palominas and San Pedro River

Photo 18.8 ■ San Pedro River and Tombstone Hills

or improving wildlife habitats, maintaining or improving species richness, maintaining the beauty of the landscape and also improving attractiveness for development—then we can begin to evaluate the alternative futures.

The first and most important relationship involves the fundamental factor for life in a desert: water. All of the scenarios-generated alternative futures, even those most restrictive of population growth and water use, result in loss of groundwater storage and in increased drying of the San Pedro River.

All the alternative futures result in a lowering of the water table near Sierra Vista and Cananea, with a drop in level around Sierra Vista of 10 to 15 m (33 to 49 ft) over the next 20 years. However, the constrained alternative futures that most restrict irrigated agriculture can result in water table gains to the north of St. David. The San Pedro River will continue to lose flow under the OPEN and PLANS futures; in the OPEN futures, the riparian habitat will continue to decline. Those futures that restrict irrigated agriculture and especially those that also concentrate development, however, can increase streamflow and improve riparian habitat in parts of the river basin. This can maintain or improve species diversity in the region and benefit those species that depend on this habitat, such as the southwestern willow flycatcher.

There will be an increasingly fragmented pattern of habitat patches that will cause decline in the quality of the region's landscape ecology. This effect is particularly noticeable in alternative futures that create development on and around the lower slopes of the mountains in the region. Habitat for the pronghorn declines in all the alternative futures, because groundwater losses and changes in grazing and fire management cause the region's extensive grasslands to decline.

The area will experience a substantial decline in its perceived beauty. This will be obvious along the major roads as they attract development, especially along State Highway 90, the major approach to Sierra Vista from the north, passing development attracted by Kartchner Caverns State Park.

Comparison of the alternative futures reveals that policy decisions affecting irrigated agriculture in Arizona cause the greatest impacts on the region's hydrology. The CONSTRAINED scenarios propose removal of all irrigated agriculture in the study area. The PLANS scenarios remove it only within 1 mi of the Upper San Pedro River, and open scenarios leave irrigated agriculture policy unchanged, except for prohibiting any agricultural expansion within 1 mi of the river.

The second most significant policy is development control. Population growth in Arizona, with its accompanying municipal and industrial water demands, is the second largest future consumer of water. It is informative to compare the two alternative futures that are most different in their impacts, CONSTRAINED 2 and OPEN 2. The OPEN 2 scenario is expected to have the highest harmful impact on the hydrology and environment of the region. It causes the most rapid depletion of groundwater of any of the alternative futures. However, these impacts are not very much more damaging than those generated by other OPEN scenarios, leading to the conclusion that the relaxation of development constraints has very powerful influences on potential negative environmental impacts.

Third in significance is growth policy in Sonora. The high growth assumed for Sonora in PLANS 2 and in OPEN 2 results in greater impacts than in their lower growth counterparts. However, the variance of their impacts is small when compared to the effects of agricultural and development policies in Arizona.

The effect of Fort Huachuca on the region was tested by comparison of three policy choices in each scenario. It would either continue as at present, double in size of on-base population, or be closed. Although local consequences in Sierra Vista may be large, when taken in the context of the Upper San Pedro River Basin, the variance associated with the fort is small when compared with variations caused by agriculture and urbanization in the Arizona portion of the study area.

Although the scenarios produce a generally negative set of impacts, there is considerable variation, especially between the extremes produced by the CONSTRAINED and OPEN scenarios. The OPEN futures result in an accelerated decline in all impact measures tested and are not significantly more attractive to development. The CONSTRAINED futures will see slower but continued lowering of the water table, and they also indicate a slowing of the processes of decline in the San Pedro River and improved wildlife habitats. The PLANS scenarios produce futures that are between the other two, but are closer to the CONSTRAINED futures in impacts. The PLANS scenarios most closely resemble the current Cochise County Plan and the most likely 2020 projections for Sonora.

If implemented and augmented with other conservation measures, the PLANS scenario will not result in a reversal of the processes of change in the Upper San Pedro River Basin. However, it could accommodate growth and be attractive to development while significantly retarding the environmental decline of this region of extraordinary ecological importance.

Many people have views on the issues facing the region and on the policies that will influence change. The alternative futures represent allocations of where development is likely to occur based on choices made in each scenario. Complex assessment of costs and benefits related to policy decisions is beyond the scope of this study. Patterns may change depending on people's actual choices about housing and on environmental policy decisions.

The findings in this study are not unexpected. The future of the Upper San Pedro River Basin is one that will bring change and environmental crisis closer to the direct perception of more people. The critical choices made over the next 20 years will determine whether the Upper San Pedro River Basin will survive as an attractive area--both for conservation and for development.

APPENDIX A

The Scenarios Guide

How would you describe the San Pedro River Basin as you think it will be in the year 2020?

Answering this question requires an understanding of the potential impacts associated with the policy choices and actions that will be made in the near future by area residents. And, in order to make this kind of assessment, the available options must first be described and then combined into sets of plans. The purpose of this document is to help define such plans.

Following are a list of issues about the built and natural landscape of this region that are currently being discussed by its residents. The topics are complicated and, in some cases, contentious. Each issue is associated with one or more questions. Each question has, in turn, two or more possible answers that define either a position on an assumption (such as the regional population forecast) or a policy option (such as fire management). When answering the questions, please check the answer provided that best reflects your view of how the future of the region should be shaped, or add your own response to the question. Taken as a set, the sum of these positions will define a scenario, or a plan, that describes a possible future for the Upper San Pedro River Basin in the year 2020. We know that the list of issues is lengthy, but the area is large and its choices are many.

The types of questions and the phrasing of each individual answer are based on two criteria. First, they represent a range of land use and environmental issues facing the region. The language used in this scenario guide has been adapted from public documents, research papers, local media reports, and comments made by area residents to a draft version of this document that was circulated in November 2001. Second, the questions and answers represent aspects of the issues that can be simulated via computer models.

Because of the large number of possible answer-position combinations, the research group cannot simulate the implications of every individual scenario guide that will be submitted by area residents. Rather, we will look for common patterns of response and, initially, simulate and compare those that illustrate the widest range of alternative futures being considered by stakeholders.

Also, please be aware that gauging public opinion is not the purpose of this study, and this guide is not a popularity poll. It is only a means to help create the scenarios. The completed guides will not be published, and statistics relating to the answers will not be calculated. Furthermore, respondents to the guide are not asked to identify themselves, and no scenario will be reported as coming from a particular individual or group.

Introduction: Creating and Using Scenarios

The word *scenario* is commonly understood to mean an outline of events, usually the plot of a story, play, or film. Similarly, for this research project, a scenario is an outline or plot for a future of the Upper San Pedro River Basin. If the future was easily knowable, there would be only one scenario and planning for it would be a relatively simple task. However, no one can tell what the actual future of the region will be; therefore, planning for the needs of next year, the next decade, or the next century is a complicated and uncertain process. Because no single vision of the future is likely to be correct, it is often more helpful to consider a set of alternative futures that encompass a spectrum of possibilities. This study will do just that: examine several alternatives that reflect the range of possible futures the region might see.

A scenario-based approach to regional land planning offers several advantages. Foremost, because it is a process that intentionally investigates several futures, different points of view (which are sometimes very different) can be accommodated within the same study. Additionally, because scenarios describe the future in terms of complete stories, there is an ability to consider the interrelationships among issues.

However, the most important reasons to use a scenario-based approach are the potential benefits to several aspects of local decision-making processes. First, for landowners interested in protecting their own property rights, scenarios can be used to understand the range of potential impacts to their lands that may be caused by regional change. Said another way, scenarios can help to assess how the multiple actions of neighboring property owners or the policies of local, regional, and national governments could affect one's own land. These changes might be measured in terms of land value or in the time it takes to commute to work. For land managers of conservation areas, these changes might be expressed in terms of habitat fragmentation. By understanding the type, location, and magnitude of the changes that might occur, property owners and managers can be better prepared to make decisions about their own land.

Second, for elected officials and public administrators, scenarios can be used to test current planning ideas. For example, how might changes in residential zoning definitions or water use change the housing pattern and service needs for the area? Scenarios can also be used to test the resilience of plans against assumptions about the stability of the future. How will regional growth change if population increases faster than expected?

Third, for all the members of a community, scenarios can be used to better understand how the presently unknowable and numerous decisions that will be—and must be—made tomorrow and the next day may add up to create a future. The use of scenarios allows communities to assess the relative impacts of several alternative sets of choices. What are the relative merits and faults of a set of policies that promote some land uses over others? Or that concentrate some land uses in a designated area rather than distribute them over the region? Given limited resources and the complexity of the issues at hand, residents and elected officials must assess these types of questions within a broad context of multifaceted needs and comprehensive solutions. Scenario analysis is one tool that can help a community to make more informed and better decisions today, for a more desirable future.

However, for scenarios to be of use in the decision-making process—be it at the individual, institutional, or community level—they must be possible, credible, and relevant. This guidebook has been created to help generate alternative scenarios that meet these requirements for Upper San Pedro River Basin. On the following pages are a series of questions regarding issues that have been discussed by neighbors, debated in municipal meetings, and reported in local media. All of the these issues are interconnected, and there is no single correct way to begin the process of plotting a course for the future. However, for purposes of convenience and clarity this guide has been divided into three general themes. Section I concerns planning goals, population growth, and the allocation of homes and industry. Section II concerns water management within the Upper San Pedro River Basin. Section III concerns land management and conservation.

The answers to the questions in this guide, when taken as a set of assumptions and choices about policy, can serve as a "script" for creating a unique future scenario. Each answer has land-use implications that can be simulated in a digital geographic information system (GIS). Translating the answers into the simulation will include aspects of both space (where certain events may occur) and time (when certain events may happen).

The date of 2020 has been selected as the scenario time frame for several reasons. First, most demographic forecasts are limited to a 20-year horizon. Second, improvements of infrastructure—roads, bridges, sewer plants, etc.—are frequently timed to 20-year periods. Third, 20 years is within the lifetime of most area residents and within the lifetime of their children and grandchildren.

Although each completed guidebook can be used as basis for a scenario, the research team does not have the resources to translate all of the many expected responses into fully-defined simulations. Instead, we will look for patterns of similar answers and create a set of composite scenarios that capture the range of opinions presented. It is not possible to know at this point in the research process how many scenarios will be created for this study. For most planning projects—whether they are for business, government, or land planning—between three and eight scenarios are developed, analyzed, and compared. The actual number in this case will depend on the range of answer-combinations to the questions in this guide.

The potential impacts from each of the wide-ranging scenarios will be compared to current conditions of the region in terms of a set of processes that will also be modeled within the GIS. The models will be created based on available literature, previous research experience, and local expert knowledge. They will include residential and commercial development, storm water runoff and infiltration, soil moisture, streamflow, groundwater head configuration, fire management, vegetation dynamics, landscape ecological pattern, species diversity, and single-species potential habitat models and visual quality.

The questions in this guide address only the part of the Upper San Pedro River within Arizona. A separate but similar question set that concerns the Sonoran part of the river system will be distributed in Mexico. However, all scenarios from the United States and Mexico will be evaluated together by the same process models.

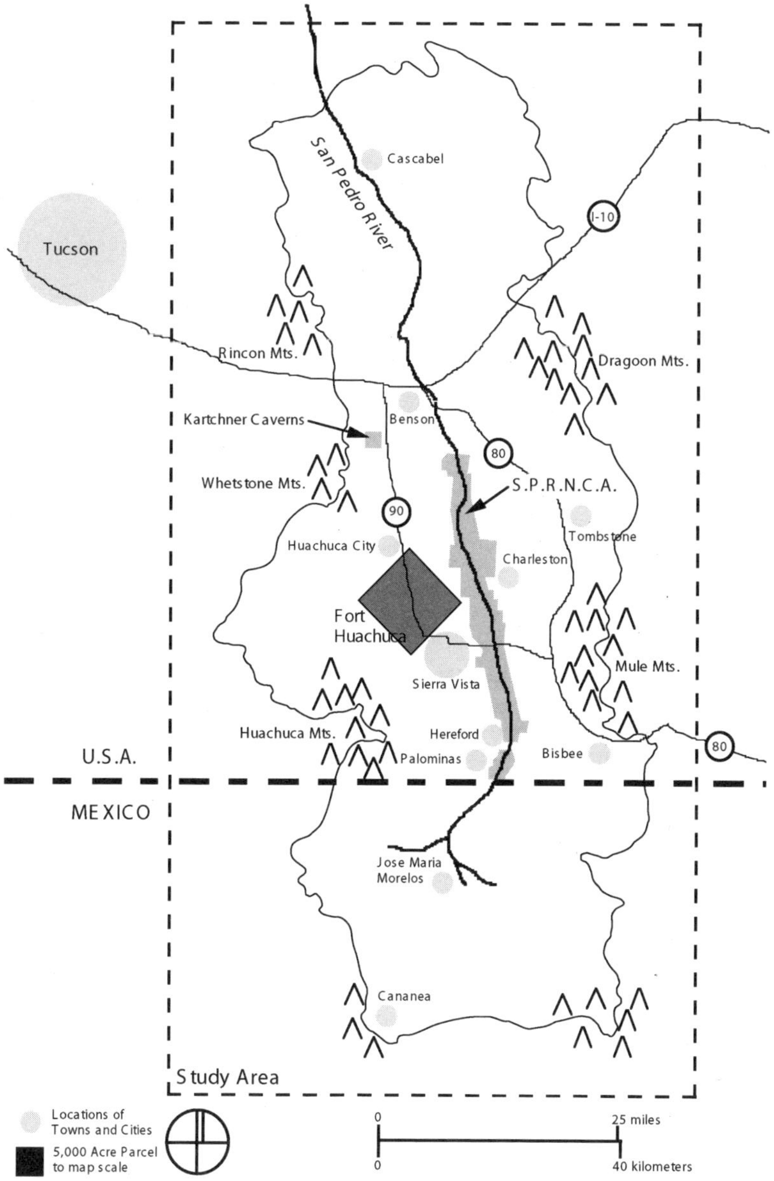
Tucson
Cascabel
San Pedro River
I-10
Rincon Mts.
Dragoon Mts.
Benson
Kartchner Caverns
80
S.P.R.N.C.A.
Whetstone Mts.
90
Tombstone
Huachuca City
Charleston
Fort Huachuca
Mule Mts.
Sierra Vista
Huachuca Mts.
Hereford
U.S.A.
Palominas
Bisbee
80
MEXICO
Jose Maria Morelos
Cananea
Study Area
Locations of Towns and Cities
5,000 Acre Parcel to map scale
0
25 miles
0
40 kilometers

Figure A.1 ■ Upper San Pedro River Basin

Section I: Planning Goals, Population Growth, and the Distribution of Homes and Industry

An Introductory Statement about the Future of the Region

On the following pages you will find detailed questions relating to policy choices for the Upper San Pedro River Basin. The answer to each of these questions is an important building block in the process of creating a scenario. But before addressing these specifics, it is usually helpful to think in more general terms. Please write a brief statement that summarizes your view of life in the Upper San Pedro River Basin in the year 2020. It may be helpful to think of this answer in terms of newspaper headlines.

Qualities of Life in the San Pedro River Basin

Many elements contribute to the quality of life in an area. Some of these are associated with a preferred lifestyle and are characteristics that residents hope to protect. Other factors call for improvement. Identifying what residents of an area consider to be the most admired aspects of life in a region and what should be changed for the better is perhaps the most important—and one of the most challenging—aspects of land planning. The following two questions address these concerns.

For the alternative future scenario you envision…

The three most important features that define the high quality of life in the Upper San Pedro River Basin and that should be protected are:

1. ______________________________
2. ______________________________
3. ______________________________

For the alternative future scenario you envision…

The three features of current life in the Upper San Pedro River Basin that should be improved for the future are:

1. ______________________________
2. ______________________________
3. ______________________________

Population Forecast

In 1990 the national census reported that more than 97,000 people lived in Cochise County. The Census Bureau estimates that by 1997, more than 112,000 people lived in the county, and a private economic and demographic consulting firm has projected that by 2020 more than 142,000 will live there. No published reports for the number of people living within the United States portion of the Upper San Pedro River Basin watershed-based study area exist. However, using information available from the above organizations and others—such as the U.S. Fish and Wildlife Service—it is possible to estimate that the 1990 population of the Upper San Pedro River Basin was approximately 62,000 people and is projected to be 95,000 by 2020.

In the alternative future scenario you envision…

[ ] Population increase should be one-half less than as forecast (to 2020 population of 78,500)

[ ] Population increase should be one-third less than as forecast (to 2020 population of 84,000)

[ ] Population increase should be as forecast (to 2020 population of 95,000)

[ ] Population increase should be one-third greater than as forecast (to 2020 population of 106,000)

[ ] Population increase should be one-half greater than as forecast (to 2020 population of 111,500)

Distribution of New Residents

The location of the new homes in the Upper San Pedro River Basin will impact the future of the region in terms of the siting of new schools and the construction or improvement of roads. For the purpose of this study, residential areas are classified into four categories: urban, suburban, rural, and exurban.

Urban homes are within an incorporated municipal boundary and are on lots smaller than 1 ac. This category includes multifamily homes. Urban homes are connected to the municipal sewer system and use the municipal water supply.

Suburban homes are built on 1 to 4 ac lots and are within 2 mi of an incorporated municipal area. Suburban homes use septic tanks and are connected to the municipal water supply.

Rural homes are built lots of 4 ac or more. They are built on generally open areas (such as ranching or agricultural areas). They have private, on-site wells and use septic tanks.

Exurban homes are also built in generally open areas (such as ranching or agricultural areas) but are built on lots of 1 to 2 ac. Typically, exurban homes are clustered in groups of five or more. Exurban homes typically use septic tanks and a common water supply (usually a private water company). Exurban homes are usually accessed by dirt roads or low-volume paved roads.

In the alternative future scenario you envision…

____ percent of the new population should live in urban homes
____ percent of the new population should live in suburban homes
____ percent of the new population should live in rural homes
____ percent of the new population should live in exurban homes
100 percent total new population

Rural Residential Zoning in the Upper San Pedro River Basin

Rural residential development and its potential impacts can be shaped by policies regulating the minimum allowable lot size. One potential strategy for protecting groundwater reserves calls for the location of single houses with individual wells on large lots. Some studies suggest that for this option to work, lots would need to be at least 25 ac. Other studies call for even larger lots of approximately 40 ac. If such a plan was adopted, it could be implemented on the Upper San Pedro River Basin as a whole, or only in part of the area such as along the San Pedro Riparian National Conservation Area (SPRNCA).

In the alternative future scenario you envision…

[ ] The minimum size of a rural residential lot should be 40 ac in the Upper San Pedro River Basin
[ ] The minimum size of a rural residential lot should be 20 ac in the Upper San Pedro River Basin
[ ] The minimum size of a rural residential lot should be 10 ac in the Upper San Pedro River Basin
[ ] The minimum size of a rural residential lot should be 4 ac in the Upper San Pedro River Basin
[ ] The minimum size of a rural residential lot should be 1 ac in the Upper San Pedro River Basin
[ ] There should be no minimum lot size for a rural residential lot in the Upper San Pedro River Basin

In the alternative future scenario you envision…

[ ] The minimum size of a rural residential lot should be 40 ac if within 1 mi of the SPRNCA
[ ] The minimum size of a rural residential lot should be 20 ac if within 1 mi of the SPRNCA
[ ] The minimum size of a rural residential lot should be 10 ac if within 1 mi of the SPRNCA
[ ] The minimum size of a rural residential lot should be 4 ac if within 1 mi of the SPRNCA
[ ] The minimum size of a rural residential lot should be 1 ac if within 1 mi of the SPRNCA
[ ] There should be no minimum lot size for a rural residential lot if within 1 mi of the SPRNCA

Providing Infrastructure

When and where urban infrastructure is developed can affect the pattern of urban and suburban growth. Constructing sewers, power and communication lines, and roads before development takes place can attract homes and businesses to an area. A policy of constructing infrastructure in anticipation of development is one means to guide what otherwise might be sprawl. However, having these amenities in place does not guarantee that development will follow. Regional economic circumstances or land-use needs peculiar to an industry or type of development may leave parcels undeveloped even though the infrastructure is already in place.

Infrastructure may also follow development that has already been established and that has reached some target density. A policy of constructing infrastructure after development has occurred can ensure that resources are allocated where needed and as needed. However, upgrading or refitting elements of urban and suburban infrastructure to existing development is usually more expensive than if the infrastructure is in place before development occurs. Furthermore, if the development is not constructed in a way that anticipates the infrastructure, it may not be possible to meet planning and zoning guidelines that are associated with higher densities.

A stated policy of not providing infrastructure improvements can be one means to discourage development.

In the alternative future scenario you envision…

[ ] Infrastructure improvements should be constructed only in the intensive growth area designated by the Cochise County Plan near Sierra Vista and should be constructed in the near future so as to attract development

[ ] Infrastructure improvements should be constructed only in the intensive growth area designated by the Cochise County Plan near Sierra Vista, but should be constructed only as development occurs

[ ] Infrastructure improvements should be constructed in the intensive growth area near Sierra Vista and within the current boundaries of the incorporated municipal areas that are expected to have "urban-style growth" (Benson, Bisbee, Tombstone, and Whetstone), and should be constructed in the near future so as to attract development

[ ] Infrastructure improvements should be constructed in the intensive growth area near Sierra Vista and within the current boundaries of the incorporated municipal areas that are expected to have "urban-style growth" (Benson, Bisbee, Tombstone, and Whetstone), but should be constructed only as development occurs

[ ] Infrastructure should follow development and be constructed anywhere in the study area

[ ] Infrastructure should not be constructed anywhere in the study area

Status of Fort Huachuca

Fort Huachuca is home to the U.S. Army Intelligence School and hosts several other military activities. In area, it occupies about 73,300 ac. Of this amount, 5270 ac is used for the airfield, base housing, offices, and instruction facilities. The remaining land is classified as training area, which includes maneuver areas and training ranges. The training area is managed in varying degrees for conservation and military training use. Approximately 7000 ac of the training area is identified as dedicated impact area, which is used for very intensive training operations and includes firing ranges.

Today, the active-duty population of the base is approximately 5700. In addition to military personnel, Fort Huachuca is also the place of work for many civilians who live in the surrounding area. A federal government study estimated that Fort Huachuca's presence accounts for more than 17,000 jobs—including active duty military personnel, civilians, and contractors. This is equivalent to approximately 45 percent of the county's working population.

Fort Huachuca has a prominent place in the history of southeast Arizona and continues to play an important role in the Upper San Pedro River Basin. However, its size and its mission could be changed as a result of the next round of the Congress' Base Realignment and Closure (BRAC) deliberations.

In the alternative future scenario you envision…

[ ] The fort remains open but is reduced to only those units and activities associated with the Electronics Proving Ground; all other units and activities are transferred to other facilities (approximately 1500 active duty troops, civilian contractors, and support personnel would remain at Fort Huachuca)

[ ] The fort remains open and should stay at its current size

[ ] The fort remains open and should double its current resident population

[ ] The fort closes and its built facilities should be reused by the Arizona National Guard; and all training areas should continue to be dual-managed for conservation and training

[ ] The fort closes and its built facilities should be used for economic growth in the civilian sector with all the training area managed for conservation

[ ] The fort closes and its built facilities should be used for economic growth in the civilian sector with half of the training area managed for conservation and half used for economic growth

[ ] The fort closes and all its built facilities and land should be used for economic growth in the civilian sector

Jobs in the Future

There are many ways to qualify or to measure the economic condition of a local economy, including average domestic income, tax revenues, housing starts, and employment rate. For the purpose of modeling the possible spatial patterns of future land development, one economic factor that is particularly important is the source of jobs. According to 1996 statistics of the U.S. Commerce Department, approximately 35 percent of Cochise County residents were employed either full-time or part-time by a government agency (including the military), 24 percent worked in services, and 18 percent worked in retail.

For the alternative future scenario you envision…

The three industries that will employ the greatest number of people are:

1. ______________________________
2. ______________________________
3. ______________________________

Kartchner Caverns

It is estimated that Kartchner Caverns, which is a part of the Arizona State Park System, will draw 200,000 visitors per year when it opens in the near future. In anticipation of the park opening, some area infrastructure has been upgraded. For example, the nearby highway has already been widened to four lanes. Depending on the popularity of the caverns in the future, additional infrastructure improvements may be necessary as new tourist-related businesses move to the area.

In the alternative future scenario you envision…

[ ] Kartchner Caverns should attract 100,000 people per year in 2020

[ ] Kartchner Caverns should attract 200,000 people per year in 2020

[ ] Kartchner Caverns should attract 400,000 people per year in 2020

[ ] Kartchner Caverns should attract 1,000,000 people per year in 2020

Visual Quality

One of the factors that contributes to the quality of life in the region of the Upper San Pedro River is the beauty of the area and especially its sense of "openness," which is created by the views of the surrounding mountains and of the San Pedro River. Zoning policies can be used to protect the visual quality of an area by defining allowable building types and controlling setbacks from property lines, the density of developments, and the height of structures. Further, areas of particular scenic beauty can be managed as "scenic viewshed districts." In such areas, additional design guidelines, such as the color of buildings and roofs and requiring screening of structures and parking lots, can be implemented to further protect the visual qualities of the area. Following are two questions that concern the conservation of the region's scenery.

In the alternative future scenario you envision…

[ ] Views of mountain ridge lines as seen from major state roads should be protected

[ ] Views of mountain ridge lines as seen from major state roads should not be protected

In the alternative future scenario you envision…

[ ] Views of the San Pedro River riparian vegetation corridor as seen from major state roads should be protected

[ ] Views of the San Pedro River riparian vegetation corridor as seen from major state roads should not be protected

Section II: Water Management in the Upper San Pedro River Basin

Domestic Water Use

Calculating domestic water use is a complicated procedure and estimates vary. As reported in the 1995 National Water-Use Data Files (compiled by the U.S. Geological Survey), per capita domestic water consumption in the Upper San Pedro River Basin is approximately 60 gallons per day for people serviced by a public supply or a water company and approximately 125 gallons per day for people who are self-supplied (that is, who have private wells).

In the alternative future scenario you envision…

[ ] Domestic per capita consumption from public/company sources should decrease from 1995 levels by 40 percent (to 36 gallons per person per day)

[ ] Domestic per capita consumption from public/company sources should decrease from 1995 levels by 20 percent (to 48 gallons per person per day)

[ ] Domestic per capita consumption from public/company sources should remain at 1995 levels (to 60 gallons per person per day)

[ ] Domestic per capita consumption from public/company sources should increase from 1995 levels by 20 percent (to 72 gallons per person per day)

[ ] Domestic per capita consumption from public/company sources should increase from 1995 levels by 40 percent (to 84 gallons per person per day)

[ ] Domestic per capita consumption from individually owned sources should decrease from 1995 levels by 40 percent (to 75 gallons per person per day)

[ ] Domestic per capita consumption from individually owned sources should decrease from 1995 levels by 20 percent (to 100 gallons per person per day)

[ ] Domestic per capita consumption from individually owned sources should remain at 1995 levels (to 125 gallons per person per day)

[ ] Domestic per capita consumption from individually owned sources should increase from 1995 levels by 20 percent

(150 gallons per person per day)

[ ] Domestic per capita consumption from individually owned sources should increase from 1995 levels by 40 percent (to 175 gallons per person per day)

Irrigated Agriculture

Much of the debate over the use of water in the Upper San Pedro Basin has focused on the demands for maintaining natural habitat; however, there are other uses of water that have been exercised in this area for many generations. One of these is irrigated farming.

In the alternative future scenario you envision...

[ ] Irrigated agriculture in the Upper San Pedro River Basin should be continued at its present level of intensity and locations

[ ] All irrigated agriculture in the Upper San Pedro River Basin should be removed

[ ] An irrigation nonexpansion area (INA) should be created within the Upper San Pedro River Basin; all existing irrigated agriculture remains, but proposed irrigated agriculture within 1 mi of the Upper San Pedro River is prohibited

[ ] An irrigation exclusion area should be created within the Upper San Pedro River Basin; all proposed irrigated agriculture within 1 mi of the Upper San Pedro River is prohibited; existing water rights for irrigated agriculture within 1 mi of the San Pedro River are purchased and retired

[ ] Irrigated agriculture in the Upper San Pedro River Basin should be increased by 50 percent (in area)

Vegetation Management for Streamflow

One suggested technique to maintain streamflow in the San Pedro is to manage the vegetation of the region, replacing those plants that transpire more water vapor into the atmosphere with plants that transpire less. Specifically, this policy option would (1) remove cottonwood and willow trees from the riparian area along the San Pedro River and/or (2) remove mesquite from the plains, restoring them to a grassland state. Recently, the U.S. Fish and Wildlife Service has reintroduced beaver to the Upper San Pedro River. It is believed by some that the actions of the beavers alone will sufficiently manage the cottonwood trees, and thus additional riparian management would not be necessary.

In the alternative future scenario you envision...

[ ] Cottonwood and willow trees in the riparian zone along the San Pedro should be removed and the land managed to maintain a grassland ecosystem

[ ] Approximately half of the cottonwood and willow trees in the riparian zone along the San Pedro should be removed by the clearing of selected areas and that land managed to maintain a grassland ecosystem

[ ] Cottonwood and willow trees in the riparian zone along the San Pedro should not be removed

In the alternative future scenario you envision...

[ ] Upland mesquite should be removed and the land should be managed to maintain a grassland ecosystem

[ ] Approximately half the upland mesquite should be removed by clearing selected areas and that land managed to maintain a grassland ecosystem

[ ] Upland mesquite should not be removed

Storm Water Management

Detention systems are intended to slow the peak flow of storm water runoff. Slowing the water allows for greater infiltration into the groundwater system. Detention systems include contour berms and check dams. Another detention system that has received significant discussion in the Upper San Pedro River Basin is the possible use of check dams to potentially increase groundwater recharge from the nearby mountains. Most of the groundwater recharge for the Upper San Pedro Basin comes from storm water runoff from the surrounding mountains. A specific idea is that groundwater recharge could be increased by constructing check dams either in mountain ravines or at the mouth of canyons (also called the alluvial fan areas).

In the alternative future scenario you envision...

[ ] Check dams for recharge should not be constructed
[ ] Check dams for recharge should be constructed only in mountain ravines
[ ] Check dams for recharge should be constructed only in canyon mouths
[ ] Check dams for recharge should be constructed in both mountain ravines and canyon mouths

Section III: Land Management and Conservation

Ranching

Ranching is currently conducted on private land and on land leased from the state and federal governments. Ranching has very low water requirements—much lower than irrigated agriculture, and lower than urban development—and contributes to the landscape's sense of openness. The continued viability of ranching depends on a variety of economic factors and on the quality of range land. Some residents have noted that it is because of the need to protect the land as a valuable and renewable resource that the area ranchers are among the best land stewards in the Upper San Pedro River Basin. Other residents, however, have voiced concern over the potential for overgrazing and argued that the practice of ranching can fragment and otherwise harm habitat needed by some native species.

In the alternative future scenario you envision...

[ ] Ranching in the San Pedro River Basin on state- and federal-owned lands should be increased to the full extent (in area) that is possible
[ ] Ranching in the San Pedro River Basin should be continued at its current intensity and locations
[ ] All ranching in the San Pedro River Basin should be removed
[ ] Ranching in the San Pedro River Basin on state-owned lands should be removed
[ ] Ranching in the San Pedro River Basin on federal-owned lands should be removed
[ ] Ranching in the San Pedro River Basin on state- and federal-owned lands should be removed

Leased Conservation Areas on State Land

Most leases for state-owned land are for the purpose of ranching. Recently, some environmental groups have sought to acquire leases of state lands for the purpose of conservation. However, current law regarding the leasing of state land does not provide a land-use category for "conservation."

In the alternative future scenario you envision…

[ ] The leasing of state-owned land in the San Pedro River Basin for conservation purposes should be allowed by competitive bidding
[ ] The leasing of state-owned land in the San Pedro River Basin for conservation purposes should not be allowed

Fire Management

Prescribing managed fires is one means to help maintain the health of native vegetation. Additionally, managed fires reduce fuel loads, lessening the risk of catastrophic fires that can harm both homes and habitat for native species. However, such management requires careful planning and the close cooperation of land-use agencies and homeowners. Fire management includes the planning of potential sites for development, allowing for burning zones and identifying fire breaks. Such planning may place restrictions on the locations of allowable development, since unplanned development can render fire management ineffective or impossible.

In the alternative future scenario you envision…

[ ] Fires should be prescribed as a part of a vegetation management plan for the Upper San Pedro River Basin
[ ] Fires should not be prescribed as a part of vegetation management plan, but when they occur, they are allowed to burn
[ ] Fires should not be prescribed, and all fires are suppressed

In the alternative future scenario you envision…

[ ] Fire management guidelines should be incorporated into the local land use plans and zoning ordinances and affect all new development
[ ] Fire management guidelines should not be incorporated into the local land use plans and zoning ordinances

San Pedro Conservation Area

In 1988 the U.S. Congress created the San Pedro Riparian National Conservation Area (SPRNCA) to protect a rare desert riparian ecosystem. The conservation area covers approximately 58,000 ac along a nearly 40-mi long stretch of the San Pedro River. According to a BLM brochure, the SPRNCA supports over 350 species of birds, over 80 species of mammals, more than 40 species of reptiles, amphibians, and fish.

In the alternative future scenario you envision…

[ ] The SPRNCA should be dissolved and the land sold to private interests
[ ] The SPRNCA should be maintained as is
[ ] Areas along the San Pedro River to the south that are not protected as part of the SPRNCA should be purchased for conservation purposes (that is, the SPRNCA will span from its current northern edge to the Mexican border)
[ ] Areas along the San Pedro River that are not protected as part of the SPRNCA between Cascabel and the Mexican border should be purchased for conservation purposes (that is, the SPRNCA will span from Cascabel to the Mexican border)
[ ] Areas along the San Pedro River that are not protected as part of the SPRNCA between Cascabel and the Mexican border should be purchased for conservation purposes (that is, the SPRNCA will span from Cascabel to the Mexican border); additionally, Mexico should establish and manage an extension of the SPRNCA in Sonora; conserved habitat should extend to the town of José Maria Morelos, Mexico (that is, near the headwaters of the San Pedro River)

Landscape Ecological Pattern

The study of landscape ecology examines the spatial patterns of the environment. Typical analysis classifies the landscape into three categories: built (suburban, urban areas), disturbed (exurban, rural residential, grazing, agricultural, and recreational areas), and natural (generally undisturbed areas). Areas are further classified by size. Discrete parcels of one classification are called "patches." "Corridors" of natural vegetation that connect patches are also classified. Determining what qualifies as a "large" patch depends on the size and features of the landscape that is being investigated. At the broad scale of states or nations, the Upper San Pedro River Basin might be considered a corridor between Mexico and the United States. At a more refined scale within the basin, the vegetation along an arroyo might be considered a corridor.

One thesis of landscape ecology is that the health of the ecosystem—which includes protecting clean water and habitat for wildlife—can best be managed by protecting large natural areas and the corridors that connect them. For this question, please consider the study area as mapped previously as the extent of landscape to be examined. Relative to this area, a large patch is defined as 5000 ac. A 5000-ac square drawn to the map scale is shown in the bottom left corner of that figure.

In the alternative future scenario you envision…

[ ] Large natural patches (natural areas that are greater than 5000 ac) and their connecting natural corridors should be protected

[ ] Large natural patches and their connecting natural corridors should not be protected

Protection of Listed Species

Some species are currently protected by federal or state law. One conservation strategy would be to concentrate on those species most at risk by protecting their potential habitat. The identification of potential habitat would be taken from the University of Arizona Species Diversity Study (discussed below). Following are the categories of protected species:

Under the Endangered Species Act, the Fish and Wildlife Service lists a species as endangered if it is in imminent jeopardy of extinction. In the Upper San Pedro River Basin, the following species are listed as endangered: Canelo Hills ladies' tresses, desert pupfish, Huachuca water umbel, lesser long-nosed bat, Sonoran tiger salamander, and southwestern willow flycatcher.

Also under the Endangered Species Act, the Fish and Wildlife Service lists a species as threatened if it is in imminent jeopardy of becoming endangered. In the Upper San Pedro River Basin, the following is listed as threatened: Mexican spotted owl.

In the alternative future scenario you envision…

[ ] Potential habitat (as defined by AZ Species Richness Analysis) for endangered species should be protected

[ ] Potential habitat (as defined by AZ Species Richness Analysis) for endangered species should not be protected (the Endangered Species Act is repealed)

In the alternative future scenario you envision…

[ ] Potential habitat (as defined by AZ Species Richness Analysis) for threatened species should be protected

[ ] Potential habitat (as defined by AZ Species Richness Analysis) for threatened species should not be protected (the Endangered Species Act is repealed)

Single-Species Habitat Models

A single-species model may also be the focus of a conservation strategy for a variety of reasons: a species may be legally protected; it may be of local importance for historic or economic reasons; and it may share the same habitat with other species (and be called an "indicator species"). Single-species habitat models differ from the species diversity models (discussed below) in the degree of detail used. Species diversity models make use of forage and breeding habitat needs, including minimum area requirements. Single-species habitat models use this information and additional behavioral characteristics such as (but not limited to) aversion to noise or light, the influence of rural residential development, and migratory patterns.

In the alternative future scenario you envision...
(check all that apply)

[ ] There is no conservation or management of individual species
[ ] Jaguar habitat should be protected (top predator in the region)
[ ] Pronghorn habitat should be protected (grassland habitat species)
[ ] Northern goshawk habitat should be protected (coniferous habitat forest species, species of concern)
[ ] Southwestern willow flycatcher habitat should be protected (riparian habitat species, endangered)
[ ] Gila monster habitat should be protected (desert scrub habitat species, species of concern)
[ ] Beaver habitat should be protected (wetland habitat)
[ ] ____________________
(Reason) ____________________

Species Diversity

The total number of vertebrate species that are expected to live in a given area based upon the type and extent of available vegetation is a measurement of species diversity (also known as species richness). Species diversity is also one measurement for biodiversity. In this case, biodiversity is defined as the variety and variability of species. Variety is a measure of how many species exist in a habitat community. Variability is a measure of how different the species are from each other. For example, a wetland that contains 150 different species of salamanders has a great amount of variety but very low variability.

One land management strategy centered on the idea of biodiversity conservation calls for the protection of those places that can support the greatest number of species and greatest diversity of species. A wildlife conservation based solely on species diversity would protect much of the biodiversity of the region, but would not protect every species.

Researchers at the University of Arizona and the Environmental Protection Agency Laboratory in Las Vegas have recently finished a species diversity assessment for the state of Arizona. Their study maps the number of species that could exist in each habitat community. Using these data it will be possible to create a conservation plan that identifies those areas with the greatest potential variety and variability of species. The final data set for Arizona has not yet been made available to the research team for this project, although we expect to have access to it soon. It is currently estimated that there are over 400 vertebrate species that potentially live in the Upper San Pedro River Basin. When the data set becomes available, this number will be revised.

In the alternative future scenario you envision...

[ ] Contiguous habitat areas that contain at least 250 vertebrate species should be protected
[ ] No areas should be protected based on species diversity

GAP Analysis

Some natural habitat in the Upper San Pedro River Basin is already managed for wildlife conservation. Such places help to ensure the continuation of many species of plants and animals. However, not all species have protected habitats. GAP analysis uses habitat information from species diversity analysis (described above) and land management information to identify areas of potential habitat for species that currently have no habitat in protected areas. That is, GAP analysis looks for "gaps" in wildlife protection plans. One proactive means to help ensure that species do not become listed by state or federal government as "of concern, threatened, or endangered" is to protect their habitat, especially that which is identified as a GAP.

Like the landscape ecological pattern model, GAP analysis can be performed at multiple scales. Typically it is done at the scale of a state, but it can also be done at a regional scale. The difference between the two scales is best explained by a hypothetical example. Reptile species Z is know to live in the Huachuca Mountains just south of Fort Huachuca and in several other parts of Arizona. One habitat patch for this species is in a biological reserve located 150 miles to the west. At the scale of the state, this species does not contribute to any GAPs because it has some habitat within a managed and protected area. However, within the Upper San Pedro River Basin, it has no protected habitat and thus its habitat in the Huachuca Mountains would be a local- or regional-scale GAP.

In the alternative future scenario you envision...

[ ] Basin scale GAPs (from Arizona GAP Analysis) should be protected

[ ] Basin scale GAPs (from Arizona GAP Analysis) should not be protected

Other Issues

Is there a land-use issue facing the Upper San Pedro River Basin that has not been addressed? If so, please describe it in the space below and include the range of policy options as well as your position on that statement.

PLEASE NOTE: Although the research team is very interested in including as many important policy questions as possible in defining the scenarios, it may not be possible to incorporate all issues and options due to constraints of the modeling process.

APPENDIX B

The Computational Process

The research has been carried out using a computer-based technical infrastructure. A series of spatial simulation models have been implemented. In several instances, the output of one model is used as the input to another. Most of these models are embedded within a geographic information system (GIS) and linked using custom programming. The models are run asynchronously, either on the central computer systems at Harvard, or at linked locations at the Desert Research Institute or at the University of Arizona.

Hardware and Software

The main GIS used for this study was Arc/Info (versions 7.2 and 8.0, ESRI, Redlands, CA). Most simulation models were programmed using Arc Macro Language (AML), although several were implemented as freestanding C programs using the "gcc" compiler (http://gcc.gnu.org). ERDAS Imagine (ERDAS, Inc., Atlanta, GA) was used for image processing and for onscreen digitizing.

A wide variety of computing systems were used, all linked using high-speed intranet or internet. Most of the intensive modeling was run on a pair of Sun Ultra-Sparc servers running Solaris version 2.6. Visualization work was done using two Silicon Graphics Windows NT workstations with dual 400 megahertz (MHz) processors and 768 megabytes of RAM. Graphics, layout, and some visualization work was done using a 500 MHz PowerMac G3 with 256 megabytes of RAM. Other processing, including the hydrological simulations, was done on other Windows NT and 98 workstations. Approximately 20 gigabytes of central disk space were allocated on a centralized disk array.

Data

Digital data have been collected from a variety of public sources, including the U.S. Geological Survey (USGS), the Environmental Projection Agency (EPA), the United States Army, the Arizona Land Resource Information System (ALRIS), the Arizona GAP Program, and the Semi-Arid-Land-Surface-Atmosphere Program (SALSA). Additional information, such as Natural Resources Conservation Service Soil Reports for the area, has been converted into digital form at the Harvard University Graduate School of Design. All original data, maps, charts, tables, and so forth are annotated by a metadata file. Information in this file includes source and other characteristics such as date, units, and resolution. Most data were processed in raster grid form at a spatial resolution of 30 m (98.5 ft) per grid cell.

Overview of the Simulation Modeling Process

A set of land use, conservation, and development constraint maps was created for each scenario. These maps were primarily based on current land management and land cover, but varied according to the policies within each scenario. For example, in the CONSTRAINED scenarios, various locations were removed from the potential development category and placed into a conservation category. The development model then allocated future residential and commercial/industrial development in 5-year increments to developable land according to simulated market preference. For each new developed area, land cover information was updated to describe the changed conditions. Where existing wells could be used to supply new development, their pumping rates were increased proportionally. In other locations, the construction of new wells to supply water to new development was simulated.

Maps of land cover and well locations for each scenario were then used as the input into a series of environmental process models. The hydrological model was run using reconstructed historic land use information and data on wells together with scenario projections. The hydrological model outputs were used to predict stream base flow and consequent vegetation changes.

The single species wildlife habitat potential models were run in order to examine the impact of predicted changes on a selected group of species. Aggregate measures of ecological function, including overall terrestrial vertebrate species richness and landscape ecological pattern, were also calculated and mapped. Predicted impacts on visual preference were assessed relative to a visual preference survey.

Outputs of the simulation models are summarized and visualized in several ways. A system was developed to generate comparable maps and charts for a particular theme across the scenarios. These can be output as hard copy plots at a variety of scales, or as digital images that are then further processed within landscape visualization systems.

A landscape scale visualization was constructed for each alternative future in both World Construction Set (3dNature LLD, Boulder, CO) and Maya (Alias/Wavefront, Toronto, Canada). For World Construction Set, the inputs to each visualization are a land cover classification exported from GIS as a raster image and vector point files describing development and well locations. For each vegetation type, a set of images representing typical ecosystem components was gathered. For example, the oak woodland category contained a series of images of oaks of various ages as well as a grass understory. Where available, images from existing vegetation image libraries were used. When necessary, imagery was captured from scanned 35-mm slides. Rules were constructed that described the typical density and size of various ecosystem components as well as the relative influence of topography on elements of that ecosystem. For example, areas of relatively low elevation compared to the surrounding terrain were more likely to support a higher density of plants as well as those known to require more moisture.

Other visualizations were generated using the three-dimensional modeling package Maya (Alias/Wavefront, Toronto, Canada). Multiple methods were used to convert geospatial data into Maya-compatible formats. For wells, an ArcView (ESRI, Redlands, CA) script was written that generates instances of three-dimensional geometry at locations specified in a GIS point file. Aquifer depth levels were exported from GIS as grayscale images and used to displace Nonuniform Rational B-Splines (NURBs planes) using Maya's "Artisan" module. Terrain elevation data in USGS Digital Elevation Model (DEM) format were converted to three-dimensional polygon surfaces using the Polytrans software and Maya plugin (Okino Computer Graphics, Mississauga, Ontario, Canada). This software tiles the terrain as it is converted, which is necessary for efficient representation within Maya. Polygon reduction techniques were then applied to each tile as a function of the distance to the camera.

For each impact model, a color overlay map was produced and exported from the GIS. This image was draped over the previously constructed landscape visualization for that scenario using a semi-transparent overlay.

References

Adams, C., and C. Steinitz. 2000. An alternative future for the region of Camp Pendleton. In V. Mander and R. H. G. Jongman, *Landscape Perspectives of Land Use Changes.* Southhampton, U.K.: WIT Press.

Apple, L. L., B. H. Smith, J. D. Dunder, and B. W. Baker. 1984. The use of beavers for riparian/aquatic habitat restoration of cold desert, gully-cut stream systems in southwestern Wyoming. G. Pilleri (ed.). *Investigation on Beavers* 4:123–130.

Alberta Environment and Olson and Olson Planning and Design. 2000. *The Southern Rockies Landscape Planning Pilot Study: Summary Report.* Alberta Environment, Land and Forest Service, Integrated Resource Management Division, Edmonton, Canada.

Arizona Department of Community Affairs and Economic Development. 1996. *Arizona's Growth and Environment: A World of Difficult Choices.* Phoenix: 68th Arizona Town Hall.

Arizona Department of Game and Fish. 1999. *The Arizona Game and Fish Department's Jaguar Page.* www.gf.state.az.us/frames/fishwild/jaguar.htm.

———. 1998. *Special Status Species for the Upper San Pedro Watershed (HUC 15050202). Heritage Data Management System.* Arizona Game and Fish Department.

Arizona Department of Water Resources. 1991. *General Assessment.* Vol. 1, *Hydrographic Survey Report for the San Pedro Watershed.* Phoenix: Arizona Department of Water Resources.

Arizona State University School of Planning and Landscape Architecture. 1997. San Pedro River watershed. Unpublished studio report.

Bahre, C. J. 1991. *A Legacy of Change: Historic Human Impact on Vegetation in the Arizona Badlands.* Tucson: University of Arizona Press.

Barnes, D. M., and A. V. Mallik. 1997. Habitat factors influencing beaver dam establishment in a northern Ontario watershed. *Journal of Wildlife Management* 61(4):1374–1377.

Bassett, S. D. 2001 *Conservation Strategies Combining Species Richness with Visual Value.* D.Des. thesis, Harvard University Graduate School of Design.

Beck, D. D. 1990. Ecology and behavior of the Gila monster in southwestern Utah (USA). *Journal of Herpetology* 24(1):5468.

Behler, J. L., and F. W. King. 1995. *National Audubon Society Field Guide to North American Reptiles and Amphibians.* New York: Knopf.

Belovsky, G. E., and J. B. Slade. 1979. Body size: Home range area patterns and an energy-maximizing explanation. Harvard University and University of Washington. Unpublished.

Bennett, P. S., M. R. Kunzmann, and L. A. Graham. Descriptions of the Arizona vegetation represented on the GAP vegetation map. U.S. Geological Survey Biological Resources Division. Unpublished.

Bogert, C. M., and R. M. Del Campo. 1956. The Gila monster and its allies: The relationships, habits and behavior of the lizards of the family Helodermatidae. *Bulletin of the American Museum of Natural History* 109(1):1–238.

Brown, D. E., C. H. Lowe, and C. P. Pase. 1979. A digitized classification system for the biotic communities of North America, with community (series) and association examples for the Southwest. *Journal of the Arizona Nevada Academy of Science* 14(suppl. 1):1–16.

Burt, W. H. 1943 . Territoriality and home range concepts as applied to mammals. *Journal of Mammalogy* 24:346–352.

Burt, W. H., and R. P. Grossenheider. 1980. *A Field Guide to the Mammals.* 3rd ed. New York: Houghton Mifflin.

Clemente, F., R. Valdez, J. L. Holechek, P. J. Zwank, and M. Cardenas. 1995. Pronghorn home range relative to permanent water in southern New Mexico. *Southwestern Naturalist* 40(1):38–41.

Commission for Environmental Cooperation. 2002. *The North American Mosaic.* Montreal: Commission for Environmental Cooperation. See also www.CEC.org/SOE.

———. 1999. *Ribbon of Life. An Agenda for Preserving Transboundary Migratory Bird Habitat on the Upper San Pedro River.* Montreal: Commission for Environmental Cooperation.

Corcuera, E., F. Steiner, and S. Guhathakurta. 2000. Potential use of land trust mechanisms for conservation on the Mexican-U.S. border. *Journal of Borderland Studies* 15(1):1–22.

Correll, S. W., F. Corkhill, D. Lovvik, and F. Putnam. 1996. *A Groundwater Flow Model of the Sierra Vista Subwatershed of the Upper San Pedro Basin-Southeastern Arizona.* Phoenix: Arizona Department of Water Resources.

Crawshaw, P. G., Jr., and H. B. Quigley 1991. Jaguar spacing, activity and habitat use in a seasonally flooded environment in Brazil. *Journal of Zoology (London)* 223:357–370.

Crandall, K. J. 1992. *Nature-Based Tourism and the Economy of Southeastern Arizona: Economic Impacts of Visitation to Ramsey Canyon Preserve and the San Pedro Riparian National Conservation Area.* Ph.D. dissertation, University of Arizona, Tucson.

Crocker-Bedford, D. C. 1990. Goshawk reproduction and forest management. *Wildlife Society Bulletin* 18:262–269.

Dramstad, W. E., J. D.Olson, and R. T. T. Forman. 1996. *Landscape Ecology Principles in Landscape Architecture and Land Use Planning.* Washington, D.C: Island Press.

Dunning, J. B., Jr. 1993. *CRC Handbook of Avian Body Masses.* Boca Raton: CRC Press.

Edwards, T. C., Jr., J. M. Scott, C. G. Homer, and R. D. Ramsey. 1993. Gap analysis: A geographical approach for assessing national biological diversity. *Natural Resources and Environmental Issues* 2:65–72.

Farrand, J., Jr. 1988. *Western Birds: An Audubon Handbook.* New York: Chanticleer Press.

Findley, J. S. 1987. Beaver. In *The Natural History of New Mexican Mammals,* 85–88. Albuquerque: University of New Mexico Press.

Forman, R. T. T. 1995. *Land Mosaics: The Ecology of Landscapes and Regions.* Cambridge: Cambridge University Press.

———. 1995. Some general principles of landscape and regional ecology. *Landscape Ecology* 10(3):133–142.

Forman, R. T. T., and M. Godron. 1986. *Landscape Ecology.* New York: Wiley.

Franklin, J. F. 1993. Preserving biodiversity: Species, ecosystems or landscape? *Ecological Applications* 3:202–295.

Freethy, Geoffrey W. 1982. *Hydrologic Analysis of the Upper San Pedro Basin from the Mexico–U.S. Boundary to Fairbank, Arizona.* U.S. Geological Survey Water-Supply Paper 1819-D.

Glinski, R. L. 1992. *The Raptors of Arizona.* Tucson: University of Arizona Press.

Goode, T. C., and T. Maddock III. 2000. Simulation of groundwater conditions in the Upper San Pedro Basin for the evaluation of alternative futures. Arizona Research Laboratory for Riparian Studies, Department of Hydrology and Water Resources, University of Arizona. Unpublished.

Goodrich, D. C., et al. 2000. Preface to Semi-Arid Land-Surface-Atmosphere Program (SALSA). *Agricultural and Forest Meteorology* 105:4–20. Special issue.

Gray, R. S. 1965. *Late Cenozoic Sediments in the San Pedro Valley Near St. David, Arizona.* Tucson: University of Arizona.

Hadley, Diane. 1999. Historic land use context for the upper San Pedro River basin. In *Proceedings of the San Pedro Conference: Divided Waters—Common Ground,* 15–20. Tucson: SALSA.

Hastings, J. R., and R. M. Turner. 1965. *The Changing Mile.* Tucson: University of Arizona Press.

Herberger Center for Design Excellence, Arizona State University. 2000. *A Watershed for a Watershed: Strategies for Sustainability in the Upper San Pedro River Drainage Basin.* Tempe: Arizona State University.

Hoogesteign, R., and E. Mondolfi. 1992. *The Jaguar.* Caracas: Armitano.

Huckleberry, Gary. 1996. *Historical Channel Changes on the San Pedro River, Southeastern Arizona.* Arizona Geological Survey Open File Report 96-15.

Hulse, D., et al. 1997. *Possible Futures for the Muddy Creek Watershed, Benton County, Oregon.* Eugene: Institute for a Sustainable Environment.

Hulse, D., J. Eilers, K. Freemark, D. White, D. Hummon. 2000. Planning alternative future landscapes in Oregon: Evaluating effects on water quality and biodiversity. *Landscape Journal* 19(2):1–19.

Hulse, D., and S. V. Gregory. 2001. Alternative futures as an integrative framework for riparian restoration of large rivers. In V. H. Dale and R. Haeuber (eds.), *Applying Ecological Principles to Land Management,* 194–212. New York: Springer-Verlag.

Hulse, D., J. Baker, and S. Gregory (eds.). 2002. *Willamette River Planning Basin Atlas: Trajectories of Environmental and Ecological Change.* 2nd ed. Corvallis: Oregon State University Press.

Jahnke, Philip. 1994. *Modeling of Groundwater Flow and Surface/Groundwater Interaction for the San Pedro River Basin from Fairbank to Redington, Arizona.* M.S. thesis, Department of Hydrology and Water Resources, University of Arizona.

Jerrick, N., P. Risser, and R. Bastasch. 2001. *Restoring a River of Life: The Willamette Restoration Strategy Overview.* Salem: Willamette Restoration Initiative. www.oregonwri.org/basin_strat.html.

Karalus, K. E., and A. W. Eckert. 1974. *The Owls of North America.* New York: Doubleday.

Kent, Gretchen. Fort Huachuca water resource management. In *Proceedings of the San Pedro Conference: Divided Waters—Common Ground,* 88. Tucson: SALSA.

Kepner, W. G., C. J. Watts, C. M. Edmonds, D. T. Heggem, and T. G. Wade. 2000. A landscape approach for detecting and evaluating change in a semi-arid environment. *Environmental Monitoring and Assessment* 64:179–195. Also, U.S. Environmental Protection Agency, Environmental Sciences Division (CD-ROM). www.epa.gov/crdlvweb/land-sci/san-pedro.htm.

Kunzmann, M. N.d. Terrestrial vertebrate species data dictionary: Arizona GAP Analysis Project. Unpublished.

Leslie, M., G. K. Meffe, J. L. Hardesty, and D. L. Adams. 1996. *Conserving Biodiversity on Military Lands: A Handbook for Natural Resource Managers.* Arlington, Va.: Nature Conservancy.

Lopez, Isaac. 1999. Water issues related to mining in the San Pedro River basin. In *Proceedings of the San Pedro Conference: Divided Waters—Common Ground,* 47–50. Tucson: SALSA.

Lowry, I. S. 1965. A short course in model design. *Journal of the American Institute of Planners,* May, 158–166.

———. 1964. *A Model of Metropolis.* Santa Monica: Rand Corporation.

Lozar, R., J. Wickizer, S. Stone, D. Mouat, C. Steinitz, G. Kent, W. Hodge, and R. Anderson. 1998. Digital geographic data to support long-term ecosystem management planning for the region of Fort Huachuca. Unpublished.

McClaran, M. P., and T. R. Van Devender (eds.). 1995. *The Desert Grassland.* Tucson: University of Arizona Press.

McDonald, M. G., and A. W. Harbaugh. 1988. *A Modular Three-Dimensional Finite-Difference Ground-Water Flow Model.* U.S.G.S. TWI 6-A1.

McGuire, C. 1997. *Soil Survey of the San Pedro Valley, Arizona.* United States Department of Agriculture, Natural Resource Conservation Service.

McHarg, I. 1969. *Design with Nature.* Garden City, N.Y.: Natural History Press. Published for the American Museum of Natural History.

Monson, G. 1968. The desert pronghorn. In *Desert Bighorn Council Transactions,* 63–69. April 10–12, 1968, Las Vegas, Nev.

Mouat, D. A. 1974. *Relationships between Vegetation and Terrain Variables in Southeastern Arizona.* Ph.D. dissertation, Oregon State University, Corvallis.

Mouat, D. A., et al. 1998. *Analysis and Assessment of Impacts on Biodiversity: A Framework for Environmental Management on DoD Lands within the California Mohave Desert: A Research Plan.* Corvallis: Regional Ecology Branch/Western Ecology Division, U.S. Environmental Protection Agency.

Mouat, D. A., and J. Lancaster. 1996. Use of remote sensing and GIS to identify vegetation change in the Upper San Pedro River Watershed, Arizona. *Geocarto International* 11(2):55–67.

Mouat, D., R. Kiester, R. Toth, M. Cablk, J. DeNormandie, T. Edwards, R. Fisher, M. Gonzales, J. Heaton, L. Hunter, K. Karish, R. Lilieholm, M. Meyers, and M. Stevenson. 2002. *Analysis and Assessment of Military and Non-Military Impacts on Biodiversity: A Framework for Environmental Management on DoD Lands Using the Mojave Desert as a Regional Case Study.*

Nassauer, J., R. Corry, and R. Cruse. 2002. Alternative Future

Landscape Scenarios: A Means to Consider Agricultural Policy. *Journal of Soil and Water Conservation* 57(2):44–53.

Nature Conservancy. www.lastgreatplaces.org.

Oliviera, T. G. 1994. Jaguar. In *Neotropical Cats: Ecology and Conservation,* 75–88. San Luis, Brazil: Edufma.

Parnell, M. 2000. Ninth beaver released at the San Pedro River. *Sierra Vista Herald,* June 1.

Peterson, R. T. 1990. *A Field Guide to Western Birds.* 3rd ed. New York: Houghton Mifflin.

Pool, D. R., and A. L. Coes. 1999. *Hydrogeologic Investigations of the Sierra Vista Subwatershed of the Upper San Pedro Basin Cochise County, Southeast Arizona,* 99–4197. Tucson: USGS Water Resources Investigations Report.

Reijnen, M. J. S. M., G. Veenbaas, and R. P. B. Foppen. 1995. *Predicting the Effects of Motorway Traffic on Breeding Bird Populations.* Wageningen, Netherlands: DLO Institute for Forestry and Nature Research.

Reijnen, R., R. Foppen, and H. Meeuwsen. 1996. The effects of traffic on the density of breeding birds in Dutch agricultural grasslands. *Biological Conservation* 75(3):255–260.

Robinson, M. 1999. Jaguar and wolf recovery in the American Southwest. *Wild Earth,* winter, 62–67.

Rodriguez Aguero, A. 1999. Historical perspectives of the basin. In *Proceedings of the San Pedro Conference: Divided Waters—Common Ground,* 8–14. Tucson: SALSA.

SALSA (Semi-Arid Land-Surface-Atmosphere Program). 1999. *Proceedings of the San Pedro Conference: Divided Waters—Common Ground.* Cananea, Sonora, and Bisbee, Arizona, November 8–10, 1999. Tucson: SALSA.

San Pedro Expert Study Team. 1999. *Sustaining and Enhancing Riparian Migratory Bird Habitation on the Upper San Pedro River.* Final Draft. Montreal: Commission for Environmental Cooperation.

Santelmann, M., K. Freemark, D. White, J. Nassauer, R. Cruse, S. Galatowitsch, S. Polasky, K. Vache, and J. Wu. 2001. Applying ecological principles to land-use decision making in agricultural watersheds. In V. H. Dale and R. Haeuber (eds.), *Applying Ecological Principles to Land Management,* 194–212. New York: Springer-Verlag.

Sauer, C. O. 1935. *Aboriginal Population of Northwestern Mexico.* Berkeley: University of California Press.

Sayer, R. A. 1999. A critique of urban modeling. In D. Bannister, K. Button, and P. Niojkamp (eds.), *Environment, Land Use and Urban Policy.* Cheltenham, U.K.: Edward Elgar.

Scott, J. M., F. Davis, B. Csuti, R. Noss, B. Butterfield, S. Caicco, C. Groves, T. C. Edwards Jr., J. Ulliman, H. Anderson, F. D'Erchia, and R. G. Wright. 1993. Gap analysis: A geographic approach to protection of biological diversity. *Wildlife Monographs,* no. 123.

Scott, J. M., B. Csuti, J. D. Jacobi, and J. E. Estes. 1987. Species richness: A geographical approach to protecting future biological diversity. *BioScience* 37:782–788.

Sheviak, C. J. 1990. A new Spiranthes (Orchidaceae) from the cienegas of southernmost Arizona. *Journal of the New England Botanical Club* 92(872):213–231.

Sogge, M. K., R. M. Marshall, S. J. Sferra, and T. J. Tibbitts. 1997. *A southwestern willow flycatcher natural history summary and survey protocol.* National Park Service Technical Report, NRTR-97/12.

Snyder, N. F. R., and H. A. Snyder. 1998. Northern goshawk. In R. L. Glinski (ed.), *The Raptors of Arizona,* 68–72. Tucson: University of Arizona Press.

Stebbins, R. C. 1985. *A Field Guide to Western Reptiles and Amphibians.* 2nd ed. New York: Houghton Mifflin.

Steinitz, C. 1993. A framework for theory and practice in landscape planning. *GIS Europe* 2(6):42–45.

Steinitz, C. 1990. A framework for the theory applicable to the education of landscape architects (and other design professionals). *Landscape Journal* 9(2):136–143.

Steinitz, C., E. Bilda, J. S. Ellis, T. Johnson, Y.-Y. Hung, E. Katz, P. Meijerink, A. W. Shearer, H. R. Smith, A. Sternberg, and D. Olson. 1994. *Alternative Futures for Monroe County, Pennsylvania.* Cambridge: Harvard University Graduate School of Design. See also www.gsd.harvard.edu/depts/larchdep/research/monroe.

Steinitz, C., and S. McDowell. 2001. Alternative futures for Monroe County, Pennsylvania: A case study in applying ecological principles. In V. H. Dale and R. Haeuber (eds.), *Applying Ecological Principles to Land Management,* 165–193. New York: Springer-Verlag.

Steinitz, C., M. Binford, P. Cote, T. Edwards Jr., S. Ervin, R. T. T. Forman, C. Johnson, R. Kiester, D. Mouat, D. Olson, A. Shearer, R. Toth, and R. Wills. 1996. *Biodiversity and Landscape Planning: Alternative Futures for the Region of Camp Pendleton, California.* Cambridge: Harvard University Graduate School of Design.

Steinitz, C., and P. Rogers. 1970. *A Systems Analysis Model of Urbanization and Change.* Cambridge: MIT Press.

Stoops, E. D., and A. Wright. 1993. *Snakes and Other Reptiles of the Southwest.* 2nd ed. Phoenix: Golden West.

Taber, A. B., A. J. Novaro, N. Neris, and F. H. Colman. 1997. The food habits of sympatric jaguar and puma in Paraguayan Chaco. *Biotropica* 29(2):204–213.

Toth, R. E., T. C. Edwards, Jr., R. J. Lilieholm, L. M. Hunter, 2002, *The Development of Alternative Future Growth Scenarios for the California Mojave Desert.* Final Project Report No. 1, Utah Cooperative

Fish and Wildlife Research Unit, Utah State University, Logan, UT, USA

Udall Center for Studies in Public Policy. 1997–2001. *San Pedro News and Comment.* Tucson: University of Arizona.

Udvardy, M. D. F., and J. Farrand Jr. 1994. *National Audubon Society Field Guide to North American Birds: Western Region.* New York: Chanticleer Press.

U.S. Army Garrison, Fort Huachuca, Directorate of Engineering and Housing, Environment and Natural Resources Division. 1998. Approval of long-range land use and real estate investment strategy in support of real property master planning environmental impact statement. Unpublished.

U.S. Department of Agriculture Forest Service. 1995. *Landscape Aesthetics: A Handbook for Scenery Management.* Handbook no. 701, Washington, D.C.

———. 1974. *The Visual Management System National Forest Landscape Management Handbook No. 462.* Vol. 2. Washington, D.C.

U.S. Department of Agriculture Research Service (Southwest Watershed Research Center) and U. S. Environmental Protection Agency. N.d. *San Pedro River Basin Spatial Data Archive.* CD-ROM. Tucson: USDA-ARS Southwest Watershed Research Center.

U.S. Department of Agriculture, Soil Conservation Service, Economic Research Service, and Forest Service with Arizona Water Commission. 1977. *Santa Cruz-San Pedro River Basin Arizona Main Report (pursuant to Section 6 of the Watershed Protection and Flood Prevention Act).*

U.S. Department of the Interior, Bureau of Land Management, Arizona State Office. 1998. *The Upper San Pedro River Basin of the United States and Mexico.* Tucson: BLM.

U.S. Department of the Interior, Bureau of Land Management. 1980. *Visual Resources Program.* Washington, D.C.

U.S. Department of the Interior, Fish and Wildlife Service, Division of Fisheries, Southwest Region. 2000. *Facts About Fish in the Southwest: Pupfish.* ifw2irm2.irml.r2.fws.gov/fishery/species/pupfish.htm.

U.S. Department of the Interior, Fish and Wildlife Service. 1999. Endangered and threatened wildlife and plants: Designation of critical habitat for the Huachuca water umbel, a plant. *Federal Register* 64(132):37441–37453.

———. 1998. *Final Revised Sonoran Pronghorn Recovery Plan.* Albuquerque, New Mexico.

———. 1997a. Endangered and threatened wildlife and plants: Determination of endangered status for three wetland species found in southern Arizona and Northern Sonora, Mexico. *Federal Register* 62(3):665–689.

———. 1997b. *Lesser Long-Nosed Bat Recovery Plan.* Albuquerque, New Mexico.

———. 1995. Listing of the Southwestern Willow Flycatcher as an endangered species. *Federal Register* 60:10694–10715.

U.S. Department of the Interior, Fish and Wildlife Service, Division of Ecological Services. 1980. *Standards for the Development of Habitat Suitability Index Models.* Washington, D.C.

U.S. Environmental Protection Agency. 2000. *Environmental*

Planning for Communities: A Guide to the Environmental Visioning Process Utilizing a Geographic Information System (GIS). Cincinnati: EPA Office of Research and Development.

Unitt, P. 1987. *Empidonax Traillii Extimus:* An endangered subspecies. *Western Birds* 18:147–162.

Vionnet, Leticia Beatriz, and Thomas Maddock III. 1992. *Modeling of Groundwater Flow and Surface/Groundwater Interaction for the San Pedro Basin: Part 1, Mexican Border to Fairbank, Arizona.* Department of Hydrology and Water Resources, University of Arizona, HWR no. 92-010.

Wheatley, M. 1997. Beaver, *Castor Canadensis,* Home Range Size and Patterns of use in the taiga of Southeastern Manitoba. 1: Seasonal variation. *Canadian Field Naturalist* 111:204–210.

Wheeler, B. K., and W. S. Clark. 1995. *A Photographic Guide to North American Raptors.* London: Academic Press.

Whitfield, M. J., and K. M. Enos. 1996. *A Brown-Headed Cowbird Control Program and Monitoring for the Southwestern Willow Flycatcher, South Fork Kern River, California.* Final Report to the U.S. Army Corps of Engineers.

Wood, A. K. 1989. Comparative distribution and habitat use by antelope and mule deer. *Journal of Mammalogy* 70(2):335–340.

Woodroffe, R., and J. R. Ginsberg. 1998. Edge effects and the extinction of populations inside protected areas. *Science* 280:2126–2128.

Acknowledgments

The Research Team wishes to acknowledge assistance of the following people in the preparation of this study:

Mark Apel
Judy Anderson
Joseph Balsama
Greg Block
Col. Michael Boardman
Robert Bridges
Mary Cablk
Tess Canfield
Ghani Chehbouni
Col. Ted Chopin
Thomas Cochran
Doug Cogger
Paul Cote
Shelley Danzer
Michael Doyle
Sam Drake
Barbara Eisworth
Stephen Ervin
Tereza Flaxman
Richard Forman
David Frodsham
Randy Gimblett
Bruce Goff
David Goodrich
Beth Gould
Col. Brent Green
Heather Gross
Russell Harmon
Jim Hessil
David Hulse
Shusak Janpathompong
Arthur "Casey" Jones
Kimberly Karish
Gretchen Kent
William G. Kepner
Rick Koehler
David J. Krupper
Craig Krumwiede
Mike Kunzmann
Robert Lozar
Robert McNish
Stuart Marsh
David Mehl
Barbara Najarian
Joan Nassauer
Douglas Olson
Joelle Pelletier
Robin Pinto
Holly Richter
Winnifred Rose
Russell Sanna
Sabra S. Schwartz
Robert Sharpe
Susan Skirvin
Sheridan Stone
Maj. Gen. John D. Thomas, Jr.
Kathryn Thomas
Richard Toth
Raymond Turner
Christopher Watts
Joseph Watts
Gordon Wicker
John Wickizer
Maj. Dan Williams
Bob Workman

And the many persons in Arizona and Sonora who participated anonymously in the creation of the scenarios.

Editing: Carl Steinitz, Tess Canfield, Julie DuSablon
Graphics: Scott Bassett, Michael Flaxman, Tereza Flaxman, Michael Doyle, Tomas Goode, Kimberly Karish, Shusak Janpathompong, Carl Steinitz
Photographs: Robert Anderson, Tess Canfield, Scott Bassett. All photographs of individual species in chapter 12 are courtesy of the U.S. Fish and Wildlife Service.

About the Authors

CARL STEINITZ is the Alexander and Victoria Wiley Professor of Landscape Architecture and Planning at Harvard University Graduate School of Design. He received a Ph.D. degree in City and Regional Planning from M.I.T., an M. Arch. from M.I.T., and a B. Arch. from Cornell. His interests include theories and methods of landscape planning, and visual resource analysis and management. He has directed several landscape planning studies of highly valued landscapes under pressures for change. He received the 1996 Distinguished Practitioner Award from the International Association for Landscape Ecology (USA). As principal investigator, Steinitz was responsible for the framework and organization of the study and contributed to the design of several of the process models.

HECTOR MANUEL ARIAS ROJO received a B.Sc. in Chemistry from the University of Mexico, an M.Sc. in Soil Physics from Colegio de Postgraduados, Chapingo, Mexico, and a Ph.D. in Watershed Management from the University of Arizona, Tucson. From 1992 to 1999, he was Director of Sustainable Development for Instituto del Medio Ambiente y el Desarrollo Sustenable del Estado de Sonora (IMADES) in Hermosillo, Sonora. He is currently Vision and Planning Officer for the World Wildlife Fund Gulf of California Program based in Guaymas, Sonora. Arias coordinated the study activities in Sonora.

SCOTT BASSETT is a postdoctoral fellow in the Division of Earth and Ecosystem Sciences at the Desert Research Institute, Reno, Nevada. He received his D.Des. at Harvard University. He holds a B.S. in Geography and Anthropology and an M.S. in Fisheries and Wildlife Ecology from Utah State University. His research concentrates on computer simulation of spatial patterns relevant to conservation. Bassett prepared the habitat models, and the species richness and landscape ecology models. He was also responsible for the visual surveys and their modeling, and contributed to the hydrology and the housing and development models.

MICHAEL FLAXMAN is a Lecturer at the Harvard University Graduate School of Design, where he received his D.Des. degree. His work focuses on the development of advanced simulation and visualization methods for landscape planning. His research is on the effects of fire management policies on the occurrence and behavior of fires. He received his Master's in Community and Regional Planning from the University of Oregon, and his Bachelor's in Biology from Reed College, Oregon. Flaxman was responsible for implementing the development model.

TOMAS GOODE is a consulting groundwater hydrologist with HydroSystems, Inc., Tempe, Arizona. He received a Master's degree in Hydrology at the University of Arizona. He holds a B.S. in Environmental Geoscience and History from Weber State University, Utah, where he was named outstanding graduate in the Department of Geosciences. Goode was responsible for implementing the hydrology model and its analyses.

THOMAS MADDOCK III is Professor of Hydrology and Water Resources at the University of Arizona and Co-director of the Research Laboratory for Riparian Studies. He has served on the Hydrology Committee of the Lower Rio Grande Adjudication and on the former San Pedro Negotiation Technical Committee. He has won the Joseph Wood Krutch Award for

Environmental Service from the Nature Conservancy and the Udall Fellowship from the Udall Center for Studies in Public Policy. He received his B.S. in Mathematics from the University of Houston and his M.S. in Applied Mathematics and his Ph.D. in Environmental Engineering from Harvard University. Maddock, as principal investigator at the University of Arizona, was responsible for the extension and development of the hydrology model.

DAVID MOUAT is an Associate Research Professor in the Division of Earth and Ecosystem Sciences at the Desert Research Institute, Reno, Nevada. His interests include relating ecological characteristics, including vegetation composition and distribution, to issues of ecosystem health, land degradation, and environmental toxicity. He has developed an integrated environmental assessment model for desertification evaluation. He managed the Department of Defense Strategic Environmental Research and Development Program (SERDP) Project "Assessment and Management of Risks to Biodiversity and Habitat." His Ph.D. is from Oregon State University. He holds a B.A. in Physical Geography from the University of California (Berkeley). Mouat, as principal investigator at the Desert Research Institute, was responsible for modeling vegetation change, and for U. S. Government interagency coordination.

RICHARD PEISER is the Michael D. Spear Professor of Real Estate Development at the Harvard Graduate School of Design, where he teaches real estate finance and development. He was founder and director of the University of Southern California's Master of Real Estate Development Program. He is a trustee and senior fellow of the Urban Land Institute. Peiser received his B.A. from Yale University, his M.B.A. from Harvard, and his Ph.D. in Land Economy from Cambridge University (U.K.). He is the author of *Professional Real Estate Development: The ULI Guide to the Business* and was Executive Editor of the *Lusk Review for Real Estate Development and Urban Transformation.* Peiser was responsible for the design of the development model and for the surveys that defined attractiveness for development within the region.

ALLAN SHEARER is a Research Fellow at Harvard University. He received his A.B. from Princeton University and a Master's in Landscape Architecture and Master of Arts from Harvard University. He has taught landscape history at the Boston Architectural Center, has practiced landscape architecture, and was project coordinator for the Camp Pendleton research project. Shearer was executive officer for this study and contributed in many ways to all of its aspects. He was responsible for the Scenario Guide.

Index

Note: page numbers in italics indicate illustrations